Interpreting Ancient Israelite History, Prophecy, and Law

Interpreting Ancient Israelite History, Prophecy, and Law

John H. Hayes

Edited and Introduced by
Brad E. Kelle

CASCADE *Books* • Eugene, Oregon

INTERPRETING ANCIENT ISRAELITE HISTORY, PROPHECY, AND LAW

Copyright © 2013 John H. Hayes. All rights reserved. Except for brief quotations in critical publications or reviews, no part of this book may be reproduced in any manner without prior written permission from the publisher. Write: Permissions, Wipf and Stock Publishers, 199 W. 8th Ave., Suite 3, Eugene, OR 97401.

Scripture quotations from the New Revised Standard Version of the Bible are copyright © 1989 by the Division of Christian Education of the National Council of the Churches of Christ in the United States of America and are used by permission.

Cascade Books
A Division of Wipf and Stock Publishers
199 W. 8th Ave., Suite 3
Eugene, OR 97401

ISBN 13: 978-161097-883-5

Cataloging-in-Publication data:

Hayes, John Haralson, 1934–

    Interpreting ancient Israelite history, prophecy, and law / John H. Hayes ; edited and introduced by Brad E. Kelle.

    ISBN 13: 978-161097-883-5

    xxiv + 296 p. ; 23 cm. Includes bibliographical references and indexes.

    1. Bible O.T.—Criticism, interpretation, etc. 2. Jews—History—To 70 A.D. 3. Bible O.T. Prophets—Criticism, interpretation, etc. 4. Law (Theology)—Biblical teaching. I. Kelle, Brad E., 1973–. II. Kuan, Jeffrey K. III. Title.

BS1188 H35 2013

Manufactured in the USA

To
J. Maxwell Miller

a longtime colleague at Emory University
and coauthor over many years

Contents

Preface / ix
Introduction by Brad E. Kelle / xi
Abbreviations / xxiii

1. The History of the Study of Israelite and Judean History / 1
2. Wellhausen as a Historian of Israel / 81
3. The Twelve-Tribe Israelite Amphictyony: An Appraisal / 111
4. The Final Years of Samaria (730–720 BC) / 134
5. The History of the Form-Critical Study of Prophecy / 162
6. The Usage of Oracles against Foreign Nations in Ancient Israel / 218
7. Amos's Oracles against the Nations (1:2—2:16) / 235
8. Restitution, Forgiveness, and the Victim in Old Testament Law / 254
9. Covenant / 269
10. Covenant and *Hesed*: The Status of the Discussion / 282

Acknowledgments / 295

Preface

NONE OF THE ESSAYS in this volume have undergone any major revision or updating. A very few changes and additions have been made, mostly in the footnotes and bibliographies

I am greatly indebted to K. C. Hanson and the staff at Cascade Books and Wipf and Stock Publishers for reformatting all of the essays and for producing a very handsome volume. I hope the volume will sell sufficiently to repay their efforts and expenses.

Special thanks go to Brad E. Kelle, my former student, who I have often said knows more about what I think than I do myself. He helped select the essays, provided the press with copies, secured permissions to reprint, and wrote the introduction.

—John H. Hayes

Introduction
Brad E. Kelle

JOHN HAYES'S SCHOLARSHIP HAS had an important and wide-ranging influence on scholars and students in the field of Hebrew Bible study for more than five decades. Many of his published works on Israelite history, prophecy, law, and the history of biblical interpretation made timely contributions at crucial moments in the field and have proven to have lasting value for scholars working in those areas today.

Hayes began life as the seventh of eight children born into an Alabama sharecropper's home in 1934. Seventy-three years later, he retired in 2007 as the Franklin N. Parker Professor of Old Testament at the Candler School of Theology at Emory University. In the intervening years, he served Baptist congregations in three states, earned degrees from three institutions, taught at two universities, published over forty books and numerous scholarly articles, and even operated a small beef-cattle farm in rural Alabama, where he continues to enjoy his retirement years. This unique blend of personal and professional experiences gave Hayes an approach to Hebrew Bible scholarship that not only resulted in new ideas that continue to inform the scholarly conversation today but also provided needed clarity on developments that were occurring in the field at various moments and turned out to be of continuing importance in the early decades of this new millennium.

This volume collects ten scholarly essays written by Hayes from 1968 to 1995. Some of these originated as papers given at scholarly meetings such as the Society of Biblical Literature or addresses delivered in public lecture series. Others represent essays solicited for particular volumes or articles from major scholarly journals in Hebrew Bible study. The pieces here are organized loosely in three topic areas, corresponding to each piece's primary focus: Israelite/Judean history, prophets, and law. During the later phases of his teaching career, Hayes was famous in the classroom for his graduate seminars on the History of Hebrew Bible Interpretation, Leviticus, Deuteronomy, and Isaiah. Students knew each of these seminars to bring a new breadth and depth to the material, and many of the articles in the present volume reflect these long-standing interests and the unique, sometimes provocative, approaches that Hayes employed. The goal of this volume is to make available some of Hayes's scholarly articles that provided important perspectives within mid- to late-twentieth-century interpretation when they first appeared and helped to shape the scholarly discussion of these topics that one now finds in the field. These articles allow current scholars to see the emergence and development of some important ideas and trends still present in contemporary scholarship and to envision potentially new avenues and perspectives for advancing the critical discussion.

The contemporary relevance of the articles included here is apparent on several counts. At the most basic level, some of the articles proposed new theories, explanations, and interpretations of issues that were at the center of Hebrew Bible scholarship throughout the last half of the twentieth century (e.g., the formation of early Israel, form-criticism of the prophetic literature, the history of the Israelite and Judean kingdoms). Some of Hayes's proposals helped to solidify emerging consensuses, while others offered new, sometimes daring interpretations. He exemplified a scholar who is willing to move outside of and challenge the mainstream of scholarship, nudging his field toward greater self-reflection. While Hayes's specific proposals concerning such things as historical reconstruction or prophetic interpretation received a variety of responses from acceptance to modification to rejection, each helped to move the critical conversation of its topic forward toward some of the forms one sees today. One such specific proposal evidenced in some of the articles included here is Hayes's unique approach to understanding the prophets and the importance of history for them, an approach that might be called the direct rhetorical-historical approach.[1] In this view, nearly every element of books such as Amos and Isaiah needs to be understood as connected to a particular historical occasion, with much of the material constituting rhetorical compositions that reference a chain of closely related political-historical circumstances in the ancient Near

---

1. See Kelle and Moore, "Introduction," in *Israel's Prophets and Israel's Past*.

Introduction

East. While not immune to disagreement, the manifestations and ramifications of Hayes's specific proposals have been evidenced in relevant scholarly work up to the present.

Beyond the first level of the specific proposals made in some of Hayes's work, the timing and context of many of the articles included here constitute a second, broader factor that commends their ongoing consideration. Several of these articles emerged at crucial moments in the discipline of Hebrew Bible study, when many long-standing interpretive settlements were being reconsidered and, in some cases, set aside. These essays identified, clarified, and further developed several of the major trends that have shaped the study of Israelite history, prophets, and law throughout the later twentieth and now early twenty-first century. Regardless of the specific proposals advanced by a particular article, Hayes's work in this way provides contemporary interpreters with glimpses of key moments in the development of particular methods, trends, and models that have given shape to current approaches in Hebrew Bible study. For instance, in the mid-1970s and 1980s, the discipline of Israelite history (and the question of the usefulness of the Hebrew Bible as a historical source) was entering a time of unprecedented change, a period in which Hayes (along with his colleague, J. Maxwell Miller) would make several significant contributions.[2] During this time, various perspectives and approaches emerged that ultimately came to fruition in the so-called "minimalist controversy" of the 1990s.[3] Several of Hayes's articles in this volume originated during this crucial period of the 1970s, 80s, and 90s, and still offer valuable, often uniquely clear insights that help contextualize developments whose effects remain formative in historical study today.

A third, and perhaps most significant, factor that commends this volume's articles for renewed consideration is the potential importance of the general *way* in which Hayes approached the study of Israelite history, prophecy, and law and the model it may provide. The diverse topics covered by the included articles find their unity in a particular posture and ethos from which Hayes's work operated. Hayes consistently engages in a "thick analysis" that embeds the topic under consideration within broader interpretive contexts. More so than any one particular proposal, this way in which Hayes approached the study of specific methods, seminal

---

2. See, for example, the comprehensive history volume originally published in 1986: Miller and Hayes, *A History of Ancient Israel and Judah*.

3. See Moore and Kelle, *Biblical History and Israel's Past*.

figures, biblical texts, and historical reconstructions has potentially lasting implications for contemporary scholarship. The thick, embedded analysis represented by Hayes's articles here takes two forms. First, one finds in Hayes's work a dogged insistence that biblical texts must be understood as firmly embedded within particular historical, social, cultural, and political matrices out of which they emerged and within which they functioned. Following from this, at times when it was not always popular to do so, Hayes argued that the biblical texts must be taken seriously (but not uncritically) as yielding important data to be used in various ways for historical interpretation. Whether exploring the social formation of early Israel, the final years of Samaria, or the social concept of covenant, Hayes demonstrated a textually focused and exegetically based approach. In this way, several of the articles included here both anticipated and helped to shape the robust discussions about the nature and usefulness of the biblical texts that came to dominate the last years of the 1990s and the opening decades of the 2000s.

A second manner in which Hayes's work models a thick and embedded approach to the critical study of ancient Israelite history, prophets, and law appears in the way that these articles consistently, often comprehensively, place the topic being considered within the long-view of the history of interpretation, both ancient and modern, Christian and Jewish, and otherwise.[4] While Hayes cannot be said to have moved outside of a historicist framework, his work displays sympathy to certain trends in postmodernist interpretation, particularly the contextual and constructed nature of knowledge. Hayes repeatedly seeks to move every topic of discussion from the general to the specific, embedding it not just into the immediate context of scholarship at the time, but into the larger intellectual currents that both shaped that topic and render it understandable within different intellectual discourses. In this way, Hayes often accomplishes the desired outcome of providing insights from the history of so-called "pre-modern" interpretation and Jewish exegesis, two areas often neglected by modern biblical criticism. The comprehensiveness with which Hayes's work embeds figures, theories, and trends within a fully orbed history of interpretation constitutes an impressive intellectual endeavor and a needed model for today's increasingly specialized biblical criticism.

4. This characteristic of Hayes's scholarship finds its fullest expression in his work as general editor on a major reception history resource. See Hayes, ed., *Dictionary of Biblical Interpretation*.

Introduction

Each article in this volume contributes in some way to the lines of significance outlined above. The articles do not proceed in strict chronological order, nor does the diversity of materials lend itself to systematic description. Hence, it may be helpful to conclude this introduction by briefly locating each article within the larger landscape of the interpretive currents of its time and the contours of Hayes's work more broadly.

The first four articles relate to the study of Israelite and Judean history in the second half of the twentieth century. "The History of the Study of Israelite and Judaean History" (orig. 1977) served as the introductory essay for the ground-breaking *Israelite and Judaean History* that Hayes co-edited with J. Maxwell Miller.[5] This comprehensive essay provided the context for the discussions of the current state of research on each of the major eras of Israelite and Judean history that followed in the volume. This work appeared at a time when the study of the history of Israel and Judah was entering a type of adolescence, and Hayes's article still offers one of the most comprehensive examinations of the development of that field through the mid-1970s.[6] At the time of the essay's appearance, the two schools of thought that had dominated academic discussions related to biblical archaeology and history from the 1940s to the 1960s—largely associated with Albrecht Alt and Martin Noth on the one hand and William Foxwell Albright and his students on the other hand—were coming under increasing methodological scrutiny and losing their epistemological hegemony in the field. The time was ripe for a volume that would evaluate the current status of research and gesture toward new directions. Hayes's opening article offered a rare moment of comprehensive self-reflection for the discipline, outlining the development of the study of Israelite and Judean history from its origins and locating it within the intellectual currents of the first half of the twentieth century. The essay embeds the modern critical discipline within the trends of history writing that existed from the time of the earliest Jewish, Christian, and other thinkers, including special consideration of historiography's interests and aims in various time periods. In Hayes's discussion of the field, one sees a helpful snapshot of where the study of Israelite and Judean history was as it entered the last few decades of the twentieth century. At the time, as Hayes indicates, four main approaches (conservative, archaeological, tradition-critical, and socio-economic) set the framework for most

5. Hayes and Miller, eds., *Israelite and Judaean History*.

6. For the continuation of this kind of survey up to the present, see Moore and Kelle, *Biblical History and Israel's Past*.

xv

Introduction

scholarship and the pre-monarchical period was the primary focus of attention. These realities soon became the starting point for the robust and contested debates over history that emerged in the following decades. In this article, Hayes already identified several of the changing trends that would come to fruition throughout the 1980s and 1990s, most notably the problem of the character and usefulness of the biblical texts within historical study.

The second article related to historical study, "Wellhausen as a Historian of Israel," originated as a presentation given at the 1978 Society of Biblical Literature meeting (later published in 1982) as part of the 100th anniversary celebration of the publication of Wellhausen's *Geschichte Israel*. It reflects a time of new directions in the field of Israelite and Judean history prompted especially by the appearance of Thomas Thompson's *The Historicity of the Patriarchal Narratives* (1974) and John Van Seter's *Abraham in History and Tradition* (1975).[7] These works were among the catalysts that loosened the dominance of the older Alt-Noth and Albright paradigms for historical study and featured a reworking of some of Wellhausen's older perspectives on questions such as the historicity of the patriarchs and matriarchs. In this climate, Hayes's article embedded one of the seminal figures in the history of the discipline within the intellectual and interpretive currents that shaped his methods and conclusions. By offering this long view, Hayes located Wellhausen's work as a historian within the context of his work as a literary (source) critic, demonstrating the unity of these two activities in Wellhausen's intellectual climate and interpretive approach. The article provides today's readers with a sense of the development present within Wellhausen's work and cautions against seeing him as an isolated figure with static ideas.

The third article related to historical study, "The Twelve-Tribe Israelite Amphictyony: An Appraisal," provides an illuminating glimpse into the new assessments and challenges that emerged in the 1970s to this long-dominant interpretive notion in the field. The article originated in 1972 as a paper delivered to the departmental faculties at Trinity University and St. Mary's University (later published in 1975). The original goal was to describe and contribute to the then-current rethinking of early Israelite history. The article appeared at the time when long-regnant theories from the work of Alt and Noth concerning the origins and sociological realities of early Israel were being subject to intense methodological

---

7. Thompson, *The Historicity of the Patriarchal Narratives: The Quest for the Historical Abraham*; Van Seters, *Abraham in History and Tradition*.

Introduction

scrutiny. Hayes's work captured the major criticisms that precipitated this change, assessed their weight, and, rightly, pronounced the collapse of the older theory. By comparing this essay with the preceding examination of Wellhausen, readers can identify important ways in which Noth both built upon and moved beyond Wellhausen's approaches. Moreover, this essay once again embeds a seminal figure and theory within the context of the wider interpretive trends that preceded and gave shape to more well-known formulations.

The last article related to historical study, "The Final Years of Samaria (730–720 BC)" (co-authored with Jeffrey K. Kuan in 1991), has become established as one of several major studies that deal with the historical reconstruction of the fall of the northern kingdom of Israel in the late eighth century BCE.[8] What made this study unique, however, was that it emerged directly from work Hayes had recently undertaken on the historical background of the prophetic literature.[9] Hence, in addition to embedding this topic into historical perspectives informed by Assyrian royal inscriptions, Hayes's approach featured extensive and bold use of Hebrew Bible prophetic texts for historical reconstruction, with a willingness to take these texts—and the specificity one finds within them—seriously as some kind of data for historical reconstruction. This approach rested on Hayes's conviction that the prophetic literature could best be thought of as rhetorical discourses shaped to function within particular social and political circumstances. The article thus provides contemporary readers with an example of the way some scholars employed certain biblical texts just prior to the full outbreak of the so-called minimalist controversy in the 1990s. Additionally, it makes a thought-provoking case for approaching topics of historical reconstruction from a different angle than that provided by the use of archaeology or an emphasis on the Hebrew Bible's historiographical texts.

The first article devoted specifically to prophetic interpretation, "The History of the Form-Critical Study of Prophecy," reflects one of the

---

8. Along with the Hayes and Kuan article, discussions of the final years of the northern kingdom commonly cite the following among others: Na'aman, "The Historical Background to the Conquest of Samaria (720 BC)"; Becking, *The Fall of Samaria*; Younger, "The Fall of Samaria in Light of Recent Research"; Tetley, "The Date of Samaria's Fall as a Reason for Rejecting the Hypothesis of Two Conquests." See also Kelle, "Hoshea, Sargon, and the Final Destruction of Samaria"; and Kelle, "What's in a Name?" Most recently, see Park, "A New Historical Reconstruction of the Fall of Samaria."

9. E.g., Hayes and Irvine, *Isaiah, the Eighth Century Prophet*; and Hayes, *Amos*.

Introduction

primary areas of scholarship to which Hayes contributed over his career. Hayes wrote this essay while editing a volume devoted to new approaches to Hebrew Bible form criticism, and the paper served as the basis for discussion in the form criticism section at the 1973 Society of Biblical Literature Annual Meeting.[10] At a crucial moment in the reconsideration of methods and practices related to prophetic interpretation, the paper embedded this important method and its major practitioners within the full context of the history of scholarship up through the 1970s. Hayes highlighted the place of Hermann Gunkel within the larger intellectual movements of the early nineteenth century and provided a thick description that illuminated other important, but perhaps lesser known, figures. He demonstrated their connections to one another and their significance for the method that became established in modern scholarship. This article familiarizes contemporary readers with the major developments in form-critical study from the 1940s to the 1970s and reveals some of the background that helps to contextualize new approaches to form criticism that have emerged in the 1990s and beyond.[11]

In relationship to the general discussion of the previous article, the next two studies represent form-critical analyses that helped to shape scholarship's approaches to one prophetic genre in particular, namely, the oracles against the nations. The first article, "The Usage of Oracles against Foreign Nations in Ancient Israel," constituted a summary of Hayes's unpublished 1964 Princeton dissertation and remains one of the most commonly cited sources in discussions of this particular prophetic genre. This genre provided key material for early form-critical explorations, with Gunkel and others proposing that the oracles against the nations were the oldest form of prophetic material. Hayes built upon earlier scholarship to propose that the rhetorical function of these oracles within ancient Israelite society was linked with the preparation and execution of warfare. Through comparison with a variety of ancient Near Eastern textual traditions, he further suggested that this genre typically functioned in cultic lamentation services or royal contexts such as coronation rituals. Similarly, in the next article, "Amos's Oracles against the Nations (1:2—2:16)," Hayes applied his general treatment of the rhetorical function of the oracles against the nations to the specific collection in the opening chapters of Amos. The article (published in 1995) originated as

10. See Hayes, ed., *Old Testament Form Criticism*.

11. See, for example, Sweeney and Ben Zvi, eds., *The Changing Face of Form Criticism for the Twenty-first Century*.

Introduction

an invited follow-up to Hayes's then recently published commentary on Amos.[12] The discussion remains one of the clearest examples of a rhetorical-historical approach to the prophetic texts. This approach, which has generated a number of similar studies by Hayes's students and colleagues, seeks to identify the rhetorical functions of the prophetic speeches as embedded within the historical-political realities of their time.[13] The article provided a new perspective on Amos's use of the oracles against the nations genre by approaching Amos 1:2—2:16 as a coherent unit with specific rhetorical purposes related to political developments in the mid-eighth century BCE.

The final three articles in this collection relate to Hayes's work on the legal texts in the Hebrew Bible, exemplified throughout his teaching career by his popular graduate seminars on Leviticus and Deuteronomy. "Restitution, Forgiveness, and the Victim in Old Testament Law" originated in 1982 as part of a Festschrift for a retiring colleague at Trinity University and appeared in *Trinity University Studies in Religion*. Given his colleague's interest in Christian ethics, the article adopted an explicitly ethical engagement with the Hebrew Bible laws concerning cases between persons, and it remains a suggestive model of what such engagement may look like. Hayes proposed that the focus of the Hebrew Bible's formulations in such cases was primarily, if not solely, on the restoration of the victim rather than the punishment of the perpetrator. The article once again exemplifies the effort to embed such analysis within the reception history of the relevant laws, with a special eye to post-biblical Jewish writings.

The remaining two articles in the volume offer a similar reexamination of the interpretive issues connected with the long-standing scholarly notion of covenant and its origins within ancient Israelite culture and the biblical literature. The first article originated as the dictionary entry for "Covenant" in the *Mercer Dictionary of the Bible* (1990). Following his thick-description approach to the history and formulation of such concepts, Hayes offered a general survey of covenant as both a term and idea within the Hebrew Bible and its ancient Near Eastern background. The discussion remains one of the clearest surveys of the concept, which stresses the diversity of the ways covenant was understood and employed. Moreover, Hayes advanced a theory that remains significant for current study of covenant as an idea, as well as the

12. Hayes, *Amos*.

13. See also Gitay, *Prophecy and Persuasion*; Shaw, *The Speeches of Micah*; Kelle, *Hosea 2*.

conceptual background of the prophets in particular. The historical and literary analysis led Hayes to endorse the conclusion that the idea of a bi-lateral covenant between Yahweh and Israel was not known before the work of deuteronomistic circles of the seventh century BCE. Rather, the eighth-century prophets in particular drew upon conceptions associated with international political treaties and assumed a triangular covenant notion in which Yahweh was the guarantor of Israel's treaty with partners such as Assyria and Babylonia.

Similarly, the final essay here, "Covenant and *Hesed*: The Status of the Discussion," provided a critical evaluation of the popular connections long-made in scholarship between the concept of covenant and the Hebrew term, *hesed*. This piece is the only article included in the volume that was not published previously. It originated as the Boone M. Bowen lecture given at the First Methodist Church in Clemson, South Carolina shortly after Bowen's death in 1987. In the true spirit of Hayes's consistent emphasis on evaluating ideas of scholarship within their formative intellectual currents, the article offers one of the most comprehensive assessments of the development of the notion of covenant within Hebrew Bible scholarship from the 1920s to the mid-1980s—a virtual snapshot of how covenant as a theological, social, and institutional concept emerged from Max Weber forward and where that discussion stood near the end of the twentieth century. Additionally, Hayes successfully set out the history of the connection of the term *hesed* with the concept of covenant before explaining the more recent challenges to this association. For today's reader, this article, like several others included here, provides the background for understanding much of what one finds in current scholarly discussions of covenant and *hesed*.

Taken together, the articles included in this volume provide a valuable resource to today's students and scholars working with Israelite history, prophecy, and law. At a number of points, they provide succinct yet comprehensive snapshots of the background of ideas that underwent significant changes in the field in the late twentieth century and help to explain some of the methods and perspectives that characterize current scholarship. At other points, they propose innovative approaches that were new at the time and have since become part of theories and proposals whose weight is still recognizable today. In every case, however, Hayes's work in these studies encourages both present and future scholars to be candid and courageous, to undertake their task with a healthy, gadfly-like skepticism toward taken-for-granted settlements and consensuses,

Introduction

and to offer boldly new ideas that, at times, go against the mainstream of scholarly opinion. Even more, throughout the articles included here one senses a kind of good humor that characterized Hayes's career as a scholar and teacher. This good humor is a spirit that refuses to take any concept or convention—including one's own, sometimes innovative and daring, proposals—as unquestionable "givens" that stand apart from the human, social, and intellectual influences that shaped them. Surely this kind of good humor and broad perspective is a happy byproduct of a life lived in settings as wide-ranging as an academic classroom and a sharecropper's field, a university faculty and a rural beef-cattle farm. It represents a healthy understanding of the human and embedded nature of all scholarly pursuits—an understanding that Hayes has expressed even more explicitly in his post-retirement writings, producing a witty book of earthy thoughts about the road of life and a novel reflecting the struggles and triumphs of life in rural southern cultures.[14] Seen in Hayes's way, all students and scholars should approach the past, present, and future ideas of their discipline for what they are—honest, but limited efforts to make sense of available data undertaken by real-life human beings, who are embedded in a host of social, cultural, and intellectual realities.

Bibliography

Becking, Bob. *The Fall of Samaria: An Historical and Archaeological Study*. Studies in the History of the Ancient Near East 2. Leiden: Brill, 1992.
Gitay, Yehoshua. *Prophecy and Persuasion: A Study of Isaiah 40–48*. Forum Theologiae Linguisticae 14. Bonn: Linguistica Biblica, 1981.
Hayes, John H. *Abanda: A Novel*. Eugene, OR: Wipf & Stock, 2012.
———. *Amos, the Eighth Century Prophet: His Times and His Preaching*. Nashville: Abingdon, 1988.
———, editor. *Dictionary of Biblical Interpretation*. 2 vols. Nashville: Abingdon, 1999.
———. *If You Don't Like the Possum, Enjoy the Sweet Potatoes: Some Principles for Travel Along the Road of Life*. Eugene, OR: Cascade Books, 2009.
———, editor. *Old Testament Form Criticism*. TUMSR 2. San Antonio: Trinity University Press, 1977.
Hayes, John H., and Stuart A. Irvine. *Isaiah, the Eighth Century Prophet: His Times and His Preaching*. Nashville: Abingdon, 1987.
Kelle, Brad E. *Hosea 2: Metaphor and Rhetoric in Historical Perspective*. Society of Biblical Literature Academia Biblica 20. Atlanta: Society of Biblical Literature, 2005.
———. "Hoshea, Sargon, and the Final Destruction of Samaria: A Response to M. Christine Tetley with a View Toward Method." *SJOT* 17 (2003) 226–44.

14. Hayes, *If You Don't Like the Possum, Enjoy the Sweet Potatoes*; Hayes, *Abanda: A Novel*.

Introduction

———. "What's in a Name? Neo-Assyrian Designations for the Northern Kingdom and Their Implications for Israelite History and Biblical Interpretation." *JBL* 121 (2002) 639–66.

Kelle, Brad E., and Megan Bishop Moore. "Introduction." In *Israel's Prophets and Israel's Past: Essays on the Relationship of Prophetic Texts and Israelite History in Honor of John H. Hayes*, edited by Brad E. Kelle and Megan Bishop Moore, 1–5. Library of Hebrew Bible / Old Testament Studies 446. New York: T. & T. Clark, 2006.

Miller, J. Maxwell, and John H. Hayes. *A History of Ancient Israel and Judah*. Philadelphia: Westminster, 1986; 2nd ed. Louisville: Westminster John Knox, 2006.

Moore, Megan Bishop, and Brad E. Kelle. *Biblical History and Israel's Past: The Changing Study of the Bible and History*. Grand Rapids: Eerdmans, 2011.

Na'aman, Nadav. "The Historical Background to the Conquest of Samaria (720 BC)." *Bib* 71 (1990) 206–25.

Park, Sung Jin. "A New Historical Reconstruction of the Fall of Samaria." *Bib* 93 (2012) 98–106.

Shaw, Charles S. *The Speeches of Micah: A Rhetorical-Historical Analysis*. JSOTSup 145. Sheffield: JSOT Press, 1993.

Sweeney, Marvin A., and Ehud Ben Zvi, editors. *The Changing Face of Form Criticism for the Twenty-first Century*. Grand Rapids: Eerdmans, 2003.

Tetley, M. Christine. "The Date of Samaria's Fall as a Reason for Rejecting the Hypothesis of Two Conquests." *CBQ* 64 (2002) 59–77.

Thompson, Thomas L. *The Historicity of the Patriarchal Narratives: The Quest for the Historical Abraham*. BZAW 133. 1974. Reprinted, Harrisburg, PA: Trinity, 2002.

Van Seters, John. *Abraham in History and Tradition*. New Haven: Yale University Press, 1975.

Younger, K. Lawson. "The Fall of Samaria in Light of Recent Research." *CBQ* 61 (1999) 461–82.

Abbreviations

AB	Anchor Bible
ANECS	Ancient Near East: Classic Studies
ANET	*Ancient Near Eastern Texts Relating to the Old Testament.* Edited by James B. Pritchard. 3rd ed. Princeton: Princeton University Press, 1969
Ant.	Josephus, *Antiquities*
ARAB	*Annals and Records of Assyria and Babylonia.* Translated by D. D. Luckenbill. Chicago: University of Chicago Press, 1926–27
b.	Babylonian Talmud tractates
BA	*Biblical Archaeologist*
Bib	*Biblica*
BWANT	Beiträge zur Wissenschaft vom Alten und Neuen Testament
BZAW	Beihefte zur Zeitschrift für die alttestamentliche Wissenschaft
CBQ	*Catholic Biblical Quarterly*
EvTh	*Evangelische Theologie*
FRLANT	Forschungen zur Religion und Literatur des Alten und Neuen Testaments
HKAT	Handkommentar zum Alten Testament
HTR	*Harvard Theological Review*
HUCA	*Hebrew Union College Annual*
ICC	International Critical Commentary
IDB	*The Interpreter's Dictionary of the Bible.* Edited by George Arthur Buttrick. 4 vols. Nashville: Abingdon, 1962
IDBSup	*The Interpreter's Dictionary of the Bible Supplementary Volume.* Edited by Keith R. Crim. Nashville: Abingdon, 1976

Abbreviations

JB	Jerusalem Bible
JBL	*Journal of Biblical Literature*
JCS	*Journal of Cuneiform Studies*
JSOTSup	Journal for the Study of the Old Testament Supplement Series
KJV	King James Version
LCL	Loeb Classical Library
m.	Mishnah tractates
Mek.	*Mekilta de-Rabbi Ishmael*
MT	Masoretic text
NAB	New American Bible
NCB	New Century Bible
NEB	New English Bible
NJPS	New Jewish Publication Society Version
NRSV	New Revised Standard Version
OTL	Old Testament Library
OTS	*Oudtestamentische Studiën*
RGG	*Die Religion in Geschichte und Gegenwart*
RSV	Revised Standard Version
SAT	Die Schriften des Alten Testament
SBLDS	Society of Biblical Literature Dissertation Series
SBT	Studies in Biblical Theology
SJOT	*Scandinavian Journal of the Old Testament*
ThBü	Theologische Bücherei
TLZ	*Theologische Literaturzeitung*
TUMSR	Trinity University Monographs Series in Religion
VT	*Vetus Testamentum*
VTSup	Vetus Testamentum Supplements
War	Josephus, *Jewish War*
WMANT	Wissenschaftliche Monographien zum Alten und Neuen Testament
ZAW	*Zeitschrift für die alttestamentliche Wissenschaft*
ZTK	*Zeitschrift für Theologie und Kirche*

1

The History of the Study of Israelite and Judean History

The Earliest Treatments of Israelite and Judean History

THE WRITING OF HISTORY as a narrative about past events is a very ancient undertaking. Its roots, so far as Western historiography is concerned, are anchored in the cultures of Israel and Greece.

History, as a genre or literary type, is found in much of the Hebrew Scriptures where events are understood in a theological or, to use Collingwood's terminology,[1] "theocratic" perspective. In spite of this perspective, much of the narrative material in these Scriptures is historiographical in intent in so far as it attempts a narrative account of past events. To suggest, as is frequently done, that Israel was the creator of historical writing[2] probably goes beyond the evidence. Egyptian, Mesopotamian, and Hittite inscriptions, annals, chronicles, narratives, and art in many ways approach genuine historical thought and writing[3] and tend to moderate extravagant claims about the originality and priority of Israelite historical writing. In addition, the origins and character of historical

---

1. Collingswood, *The Idea of History*, 14.
2. Pfeiffer, *Introduction*, 357.
3. See Dentan, ed., *The Idea of History*; Otto, "Geschichtsbild"; Kramer, "Sumerian Historiography"; Olmstead, *Assyrian Historiography*; Gese, "The Idea of History"; and Moscati, *Historical Art*.

writing in Israel, especially with regard to the materials in the Pentateuch remain a much debated and unsettled issue.[4] Since the Hebrew Scriptures have been and remain the primary sources for reconstructing the history of Israel and Judah, questions regarding the nature, character, and antiquity of these traditions will be discussed in various places in the following chapters.[5]

The first discussions of Israelite and Judean history, apart from the biblical traditions, stem from the Hellenistic Age and were the products of both Jewish and non-Jewish authors. In the early Greco-Roman period, Jewish–Roman relations and Jewish apologetic concerns engendered several treatments of Jewish history and life. From the second to the fifth century CE, with the emergence and dominance of rabbinic Judaism and the growth and state recognition of Christianity, concern with and interpretation of earlier Israelite and Judean history passed into the hands of Christian historians and theologians whose assumptions and descriptions set a pattern that remained basically unchallenged throughout the Middle Ages. These three phases of the discussion are the concern of this section.

Much of the literature dealing with Israelite and Judean history from the Hellenistic Age either did not discuss the subject in any great detail or, more probably, has been irretrievably lost. Except for the biblical book of Daniel and the apocryphal books of 1 and 2 Maccabees, only the fragments of this Hellenistic literature preserved in the works of Josephus, in Eusebius's *Praeparatio Euangelica*, and in a few other Greco-Roman writers survive.[6] Nonetheless, it is highly probable that most Hellenistic universal historians included a section on the history of the Jews in their works.

Among pagan authors, discussions of the origin of the Jews and the figures of Abraham and Moses dominate. Both favorable and slanderous treatments appear. Hecataeus of Abdera (about 300 BCE), in his work on the culture, history, politics, and religion of ancient Egypt, discussed the origins of the Jews in terms of their expulsion from Egypt at divine urging and their subsequent colonization of Judea. Josephus (*Contra Apionem* 1.183–204) quotes from a work by Hecataeus which was wholly concerned with the Jews, although Josephus's passage only contains

---

4. See von Rad, "The Beginnings"; Cassuto, "The Beginning"; Winnett, "Re-examining"; Mowinckel, "Israelite Historiography"; and Schulte, *Die Entstehung*.

5. Referring to Hayes and Miller, eds., *Israelite and Judaean History*.

6. See Stern, *Greek and Latin Authors*, for non-Jewish writers.

miscellaneous material about Jewish matters during the early Hellenistic Age. Hecataeus's treatment of the Jews and their history was generally favorable and, while praising Moses as a cult founder and lawgiver, he shows little, if any, direct knowledge of the Jews and their sacred writings. Hecataeus's description of Moses and subsequent Jewish history that tended to telescope everything around Moses was highly influential upon practically all Hellenistic and even Greco-Jewish writers.[7]

Over against the material in Hecataeus (and Theophrastus, Megasthenes, and Clearchus), which took a favorable attitude towards the Jews, one finds widespread use of a version of the exodus and the career of Moses that heaps calumny upon the Jews. Utilizing an old story form that told of a foreign invasion of Egypt,[8] a reign of terror by outsiders, and a triumph over this dominance by a hero-king,[9] these descriptions of Jewish history depicted the Hebrews as an impure people, Moses as a polluted Egyptian priest, and portrayed Jewish life and practices as hostile to everything non-Jewish.[10] This hostile propaganda was basicaly centered in Alexandria and reflects the tension between Jews of the Egyptian diaspora and the native, especially priestly, Egyptian population. The roots of this anti-Jewish polemic were no doubt multiple,[11] and the tension is already reflected in Aramaic papyri of the fifth century BCE from Egypt. Variations on this theme of Jewish origins are reflected in Egyptian literature for over six centuries[12] and no doubt formed a vital part of the arsenal of anti-Jewish propaganda offering a supportive rationale for repressive measures.

Perhaps the most significant example of this anti-Jewish version of Moses and the origins of the Jews is that attributed to Manetho (third century BCE) by Josephus (*Contra Apionem* 1.73–91, 93–105, 228–52), who claims to be quoting from Manetho's *Aegyptiaca*, although Josephus seems to retell Manetho's treatment in two different versions.[13] Manetho's phil-Egyptian version or Josephus's interpretation of it identified or associated the expulsion of the Hyksos with the biblical account of

---

7. Wacholder, *Eupolemus*, 85–96.
8. Yoyotte, "L'Egypte ancienne."
9. See *ANET*, 231–34, 260.
10. Gager, *Moses*, 113–33.
11. Sevenster, *The Roots*.
12. Gager, *Moses*, 113.
13. Stern, *Greek and Latin Authors*, 62–65.

the Hebrew departure from Egypt, an interpretation sometimes found in modern histories of ancient Israel.

Among the materials preserved by Eusebius from the collective work of Alexander Polyhistor (*Concerning the Jews*) are fragments of a historical work by the so-called Pseudo-Eupolemus (*Praeparatio Evangelica* 9.17–39). This writer was apparently a Samaritan and one of the first to present biblical history under the form of Hellenistic historical writing.[14] Some time near the beginning of the second century BCE, he combined biblical materials with traditions from non-Jewish writers such as Berossus and Hesiod in order to show Abraham as the source of the culture of the Phoenicians and Egyptians, and thus indirectly the source of Greek culture, since Herodotus, Plato, and Hecataeus had argued that the Greeks had acquired much wisdom from the Egyptians. Such a position carried the assertion that the biblical tradition represented the oldest wisdom of humanity. Abraham was the teacher of a multitude of nations (see Gen 17:5)! Pseudo-Eupolemus utilized various elements of Babylonian and Greek mythology, perhaps the pseudepigraphical Enoch tradition, and haggadic traditions about Abraham. His work depicts Abraham in universalistic categories and is clearly concerned with apologetic interests.

Shortly after Pseudo-Eupolemus, and perhaps partially dependent upon him, the Alexandrian Jewish philosopher Aristobulus (see 2 Macc 1:10) expounded Judaism as a philosophy and sought to show that the Mosaic law was a true philosophy and in no way contradictory to philosophical wisdom.[15] His work was apparently addressed to the young King Ptolemy VI Philometor (181–145 BCE) but may have been intended for a larger, even predominantly Jewish audience. Such apologetic works—both historical and philosophical—must have been addressed, at least in a limited way, to non-Jewish pagans[16] and not just to renegade Jews who had forsaken Judaism or were strongly tempted by the option of apostasy.[17] The work of Pseudo-Eupolemus suggests that historical writing as an apologetic concern addressed to non-Jews developed in Palestine in

---

14. Wacholder, "Pseudo-Eupolemus"; Walter, "Zu Pseudo-Eupolemus."
15. See Walter, *Der Thoraausleger Aristobulos*.
16. So Gager, *Moses*, 78–79.
17. So Tcherikover, "Jewish Apologetic Literature."

Hellenistic circles before the Maccabean Revolt and probably not just in Samaria.[18]

The Maccabean struggles against the Seleucids triggered extensive Jewish historical writing. Eupolemus,[19] probably shortly after the Maccabean Revolt (see 1 Macc 8:17; 2 Macc 4:11), wrote a work on Jewish history that discussed, among other matters, the date of the exodus and the figure of Moses (dated chronologically much earlier than in the MT), the Solomonic temple, and the Davidic–Solomonic state where the discussion reflects the influence of the expansion of the Hasmoneans and their international political relations. Eupolemus, as a Hellenized, priestly supporter of the Maccabees, demonstrates a strong patriotic and nationalistic interpretation of Jewish history and less of the universalistic spirit that characterized Pseudo-Eupolemus. According to Clement of Alexandria (*Stromata* 1.141), Eupolemus calculated the time between Adam and the fifth year of Demetrius I Soter (162–150 BCE) as 5,149 years. In his chronological concerns, Eupolemus expressed the widespread interest in world chronology that was characteristic of many Hellenistic writers.[20] Jason of Cyrene, about whom nothing is certainly known, produced a five-volume history of the early Maccabean struggles (see 2 Macc 2:23), probably covering the years 176–160 BCE. His work has been summarized as 2 Maccabees[21] by an unknown epitomizer who probably not only condensed the massive work but added some popular haggadic legends (2 Macc 1:11–18), supernaturalistic touches, and martyrological stories (2 Maccabees 6–7). Second Maccabees is more akin to Hellenistic than biblical historiography—in its direct address to the reader, its edifying quality, its conscious literary strivings, and its concern to entertain and enhance the reader's enjoyment (see especially 2 Macc 1:1–6; 15:38–39).

First Maccabees, like 2 Maccabees, may be classified as contemporary history since its focus of concern is the Maccabean struggles down to 134 BCE, probably near the book's date of composition. This work is more similar to the narrative style of Kings and Chronicles, that is to biblical historiography, than 2 Maccabees, although the work is in some regards more pro-Hasmonean than the latter.

18. See Wacholder, "Pseudo-Eupolemus," 112–13.
19. See Wacholder, *Eupolemus*.
20. See Wacholder, "Biblical Chronology."
21. Momigliano, "The Second Book of Maccabees."

One further work engendered by the Maccabean struggles should be noted, namely the book of Daniel. While apocalyptic rather than purely historical in form, the book of Daniel does, however, reflect a concern widespread in Hellenistic historiography—the concern with universal history which has already been noted in the work of the Samaritan Pseudo-Eupolemus. Daniel utilized the concept of four world monarchies in discussing universal history, a concept widely and earlier employed by Greek and Hellenistic writers as well as later Roman authors.[22] In Daniel one can discern a tripartite division in the author's treatment of world history: (1) the time before the capture of Jerusalem, known from the biblical historical works (more assumed than discussed by the author); (2) the era of the four world empires manifesting a great decline in civilization; and (3) the futuristic eternal kingdom about to dawn.[23] This understanding and schema of history, later adopted and adapted by Christian historians, were to dominate historical treatments of Israelite and Judean history until the post-Reformation period.

Four writers of Jewish history from the Greco-Roman period deserve attention: Alexander Polyhistor (first century BCE), Nicolaus of Damascus (born about 64 BCE), Justus of Tiberias (first century CE), and Flavius Josephus (about 37–100 CE). Alexander was from Miletus, although he wrote in Rome where he had been taken by Lentulus during Sulla's eastern campaign. The latter manumitted and appointed him a pedagogue. Among Alexander's more than twenty-five works, one was titled *Concerning the Jews*, fragments of which have been preserved in Eusebius's *Praeparatio Evangelica*. Much of his writings apparently consisted of compilations. His writing on the Jews probably belongs to the period shortly after Pompey's conquest of the Seleucid empire and reflects the Roman fascination with and curiosity about things Eastern. In the preserved fragments, Alexander, who was not Jewish, quotes Jewish and pro-Jewish as well as non-Jewish and anti-Jewish authors, seemingly adhering faithfully and undiscriminatingly to his sources. His account of Jewish history began with the pre-patriarchal ancestors and may have extended down to his own day. The order of the events narrated follows the sequence of the biblical books, beginning with Genesis and extending through Kings and Chronicles, which might suggest that he was familiar with the biblical books in translation. His quotations from some rather

---

22. See Trieber, *Die Idee*; and Swain, "The Theory."
23. So Koch, "Spätisraelitisches Geschichtsdenken," 28.

obscure writers would indicate his utilization of a significant Roman library. An important feature of Alexander's work is its reflection of the extensive chronological synchronization of Egyptian, Babylonian, Greek, and biblical history and data. For example, Alexander associated the biblical flood and Noah with Berossus's Babylonian flood story and Xisuthrus. Already in the second and first centuries BCE, numerous attempts had been made to produce a world chronology and an Alexandrian biblical chronological 'school' can perhaps be traced back to the Hellenistic Jewish writer Demetrius, who wrote during the reign of Ptolemy IV Philopator (221–204 BCE).[24] The Greek version of the Pentateuch certainly reflects the activity of such a chronological school.

Nicolaus of Damascus, who had served as tutor to Cleopatra's children and written a biography of Augustus, became a court official and counsellor to Herod the Great some time before 14 BCE probably as part of the latter's desire to turn Jerusalem into a major literary center. Among his works were an autobiography and a world history composed in 144 books. Nicolaus's history, written in Jerusalem and under the patronage of Herod, to whose reign about one-fifth of the work was devoted, was a true universal history that integrated Jewish history into the larger context of world history, which was traced back to the times of mythical origins. With the exception of Josephus, Jewish and Christian historians seem to have made little use of Nicolaus's work, although extensive portions were available to Photius, the ninth-century anthologist and patriarch of Constantinople.

Justus of Tiberias, a contemporary and antagonist of Josephus and like him apparently an unenthusiastic supporter of the revolt against Rome, produced not only a history of the Jewish War but also a chronicle of the Jewish kings extending from Moses to the time of Agrippa II. Justus seems to have made extensive use of Hellenistic universal chronicles, synchronizing the date of the exodus with the assumed contemporary Attic and Egyptian rulers. Justus's extensive chronological synchronization, through the work of Julius Africanus, exercised a significant influence upon Christian biblical chronography.

Pride of place among Greco-Roman Jewish historians must be assigned to Flavius Josephus, although this may be as much due to the accident of historical preservation as to the excellence of historical presentation in his works. In the last quarter of the first century BCE,

---

24. Wacholder, *Eupolemus*, 98–104.

Josephus produced four major writings: *Bellum judaicum*, a history of the Jewish War in seven books; *Antiquitates Judaicae*, a history of the Jewish people from earliest times down to the outbreak of the Jewish–Roman War in 66 BCE in twenty books; *Vita*, an autobiographical work primarily describing Josephus's role in the war; and *Contra Apionem*, a treatise on the antiquity of the Jewish people in two books. All of Josephus's works were written for apologetic or polemical purposes, a factor that exercised significant influence and perhaps frequently produced distortions in his presentations. Whether Josephus was a traitor to his own people or a nationalist with loyalties that transcended the passion of Zealotism has been much debated, but that he was a sagacious opportunist has seldom been doubted.

In spite of Josephus's argument that "the industrious writer is not one who merely remodels the scheme and arrangement of another's work, but one who uses fresh materials and makes the framework of the history his own" (*War* 1.15), much of his historical work relied heavily upon previous authors, a factor sometimes acknowledged, sometimes not.[25] Josephus was consciously aware of his interest, apologetic concerns, and the need to justify his presentations, and he commented briefly on his historiographic method. The account of the Jewish war, his finest work, was written to demonstrate that the Jewish revolutionary party was the dominant factor in the Jewish–Roman strife and the cause of the destruction of the temple and to correct previously published non-Jewish versions of the conflict (*War* 1.1–18). As to the first purpose, Josephus informed his Greek and Roman readers that, in spite of his desire to "recount faithfully the actions of both combatants" (*War* 1.9), his own reflections and private sentiments held that his country "owed its ruin to civil strife, and that it was the Jewish tyrants who drew down upon the holy temple the unwilling hands of the Romans" (*War* 1.10). As to the second purpose, Josephus felt that he had to correct the view that the Romans were "the conquerors of a puny people" (*War* 1.8) and to combat ill-informed historians: "As for the native Greeks, where personal profit or a lawsuit is concerned, their mouths are at once agape and their tongues loosed; but in the matter of history, where veracity and laborious collection of the facts are essential, they are mute, leaving to inferior and ill-informed writers the task of describing the exploits of their rulers.

---

25. See Schürer, *History*, 43–63, on his sources.

Let us at least hold historical truth in honour, since by the Greeks it is disregarded" (*War* 1.16).

In the *War*, Josephus's interpretation of the events of his day is presented, in Thucydidean fashion, in three speeches attributed to Agrippa (2.345–401), Josephus himself (5.362–419), and Eleazar, the leader of the Masada rebels (7.323–36, 341–88).[26] The central elements in Josephus's interpretations were twofold. (1) As in Polybius, Roman dominance was understood as the work of providence or God. Josephus has Agrippa declare: "Divine assistance . . . is ranged on the side of the Romans, for, without God's aid, so vast an empire could never have been built up" (2.391). Josephus reports that in his speech to the defenders of Jerusalem, he, after surveying the history of Israel's suffering, sought to convince the Jews that "the Deity has fled from the holy places and taken His stand on the side of those with whom you are now at war" (5.412). Thus, like the prophets of old, Josephus applied a theological rationalization to explain the conditions of history. (2) The decimation of the nation and the trauma of the temple's destruction were interpreted by Josephus as divine recompense (5.413–19). Josephus has Eleazar declare: "We have been deprived, manifestly by God Himself, of all hope of deliverance," for God was expressing his "wrath at the many wrongs which we madly dared to inflict upon our countrymen." He even has Eleazar interpret the rebels' suicidal death as a form of payment to God: "The penalty for those crimes let us pay not to our bitterest foes, the Romans, but to God through the act of our own hands" (7.331–33). With good Deuteronomistic theology, Josephus explained the calamity that befell the Jews as divine punishment for the sins of the people, though as the sins of a minor element in the population.

Josephus's other major historical work, his magnum opus, was titled *Jewish Antiquities* (or, literally translated, *Jewish Archaeologies*). Involved in Josephus's presentation of the "ancient history and political constitution" of the Jews to the Greek-speaking world (*Ant.* 1.5) were two subsidiary influences, one clearly expressed and the second clearly deducible. In the first place, the translation of the Pentateuch into Greek in Alexandria, as reported in the *Letter of Aristeas*, and the assumed Greco-Roman interest in this work on Jewish history led Josephus to hope that a widespread interest in Jewish history in its entirety existed among non-Jews (1.10–14). The curiosity and encouragement of his patron, Epaphroditus,

---

26. See Lindner, *Die Geschichtsausfassung*.

reinforced his hope. Josephus's model led him to approach the topic in terms of translating the Hebrew records (1.5), although his work can in no way be classified as a translation and even to designate it a paraphrase is misleading.

Secondly, in 7 BCE, Dionysius of Halicarnassus had published in twenty books a work on Roman archaeologies (*Antiquitates Romanae*), written in Greek, in which he utilized various types of source material in order to demonstrate the great antiquity of Rome in line with the general interest in antiquity reflected in Hellenistic writers who, however, stressed Babylonian, Greek, Egyptian, or Jewish antiquity rather than Roman. Josephus seems to have adopted consciously the pattern and interest of Dionysius in the general structure of his work in order to demonstrate that Jewish history was able to stand on an equal footing with that of any other culture in terms of both antiquity and intrinsic interest.

In the present discussions, only a few general characteristics of Josephus's history can be noted:

1. Although Josephus declares that his aim is to set forth "the precise details of our Scripture records neither adding nor omitting anything" (*Ant.* 1.17), he did deliberately omit some traditions as well as supplement the biblical materials. Some of his conscious omissions were clearly calculated to avoid providing anti-Jewish protagonists with any material that might be used to support the scurrilous claims that the Jews worshipped God in animal form, specifically the ass. One of the prominent concerns in his *Contra Apionem* is the refutation of this accusation. Noteworthy in this regard is his omission of any reference to the story of the Israelite worship of the golden calf (Exodus 32) in his history. Numerous non-biblical legends, many with parallels in rabbinic and Hellenistic haggadah, were added to his presentation. Among these are the stories of Moses's command of the Egyptian army in expelling the Ethiopians (*Ant.* 2.238–53; a similar but not identical version appears in the second-century BCE writings of the Alexandrian Artapanus), the worship of Alexander the Great in the Jerusalem temple and his special favors to the Jews (*Ant.* 11.329–45; a very popular theme in later rabbinic tradition), and numerous less significant stories. Josephus does not explicitly differentiate between the biblical and the haggadic non-biblical traditions; the two seem to stand on an equal footing in his work.

2. In his discussion of Abraham and Moses, Josephus glorifies both characters, but at the same time he stops short of portraying them as immortals. Abraham is depicted as the first monotheist whose monotheism

was derived from his speculation on the irregularity of natural and astronomical phenomena and was responsible for his persecution in Mesopotamia and subsequent settlement in Canaan (*Ant.* 1.154–57). In Egypt, Abraham taught astronomy (already discovered by the antediluvian ancients; *Ant.* 1.69–71) and arithmetic to the ignorant Egyptians, who subsequently passed along this learning to the Greeks (*Ant.* 1.166–68; somewhat similarly Artapanus, see Eusebius, *Praeparatio Evangelica* 9.18). Josephus presents Moses, whose birth and significance were revealed to Pharaoh and Amram (*Ant.* 2.205–16), as a philosopher, lawgiver, statesman, and military hero (see especially *Ant.* 1.18–26; 2.238–53; 3.179–87; 4.176–95). Josephus stresses not only Moses's death but Moses's authorship of the account of his death so that none could claim that, like Enoch (*Ant.* 1.84), "by reason of his surpassing virtue he had gone back to the Deity" (*Ant.* 4.326; see 396; and compare Philo, *De Vita Mosis* 2.288–91) and thus been granted special immortality, as seems to have been claimed in certain circles (see Origen, *Contra Celsum* 1.21).

3. Although Josephus declares that "some things the lawgiver Moses shrewdly veils in enigmas, others he sets forth in solemn allegory" (*Ant.* 1.24), his work is surprisingly free of allegorical interpretation, in strong contrast to the work of Philo (see, for example, Philo's *De Migratione Abrahami*). Josephus, however, sought to show the correlation between Moses's writing and natural philosophy, for example, in the depiction of the tabernacle and priestly garments as "an imitation of universal nature" (*Ant.* 3.123, 179–87).

4. A further noteworthy characteristic in Josephus's history is his recognition of many of the critical problems and difficulties in the biblical text, a characteristic shared by many of his Jewish contemporary and later rabbinic interpreters of the Scriptures. His work demonstrates that the ancients perceived many of the issues that were to occupy scholarly investigations centuries later. Working within a framework that accepted the inspiration and veracity of the Scriptures and gave no thought to the possibility of diversity and development in the literary text, Josephus handled these problems through supplementation and harmonization. A few examples will suffice as illustrations. In discussing Cain, for example, Josephus is careful to point out that Adam and Eve had not only sons but daughters as well (*Ant.* 1.52; cf. *Jubilees* 4.1–8) and that Cain feared that he would be a prey to wild beasts in his wanderings and thus needed a protective marking (*Ant.* 1.59). In the discussion of the tribal allotments in the book of Joshua, one should logically conclude that since

the distribution was an ad hoc operation by lot, then equality in tribal territories should be expected. Josephus knew that this had not been the case and this he explained in terms of land valuation and tribal population (*Ant.* 5.76–80). In discussing the capture of Jerusalem, Josephus was aware of the contradictions in Josh 15:63; Judg 1:8, 21; and 2 Sam 5:1–10 and the need to harmonize such contradictions. Josephus accomplished this task by having two Jerusalems—a lower city captured as noted in Judg 1:8 and an upper city not taken until the time of David (*Ant.* 5.124; 7.61–64). In the stories of David's first association with Saul, the biblical text has David entering Saul's service as a musician and armor-bearer (1 Samuel 16) whereas the subsequent story of David's combat with Goliath depicts Saul as unaware of David's identity. Josephus harmonizes the traditions by playing down the identity problem, omitting any reference to 1 Sam 17:55–58 (perhaps due to his dependence upon the Greek text where these verses do not appear), and by suggesting that David had previously been placed on furlough by Saul (*Ant.* 6.175). Second Samuel 21:19, where Elhanan is said to have killed Goliath, is harmonized with 1 Samuel 17 by Josephus's omission of the name of Goliath in the former.

5. Another notable feature of Josephus's historical treatment is his rationalization of miraculous and extraordinary events. Josephus was somewhat troubled by Old Testament miracles (as was apparently the author of Wisdom of Solomon 19:6–21), or at least wondered about the incredulity of Gentile readers. Josephus dealt with the miraculous by carefully guarding himself and his own opinion and/or by explaining the miraculous through rationalization. When speaking of accounts in which miracle played a significant role, Josephus frequently pointed out that he was merely recounting the story as he "found it in the sacred books" (see *Ant.* 2.347). At other times, he used a rather set formula suggesting that on these matters "everyone should decide according to his fancy" or "everyone is welcome to his own opinion" (see *Ant.* 1.108; 2.348 and frequently elsewhere). This tendency to point the reader to his own opinion was already used by Dionysius of Halicarnassus (*Roman Antiquities* 1.48), from whom Josephus may have borrowed it, and was later stated as a rule for historians by Lucian in his third-century CE work, *How to Write History*: "Should any myth come into question, it should be related but not wholly credited: rather it should be left open for readers to conjecture about it as they will, but do you take no risks and incline neither to one opinion nor to the other" (60).

The History of the Study of Israelite and Judean History

On several occasions, Josephus offers a rationalistic or naturalistic explanation for the unusual. The great longevity of the antediluvians was due not only to their being "beloved of God" but also to their use of astronomy and geometry and a diet "conducive to longevity" (*Ant.* 1.104–8). The Hebrew passage through the sea is paralleled by the retirement of the Pamphylian Sea before Alexander (*Ant.* 2.347–48).The purification of the bitter waters of Marah was due to the draining off of the contaminated part (*Ant.* 3.8). Josephus pointed out that quail were abundant around the Arabian Gulf and that manna was still a phenomenon in that region (*Ant.* 3.25, 31). Even natural causes are offered as one solution to the plagues that beset the Philistines after their capture of the ark (*Ant.* 6.9). In explaining the rescue of Jerusalem and the slaughter of 185,000 Assyrians in a single night, Josephus drew upon the story of Herodotus, which told of an invasion by mice of the Assyrian military camps (*Ant.* 10.18–22). Josephus, however, was no thoroughgoing rationalist who shied away from references to the miraculous. In his description of the fall of Jerusalem (*War* 6.288–300), he refers to numerous miraculous portents that heralded the fall of the holy city. Whether he believed these to be actual occurrences or was merely seeking to emphasize for his audience the gravity of the occasion with rhetorical exaggeration is, of course, beyond the realm of solution.

6. A final characteristic of Josephus's account of Israelite and Judean history is his lack of any sense of development in the people's institutions and religion. The orthodox practices, beliefs, and institutions of his day were assumed to have existed from the time of Moses (see the book of *Jubilees* where the patriarchs are depicted as exemplary practitioners of the Mosaic law). That the whole of Jewish law and the institutional structure of Judaism had been given on Mount Sinai was a firmly anchored concept in later rabbinic Judaism. Josephus certainly operated with a very similar assumption.

After Josephus, ancient Judaism produced no historian in any way comparable. Very few Jewish writings from the rabbinic and Talmudic periods can be called historical works. Three perhaps should be noted. The *Megillat Taanit* ("The Scroll of Fasts") is an Aramaic document probably written near the beginning of the second century CE. Containing a list of thirty-six days on which Jews were not to fast because of the joyous events that occurred on those days, the work provides some narrative material on events during the period of the second temple. However, in no way can it really be designated a real history. The *Seder Olam Rabbah*

("The Order of the World"), probably from the second century CE, is a chronological work generally ascribed to Rabbi Yose ben Halafta.[27] The work established a chronology based on the calculation of dates from the creation of the world (*libriath ha'olam* or *anno mundi*). While it is primarily concerned with the dating of biblical events, a final chapter surveys the period from Alexander the Great to the revolt of Bar Kokhba in 132–135 CE. Meyer has summarized the value of this work in the following terms: The author's

> endeavour to establish a single consistent chronology, reconciling apparent variations in the biblical text, would place his work very much in the rabbinic tradition of seeking to resolve scriptural contradictions which might otherwise create some doubt about the accuracy of the text. Though he confined himself almost entirely to biblical history, mixed chronicle with midrash, and sometimes departed from chronological sequence, the author of *Seder Olam* did evince a desire to establish a sequential framework for Jewish history. His concern was unusual for that time.[28]

Pseudo-Philo's *Liber antiquitatum biblicarum* was apparently produced in the first century CE as a Jewish handbook on biblical history.[29] The work is primarily a midrashic chronicle of biblical history from Adam to David characterized by extensive omissions, modifications, and additions to the biblical texts. Its exact purpose is unknown. Many of its additions have parallels in other Jewish haggadah. The work was translated into Greek and subsequently into Latin, perhaps in the process being turned into a Christian handbook.

The sudden cessation of the writing of historical works by the Jews has been explained in various ways. The causes of this phenomenon were probably multiple; among them were the Jewish loss of a national and cultic center, the sense of a demise of sacred history with the destruction of the temple, the further scattering of the Jews in the diaspora that intensified the dissipation of any concept of continuing political history, the canonization of Scripture that presented the Jews with a closed sacred past, the general disillusionment with historical processes attendant upon the failure of two major Jewish revolts against Rome, and the rabbinical

---

27. For the chronological scheme, see Finegan, *Handbook*, 123–30.
28. Meyer, *Ideas of Jewish History*, 14.
29. On the text, see Kisch, *Pseudo-Philo's*; and Harrington, *The Hebrew Fragments*.

orientation towards the law and its application and the rabbinical demands for total purity of life and separation from the world. Jewish historians in the Hellenistic and Greco-Roman world had borrowed the forms and interests of Hellenistic historiography and ethnography and utilized these for apologetic, propaganda, and polemical purposes. Josephus was a primary example. After the Bar Kokhba Revolt, these purposes seem to have lost their appeal. Jewish apocalyptic, with its special historical concerns, was reduced to only a glowing ember in the Hadrianic fires.

The early Christian church inherited from Judaism a collection of Scriptures strongly oriented to history. This combined with the belief that God had finally and fully revealed himself in the historical person, Jesus of Nazareth, meant that Christians could not ignore past history; in fact it had to claim the history of the old covenant as its own. The apologetic desire to present Christianity as the true heir of Old Testament faith and the evangelistic-confessional proclamation of the church as the special object of God's providence led to the attempt to view "theocratic" history in systematic form. This systematization of history took both chronological and philosophical forms, although even the chronological perspectives were undergirded with major theological claims. The earliest specimens of Christian interpretation and systematic treatments of history were more chronological than historiographic in form.

The Christian chronographers had to summarize the history that the converts were now supposed to consider their own; they had also to show the antiquity of the Jewish–Christian doctrine, and they had to present a model of providential history. The result was that, unlike pagan chronology, Christian chronology was also a philosophy of history. Unlike pagan elementary teaching, Christian elementary teaching of history could not avoid touching upon the essentials of the destiny of man.[30]

Little is known of the Christian chronographers and their works prior to the establishment of Christianity as the state religion in the fourth century CE. Among the most important of these pre-Constantinian Christian 'historians' were Clement of Alexandria, Julius Africanus, and Hippolytus of Rome. Their concerns were primarily apologetic—to counter the contempt of Christianity as a novelty; and their methods were primarily those of their precursors, the Greco-Jewish historians and Hellenistic chronographers.

---

30. Momigliano, "Pagan and Christian Historiography," 83.

The work of Julius Africanus (about 170–245 CE), of which only fragments have survived, will illustrate the approach of these Christian chronographers.³¹ Africanus's work, which was still available to Jerome (*De viris illustribus*, 63), consisted of five volumes. He treated the history of the world from creation until his own day and like practically all patristic writers saw chronology in eschatological perspectives. He allotted 6,000 years for the world's duration and dated the birth of Jesus to 5500 *anno mundi*. Such time schemes or world ages were common in Jewish apocalyptic writings and are even found in rabbinic sources.³² Africanus did not share the view of his North African contemporary Tertullian, who claimed that "to be ignorant of everything outside the rule of faith is to possess all knowledge." He worked out an elaborate synopsis of sacred and profane history, using as a fixed point the accession of Cyrus, and sought to collaborate his synchronisms with quotations from secular sources. He dated the flood to 2,262 after creation and apparently placed the exodus in the year 3,707. The first of these reckonings differs from the LXX, which places the flood 2,242 years after creation, and the date of the exodus was correlated with a Greek version of the flood assigned to the time of Ogygos, the legendary first king of Thebes. The date of Cyrus's accession was derived from Diodorus of Sicily, who had stated that Cyrus became king of the Persians in the opening year of the fifty-fifth Olympiad. The Olympiad system was based on the quadrennial celebration of the Olympic games, with the first of these supposedly held in what would be our 776/775 BCE.³³

In Africanus, one sees a flicker of textual criticism, so essential to scientific historiography. In a letter to Origen, he outlined seven reasons for considering the story of Susanna as late and fictitious and thus as no original part of the book of Daniel. He also noted and discussed the differences in the Matthean and Lukan genealogies of Jesus. Africanus's textual criticism and skepticism of sources, however, nowhere approached that of the non-Christians Celsus and Porphyry. In their attacks on Christianity, the former criticized the miraculous and absurd in the Bible and the latter denied the Mosaic authorship of the Pentateuch, pointed out inconsistencies in Genesis, understood the book of Daniel against the

---

31. See Gelzer, *Sextus Julius Africanus*.

32. Rabbi Katina, in *b. Sanhedrin* 97a, spoke of a 6,000-year scheme: 2,000 years of *tohu* (chaos), 2,000 years of torah, and 2,000 years in the messianic age.

33. For Africanus's chronological system, see Finegan, *Handbook*, 140–46.

times of Antiochus Epiphanes, and called attention to major disagreements in the Gospels.

Eusebius of Caesarea, who died about 340 CE, utilized the works of his Christian and pagan predecessors in the study of chronography and produced an extensive chronology of world history. Although especially indebted to the work of Africanus, Eusebius frequently deviated from him and developed a new system for synchronistic tabulation. Unfortunately, Eusebius's chronographic work has survived only in Jerome's Latin translation and adaptation and in an anonymous Armenian translation. In his so-called *Chronographia*, he produced an outline of the history of five major nations: the Assyrians, Hebrews, Egyptians, Greeks, and Romans. In calculating the reigns of these nations' rulers, he engaged in some critical discussions of the systems used for dating. The chronological differences among the Greek, Hebrew, and Samaritan texts were discussed with Eusebius generally opting for the LXX calculations. In his so-called *Chronicon*, Eusebius utilized a series of parallel columns for presenting the synchronism of the various empires. He took the birth of Abraham as his fixed point for reckoning and placed this in 3,184 *anno mundi*. The flood was dated to 2,242 and the exodus 505 years after the birth of Abraham. By choosing Abraham as the beginning point in his calculations, Eusebius thus partially sidestepped the LXX/Hebrew chronological problems, since the major differences are found in the early chapters of Genesis.[34]

Eusebius did not produce his chronology in any hope of detailing the coming of the eschatological end-time, nor did he, like Africanus, work with any world-age scheme. Uncertainty about the times and seasons, he wrote, applies "not merely to the final cataclysm but to all times." For him, "chronology was something between an exact science and an instrument of propaganda."[35] Eusebius's career spanned the time that saw the church move from a persecuted sect to a state institution. His days were times of triumph for Christianity and Eusebius's writings affirm this as the providential purpose of God whose action in human affairs was the real nucleus of the historical process.

Eusebius was not only the ablest of the ancient Christian chronographers, he was also the father of ecclesiastical history. Eusebius was the first to produce a history of the church—which for him extended from

---

34. For Eusebius's chronological reckonings, see ibid., 147–87.
35. Momigliano, "Pagan and Christian Historiography," 85.

the incarnation until his own day, in which the savior had wrought a great and final deliverance and destroyed the enemies of true religion. In approaching his subject, Eusebius confessed, in the first chapter of his *Ecclesiastical History*, that "as the first of those that have entered upon the subject, we are attempting a kind of trackless and unbeaten path." In executing his narration of church history, Eusebius spoke of the fragmentary knowledge of the past and the evidence available.

> We are totally unable to find even the bare vestiges of those who may have travelled the way before us; unless, perhaps, what is only presented in the slight intimations, which some in different ways have transmitted to us in certain partial narratives of the times in which they lived; who, raising their voices before us, like torches at a distance, and as looking down from some commanding height, call out and exhort us where we should walk, and whither direct our course with certainty and safety. Whatsoever, therefore, we deem likely to be advantageous to the proposed subject, we shall endeavour to reduce to a compact body by historical narration. For this purpose we have collected the materials that have been scattered by our predecessors, and culled, as from some intellectual meadows, the appropriate extracts from ancient authors. (1.1)

In carrying out this procedure, Eusebius made a lasting contribution to Western historiography.

A new chapter of historiography begins with Eusebius not only because he invented ecclesiastical history, but because he wrote it with a documentation that is utterly different from that of pagan historians.[36]

Over one hundred works are cited directly or referred to as read by Eusebius. It is true, as Eusebius's critics have frequently noted, that his intellectual qualifications were somewhat defective, that he sometimes suppressed that which might disgrace religion, that he occasionally misquoted sources, and that he sometimes failed to note that his quoted documents were contradictory. Nonetheless, Eusebius realized that the writing of history is dependent upon the reading and discriminating study of the documents of the past. Considering the number of spurious documents he chose not to utilize, one must judge Eusebius an outstanding source critic for his age.

Eusebius wrote his works in the glow of Christianity's newly acquired status. In the glare of the conflagration kindled by the barbarian

---

36. Ibid., 92.

invasion of the Roman empire, Augustine (354–430 CE), the converted ex-teacher of rhetoric, sought to gather the whole of human history into a theological-eschatological framework. Christianity, like the empire, found itself on the defensive in the days of Augustine, and he launched a counter-offensive against paganism's attempts to lay the blame for the empire's troubles on the steps of the church. For the later Augustine, any attempt to present the Roman empire in messianic terms would have constituted a heresy of the first order.

Augustine took the six-day scheme of creation and transposed these into a sixfold periodization of sacred history, the history of *De civitate dei* versus *De civitate terrena*: Just as there were six days of creation, so there were six ages of history: the first from Adam to the flood, the second from the flood to Abraham, the next three (as outlined in St Matthew's gospel) from Abraham to David, from David to the Babylonian captivity, and from the Babylonian captivity to the birth of Christ. Then came the sixth age, in which the human mind was recreated in the image of God, just as on the sixth day of creation humandkind was created in the image of God. In this age men now lived (*De civitate dei* 22.30). The time from Adam to Noah constituted the first day and saw the light of a promised redeemer given to the fallen parents of the human race. The second day—the period of childhood—extended from Noah to Abraham with the ark as the symbol of the promise of salvation. From Abraham to David was the third day of youthful adolescence, and, as God has separated the waters on the third day, so he in this age separated the chosen people from the heathen masses. From David to the exile was the day of early manhood. The period of full manhood—the fifth day—extended from the scattering of the chosen people until the coming of the Messiah. The period of old age—the sixth day—was the age of Christian salvation with its new Adam (Jesus) and its new Eve (the church). The seventh day, corresponding to the divine sabbath, would dawn with the return of Christ in glory to establish a peace that would know no end. Augustine thus placed his own time within the waning period of the sixth day. That day had dawned with John the Baptist, with Christ's incarnation the sun had risen, and with the spread of Christianity noonday had arrived. The sun had now begun its descent and senility set in but Augustine warned against precise speculation on the arrival of sunset.

In Augustine's schematization, a number of factors are of significance. (1) He is not so much concerned with history as with the philosophy of history. (2) It is sacred history, the history of *De civitate dei*, that is important, not the outer events or occurrences nor human actions and causality. (3) The past of humankind and of Israel and Judah are of importance only as the prelude to the age of redemption, which itself is only a prelude to that final timeless period of total salvation and damnation. (4) Augustine's vision embodies a penultimate pessimism about his own day, which was the age of senility, the time before the end. (5) Augustine sought "to direct man's gaze from the contemplation of himself and the achievements of his reason upwards to the majesty of God."[37]

In *The City of God*, Augustine had attempted to prove that the calamities that had befallen the Romans were not limited to the period of the church and, whenever they had occurred, were the result of the corruption of manners and the vices of the soul. The expansion of this thesis he bequeathed to his contemporary and admirer, Orosius. The latter's *Historiarum adversus paganos libri septem*, completed in 418 CE, was an attempt "to trace the beginning and man's wretchedness from the beginning of man's sin" (1.1). Orosius prefaced his main discussion with a description of Asia, Europe, and Africa, thus manifesting a recognition of the importance of geography for history (as had Caesar, Cicero, and Sallust). Orosius's work is important for subsequent historiography not because he "set forth . . . the desires and punishments of sinful men, the struggles of the world and the judgments of God, from the beginning of the world down to the present day, that is, during five thousand six hundred and eighteen years" (7.43), but because of his particular periodization of world history. According to Orosius, there had existed four world empires: Babylon, Macedon, Carthage, and Rome. His thesis is no doubt based on a particular interpretation of the four empires in Daniel (Babylonian, Persian, Median, and Greek), which identified the fourth empire with Rome. However, Orosius took a far more favorable attitude towards the Roman empire than his idol Augustine. For him, the iron teeth and claws of the fourth beast were a deterrent to the barbarians and the antichrist.

Before summarizing the early church's historiographic legacy to the Middle Ages, three additional factors should be noted. In the first place, the theory of the plenary inspiration of Scripture had become widespread by the fifth century CE. Such a view of the origin and nature of the Bible stifles any drastic critical approach to the biblical materials. Since the Bible was and remains the basic source material for the history

---

37. Milburn, *Early Christian*, 85.

of Israel and Judah, such a position almost by necessity means that the historian retells, expands, elucidates, and harmonizes the biblical source material but does not deal with it critically. Secondly, the hermeneutical principles widely employed in the church allowed the interpreter to find several meanings in any given text: the historical and various mystical, analogical, figurative, and allegorical senses. This multiple layer method of interpretation was indebted not only to Greek allegorical treatments of epic and mythical materials and to rabbinic exegesis but also to the philosophical–allegorical interpretation of Aristobulus and Philo of Alexandria.[38] The allegorical approach to biblical interpretation meant that interpreters did not have to confront directly the problems and difficulties within the biblical text. When in doubt, appeal could be made to the rule of faith and the established tradition: *Quod ubique, quod semper, quod ab omnibus creditum est.*

Thirdly, hagiography (the writing of accounts of the lives and sufferings of saints) had become widespread in the fourth and fifth centuries, perhaps influenced to a degree by the Hellenistic conception of the divine man. Athanasius's *Life of St. Anthony* and Sulpicius Severus's *Life of St. Martin of Tours* are good examples. These hagiographies were eulogistic and rhetorical biographies that offered a sort of dateless and timeless semi-historical work. They actually functioned to draw people away from the matter-of-fact world and pointed to that transcendental realm that impinged upon historical reality. Eusebeius, in his life of Constantine, demonstrated how difficult it was to write a Christian biography of a person involved in affairs military, political, and economic. Hagiography was concerned with different matters. Yet hagiography was to be standard fare in medieval times and in its own way an impediment to the development of serious historiography.

What the early church transmitted to the Middle Ages did not encourage the development of serious historiography. No developed Christian historiography comparable to the work of Herodotus, Thucydides, or even Livy, Tacitus, and Josephus, was passed on unless Eusebius's *Ecclesiastical History* be the exception. Augustine, Orosius, and their contemporaries had not dialogued with the secular historians of the pagan revival in the late fourth and early fifth centuries, such as Ammianus Marcellinus. These were left "to die from natural causes."[39] The works of

---

38. See Grant, *The Letter and the Spirit.*
39. Momigliano, "Pagan and Christian Historiography," 99.

the Greek and Hellenistic historians belonged to the pagan past and in the West could quickly sink into a long dormant eclipse. Source and textual criticism were suffocated by the weight of a totally inspired collection of Scriptures, and allegorical interpretation was at hand to provide any needed escape valve. Concern with the transcendental, with the sacred side of the historical process, with the philosophical-eschatological dimensions oriented people towards the other world and away from the questions of human causality and action.

The Medieval Period

Three major types of historical tradition during the medieval period have been distinguished by Southern: classical, early scientific, and prophetic.

> The aim of the classical imitators was to exemplify virtues and vices, for moral instruction, and to extract from the confusion of the past a clear picture of the destinies of peoples. The aim of the scientific students of universal history was to exhibit the divine plan for humanity throughout history, and to demonstrate the congruity between the facts of history revealed in the Bible and the facts provided by secular sources. As for the prophetic historians, their aim was first to identify the historical landmarks referred to in prophetic utterances, then to discover the point at which history had arrived, and finally to predict the future from the still unfulfilled portions of prophecy.[40]

Much of medieval historiography can be analysed in these categories.

A characteristic of practically all historical works during the Middle Ages is what has been called "history without historical perspective."[41]

> The student of medieval historiography must learn to do without perspective in historical presentation. A medieval writer could distinguish stages in the history of salvation, but they were religious stages. He did not discern change or development in temporal history. He saw continuity in customs and institutions ... Roman emperors are made to talk and behave like medieval rulers. Alternatively, a writer learned in the Latin classics tended to make medieval rulers talk and behave like the Caesars. The historian did not only look back to the Old and New Testaments for parallels and precedents; he lived in an expanding Bible. The

---

40. Southern, "4. The Sense of the Past," 242.
41. Smalley, *Historians in the Middle Ages*, 50.

writer of a saint's *Life* felt that he was adding a new page to the Gospel story; the recorder of a warrior's deeds was continuing the tale of ancient and Old Testament heroes. Past and present interlock: ancient precedents imposed themselves on the present; the past resembled the present as the historian saw it. He had no sense of anachronism.[42]

This lack of any sense of the past as past is vividly reflected in medieval art, which portrayed ancient kings, prophets, and saints in the dress, armament, and physical setting of medieval times.

Before examining some of the historical works of this period related to the history of the study of Israelite and Judean history and to historiography in general, some particular comments should be made. First of all, distinction must be made between the European West and the Byzantine East. In the West, Greek literature fell into temporary oblivion; in addition to the basic patristic literature, the primary classical sources used and imitated were Roman. The most widely used of Roman writers were Suetonius, Sallust, Cicero, Virgil, Ovid, and Livy. This meant, of course, a strong emphasis on rhetoric to which history was a sub-genre. In the East, the Byzantine scholars were heirs to the classical Greek traditions, Hellenistic historiography, and early Christian historical writings due to the survival of the Greek language. In the East, however, the writings of Polybius and Plutarch had a significant impact that influenced historical writing towards contemporary history and biography. In the West, the lower level of literacy prejudiced much historiography towards the miraculous and mythical. The rise of territorial states in the West produced a desire to relate national and contemporary history to the general sweep of sacred history.

Secondly, medieval historical works as a rule dealt with pedestrian matters such as city and monastic records and annals, with propagandistic concerns as in the case of royal biographies, or with pietistic orientations exemplified in the lives of saints and other writings of a hagiographic character, as well as in the devotional use made of the biblical traditions. Most of these works contribute little or nothing to either the development of historiographic methodology or to the study of Israelite and Judean history.

Thirdly, the medieval period was no cultural and educational monolith. The concept of the Middle Ages as a barbarian period of constant

---

42. Ibid., 63.

decline is a legacy from Renaissance historiography. Two periods, the Carolingian in the late eighth and early ninth centuries, and the twelfth century have rightly been described as periods of true renaissance.

In the early medieval period, four historians are pre-eminent: Gregory of Tours (about 540–94), Isidore of Seville (about 560–636), the Venerable Bede (about 673–735), and Paul the Deacon (about 720–800). Each of these produced histories that, to a lesser or greater degree, filled out the shadowy past of their people by drawing up a historical pedigree that traced its origins to some great but misty figure or people of the past. (Virgil had done this for the Romans in his account of Aeneas and the Trojans who settled in Latium; and Jordanes, who died about 554, had traced the Goths back to the biblical Magog and the Scythians in his rewriting of Cassiodorius's *De Origine Actibusque Getarum*.) Of these, Isidore and Bede are of interest for the history of the biblical period.

In his *Chronica Majora*, Isidore borrowed from several earlier Christian chronographers and produced a chronology extending from creation to 615 CE. In his universal scheme, Isidore devised the practice of dating everything backward and forward from the birth of Jesus. In his *Etymologiae*, an encyclopedia summarizing the known information on topics as diverse as grammar, mathematics, and medicine, Isidore discussed the topic of history writing.

> Predictably, history is seen as a subsection of grammar, which itself is part of rhetoric. Grammar Isidore defines as "the art of writing," and history as "a written narrative of a certain kind." He distinguishes history from fable and myth: fable expresses truth by means of fiction . . . while poetic myth expresses truth by means of fictions about the gods . . . History differs from these kinds of narrative in being true in itself. It is "the narration of deeds done, by means of which the past is made known."[43]

Isidore went on to argue that history must depend upon the account of eyewitnesses. He writes: "None of the ancients would write history unless he had been present and had seen what he narrated; we grasp what we see better than what we gather from hearsay. Things seen are not represented falsely."[44] A historian writing about the past is thus basically forced to be a compiler dependent upon his sources, which hopefully are or rely upon eyewitness accounts.

---

43. Ibid., 22.
44. Quoted in ibid., 24.

The History of the Study of Israelite and Judean History

By all standards, Bede was the most outstanding historian of the early Middle Ages. In his *Ecclesiastical History of the English People* (*Historia ecclesiastica gentis Anglorum*), he adopted a Eusebian approach to church history, listing and quoting from his sources "in order to remove all occasions of doubt about those things I have written, either in your mind or in the minds of any others who listen to or read this history," as he wrote in his dedication to King Ceolwulf of Northumbria. In his treatment of the biblical period, Bede stood within what Southern has called the scientific tradition of medieval historiography.[45] Bede adopted the six-age scheme of Augustine[46] and popularized Isidore's BC/AD dating. Within the six-age pattern, Bede incorporated a genuine concept of autonomous development in history. Southern has described Bede's originality in the following manner:

> Just as the first Day began with the separation of light from darkness, and ended with the fall of Night, so the first Age began with the creation of man, continued with the separation of the good from the bad, and ended with the destruction of the universal Flood. Bede applied this form of exegesis to each of the six ages. As a result, each age acquired a distinct momentum, similar in pattern but distinct in its results: at the beginning of each there was an act of restoration, succeeded by a period of divergent development, leading to a general disaster which set the scene for a new act of restoration. I think that Bede is quite original in giving to each Age this rhythm of dawn, growth, and destruction, containing the promise of a new dawn. It is a rhythm which has some faint similarity to the Hegelian dialectic of history, and this similarity is strengthened by the way in which Bede ties his ages of history together in a movement analogous to the seven ages in the life of man. The first age, Infancy, is the time beyond the reach of memory before the Flood; the second, Childhood, is the time before Abraham when human language was first formed; the third, Adolescence, is the time of potency, when the generation of the Patriarchs began; the fourth, Maturity, is the time when mankind became capable of kingly rule; the fifth, Old Age, is the time of growing afflictions; the sixth, Senility, is the time in which the human race moves into the decrepitude which precedes the age of eternal rest . . . Bede brought history to the point at which it could be looked on not only as a

---

45. Southern, "2. Hugh of St. Victor," 161.
46. On this scheme, see Schmidt, *Aetates Mundi*; and Luneau, *L'histoire du salut*.

succession of distinct ages with development of their own, but also as a kind of biological process preceding from age to age.[47]

Although Southern has here probably overstated the originality of Bede,[48] this medieval historian certainly grasped something of the developmental process in human affairs and pondered deeply over the shape of universal history. In most of his works, however, Bede manifests the medieval fascination with the miraculous and the visionary, but it must be remembered that he, especially in the ecclesiastical history, was writing for the edification of his audience and was stressing the role of divine providence in Anglo-Saxon conversion to Christianity.

In the Carolingian period, under the Frankish rulers Charlemagne (768–814) and his son Louis the Pious (814–40), significant intellectual and educational developments occurred. Royal prescription decreed that monasteries and bishops' houses should be centers of education. At Charlemagne's palace school, the seven liberal arts—the Trivium (grammar, rhetoric, and dialectic) and the Quadrivium (music, arithmetic, geometry, and astronomy)—were cultivated. Latin was restored to the position of a literary language, and there was a revival of interest in classical texts, both Christian and pagan. The works of Sallust and Suetonius were especially influential. Einhard drew upon Suetonius's *Lives of the Caesars* for his life of Charlemagne and thus chose to imitate a style that differed radically from general medieval hagiography and biography and allowed for a rather secular and critical interpretation. Einhard's treatment of Charlemagne gave impetus to numerous royal biographies; but biography as a form became an instrument of the church, and rulers tended to be treated from clerical perspectives. Thus they hardly advanced the general cause of historiography. The classical eulogy and the Christian tradition of saints' *Lives* combined to reduce the amount of factual information required in biography.

> The Suetonian model permitted more precision, but it proved to be too bare for medieval taste. The rhetorical tradition defeated it. We cannot expect to find objectivity either; biographers wanted to praise or excuse. Their saving grace is that they remember the traditional advice to the historian to tell the truth and to report events as an eyewitness wherever possible . . . Sudden

---

47. Southern, "2. Hugh of St. Victor," 162–63.

48. See Markus, *Saeculum*, 17–28, where Augustine's scheme is discussed in both creation-week and biological terms.

flashes of realism light up their most conventional stories. If we judge them as propagandists, we have to admire their ingenuity. All do their best for rulers who fell short of what was expected of a Christian hero.[49]

Historians who quoted and imitated Sallust's *Catiline Conspiracy* and *Jugurthan War* failed to make use of a significant factor in his works: 'there is no sign of any interest in Sallust's theory of historical causation . . . none of them so much as noticed that he had an overall theory of the development and decline of political societies.'[50]

The Carolingian revival of learning was oriented towards preparation for Bible study. During the reign of Charlemagne, several attempts were made to revise the Latin text of the Bible.[51] The most important was that of Alcuin, presented to the king at his coronation as emperor on Christmas Day 800. Alcuin was certainly familiar with the Greek text and used this occasionally to correct the Latin. Some evidence exists to suggest that at least some Christian scholars were acquainted with Jewish interpretations of the Old Testament—with their emphasis on a literal reading of the text—if not with Hebrew itself.[52] During this period "there begins a veneration for the Fathers that invests their views on the meaning of Scripture with dogmatic authority."[53] Commentaries produced by piecing together excerpts from the fathers were common in the ninth century. Such commentaries not only served the devotion of the faithful but also brought to attention "the inconsistencies and gaps in the patristic tradition."[54] Differences among the patristic authorities meant that attempts had to be made at reconciliation or harmonization or, as in the case of Paschasius and John the Scot—who was familiar with Greek theology—one might be led to compare, criticize, and even discuss the differences and the meaning of the text.

The primary concern of historians during the Carolingian period was contemporary history. Royal historiography possessed a commanding subject in Charlemagne and his family. During the period, "a new form of historical writing is evolved in the *Annales*, which develop

---

49. Smalley, *Historians in the Middle Ages*, 78.
50. Southern, "1. The Classical Tradition," 179–80.
51. See Loewe, "Medieval History," 133–40.
52. See Smalley, *The Study of the Bible*, 37–46.
53. Loewe, "Medieval History," 140.
54. Smalley, *The Study of the Bible*, 38.

gradually from entries in a liturgical calendar to an increasingly fuller narration";[55] but this too was oriented towards contemporary events. Nothing comparable to the works of Augustine, Orosius, or Bede were produced during this time.

What might be called national history continued as a major concern of the post-Carolingian period as it had been in the early medieval period. "The lesson that destiny of nations is the noblest of all historical themes" was not lost.[56] Most of these works were similar in intent to the earlier histories of Jordanes, Gregory of Tours, Bede, and Paul the Deacon. "A whole series of attempts was made to apply to other races the theme in Virgil's *Aeneid* of a noble group of people guided by the gods towards a splendid destiny."[57] Widukind produced his work on Saxon history, Dudo wrote about the Normans, and Richer about the Franks. This form of writing reached its apogee in the romantic and fantastic *Historia regum Britanniae* by Geoffrey of Monmouth (about 1100–1154). He attempted to establish for the Celts a more illustrious and detailed past and a more glorious and consequential destiny than was the case of any other national historian. Trojan origins, visions and heavenly visitations, and Arthur and his Knights of the Round Table are described in imaginary and graphic contours. "Although some, even contemporary, readers were not deceived by the work, and William of Newburgh, one of the best English historians of the 12th century, denounced it as a tissue of absurdities, many seriously accepted it as history."[58]

Scholars are accustomed to speak of the late eleventh and twelfth centuries as a proto-Renaissance, as a time of great progress in learning and culture. Knowles has summarized the humanism of this period by outlining its three dominant characteristics: "first, a wide literary culture," which demonstrated itself in a "capability of self-expression based on a sound training in grammar and a long and often loving study of the foremost Latin authors"; "next, a great and what in the realm of religious sentiment could be called a personal devotion to certain figures of the ancient world; and, finally, a high value set upon the individual, personal emotions, and upon the sharing of experiences and opinions within a

---

55. Lacroix, "The Notion of History," 222.
56. Southern, "1. The Classical Tradition," 188.
57. Fryde, "Historiography," 949.
58. Ibid.

small circle of friends."[59] During this period, the universities at Paris, Bologna, and Oxford were founded. The Crusades to recover the holy land from the Seljukian Turks reached their culmination in the establishment of the Latin kingdom of Jerusalem. Contacts between the East and West, in spite of the church split in 1054, produced cross-fertilization between Byzantium and Latin Europe. Aristotelian logic and philosophy, partially through the mediation of the Arabs, began to dominate Western thought through translations and the greater availability of his works.

> The introduction of the whole canon of Aristotle to the West was a process continuing over a hundred years. The first wave, that of the logical works, was absorbed easily and avidly... The second wave, that of the difficult and profound philosophical works, gave more trouble and was less easily absorbed, though its effects were epoch-making. Finally, the ethical and political and literary treatises presented Europe with a philosopher who regarded human life from a purely naturalistic, this-world point of view... the atmosphere, the presuppositions of this great body of thought were not medieval and Christian, but ancient Greek, not to say rationalistic in character.[60]

Aristotelian thought made possible the birth of 'theology' in the systematic and scholastic sense that was to dominate religious studies in the thirteenth to fifteenth centuries.[61]

Aristotle's thought, it should be recalled, did not encourage historiographic studies. For Aristotle, history was too chaotic: "The historian has to expound not one action, but one period of time and all that happens within this period to one or more persons however disconnected the several events may be" (*Poetics* 1459a). History also lacked the element of universality: "The historian describes the thing that has been; the poet the kind of thing that might be. Hence poetry is more important and philosophic than history, for its statements have universal validity, while those of the historian are valid only for one time and one place" (*Poetics* 1451b). The urge to systematization is basically anti-historical in perspective.

This period of the proto-Renaissance, in its earliest phase, also witnessed some significant developments in historiography. In England, after the Norman Conquest of 1066, radical changes characterized society

---

59. Knowles, *The Historian*, 19–20.
60. Knowles, *The Evolution*, 193.
61. See Köpf, *Die Anfänge*.

and the old cultural systems were challenged. In response to the threat of change, English monastics saw themselves as the custodians of the past and to preserve that past monasteries became the centers of antiquarian concerns.[62] Monastic charters were collected, documents transcribed, historical and annalistic texts assembled, buildings and inscriptions studied, and the remains of saints gathered. "The post-Conquest monks were sure that they had a great past, but they were uncertain of their present and future . . . The monastic antiquaries searched the records to give detail and lucidity to their inherited conviction of greatness . . ."[63]

William of Malmesbury (about 1080–1143), in his ecclesiastical and secular histories of England, demonstrated how such antiquarian material could be used to reconstruct a realistic view of the past. No parallel to such antiquarianism exists before the sixteenth and seventeenth centuries, but the latter was to lack both the passion and purpose of the former.

At least two major theologians and canonists of the twelfth century worked with a concept of development and change in history.[64] These were Hugh of St. Victor (about 1096—1141), and Otto of Freising (about 1115–58). Hugh was not strictly a historian, although he wrote a chronicle of world history for use as a student's handbook in which he stressed the importance of time, place, people, and events for the understanding of history. In his theological works, a dynamic view of history pervades his discussions. His arguments rest on the presupposition that humandkind moved in history from the primitive and simple to the more sophisticated and developed. He sought to outline the various stages, for example, in the history of the sacrament of penance showing that its final form was the product of the needs of the early church. Thus doctrine goes through developmental stages and the needs of human institutions play a role. In his description of the world ages, Hugh's thought has a certain evolutionary ring. The first age of man, from the fall to Abraham, was "the age of natural law when men groped around for remedies for their ills by the light of reason and experience." Primitive humandkind developed various sacraments, sacrifices, and offerings to present to their gods. The second age, which began embryonically with Abraham and fully with Moses, was "the age of written law when God intervened actively in human history" and provided humanity with the means of

---

62. See Southern, "4. The Sense of the Past."
63. Ibid., 262.
64. See Southern, "2. Hugh of St. Victor."

education and sacramental union. In the third age, which began with Christ, grace replaced law and the inspirations of the spirit supplanted the commandments.[65] In these ages, humans cooperated with God in a forward movement towards higher forms of human existence. Hugh, in his writings on the liberal arts, argued again for stages in human development from the primitive to the advanced. He declared: "Men wrote and talked before there was grammar; they distinguished truth from falsehood before there was dialectic; they had laws before there was rhetoric; they had numbers before there was arithmetic; they sang before there was music; they measured fields before there was geometry; they observed the stars and seasons before there was astronomy."[66]

In technology, it was the operation of human reason that functioned to meet the needs of humans. Physical necessity prompted humanity towards achievement. "There arose the theoretical sciences to illuminate ignorance, ethics to strengthen virtue, and the mechanical arts to temper man's infirmity."[67] Hugh's sense of historical development in all categories of life presented a rather optimistic view of the historical process, a view in which novelty was not only accepted but also declared good.

Otto, the bishop of Freising in Bavaria and a member of the imperial family, produced a universal history from creation to his own day relying on the schemes of six ages and four world monarchies. The work is basically Orosian in orientation. In a number of ways, Otto differed from or extended the thought of Augustine and Orosius. He identified the city of God with the church and in Henry IV's submission to Pope Gregory VII at Canossa in 1077 he saw the triumph of the 'heavenly' over the 'earthly' city. Although Otto shared the Orosian view of the decline of human rule, he was nonetheless able to affirm, especially in his work on Frederick I, that history was not a tragedy and that empire could be an instrument of peace. Otto gave detailed treatment to the so-called 'transfer thesis,' the idea that civilization and empire moved from East to West. The idea was implicit already in Eusebius and perhaps already used at the Frankish court before Otto. He, however, worked out analogies between the ancient empires and those in Europe. The empire of his day was understood as the continuation of the fourth empire—the Roman—which had simply moved westward. Otto applied the transfer theory not only to

---

65. Ibid., 166–67
66. Quoted in ibid., 171.
67. Quoted in ibid., 170.

political power but to religion and education as well: "Note well that all human power and knowledge began in the East and end in the West, so that in this way the variability and weaknesses of all things may be made clear."[68]

The Middle Ages witnessed the blossoming of what might be called 'prophetic' or 'apocalyptic' historiography. The six-age scheme and the four monarchies theory of world history were, of course, derived from biblical texts that were either taken as prefigurations or as predictions. Biblical commentators had solved to their own and their contemporaries' satisfaction most of the assumed predictions in the biblical texts. Numerous attempts were made, however, to define more closely some of the loose ends, especially the interpretation of Daniel 7, Revelation 6, and the appearance of the antichrist. The general ambiguity of apocalyptic texts tends to allow for their constant reinterpretation by those disposed to see themselves living in the last days and to see their enemies as the antichrists. The ambiguity of the biblical texts had even been heightened in some cases by patristic exegesis. Jerome, for example, had suggested that the ten horns in Daniel 7 might refer to the ten kings who would be the instruments of the Roman empire's destruction and would be followed by the antichrist. If the Bible were the inspired truth, then these prophecies must have some concrete historical referent, or so reasoned medieval lovers of prophecy.

In addition to biblical prophecies, various other elements contributed to medieval prophetical historiographic interests: numerous Sibylline documents, developing astrological investigations stimulated by Islamic science and the introduction of the astrolabe and the improved ability to calculate astronomical phenomena, and the prophecies of such figures as Merlin and Hildegard of Bingen.[69] The most famous apocalyptic historian of the time was Joachim of Fiore (about 1132–1202), whose fame and thought endured long after his passing. Joachim advanced a trinitarian conception of history. The time of ancient Israel and Judah was the age of God the Father, the second age of God the Son began with Jesus, and the age of the Holy Spirit was soon to dawn. The world of the new age was to be the time of the monks and was to be inaugurated by the appearance of a new Elijah and twelve holy men. (Many saw in the mendicant friars of the following decades a fulfilment of his prophecies.) The antichrist was

---

68. Quoted in ibid., 177.
69. See Reeves *The Influence*; and Southern, "3. History as Prophecy."

to appear for the first time before the dawn of the final age and the reign of the Spirit. Needless to say, many were later seen as the embodiment of the antichrist; the most frequent candidate being the Muslims, a view already expounded by ninth-century Spanish theologians. The views of Joachimism and prophetic historiography scarcely advanced the cause of Israelite and Judean historiography. They did, however, tend to dispose people towards the future and hope and for several generations occupied the thoughts of many, not the least of whom was Sir Isaac Newton.

Before leaving this section, a few comments should be made about Jewish historiography in the Middle Ages. The surprising factor is that nothing comparable to Christian and Muslim historiography existed in Judaism during this period.[70] The primary concerns of medieval Judaism centered upon either halakhic or philosophical-ethical matters. When they appear, historical matters in the Talmud are anecdotal. When the Jewish authorities "discussed the past, particular incidents, rather than its totality, caught their attention."[71] It is possible to take the various writings of a Jewish scholar like Maimonides (1135–1204) and distill from these his comments on and interpretations of various historical events reported in the Bible.[72] These are basically retelling, with commentary, of the biblical narratives supplemented by haggadah and chronological notations. From these it is possible to reconstruct Maimonides's historical worldview, but this is hardly historiography.

One special work deserves mention. This is the Hebrew writing called *Josippon*, so named because of its association with Josephus. Written in southern Italy in the mid-tenth century, *Josippon* begins with the table of nations in Genesis 10, contains a discussion of the founding of Rome, and provides a history of the Jews, primarily of the second temple period down to the fall of Masada. The unknown author made use of the Latin version of most of the books in Josephus's *Antiquities* and a Latin adaptation of Josephus's *War*. The book was widely used in the Middle Ages, was even translated into Arabic in the eleventh, and apparently was supplemented in the twelfth century.[73]

---

70. For the Muslim historiography, which had no influence on Western historiography, see Rosenthal, *A History*.

71. Meyer, *Ideas of Jewish History*, 71.

72. Baron, *History*, 109–63.

73. On Jossipon, see Flusser, "Jossipon."

From the Renaissance to the Enlightenment

The foundations of modern historiography were laid in the Renaissance, which began in Italy in the fourteenth century and spread northward. The militant humanism of this period certainly had its roots in medievalism, in spite of its scorn for the Middle Ages; but its intellectual and technological accomplishments were revolutionary both in themselves and in their implications. One of the products of the Renaissance was history as an independent discipline. A second result was a critical approach to many of the problems and issues of life. The radical consequences of these two developments for the study of Israelite and Judean history, however, were not to be developed fully until the nineteenth century.

During the Renaissance, four elements that pervaded much of the intellectual activity were generative of momentous consequences for future historiography. These were a true sense of anachronism, a renewed interest in antiquarianism, a critical stance towards the literary evidence from the past, and the attempt to understand the causation of historical events through reason.[74] One must not, of course, assume that a majority of the educated and scholarly figures of the Renaissance period shared these perspectives, any more than one should assume that after the publication of Darwin's *Origin of Species* everyone gave up the idea that God created humankind in a paradise state.

As was noted earlier, medieval writers as a rule lacked a historical perspective on the past as past, as different in space and time from the contemporary. In the fourteenth century, a historical sensibility began to develop. This appears, for example, in Giotto's fresco painting in the Arena Chapel at Padua (about 1305), which depicts Pontius Pilate cleanshaven, with garlanded head, and wearing a Roman robe embossed with a golden, imperial eagle. He appears as a figure from the past, not as a contemporary. Petrarch (1304–74) was well aware of the differences between his own day and those of his beloved Rome before the conversion of Constantine. So much so that he described his own times as barbarian and wrote 'nostalgic' letters to the classical authors expressing his longing to escape from the present and to find solace in those happier bygone days of old. Renaissance authors slowly recognized that everything had changed over time—laws, words, clothes, customs, arts, and buildings.[75] There was, in other words, a historical relativity to all things.

74. See Burke, *The Renaissance*.
75. See ibid., 39–49.

The History of the Study of Israelite and Judean History

Antiquarianism was a natural accompaniment to the revived interest in the past.[76] In the Renaissance, men like Petrarch were not only interested in ancient literary works but in what would be called archaeological remains. Coins, inscriptions, and ancient ruins were of interest not just as relics from the past but as means to reconstruct the past. Petrarch used coins to discover what Roman emperors looked like and in his epic poem *Africa* drew upon the ruins of Rome, which he had visited, in describing the city at the time of the Carthaginians' visit. In 1446, Flavio Biondo produced a topographical description of Rome dependent upon both the literary sources and his personal visits to the ruined sites. The fact that Renaissance scholars frequently misinterpreted antiquities or distorted their antiquarian knowledge is beside the point, for the issue is not their correctness in detail but their methodological procedure.

The discipline of documentary criticism was a speciality of many Renaissance scholars, The most outstanding and influential early Renaissance literary critic was Lorenzo Valla (about 1406–57). Petrarch, however, had already (in 1355) used internal and external evidence to prove that a document exempting Austria from the jurisdiction of the Emperor Charles IV was a forgery.[77] In 1439, Valla disproved the authenticity of the Donation of Constantine in which Constantine had supposedly assigned temporal power over Italy to Pope Sylvester I and his successors. (Otto of Freising and other medieval authors had suspected that the document was a forgery, as did Valla's contemporaries Nicholas of Cusa and Reginald Pecock, independently.) "The significance of Valla's declamation was neither in applying philological criteria, for Petrarch and others, including canonists, had taken this step, nor in denying the authenticity of the document, which had already been placed in doubt; rather it was in exhibiting the whole array of humanist weapons—polemic and personal vituperation as well as criticism stemming from grammar, logic, geography, chronology, history, and law."[78] Valla and others applied their literary criticism to numerous documents, both classical and Christian, to prove their inauthenticity or to elucidate their origin and history. "In 1460, Nicholas of Cusa wrote the *Sieving of the Koran* (*Cribratio Alcoran*) which treated the Koran as Nicholas had already treated the *Donation*. He identified three elements in its composition: Nestorian Christianity, a

---

76. See Momigliano, "Ancient History"; and Weiss, *The Renaissance Discovery*.
77. See Burke, *The Renaissance*, 50–54.
78. Kelley, *Foundations*, 38.

Jewish adviser of Muhammad, and the corruptions introduced by Jewish 'correctors' after Muhammad's death. This was to treat the Koran as a historical document, and to write the history of its leading ideas."[79] The status of the Bible as the word of God exempted it from such treatment for the moment.

The literary legends about national origins and hagiographic legends about the saints were open to criticism by the humanists. Two examples will suffice. The Italian historian, Polydore Vergil, published a history of England in 1534 in which he took up the older attack on Geoffrey of Monmouth's depiction of the Trojan Brutus as the founder of Britain. His basic argument rested on an appeal to the ancient sources: none of the ancient Roman authors and sources make any reference to this Brutus.[80] In a short biography prefaced to his edition of Jerome's works, Erasmus (in 1516) argued that many of the legendary traditions "contaminate the saints with their old wives' tales, which are childish, ignorant, and absurd" and that the best source for knowledge about Jerome was the humandkind himself.

> For who knew Jerome better than Jerome himself? Who expressed his ideas more faithfully? If Julius Caesar is the most reliable source for the events of his own career, is it not all the more reasonable to trust Jerome on his? And so, having gone through all his works, we made a few annotations and presented the results in the form of a narrative, not concealing the fact that we consider it a great enough miracle to have Jerome himself explaining his life to us in all his famous books. If there is anyone who must have miracles and omens, let him read the books about Jerome which contain almost as many miracles as they do sentences.[81]

The literary study of the early Renaissance humanists was not oriented merely to the detection of forgery and the exposure of many venerated traditions as nonhistorical legends. There was a very positive side to the focus on documentary evidence. "The mere problem of gaining access to the past began to supersede the problem of how to make use of it."[82] The humanists stressed that the recovery of the past through

79. Burke, *The Renaissance*, 59.

80. Similar attacks were made on other national and foundational legends; see ibid., 71–75.

81. Text in ibid., 70.

82. Kelley, *Foundations*, 24.

documentary sources had to depend upon philology and grammar. This meant a literal and realistic reading of the sources and at times textual criticism to restore the sources. Valla, in his *Annotations on the New Testament* published by Erasmus in 1505, came close to placing the biblical sources on the same footing with other ancient documents. Valla had also concluded that "none of the words of Christ have come to us, for Christ spoke in Hebrew and never wrote down anything."[83] Erasmus, who argued for a "return to the sources" (*versetur in fontibus*), defended Valla's position on the need for textual criticism to restore the sources of theology.[84] This meant that the reliability of the Old Testament versions must be established on the basis of Hebrew and the New Testament on the basis of Greek. (Pope Clement V and the Council of Vienne in 1311–12 had called for the training of teachers in three languages—Arabic, Hebrew, and Aramaic or Chaldee.) In interpreting the Bible, Erasmus argued that the role of the grammarian was more important than that of theologian.

> Nor do I assume that theology, the very queen of all disciplines, will think it beneath her dignity if her handmaiden, grammar, offers her help and the required service. For even if grammar is somewhat lower in dignity than other disciplines, there is no other more necessary. She busies herself with very small questions, without which no one progresses to the large. She argues about trifles which lead to serious matters. If they answer that theology is too important to be limited by grammatical rules and that this whole affair of exegeting depends on the inspiration of the Holy Spirit, then this is indeed a new honor for the theologian that he alone is allowed to speak like a barbarian.[85]

In spite of Erasmus's emphasis on grammar in the understanding of the biblical text, he refused to disavow allegorical interpretation, although he warned that it should not be overdone, should apply everything to Christ, and requires a pious mind.[86] Here he shows himself closer kin to Augustine than to Valla.

The trivial concerns of the grammarian or the "very small questions" grammar asks—to use Erasmus's terminology—were part of a major revolution in thought. The difference between the medieval interpretative gloss on a text and the grammatical analysis of a text is

---

83. Quoted in Fryde, "Historiography," 952.
84. See Rabil, *Erasmus*, 58–61.
85. Quoted in ibid., 59.
86. See ibid., 109–13.

enormous; they belong to two different worlds of thought. The humanists of the Renaissance openly broke with the scholastic method, caustically opposed it, and asserted the superiority of their new methods. Valla declared: "The discourse of historians exhibits more substance, more practical knowledge, more political wisdom . . . , more customs, and more learning of every sort than the precepts of any philosophers. Thus we show that historians have been superior to philosophers."[87] The difference between scholasticism and humanism in the Renaissance period has been described in the following terms: "By proliferating abstractions and superfluous distinctions, scholastic philosophy had lost contact with concrete reality. It had cut men off from meaning, hence from their own humanity. Valla's philosophy, on the other hand, emphasized precisely these standards—concreteness, utility, and humanity . . . Indeed, a return to reality may be taken as the slogan of Valla's entire philosophy."[88]

The quest or return to reality was not only the source of the humanistic or historical revolution of the Renaissance but also the basis for the scientific revolution that has its roots in the same period.[89] Science had to overcome the legacy of Aristotelian scholasticism. It is difficult to overstate the importance of the scientific revolution, which reached a climax in the sixteenth and seventeenth centuries, for all aspects of life including biblical studies, although Butterfield seems to have been successful in this regard: "Since that revolution overturned the authority in science not only of the middle ages but of the ancient world—since it ended not only in the eclipse of scholastic philosophy but in the destruction of Aristotelian physics—it outshines everything since the rise of Christianity and reduces the Renaissance and Reformation to the rank of mere episodes, mere internal displacements, within the system of medieval Christendom."[90] Mechanics and astronomy were the first scientific disciplines to develop.

These new approaches to reality were concerned with questions of explanation and causation in both natural and human orders. The way was opened for a view of the world that operated according to 'natural law' even if that law be understood as the will of God. The historical implication of such a view is enormous: humans can understand past events

---

87. Quoted in Kelley, *Foundations*, 19.
88. Ibid., 29.
89. See Grant, "Late Medieval Thought."
90. Butterfield, *The Origins*, vii.

as analogous to present events. Human, climatic, geographical, and other factors could be viewed as causal elements in historical events both past and present. This rise of explanation in historical studies marked a significant development in historiography.

"In medieval historical writing there are explanations of an extremely specific kind, in terms of the motives of individuals; there are also explanations of an extremely general kind, in terms of the hand of God in history, or the decay of the world; but middle-range explanations are lacking."[91] These "middle-range explanations"—what today we would call sociological, economic, geographical, and climatic considerations—have their beginnings in the Renaissance.[92]

The Protestant Reformation of the sixteenth century, which in many ways represents merely a radical and religious application of Renaissance principles and aims, made at least four significant contributions that were ultimately of great importance in the history of Hebrew historiography.

First of all, the reformers placed the Bible at the center of the theological enterprise. *Sola scriptura* was the keynote of the Reformation.[93] In emphasizing the Bible as the rule and norm of faith, the reformers stressed a literal interpretation of the Scriptures. Luther wrote:

> The Holy Spirit is the plainest writer and speaker in heaven and earth, and therefore His words cannot have more than one, and that the very simplest, sense, which we call the literal, ordinary, natural sense.
>
> All heresies and error in Scripture have not arisen out of the simple words of Scripture ... All error arises out of paying no regard to the plain words and, by fabricated inferences and figures of speech, concocting arbitrary interpretations in one's own brain.
>
> In the literal sense there is life, comfort, strength, learning, and art. Other interpretations, however appealing, are the work of fools.

In addition to an emphasis on the literal reading of Scripture, the reformers argued that Scripture is its own interpreter. Luther declared: "Scripture itself by itself is the most unequivocal, the most accessible, the most

---

91. Burke, *The Renaissance*, 77.
92. See the collection of texts in ibid., 77–104.
93. See Kraus, *Geschichte*, 6–9.

comprehensible authority, itself its own interpreter, attesting, judging, illuminating all things."[94]

This emphasis upon a literal reading of the Scriptures, which had earlier been stressed in Judaism over against a christocentric reading of the Old Testament, did not immediately produce any critical-historical approach to the Bible. Even Luther retained a prophetic-christocentric attitude towards the Old Testament. The idea of the divine inspiration of Scripture or the Bible as the word of God halted the reformers short of any really critical approach, although Luther relegated Hebrews, James, Jude, and Revelation to an appendix in his New Testament translation primarily because of theological reasons, which he buttressed with an appeal to the dispute over these documents in the early church.[95] Matthias Flacius Illyricus's *Claris scripturae sacrae* (1567), one of the first handbooks on biblical hermeneutics, is representative of Protestantism's stress on the importance of the literal or grammatical sense, but warns that there are no contradictions in Scripture and that exegesis must be in agreement with faith.[96] This emphasis on the literal reading of the biblical materials was ultimately to make literary-critical analysis not only possible but also necessary.

A second contribution of the reformers was an iconoclastic attitude towards tradition. This phenomenon was widely current in many circles during the times as previous examples have shown. The reformers sought to restore the purity of the church and return to the origins; components and traditions that appeared to have intervened extraneously could be repudiated. Such attitudes, however, fostered a sense of criticism although it was much easier to be critical of post-biblical than biblical traditions. An example of a significant critique of an ancient and venerated tradition is represented by Carolus Sigonius who challenged the traditional Jewish view of the origin of the synagogue. An expert on Greek and Roman institutions, Sigonius, in his *De republica Hebraeorum libri VII* (1583), argued as follows regarding the antiquity of the synagogue:

> The origin of the synagogue is by no means an old one. We find, indeed, no mention of it [in Scripture] either in the history of the Judges or in the history of the Kings. If it is at all admissible to venture a conjecture in this kind of antiquity, I would surmise

---

94. For all these texts, see Kümmel, *The New Testament*, 20–23.
95. See ibid., 24–26.
96. For excerpts from his work, see ibid., 27–30.

that synagogues were first erected in the Babylonian exile for the purpose that those who have been deprived of the temple of Jerusalem, where they used to pray and teach, would have a certain place similar to the temple, in which they could assemble and perform the same kind of service.[97]

Many concepts, positions, and traditions, however, were taken over uncritically by the reformers. Both Luther and Melanchthon accepted the four monarchies approach to world history. The Frenchman Jean Bodin, in his *Method for the Easy Understanding of Histories* (1566), thus sensed he was breaking new ground when he included an essay on the "refutation of those who postulate four monarchies and the golden age."

A third contribution of the Reformation and the Catholic Counter-Reformation can be seen in the fact that the history of the church became a dominant issue in the struggles within the church in the sixteenth and seventeenth centuries. Historiography was a major weapon in both arsenals. Protestants argued that the teachings of Jesus and the faith of the primitive church had become distorted by the hierarchy of the church. (They differed among themselves as to the precise date at which the apostasy began.) Catholics sought to prove that the church at the time was the true successor of primitive Christianity and that the church was basically the same as it had always been. Luther and Calvin's writings reflect the general Protestant view of church history,[98] although Luther wrote in the introduction to Robert Barnes's *Vitae Romanorurn pontificum* (1535) that it was a wonderful delight and the greatest joy to see that history, as well as Scripture, could be used to attack the papacy. In Eusebian fashion, historians on both sides turned again to the extensive study and employment of documents, to even a greater extent than many humanist historians, who, especially in Italy, were more interested in literary form than documentation, being strongly influenced by the rhetorical tradition.[99] The greatest monuments to this historical controversy are the thirteen-volume *Historia ecclesiae Christi* (1559–74) produced by the Magdeburg Centuriators, under the leadership of Matthias Flacius, and the twelve-volume rejoinder, *Annales ecclesiastici*, by Caesar Baronius.[100] As a result of this use of historiography as a battlefield, ecclesiastical history in the

---

97. Quoted by Sonne, "Synagogue," 478.
98. On Luther, see Headley, *Luther's View*.
99. See Reynolds, "Latin Historiography."
100. On the historical controversy, see Pullapilly, *Caesar Baronius*, esp. 144–77.

sixteenth and seventeenth centuries displayed a greater erudition, a more minute analysis of sources, and a more historiographic sophistication than secular history. Unfortunately none of this energy and insight was applied to the study of Israelite and Judean history, although the issue established history as an important element in religious controversy.

The fourth significant development that grew out of the Reformation was religious freedom that allowed for enormous theological diversity. The rejection of authoritarianism in tradition, priesthood, and religious practice permitted an increased appeal to private judgment, often, of course, uncompromisingly certain that it reflected the true biblical and Christian point of view. Thus theological positions were capable of absorbing modernity while claiming to be founded upon true antiquity. This permitted significant shifts on the questions of authority and revelation, which made biblical criticism not only possible but sometimes desirable. "The exercise of private judgment permitted the Protestant not so much to avoid as to conclude compromises: he could come to terms with the new ideas around him."[101] Protestantism thus had a built-in flexibility that made accommodation possible. "It is to Calvin's great credit that he recognized the discrepancy between the scientific world system of his days and the biblical text, and secondly, that he did not repudiate the results of scientific research on that account."[102]

The Italians Lelio (1525–62) and Faustus Socinus (1539–1604), with their moderate unitarian theology and their assumption that the veracity of Scripture should be subjected to rational judgment, were among the first to formulate a view of religion whose modernity even antagonized the reformers.[103]

Following the Council of Trent (1545–63), which reaffirmed the Vulgate canon and text of the Bible but recommended the latter's revision, a long debate ensued between Catholics and Protestants and among Protestants themselves over which Old Testament text—Latin, Greek, or Hebrew—was authoritative. Even the inspiration of the Hebrew vowel points became involved.[104] The attempts to decide such issues led to heated controversy and, though perhaps not widely recognized, to humans sitting in judgment over the text.

---

101. Gay, *Deism*, 19.
102. Hooykaas, "Science and Reformation," 136.
103. See Scholder, *Ursprünge und Probleme*, 34–55; Kraus, *Geschichte*, 41–43.
104. See Diestel, *Geschichte*, 253–54, 326–28; Allen, *The Legend of Noah*, 39–65.

The History of the Study of Israelite and Judean History

The reformers had argued that a person could interpret the Scriptures aided by divine light or *fides divina*. Luther, at the Diet of Worms (1521), had spoken of being "convinced by the testimony of the scriptures or by clear reason."[105] Gradually the *fides divina* had to give more and more to 'clear reason' and the divine or inward light tended to become "really the *Lumen naturale* under a mask."[106] The seventeenth century witnessed the dethronement of the Bible as the authoritative source of knowledge and understanding and saw biblical interpreters and historians utilizing the products of the *lumen naturale*.[107]

The heliocentric theory in astronomy, expounded in Copernicus's *De revolutionibus orbium coelestium* and opposed by Luther and Melanchthon, was undergirded by Kepler's mathematical work and Galileo's theory of dynamics and his invention of the telescope. Kepler suggested that science should be used in understanding the Bible and proposed (in 1606) that the Bethlehem star was due to the unusual conjunction of Mars, Saturn, and Jupiter in the sign of Taurus in 6 BCE. The discovery and exploration of new lands brought to attention the existence of peoples beyond the purview of the biblical texts. Travel accounts reported on the life and customs of distant lands. For the first time—in the writings of figures like Pietro della Valle and Michael Nau—reports on monuments, sites, and life in Palestine became known. The scientific revolution possessed its philosophical counterpart in the thought of Francis Bacon and Rene Descartes. Based on an empirical and critical approach to all knowledge, the new philosophy sought, as Bacon stated, "a total reconstruction of sciences, arts, and all human knowledge, raised upon proper foundations." The establishment of history as an independent discipline in the major universities necessitated the self-consciousness of the field as a 'science': the earliest professors of history were primarily commentators on the writings of ancient historians. The first professor of history at Cambridge University was dismissed in 1627 because his comments on Tacitus were considered politically dangerous.[108] Historians

---

105. Text in Kümmel, *The New Testament*, 20.

106. Allen, *The Legend of Noah*, 45.

107. See Scholder, *Ursprünge und Probleme*, for seventeenth-century developments and biblical studies.

108. Hobbes in *Leviathan*, written in 1651, commented: "As to rebellion in particular against monarchy, one of the most frequent causes of it, is the reading of the books of policy, and histories of the ancient Greeks, and Romans... From the reading, I say, of such books, men have undertaken to kill their kings" (ch. 29).

produced manuals on the art of history writing and the use and criticism of documents. The most important of the latter was Jean Mabillon's *De re diplomatica* (1680). Generally, in the seventeenth century, antiquarian or archaeological and historical concerns were pursued separately. The former was undertaken, with some exceptions, by dilettantes possessed by an abundance of leisure and some interest in the arts and travel. Much energy and money were expended to secure artifacts for the adornment of museums and livingrooms. Near the end of the century efforts were made to combine historical and antiquarian interests; some scholars went so far as to claim the superiority of archaeological over literary evidence in reconstructing history.[109] The seventeenth century was also a time of general questioning of authority, both political and religious, as the Puritan movement and the Cromwellian revolution in England demonstrate.

The impact of the intellectual climate of the seventeenth century upon the study of biblical history can be illustrated through the selection of three examples: the desire to produce a definitive biblical chronology, the attempt to defend a literal interpretation of biblical events through the use of the new sciences, and the growing literary-critical approach to Old Testament documents.

In 1583, Scaliger (1540–1609), the most outstanding philologist of his day, published his *De emendatione temporum*, which provided a synchronized world chronology incorporating Greek, Roman, and Jewish calculations and utilizing recent astronomical discoveries. In 1606, he published his *Thesaurus temporum*, a collection of every chronological relic extant in Greek and Latin. The most influential biblical chronology in the English-speaking world was published in 1650–54 by the Irish bishop James Ussher (1581–1656). In the preface to his *Annales Veteris et Novi Testamenti*, Ussher confidently assured the reader: "If anyone well seen in the knowledge not only of sacred and exotic history, but of astronomical calculation, and the old Hebrew calendar, should apply himself to these studies, I judge it indeed difficult, but not impossible, for such a one to attain, not only the number of years, but even of days from the creation of the world." Of the date of creation, he wrote: "In the beginning, God created Heaven and Earth, Genesis 1, verse 1, which beginning of time, according to our chronologers, fell upon the entrance of the night preceding the 23rd day of October in the year of the Julian Calendar, 710

---

109. Momigliano, "Ancient History," 14.

... Marginal note: the year before Christ, 4004."[110] Subsequently, Ussher's chronological calculations were placed in the margin of the King James Version of the Scriptures. Chronographers, of course, differed in their calculations, but many of the scientific minds of the seventeenth century sought to establish scientifically the biblical chronological data. Even so great a mathematical mind as that of Isaac Newton, in a work published posthumously in 1733, sought to demonstrate the accuracy of the predictions in Daniel when applied to papal power. He also sought to make biblical chronology agree with the course of nature, astronomy, sacred history, and the classical histories, especially Herodotus.

One of the most debated topics in the seventeenth century was Noah's flood—its historicity, nature, and extent. In a classical study, Allen has shown how all the sciences of the time were drawn upon to expound the flood in a literal sense and to explain it in rational terms. Scholars discussed the chronology of the flood, the size of the ark, the number and names of the animals, the amount of food needed to feed the ark's passengers, and so on. The most vexing problem was, of course, the question of the origin of sufficient water to flood the entire earth to a depth of fifteen cubits. With the discovery of new lands and new animals, living quarters on the ark became more crowded. Even astronomical phenomena, such as comets, were brought into the picture as explanations. A local flood theory developed when reasonable arguments for a universal flood wore thin. Such an enormous superstructure of arguments was developed to support a literal flood until the whole thing was doomed to topple from its own weight. What resulted from such attempts to support the literal historicity of biblical narratives was a "rational exegesis, a form of pious explanation that innocently damned the text that it expounded." "Theologians now required the Bible to conform to the reason of men."[111]

A third seventeenth-century development was the application of literary and documentary criticism to the Old Testament, especially the Pentateuch. Documentary criticism meant that questions about the origin, nature, and historical reliability were to be asked of the biblical materials. Earlier scholars, such as Isaac ben Suleiman in the tenth century, Ibn Ezra in the twelfth century, Carlstadt and others in the sixteenth century, had raised questions about the Mosaic authorship of the Pentateuch. The significant biblical critics of the seventeenth century were Thomas

---

110. Texts in Burke, *The Renaissance*, 471.
111. Allen, *The Legend of Noah*, 65, 89–90.

Hobbes (1588–1679), an English philosopher; Benedict de Spinoza (1632–77), a Dutch-Jewish philosopher; Hugo Grotius (1583–1645), a Dutch jurist and theologian; and Richard Simon (1638–1712), a French Catholic priest.[112]

Spinoza outlined the program of biblical criticism.

> The history of the Scriptures should ... teach us to understand the various vicissitudes that may have befallen the books of the prophets whose tradition has been handed down to us; the life, character and aim of the author of each book; the part which he played; at what period, on what occasion, for whom and in what language he composed his writings. Nor is that enough; we must know the fortune of each book in particular, the circumstances in which it was originally composed, into what hands it subsequently fell, the various lessons it has been held to convey, by whom it was included in the sacred canon, and, finally, how all these books came to be embodied in a single collection.[113]

Several assumptions can be discerned in this newly budding biblical criticism. (1) The Bible is to be subjected to critical study just as any other book. (2) The biblical material has a history of transmission that can be elucidated by determining the various circumstances through which it passed. (3) Internal statements, styles, and repetitions make it possible to deny single and Mosaic authorship of the Pentateuch. It should be noted that Grotius, Hobbes, and Spinoza had moved away from the typical Jewish and Protestant view of religious authority and revelation and that their criticism was probably the result rather than the cause of such a move.

The most important and influential seventeenth-century biblical critic was Simon.[114] As a Catholic, Simon sought to show that Protestantism's reliance upon the Bible was not as sound a principle as the Catholic reliance upon Bible, tradition, and the church. He stressed the importance of a thorough knowledge of Hebrew for Old Testament study as well as textual criticism and philology. Simon emphasized the process by which the biblical materials were transmitted, pointing to their supplementation and alteration. Claiming inspiration for the revisers of the materials, on the analogy of church tradition, Simon argued that those

---

112. See Gray, *Old Testament Criticism*, 75–115; Knight, *Rediscovering*, 39–54, and bibliography given there.

113. Spinoza, *Tractatus theologica-paliticus*, VII.

114. See Hazard, *La Crise*, 180–97, for a perceptive essay on him.

who had the power to write the sacred books also had the power to revise them. Simon deliberately stressed the words 'critic' and 'criticism' in his writing, using them in the title of practically all his works. He explained the usage this way:

> My readers must not be surprised if I have sometimes availed myself of expressions that may sound a little strangely in their ears. Every art has its own peculiar terminology, which is regarded more or less as its inviolable property. It is in this specialized sense that I have employed the words *critic* and *criticism* . . . together with some others of the same nature, to which I was obliged to have recourse in order to express myself in the terms proper to the art of which I was treating. These terms will come as no novelty to scholars, who have for some time been accustomed to their use in our language.[115]

Simon addressed his writings to the general educated audience, and wrote in French, not Latin, and his *Histoire critique du Vieux Testament*, published in 1678, had, by 1700, gone through four Latin, two English, and seven French editions. The object of multiple attacks for its questioning of venerated traditions and positions, the book was condemned by the Congregation of the Index in 1683.

The humanists' and reformers' insistence on a 'return to the sources' and a literal reading of the text had been based on the conviction that there one could find the pristine faith, piety, and history. This confidence was to be shattered on the rocks of biblical criticism. What literary criticism found in the Bible was to produce a quagmire that was increasingly to absorb scholarly attention.

In the eighteenth century, and for the first time in Western history, a diversity of philosophical-theological systems with scholarly respectability competed in the intellectual marketplace. These included a variety of approaches to Christian theism ranging from scholasticism to experiential pietism, Pyrrhonic agnosticism, atheism, and pragmatic rationalism.[116] The sanctity of tradition, the customs of culture, and the regulations of the marketplace all favored the theistic option; however, Christianity and the Bible were subjected to an unprecedented and trenchant examination and critique. The agent of this activity was deism.

---

115. Quoted from Hazard, *La Crise*, 182.
116. Gay, *Deism*, 13.

Deism's roots can be traced to various earlier influences and anticipatory figures. McKee has done this in the case of Isaac de la Peyrere, who in 1655 published a work advancing such hypotheses as the existence of men before the creation of Adam and the non-Mosaic authorship of the Pentateuch. Gay provides a good description of the exponents of the movement:

> All deists were ... both critical and constructive ... All sought to destroy in order to build, and reasoned either from the absurdity of Christianity to the need for a new philosophy or from their desire for a new philosophy to the absurdity of Christianity ... Deism ... is the product of the confluence of three strong emotions: hate, love, and hope. The deists hated priests and priestcraft, mystery-mongering, and assaults on commonsense. They loved the ethical teachings of the classical philosophers, the grand unalterable regularity of nature, the sense of freedom granted the man liberated from superstition. They hoped that the problems of life—of private conduct and public policy—could be solved by the application of unaided human reason, and that the mysteries of the universe could be, if not solved, at least defined and circumscribed by man's scientific inquiry.[117]

Various stances towards the Bible were taken by the deists, but as a rule, they sought to distill the biblical traditions; to siphon off the supernatural, the miraculous, and the unbelievable; and to leave behind the pure essence of a reasonable faith.[118]

During the height of the deistic controversy in England (1700–1750), two major studies of Israelite and Judean history were published. Prideaux's work, which covers the period from the reign of Tiglath-pileser III to the lifetime of Jesus, comprises three volumes that totaled almost 1,400 pages.[119] The work went through over a score of editions and was translated into German and French. Prideaux relied primarily upon the biblical traditions and Josephus, but made use of practically every known literary document from antiquity. Only occasionally did Prideaux take a critical attitude towards his sources. He challenged the authenticity of the letter of Aristeas and its account of the origin of the LXX and pro-

---

117. See Hazard, *La Crise*, for the general background; and Barth, *Protestant Theology*, 33–173, for a descriptive analysis.

118. On deism, see the readings in Waring, *Deism*; and Gay, *Deism*; for descriptive discussions, see Stephen *History*; and Cragg, *Reason and Authority*.

119. Prideaux, *The Old and New Testament*.

vided the reader with a history and description of the study of the LXX.[120] Prideaux disagreed with Josephus on Alexander's route to Jerusalem,[121] and argued that the synagogue had its origin in the days of Ezra.[122]

Shuckford wrote his volumes to present the history from creation to the point where Prideaux had begun. Like his predecessors, from the fourth century on, Shuckford presented universal history in a biblical perspective, beginning with Adam and Eve. This was still the classical model. Sir Walter Raleigh had started at this point in his widely used *History of the World*, published in 1614, and although unfinished it covered history down to the Roman period. Basically the same model was employed in the multi-volume *An Universal History from the Earliest Time to the Present*, written by a consortium of scholars, mostly from Oxford and Cambridge, and published in 1736–50.[123] Shuckford, like Prideaux, was thoroughly familiar with all the ancient sources as well as the historyof research. Both, for example, used, quoted, and opposed Spinoza and Simon. Shuckford's work, which was never completed beyond the time of Joshua, was, perhaps because of the biblical material covered, more influenced by the deistic controversy than that of Prideaux. In describing the magicians at the court of Pharaoh, Shuckford presents them as deistic philosophers:

> In Moses's time, the rulers of the Egyptian nation . . . were then the most learned body in the world, *beguiled by the deceit of vain philosophy* . . . The Pagan divinations, arts of prophecy, and all their sorceries and enchantments, as well as their idolatry and worship of false gods, were founded, not upon superstition, but upon learning and philosophical study; not upon too great a belief of, and adherence to revelation, but upon a pretended knowledge of the powers of nature. Their great and learned men erred in these points, not for want of freethinking, such as they called so; but their opinions upon these subjects were in direct opposition to the true revelations which had been made to the world, and might be called the deism of these ages; for such certainly was the religion of the governing and learned part of the Heathen world in these times.[124]

120. Ibid., 2.264–98.
121. Ibid., 2.132.
122. Ibid., 2.12–13.
123. See Southern, "2. Hugh of St. Victor," 178–79.
124. Shuckford, *Sacred and Profane*, 1.565–66.

Like his predecessors, Shuckford stretched his intellectual powers in defence of the biblical chronology, arguing that the antediluvians enjoyed longevity because before the flood the earth was situated so as to have a perpetual equinox, thus sparing its inhabitants the rigors of seasonal change.[125] He argued that "at the flood, the heavens underwent some change: the motion of the sun was altered, and a year, or annual revolution of it, became, as it now is, five daysand almost six hours longer than it was before."[126] However, Shuckford, who was thoroughly familiar with the problems of textual criticism, was occasionally willing to amend the Hebrew text on the basis of the Greek (for example, Deut 34:6 should read "they buried him";[127] thus Moses did not write the account of his death). He sensed the problem of the divine names in Genesis and Exodus, and devoted an extended discussion to the use of the names Jehovah, El Shaddai, and Elohim.[128] His solution tothe problem was not to postulate a multiplicity of documents but to theorize about the diversity of persons in the godhead.

Outside England, the deist impulse led to some very scathing attacks on Christianity and the Bible. The Frenchman Voltaire (1694–1778) never tired of pointing out what he called the absurdities, inconsistencies, and low morality found in the Bible. To claim that God was its author was to make "of God a bad geographer, a bad chronologist, a bad physicist; it makes him no better a naturalist."[129] To claim that Moses wrote the Pentateuch was to claim Moses to be a fool. Voltaire suggested that much of the Old Testament was borrowed by the Jews from other peoples, and proposed that Moses may have never lived: "If there only were some honest and natural deeds in the myth of Moses, one could believe fully that such a personage did exist."[130] The significance of Voltaire was his popularization, in caustic language, of many of the issues that had previously been the concerns of erudite scholars. Voltaire, however, approached the Bible and its historical materials not so much as a critic but as an assassin.

In Germany, the impact of deism can be seen in the work of H. S. Reimarus (1694–1768), who, at his death, left behind what the philosopher

---

125. Ibid., 20–21.
126. Ibid., 1.iii.
127. Ibid., 2.229.
128. Ibid., 1.517–30.
129. Quoted in Appelgate, *Voltaire on Religion*, 26.
130. Quoted in ibid., 102.

Lessing published as the *Wolfenbüttel Fragments*. One of these fragments was an essay on "the passage of the Israelites through the Red Sea."[131] Reimarus sought to show the impossibilities in a literal interpretation of the biblical description of the crossing of the sea. According to Exod 12:37–38, about six hundred thousand Hebrew men left Egypt, not counting the women, children, and mixed multitude and animals that accompanied them. Reimarus says this would give a figure of about three million people, three hundred thousand oxen and cows, and six hundred thousand sheep and goats. Approximately five thousand wagons would have been needed to carry provisions and three hundred thousand tents would have been required to house the people at ten per tent. Had the multitude marched ten abreast, the three million would have formed a column one hundred and eighty miles long. It would have required nine days as a minimum for such a group to march through the parted sea. Reimarus's arguments, and there were others who made similar points, hit at the very heart of those who took the Bible as literally inspired and as factually infallible.

Among the founding fathers of the United States were many with deistic leanings. Jefferson edited a version of the New Testament devoid of any miracles and concluding with the death of Jesus. Thomas Paine, an Englishman who spent several years in the U.S. supporting the Revolutionary War and some time in France in exile, was a brutal controversialist in his attack upon the Bible. Paine's peculiarity consists in the "freshness with which he comes upon very old discoveries, and the vehemence with which he announces them."[132] In his book *The Age of Reason*, Paine wrote:

> Whenever we read the obscene stories, the voluptuous debaucheries, the cruel and torturous executions, the unrelenting vindictiveness, with which more than half the Bible is filled, it would be more consistent that we called it the word of a demon than the word of God. It is a history of wickedness that has served to corrupt and brutalize mankind; and, for my part, I sincerely detest it, as I detest everything that is cruel. Speaking for myself, if I had no other evidence that the Bible is fabulous than the sacrifice I must make to believe it to be true, that alone would be sufficient to determine my choice.[133]

---

131. For a selection, see Gay, *Deism*, 158–63; for a study of Reimarus and the Old Testament, see Reventlow, "Die Auffassung."

132. Stephen, *History*, 1.461.

133. See the selection from Paine in Gay, *Deism*, 164–76.

The significance of the deistic movement and the Enlightenment of the eighteenth century was not in the area of historiography per se. The deists, in their discussions of the Bible and the history portrayed in the Bible, presented the issues of biblical criticism to the general public. In addition, their scathing attacks on the defences supporting a factual, literal reading of the text were devastating. It would never again be easy to present Israelite and Judean history by simply retelling and amplifying the biblical narratives.

Several developments, in addition to the deistic controversy, occurred in the eighteenth century, which should be noted since they were greatly to affect the study of Israelite and Judean history. The use of ancient literature in comparative studies of the Old Testament became more common and less apologetic. In 1685, John Spencer, of Corpus Christi College in Cambridge, published his *De legibus Hebraeorum ritualibus et earum rationibus* in which he compared the ritual laws of the Old Testament with relevant material from Egypt, Greece, and Rome. Comparative study, as the deists demonstrated, could cut in two directions; it could be used to support either the uniqueness or the dependency of the biblical materials. The study of Palestinian geography was advanced by Hadrian Reland's *Palaestina ex monumentis veteribus illustrata* (1714) and the pioneer work in Palestinian antiquities, *Compendium antiquitatum Hebraeorum*, by Johann David Michaelis, appeared in 1753.

The basic elements in the documentary criticism of the Old Testament were established during this time. The German pastor Henning Bernhard Witter (1683–1715) and the French physician Jean Astruc (1684–1766) laid down some of the criteria for source criticism of the Pentateuch. The classic four-source theory of the Pentateuch was to be worked out in the nineteenth century but the five pillars of documentary criticism were established in the eighteenth. These pillars are: (1) the use of different names for the deity, (2) varieties of language and style, (3) contradictions and divergences, (4) repetitions and duplications, and (5) indications of composite structure.

A third phenomenon to be noted is the maturation of the science of Old Testament introduction. Pioneers in this area were Michaelis and Johann Salomo Semler.[134] Both of these men were influenced by English deism.[135] With Johann Gottfried Eichhorn's *Einleitung in das Alte Testa-*

---

134. See Kraus, *Geschichte*, 97–113; Kümmel, *The New Testament*, 62–73; and on Semler, see Hornig, *Die Anfänge*.

135. See Kümmel, *The New Testament*, 415 notes 59, 63.

The History of the Study of Israelite and Judean History

ment (1780–83), the basic problems of Old Testament introduction—growth of the canon, history of the text, and origin and nature of the individual books—were discussed in handbook form. With Eichhorn, the humanistic argument that the literature of the Old Testament should be investigated like any other literature was integrated into the mainstream of Protestant biblical study.

A fourth factor in the eighteenth century was the poetic or 'romantic' reaction to the classicism and rationalism of the Enlightenment. In Old Testament studies, this movement is most closely associated with the work and thought of Johann Gottfried Herder (1744–1803) who was influenced by such figures as Jean-Jacques Rousseau (1712–78), Johann Georg Hamann (1730–88), and Robert Lowth (1710–87). The latter's *De sacra poesi Hebraeorum* (1753) studied Hebrew poetry along the lines of research applied to Greek and Latin poetry, arguing that poetry represented humandkind's earliest form of speech and was as expressive of truth as philosophy. The pietist Hamann had also expressed an emphasis on poetry as the mother-tongue of the human race and, like most pietists, stressed the reader's immediacy to the biblical materials. Rousseau glorified primitive humandkind as a free and happy being living in accordance with nature and instinct, and for whom language was his basic expression of the natural and communal spirit.[136] Herder emphasized the necessity of entering empathically into the human world out of which the Bible had come, rather than seeking understanding merely through critical and technical analysis. He was more interested in the group than the individual and in the manner in which the group gave expression to its distinctive culture, not necessarily according to any universal laws. Cultures are like plants that grow in unique ways dependent upon the situation of the place, the circumstances of the times and the generative character of the people. Whatever can take place among humankind does take place; life does not operate along rationalistic lines. Herder's approach to the human past stressed an appreciative and imaginative relationship to the 'spirit' and not a rational, judgmental relationship.[137]

A final development in eighteenth-century Old Testament research was the introduction of mythological study. The systematic study of

---

136. On Herder's broad concerns and their relationship to Enlightenment thought, see Berlin, "Herder and the Enlightenment"; on his hermeneutics, see Frei, *The Eclipse*, 183–201.

137. See Scholder, "Herder"; and Willi, *Herders Beitrag*, on Herder's general contributions to Old Testament study.

classical mythology originated with the German classicist Christian Gottlob Heyne (1729–1812) who argued that myth was one of primitive humandkind's basic modes of expressing the experiences and understanding of life and nature. The first application of mythological studies to the Old Testament was made by Eichhorn, a student of Heyne at Göttingen, who published a work on Genesis 1–3 titled *Die Urgeschichte* (1779). Eichhorn's work, which was greatly influenced by Lowth, was taken up by Johann Philipp Gabler (1753–1826). The concept of myth, when applied to parts of the Old Testament, greatly affected the manner in which scholars examined these materials and naturally led directly to the question of the historical factuality of their content. Later, what could be labeled as mythical was removed from the arena of the historical.[138]

The Nineteenth Century

Major developments in the nineteenth century that form the background for Israelite historiography may simply be noted since they have been so frequently discussed. In the first place, more liberal stances in theology came to characterize many segments of the religious communities. This liberalism was less dogmatic in its theological orientation, more progressive in its relationship to contemporary culture and thought, and more humanistic in its perspectives than previous generations. This gradual shift can be seen, for example, in the rise of the so-called *Wissenschaft des Judentums* movement, which sought "to see in Jewish history the gradual progression of Jewish religious or national spirit in its various vicissitudes and adjustments to the changing environments."[139] This liberal spirit, which was now located within the life of the religious communities themselves, was willing to break with traditional beliefs and approaches and to take a more critical attitude towards the biblical materials.

Secondly, major advances were made in general historiography. The nineteenth was the century of history. Of special importance was the development of what has been called a positivistic approach to history, which not only attempted but also believed it possible to reconstruct past history "as it had actually happened" (*wie es eigentlich gewesen*). The most prominent of these outstanding positivistic historians were Barthold

---

138. On the early stages of mythological research on the Old Testament see Hartlich and Sachs, *Der Ursprung*, 1–53; and Rogerson, *Myth*, 1–15.

139. Baron, *History*, 76.

The History of the Study of Israelite and Judean History

Georg Niebuhr (1776–1831), Leopold Ranke (1795–1885), and Theodor Mommsen (1817–1903). Practically every aspect of human life was subjected to historical exploration in the nineteenth century.[140]

Thirdly, the decipherment of ancient Near Eastern languages— opened the long-closed literary remains of Israel's neighbors to study and interpretation.[141] The full impact of these new fields of learning was not to be felt fully until the last years of the nineteenth and the first decades of the twentieth century. Nonetheless, for the first time scholars could examine the literary products of these cultures at first hand and thus were no longer dependent upon the ancient, secondary sources.

Fourthly, the exploration of the Near East and Palestine raised historical geography to a level of real competence. Explorers like the Swiss Johann Ludwig Burckhardt (1784–1817) and the American Edward Robinson (1794–1863) whose three-volume work, *Biblical Researches in Palestine, Mount Sinai and Arabia Petraea* (1841), based on his travels in 1838, reported on sites, place-names, and customs and used modern names to identify many places mentioned in the Bible. In 1865, the Palestine Exploration Fund was established and, in 1872–78, it sponsored a geographical survey of western Palestine (the Conder–Kitchener expedition). Other national societies were begun to encourage and finance exploration. Archaeological excavations at several sites in Palestine were undertaken.[142]

Fifthly, the isolation and dating of the 'documents' that went to make up the Pentateuch continued apace. The so-called four-source hypothesis that argued that four major documents (J, E, P, D) were redactionally combined to produce the Pentateuch gradually came to dominate discussions after mid-century. The character, content, and date of the individual documents were considered of great significance in understanding the religious development of Israelite and Judean life and in evaluating the historical reliability of the documentary materials.[143]

A survey of Israelite and Judean history in the nineteenth century can best be made by examining some innovative works from the period. The first work to be noted, and perhaps the first really critical history of Israel ever written, is that by Henry Hart Milman (1791–1868). Milman,

140. For the major developments and historians, see Gooch, *History and Historians*.

141. See Lloyd, *Foundations*; Bratton, *A History*; and Wilson, *Signs and Wonders*.

142. See Bliss, *The Development*; Hilprecht, *Explorations*; and Macalister, *A Century*.

143. On the development of critical research, see Briggs, *The Higher Criticism*; Carpenter, *The Bible*; Kraus, *Geschichte*, 152–308, 242–74; and Thompson, *Moses*.

55

a graduate of Oxford University, was ordained in 1816. During his early days, he wrote poetry and plays and from 1821 to 1831 held a professorship of poetry at Oxford. In 1849, he was appointed dean of St. Paul's Cathedral. Most of Milman's rather extensive literary output were works in church history. His *History of the Jews* was first published in 1829 and met with significant opposition. The work, however, was issued in a number of editions by various publishers until the first decade of the present century. Of the twenty-eight books in his three-volume history, the final ten are concerned with the history of the Jews following the Bar Kochba Revolt.

Milman's history was addressed to the general reading public and tends to be rather sketchy and to avoid any detailed discussion of controversial points or of methodology. The extent of his familiarity with Old Testament studies cannot be really determined. Only a few isolated references are made to significant figures, although Milman was acquainted with travel reports on the Near East and Palestine and makes rather frequent reference to these. Milman adopted a developmental approach to Jewish history: "Nothing is more curious, or more calculated to confirm the veracity of the Old Testament history, than the remarkable picture which it presents of the gradual development of human society: the ancestors of the Jews, and the Jews themselves, pass through every stage of comparative civilization."[144] Excepting only their knowledge of God and their custodianship of the promises, "the chosen people appear to have been left to themselves to pass through the ordinary stages of the social state."[145] Milman approached the Bible with a very limited view of inspiration and noted that "much allowance must . . . be made for the essentially poetic spirit, and for the Oriental forms of speech, which pervade so large a portion of the Old Testament"[146] and that God "addressed a more carnal and superstitious people chiefly through their imagination and senses."[147] He warned his readers that miracle would play little role in his interpretation of history, noting that those who have criticized the belief in revelation are "embarrassing to those who take up a narrow system of interpreting the Hebrew writings; to those who adopt a more rational

---

144. Milman, *History*, 1.v.
145. Ibid., 1.vi; see 3.346.
146. Ibid., 1.viii.
147. Ibid., 1.vi.

The History of the Study of Israelite and Judean History

latitude of exposition, none."[148] Whereas Prideaux and Shuckford were unwilling to accommodate their historical discussions to the views of the biblical critics, for Milman, there was no other option.

Milman began his history with the patriarchs and made no reference to the materials in Genesis 1–10. Abraham is described as an "independent Sheik or Emir"[149] or "the stranger sheik" who is allowed "to pitch his tent, and pasture his flocks and herds" in Canaan.[150] Milman considered the different stories of the endangering of the wife to be "traditional variations of the same transaction";[151] "Abraham is the Emir of a pastoral tribe, migrating from place to place . . . He is in no respect superior to his age or country, excepting in the sublime purity of his religion."[152] In describing patriarchal society, Milman wrote:

> Mankind appears in its infancy, gradually extending its occupancy over regions, either entirely unappropriated, or as yet so recently and thinly peopled, as to admit, without resistance, the new swarms of settlers which seem to spread from the birthplace of the human race, the plains of central Asia. They are peaceful pastoral nomads, travelling on their camels, the ass the only other beast of burden . . . The unenterprising shepherds, from whom the Hebrews descended, move onward as their convenience or necessity requires, or as richer pastures attract their notice.[153]

The description of the patriarchs as "the hunter, the migratory herdsman, and the incipient husbandman," suggests that the record draws upon "contemporary traditions."[154] The Israelite ancestors are thus a *Volk* who differ from their contemporaries only in their theological view of God.

In discussing the stay in Egypt, Milman argued against identifying the period with the Hyksos era but dated it later, refusing however to hypothesize a specific time.[155] He noted that biblical tradition assigns either 430 (MT) or 215 (LXX) years to the stay, but that both of these are irreconcilable with the mere two generations that separated Moses from Levi,

148. Ibid., 1.xi.
149. Ibid., 1.10.
150. Ibid., 1.20.
151. Ibid.
152. Ibid., 1.22–30.
153. Ibid., 1.29–30.
154. Ibid., 1.32.
155. Ibid., 1.40–42

a factor that also raised uncertainty about the number of Israelites leaving Egypt.[156] Milman described the plagues and the crossing of the Red Sea, but spoke of the "plain leading facts of the Mosaic narrative, the residence of the Hebrews in Egypt, their departure under the guidance of Moses, and the connexion of that departure with some signal calamity, at least for a time, fatal to the power and humiliating to the pride of Egypt."[157] In describing the crossing of the sea, he refers to a report by Diodorus Siculus concerning the erratic behavior of the water in the area.[158] The quails and manna in the desert are explained in naturalistic terms and the changing of bitter water to sweet is explained chemically. In footnotes in the second edition, Milman reports on the chemical analysis of water especially secured from a Palestinian spring called Marah that suggested high concentrations of "selenite or sulphate of lime," which could be precipitated by "any vegetable substance containing oxalic acid . . . and rendered agreeable and wholesome." He also reports that a traveler had brought him a sample of manna produced by the tamarisk tree.[159]

The pentateuchal legislation—"the Hebrew constitution"[160]—is attributed to Moses, "the legislator constantly, yet discreetly, mitigating the savage usages of a barbarous people."[161]

> The laws of a settled and civilized community were enacted among a wandering and homeless horde who were traversing the wilderness, and more likely, under their existing circumstances, to sink below the pastoral life of their forefathers, than advance to the rank of an industrious agricultural community. Yet, at this time, judging solely from its internal evidence, the law must have been enacted. Who but Moses ever possessed such authority as to enforce submission to statutes so severe and uncompromising? Yet, as Moses incontestably died before the conquest of Canaan, his legislature must have taken place in the desert. To what other period can the Hebrew constitution be assigned? To that of the judges? a time of anarchy, warfare, or servitude! To that of the kings? when the republic had undergone a total change! To any time after Jerusalem became the metropolis? when the holy city, the pride and glory of the

156. Ibid., 1.48–49, 119.
157. Ibid., 1.73.
158. Ibid., 1.72; see Herrmann, *History*, 63.
159. Ibid., 1.117.
160. Ibid., 1.79.
161. Ibid., 1.113.

> nation, is not even alluded to in the whole law! After the building of the temple? when it is equally silent as to any settled or durable edifice! After the separation of the kingdoms? when the close bond of brotherhood had given place to implacable hostility! Under Hilkiah? under Ezra? when a great number of the statutes had become a dead letter! The law depended on a strict and equitable partition of the land. At a later period it could not have been put into practice without the forcible resumption of every individual property by the state; the difficulty, or rather impossibility, of such a measure, may be estimated by any reader who is not entirely unacquainted with the history of the ancient republics. In other respects the law breathes the air of the desert. Enactments intended for a people with settled habitations, and dwelling in walled cities, are mingled up with temporary regulations, only suited to the Bedouin encampment of a nomad tribe.[162]

Milman certainly realized that the dating of the law was the central issue in Old Testament interpretation and that when one dates the law is highly determinative for how one writes the history. Also, he raised practically all the possible options for dating the law.

Milman follows the basic biblical account of the conquest and division of the land. The judges of early Israel, whose title is associated with "the Suffetes of the Carthaginians," are described as "military dictators" operating in emergencies within the "boundaries of their own tribe." Their qualifications were their "personal activity, daring, and craft," and they appear "as gallant insurgents or guerilla leaders." In the case of Deborah, several tribes came together in "an organized warlike confederacy." The tribes were disunited because of their disobedience to the Mosaic law and were compelled to arms in furthering the incomplete conquest in "war of the separate tribes against immediate enemies."[163] Although the Bible speaks of the judges being raised up by the Lord, "their particular actions are nowhere attributed to divine action."[164] The absence of Judah and Simeon from the song of Deborah (Judges 5) suggests that perhaps they "had seceded from the confederacy, or were occupied by enemies of their own."[165]

162. Ibid., 1.78–79.
163. Ibid., 1.155–56.
164. Ibid., 1.158–59.
165. Ibid., 1.160.

Enough has been said of Milman's work to suggest his approach since many of the basic issues arise in treating the period prior to David. Although Milman was probably the first to treat Israelite and Judean history from a secular orientation and in the same terms one would write a history of Greece or Rome, his name and an exposition of his position are seldom mentioned in surveys of Old Testament studies.

A second innovative work was the lengthy, multi-volume history by Heinrich Georg August Ewald (1803–75),[166] one of the most outstanding Oriental and Semitic scholars of the nineteenth century.[167] He was a student and successor of Eichhorn at Gottingen. Ewald's history is as verbose and dull as Milman's is crisp and entertaining.

Almost one half of the first volume of Ewald's history is devoted to the problem of the sources for Israelite history.[168] Ewald says his "ultimate aim is the knowledge of what really happened—not what was only related and handed down by tradition, but what was actual fact."[169] Tradition thus preserves an image of what happened, but it is also formed by imagination, which may blur the details or form of the event it remembers, and is shaped by the memory, which tends to obliterate details and contract the overall content.[170] Chronological distance from the events reduces the extent and trustworthiness of the tradition:

> The Hebrew tradition about the earliest times—the main features of which, as we have it, were fixed in the interval from the fourth to the sixth century after Moses—still has a great deal to tell about Moses and his contemporaries; much less about the long sojourn in Egypt, and the three Patriarchs; and almost nothing special about the primitive times which preceded these Patriarchs, when neither the nation, nor even its 'fathers,' were yet in Canaan. So, too, the Books of Samuel relate many particulars of David's later life passed in the splendour of royalty, but less about his youth before he was king.[171]

---

166. Ewald, *Geschichte*; ET = *History*.

167. On Ewald, see Wellhausen, "Heinrich Ewald"; Cheyne, *Founders*, 66–118; Kraus, *Geschichte*, 199–205.

168. Ewald, *History*, 1.11–203.

169. Ibid., 1.13.

170. Ibid., 1.14–16.

171. Ibid., 1.7.

The History of the Study of Israelite and Judean History

Tradition has supports in songs, proverbs, and personal names, and in visible monuments such as altars, temples, and memorials.[172] The strongest support of tradition, however, is the institution, such as annually recurring festivals that recall the incidents.[173] Foreign elements also enter traditions: names are added, numbers lose exactness, events shift their chronological moorings, and similar traditions become associated.[174] Tradition rests in imagination and feeling more than understanding and thus is closely associated with nationalistic sentiments.[175] Different events are remembered in different styles of traditions and since tradition is very plastic it may be moulded by religious interests, aetiological concerns, and mythological perspectives.[176]

The earliest Israelite historians found the tradition that they used as "a fluctuating and plastic material, but also a mass of unlimited extent."[177] At the writing-down stage, tradition went through further change. The modern historian must "distinguish between the story and its foundation, and exclusively seek the latter with all diligence."[178] "Tradition has its roots in actual facts; yet it is not absolutely history, but has a peculiar character and a value of its own ... It is our duty to take the tradition just as it expects to be taken—to use it only as a means for discovering what the real facts once were."[179]

Thus, Ewald has a high regard for tradition's relationship to historical facts and for the historian's ability to use the tradition to discover the facts. By the Mosaic era, writing was known in Israel and a historiography possible.[180]

Ewald divides the historical books into three groups: the Great Book of Origins (the Hexateuch), the Great Book of Kings (Judges–Kings + Ruth), and the Great Book of Universal History down to the Greek Times (Chronicles–Ezra–Nehemiah + Esther). Ewald then analyzes these great books as to their sources. The basic source of the Hexateuch was what Ewald called the "Book of Origins" (what is today called P), which he

---

172. Ibid., 1.17–21.
173. Ibid., 1.21–22.
174. Ibid., 1.22–26.
175. Ibid., 1.26–31.
176. Ibid., 1.31–40.
177. Ibid., 1.41.
178. Ibid., 1.45.
179. Ibid., 1.44.
180. Ibid., 1.49–51.

dated to the period of the early monarchy.[181] This book incorporated older fragments and materials and was subjected to various modifications, prophetic and Deuteronomistic, before it attained its final form at the end of the seventh or the beginning of the sixth century.[182] In similar manner, Ewald proceeds to analyze the other two historical complexes, their origin, components, modifications, and history.

Before beginning his reconstruction of the history, Ewald discussed some problems of chronology[183] and general geographical matters.[184] Ewald follows the four-age theory of P and speaks of the three ages of the preliminary history of Israel: creation to Noah, Noah to Abraham, and Abraham to Moses. In discussing the first two ages, Ewald compares the traditions with those of other peoples, discusses the ages of the characters, and avoids any real straightforward statements about the factuality of the materials. Behind the patriarchal figures are to be seen tribal groups. The oldest extant tradition about Abraham is Genesis 14.[185] The patriarchal ancestors spoke and thought monotheistically but not quite in the Mosaic form.[186] The Hebrews are pictured entering Egypt at different times in various migrations, beginning in the Hyksos period, but the exodus is not to be associated with the expulsion of the Hyksos.[187]

The Hebrew nation as a theocracy came into being under Moses in the wilderness. The event of the exodus, which inaugurated this period, cannot be fully reconstructed: "Whatever may have been the exact course of this event, whose historical certainty is well established; its momentous results, the nearer as well as the more remote, were sure to be experienced, and arc even to us most distinctly visible."[188] Under Moses, the golden theocratic age of Israel began, the law was given, and the age reached maturity under his leadership and that of Joshua. From Joshua to the monarchy was a time of the decay of the pure theocracy and the relaxation of the national bond.

181. Ibid., 1.74–78.
182. Ibid., 1.131.
183. Ibid., 1.204–13.
184. Ibid., 1.214–55.
185. Ibid., 1.307.
186. Ibid., 1.320–21.
187. Ibid., 1.388–407.
188. Ibid., 2.75.

The History of the Study of Israelite and Judean History

Enough has been said of Ewald's work to suggest its general approach. His work was innovative in that it sought to base the discussion of the history on a systematic study of the biblical traditions and sources. Ewald, however, basically adhered to the theological perspective of the biblical text while modifying the miraculous element. As in the Bible, the golden age of Israelite history is the age of Moses. After wading through Ewald's presentation, one possesses the impression of having read a historical commentary on the historical books, but not of having read a history of Israel.

A third innovative history of the nineteenth century was the work by Heinrich Graetz (1817–91). His work is not of major significance per se, but because it represents the first modern history of ancient Israel and Judah written by a Jew.[189] Graetz had been preceded by his younger Jewish contemporary, Isaac Marcus Jost (1793–1860), whose nine-volume history of the Jews from Maccabean times until the nineteenth century was the first major Jewish history in modern times.[190] The first volume of Graetz's work covered the period from Moses to the death of Simon in 135 BCE.[191] The work is primarily a rather free—at times rather romanticized—narration built upon the biblical materials. Very few of the problems are given any detailed treatment. The real importance of Graetz's work is the fact that it depicts the history free from any overriding theological stance or biblical orthodoxy.

A final nineteenth-century historian to be noted was Julius Wellhausen (1844–1918), who was the most influential and significant Old Testament scholar of the time. Before producing a reconstruction of Israelite history, Wellhausen carried out a detailed examination of the literary traditions in the Hexateuch. He accepted and supported the documentary criticism that argued that there were four sources in the Pentateuch that originated in the order J, E, D, P. In his *Prolegomena*, Wellhausen supported this theory with an incisive analysis of the history of worship and religion, which sought to demonstrate that Israelite religious life had gone through various states that are reflected in the documents of the Pentateuch. Some of Wellhausen's major conclusions on the literary and religious history were the following. (1) The theocratic organization of Israel and the priestly laws of the Pentateuch were the basis not for life in

---

189. Graetz, *Geschichte*; ET = *History*.
190. On Jost, see Baron, *History*, 240–75.
191. On Graetz, see ibid., 263–75.

the age of Moses but for post-exilic Judaism. (2) The eighth century was the age of real literary activity in Israel: "The question why it was that Elijah and Elisha committed nothing to writing, while Amos a hundred years later is an author, hardly admits of any other answer than that in the interval a non-literary had developed into a literary age."[192] (3) The Yahwistic (J) and Elohistic (E) sources came into being during the early days of classical prophetism and reflect the pre-prophetic religion of Israel.[193] (4) Under the influence of the prophets, Deuteronomy was produced in the seventh century.[194] (5) Deuteronomy was strictly a law-book and J was a history-book; the combination of these two was the beginning of the combination of law and narrative that was the pattern followed by P.[195] (6) The priestly work derives from post-exilic times and reflects the atmosphere of theocratic Judaism. (7) The presentations of the earliest phase of Israelite history, the patriarchal period, in the various sources were colored by the times in which the sources were written and thus cannot be used for historical purposes: "We attain to no historical knowledge of the patriarchs, but only of the time when the stories about them arose in the Israelite people; this later ageis here unconsciously projected, in its inner and outward features, into hoar antiquity, and is reflected there like a glorified mirage."[196] It should be noted that Wellhausen makes such a statement only for the patriarchal period, and not for the following ones. Wellhausen saw Israelite religion developing through three phases:

(a) the stage of primitive religion characterized by popular sentiments, a spontaneous and simple faith, and a nature orientation;

(b) the stage of ethical concerns and consciousness initiated by the prophets; and

(c) the stage of ceremonial and ritual religion influenced by the priestly legislation and further separated from the orientation to nature.

Wellhausen seems to have sympathized most with the religion of the earliest phase, although he shared in the general nineteenth-century excitement over the 'rediscovery' of the prophets as creative individuals and exponents of personal and ethical religion.[197]

192. Wellhausen, *Prolegomena to the History of Israel*, 465.
193. Ibid., 360–61.
194. Ibid., 487–88.
195. Ibid., 345.
196. Ibid., 318–19.
197. Ibid., 464–70; 1958 ed., 78–103.

The History of the Study of Israelite and Judean History

Various attempts were, and still are, made to counter Wellhausen's position by arguing that he imposed Hegelian philosophy or evolutionary thought on the Old Testament.[198] This attempt to condemn by association has really no foundation in fact.[199] The basic influences upon Wellhausen were the emphasis laid by Herder and by Romanticism on primitivism, with its opposition to cultic ceremonial and things priestly, the positivistic approach to history exemplified in Niebuhr, Ranke, and Mommsen, the general nineteenth-century concern with stages in the history of practically everything, which most frequently argued for progressive development (in a good sense), although this was not completely the case with Wellhausen, the Lutheran theological position vis-à-vis the problem of law and gospel, and the general philosophy of history inherent in Christianity. (Even Bright, who criticizes Wellhausen for his evolutionary thought, calls the epilogue to his history "Toward the Fullness of Time."[200]) The primary influence on Wellhausen's reconstruction of Israelite history was, of course, the results and consequences of his literary study of the Old Testament.

Wellhausen's article on Israel, published in the ninth edition of the *Encyclopaedia Britannica* in 1880, was his basic statement on the topic. His later publications expanded the content but made no substantive changes; thus this article in its 1885 reprint can serve to present his views. For him, the ancestors of Israel were part of a Hebrew group, which included the ancestors of the Edomites, Moabites, and Ammonites, who settled in southeastern Palestine. Some time in the fifteenth century BCE, a part of this Hebrew group left southern Palestine and moved into Goshen in Egypt. They were later subjected to forced labor until Moses reminded them of the God of their fathers and taught them self-assertion against the Egyptians. When Egypt was scourged by a plague, the Hebrews fled secretly to return to their old home. The fleeing Hebrews were pursued by the Egyptians but were able to ford a shallow sea that had been blown back by a high wind. A struggle ensued between the Egyptians and Hebrews but the former in their chariots were at a disadvantage and were annihilated by the returning waters.[201]

---

198. See Thompson, *Moses*, 35–49, and bibliography there.
199. See Perlitt, *Vatke und Wellhausen*.
200. Bright, *History*, 458–64.
201. Wellhausen, "Israel," in *Prolegomena*, 429–30.

After visiting Sinai, the emigrants settled at Kadesh for many years and there had their sanctuary and judgment-seat. Some attempts to move northwards into Canaan may have been made while the Hebrews pastured their flocks over an extended area around Kadesh. They left Kadesh to aid their kinsmen against Sihon in Transjordan, being joined by kindred elements. At this stage some groups—the six Leah clans and Joseph, a Rachel clan—may have already existed as organized tribes.[202] From the historical tradition in the Pentateuch, Wellhausen argued that some picture of Moses can be seen: he was the founder of Torah, called into activity the feeling for law and justice, and was the founder of the nation, but presented the Hebrews with no new concept of God.[203]

The first movement into Palestine was led by Judah; the second wave by Joseph. There the divisions of Israel and Judah developed. Joshua was the leader of the Joseph and Benjamin groups.[204] After some united effort at conquest, the tribes and families fought for their own land. Much of the indigenous population was absorbed. Gradually Israel advanced from pastoralism to agriculture.[205] Yahweh was the god of Israel and Israel the people of God in its earliest days. In origin, the name Yahweh was a special name of the god El; Yahweh was the warrior El.[206] For a time, Baalism and Yahwism existed side by side. Gradually Yahwism absorbed elements of Baalism including the main elements in the cult.[207]

This summary of Wellhausen's reconstruction of the early history of Israel sufficiently demonstrates his approach. Wellhausen refused to understand Israel's history by postulating a golden period at some point early in its history, from which subsequent generations degenerated.

Current Approaches

Subsequent chapters in *Israelite and Judaean History* discuss the modern history of research on particular periods of Israelite history.[208] At this point, a brief comment on the general methodology of the major current

---

202. Ibid., 430–32.
203. Ibid., 432–40.
204. Ibid., 441–44.
205. Ibid., 441–46.
206. Ibid., 433–34.
207. Ibid., 447–48.
208. Hayes and Miller, eds., *Israelite and Judaean History*.

The History of the Study of Israelite and Judean History

approaches to the history will be made to provide some background for those discussions.

One approach that is still used by conservative scholars is the orthodox or traditional approach. This position operates on the assumption that the Bible is of supernatural origin and in its autograph form (which is no longer available) was totally free of any error.[209] Other scholars who would classify themselves as conservative would not take so rigid a view of biblical inspiration.[210] The orthodox view, similar to mainline biblical studies of the seventeenth and eighteenth centuries, works primarily from the evidence of the biblical text, supplying this with illustrative and supportive material drawn from extra-biblical texts and archaeological data. At points, the biblical texts need to be harmonized where apparent contradictions seem to appear. This view of the biblical materials is sometimes extended to the seven-day creation scheme, to be dated about 4000 BCE, and to the flood. Wood's history supplies a good representation of this approach.[211] He is able to supply exact dates for biblical events, which are all taken as historically accurate: Abraham was born in 2166 BCE, Isaac married Rebekah in 2026 BCE, Jacob was seventy-seven years old when he went to Haran and hired himself to Laban for fourteen years, the exodus occurred in 1446 BCE, and so on. Biblical figures are accurate: over two million Hebrews left Egypt. Miracles happened as described, although God normally employed natural law when this was available: the sea was opened to approximately a mile in width to allow passage of the fleeing Hebrews,[212] and the earth "slowed, in its speed of rotation on its axis, approximately to half that of normal" in order to provide Joshua with additional daylight in his battle near Gibeon.[213] Sufficient examples have been noted to illustrate this approach. In the following chapters, practically no attention will be given to this view since it does not assume that one has to reconstruct the history of Israel; one has only to support and elucidate the adequate history that the Bible already provides.

A second approach to Israelite history is what might be called the archaeological approach, since it seeks to substantiate much of the biblical data by appeal to evidence external to but supportive of the biblical

---

209. On this view of the Bible, see Lindsell, *The Battle for the Bible*.
210. See Beegle, *The Inspiration of Scripture*.
211. Wood, *Survey*.
212. Ibid., 132–33.
213. Ibid., 181.

text. This approach to Israelite history, built on the earlier antiquarian interests, became a fully conscious approach in the late nineteenth century as a reaction to documentary criticism of the Pentateuch and the historical approaches, such as that by Wellhausen, built on documentary criticism.[214] In recent years, this approach has been associated in a special way with William Foxwell Albright (1891–1971) and his students (but see the widely popular book by Keller), although there are many archaeologists who would not share his methodological approach. Albright formulated his approach to the history and religion of Israel in the 1920s and 1930s, and this remained basically unchanged throughout his career. His methodology rests on two basic arguments. (1) The traditions of the Old Testament are generally quite reliable. One should assume that these traditions embody historical memory and that the tendency to preserve traditions rather than create them was a fundamental characteristic of Near Eastern life, including Israelite, where one finds "a superstitious veneration both for the written word and for oral tradition."[215] (2) Archaeological remains—both literary and artifactual—provide a source of material external to the Bible that can be used as a control against the unnecessary dependency upon literary, philosophical, or fundamentalist hypotheses. Since archaeology "is concrete, not speculative," it can play this role.[216] Albright and his students operated on the assumption that archaeology had and would support the historicity of the biblical traditions.

"Archaeological and inscriptional data have established the historicity of innumerable passages and statements of the Old Testament; the number of such cases is many times greater than those where the reverse has been proved or has been made probable."[217] "Before archaeology there was no adequate alternative to the creation of hypothetical frameworks for the biblical narrative; but as the factual evidence has become available, there is less and less excuse for such exercises in ingenuity, and in due course there will be none."[218]

Probably few, if any, of Albright's students would go as far as the following statement of Mendenhall on the role of archaeology, but an

---

214. See Thompson, *Moses*, 91–96, 132–39, and bibliography there.
215. Albright, "Archaeology," 183.
216. Ibid., 179; see Bright, *Early Israel*, 11–33, 111–26.
217. Albright, "Archaeology," 180.
218. Freedman, "Archaeology," 298.

The History of the Study of Israelite and Judean History

emphasis on external evidence points in this direction: "We have an abundance of documentation from excavations comprised of primary, contemporary, and datable sources that yield all kinds of information about the social, political, ethnic, and religious traits of humandkind in the Near East... Unless biblical history is to be relegated to the domain of unreality and myth, the biblical and the archaeological most be correlated. Methodologically, the archaeological documents, especially the written ones, must he given priority and considered seriously."[219]

A third typological approach to Israelite history may be called the traditio-historical approach.[220] This methodology is most closely associated with Albrecht Alt (1883–1956), Martin Noth (1902–68), and Gerhard von Rad (1901–71). The impetus for this approach goes back to Hermann Gunkel (1862–1932), who was the pioneer in Old Testament form-critical studies.[221] Gunkel's work was postulated upon a number of perspectives that were ultimately of significance in the traditio-historical study of the Old Testament.

1. The writing down of Old Testament traditions in the form of documents was a late stage in a long process, and the writers of the documents were more like redactors or editors than authors.

2. Old Testament traditions had a long history of usage in an oral stage before they were written down.

3. Traditions may be divided into genres according to the content and mood of the materials, their formal language of expression, and their setting in life.

4. The basic form of the tradition is the individual unit or genre.

5. In the patriarchal traditions, the primary unit is the saga.

6. The individual sagas had their particular function in the setting in which they were used and the function of many of these was aetiological; they were used to 'explain' the origin of some physical feature, custom, practice, or ethnic relationship.

7. The individual sagas could be combined to produce cycles of traditions.

---

219. Mendenhall, *The Tenth Generation*, 142.

220. See Knight, *Rediscovering*, for the history and description of this methodology.

221. On Gunkel, see Buss, "The Study of Forms," 39–52; Wilcoxen, "Narrative," 57–79.

8. History writing in Israel developed out of this saga tradition.

Von Rad contributed four perspectives that were to be influential in traditio-historical studies in the latter's impact on the study of Israelite history.

1. He isolated the small summaries of Israel's pre-monarchic history and related the usage of these to cultic celebrations.[222]

2. The Sinai tradition was not originally a part of the historical summaries but had a different setting in the cult.

3. The cultic summaries were seen as the basis of the Yahwist's (J) history of early Israel that incorporated the Sinai theme and was prefaced by the primeval history.

4. The time of David and Solomon was the period when Israelite historiography developed out of the narrative art of the saga.[223]

A number of preliminary stages led to Noth's history of Israel along traditio-historical lines. In 1930, he used the concept of the Greek amphictyony to explain the organization of the tribes in pre-monarchical Israel.[224] The unity of the twelve tribes during this period was primarily religious but with some legal basis as well. In 1940, Noth published his study of pentateuchal law,[225] whose origin he associated with the life of the tribal amphictyony. Noth's study of the Deuteronomistic history (1943) stressed the late editorial work in the book of Joshua and its account of the conquest.[226] His study of the pentateuchal traditions[227] argued that the major traditions in the Pentateuch can be divided into five major themes: guidance out of Egypt, guidance into the land, promise to the patriarchs, guidance in the wilderness, and revelation at Sinai. Each of these themes was originally independent of the others. These themes were first combined during the time of the tribal league—the pre-monarchical source 'G' in which these were combined was the basis for the later sources such as J from the Davidic–Solomonic period.

---

222. Von Rad, "The Form-Critical Problem," 1–50.

223. Von Rad, "The Beginnings"; so Meyer, *Geschichte*, II/2.285–86.

224. Noth, *Das System*; so already, in limited ways, Ewald, *History*, 1.370; and Haupt, "Midian und Sinai."

225. Noth, *Die Gesetze*; ET = "The Laws."

226. Noth, *Überlieferungsgeschichtliche Studien*; ET= *The Deuteronomistic History*.

227. Noth, *Überlieferungsgeschichte des Pentateuchs*; ET = *A History of Pentateuchal Traditions*.

The History of the Study of Israelite and Judean History

When these concepts are applied to the history of Israel, Noth has to begin his treatment with the tribal league.[228] Since the early themes have only been associated secondarily, their historical outline is unreliable. Nothing substantial can be known about Moses since he has been introduced secondarily into the thematic traditions. The patriarchal traditions cannot be penetrated to discover anything of real historical value. The dominant account of the conquest is Deuteronomistic, although some early, primarily aetiological, materials are found in the accounts. Since the tribes moved into Palestine separately, no united leadership of the tribes can be ascribed to Joshua. It was the amphictyonic Israel that first imposed the 'all Israel' concept upon what were originally independent traditions and independent pasts. This time of the sacral amphictyonic organization is, for Noth, something like a golden age from which the later ages deviated.

A further approach to the early history of Israel is the attempt to understand early Israelite life in socio-economic categories. The first scholar to work along these lines was the sociologist Max Weber (1864–1920) in his *Ancient Judaism*, although he was not an Old Testament specialist. This approach has been taken up by Mendenhall, Dus, Gottwald, and others.[229] Although there are some major differences within this approach, the following are generally shared convictions.

1. Israel as a people or tribal confederacy originated in the land of Canaan.

2. Her origin was primarily the product of an internal revolt within Canaan against the Canaanite city-states' economic and political structures. The peasants and pastoralists involved in this revolt sought liberation and freedom from their oppressive overlords.

3. Israel created a new order of society in its tribal and covenant relationships.

4. The idea of Israel's origin in nomadic culture and the concept of a general conquest from outside the land must be given up.

5. The establishment of the monarchy was in many ways a return to the pre-revolutionary state of affairs and thus represents a paganization of the life and faith of liberated Israel.

---

228. Noth, *Geschichte Israels*; ET = *The History of Israel*.

229. See, e.g., Mendenhall, "The Conquest"; Dus, "Mose oder Josua?" (ET = "Moses or Joshua?"); and Gottwald, *The Tribes*.

These four approaches represent the basic alternatives at present employed in reconstructing Israelite history. The crucial period is, of course, the pre-monarchic times. Obviously, different scholars utilize insights and evidence from other approaches than that which is dominant in their own methodology. Some historians, especially Herrmann and de Vaux, cannot be said to be dominated by any exclusive methodology but are more eclectic.[230]

Bibliography

Part 1: The Earliest Treatments of Israelite and Judean History

Cassuto, Umberto. "The Beginning of Historiography among the Israelites." *Eretz Israel* 1 (1951) 85–88 (Hebrew). Translated in *Biblical and Oriental Studies*, vol. 1, 7–16. Jerusalem: Magnes, 1973.

Collingwood, R. G. *The Idea of History*. London: Oxford University Press 1946.

Collomp, Paul. "La place d'Josèphe dans la technique de l'historiographie hellenistique." *EHFLS* 106 (1947) 81–92. Reprinted in *Zur Josephus-Forschung*, edited by Abraham Schalit, 278–93. Wege der Forschung 84. Darmstadt: Wissenschaftliche Buchgesellschaft, 1973.

Dentan, Robert C., editor. *The Idea of History in the Ancient Near East*. American Oriental Series 38. New Haven: Yale University Press, 1955.

Finegan, Jack. *Handbook of Biblical Chronology: Principles of Time Reckoning in the Ancient World and Problems of Chronology in the Bible*. Princeton: Princeton University Press, 1964.

Gager, John G. *Moses in Greco-Roman Paganism*. SBL Monograph Series 16. Nashville: Abingdon, 1972.

Gelzer, Heinrich. *Sextus Julius Africanus und die byzantinische Chronographie*. 2 vols. in 1. Leipzig: Teubner, 1880–98.

Gese, Hartmut. "Geschichtliches Denken im alten Orient und im Alten Testament." *Zeitschrift für Theologie und Kirche* 55 (1958) 127–45.

———. "The Idea of History in the Ancient Near East and the Old Testament." *Journal of Theology and the Church* 1 (1965) 49–64.

Glatzer, Nahum N. *Untersuchungen zur Geschichtslehre der Tannaiten: Ein Beitrag zur Religionsgeschichte*. Berlin: Schocken, 1933.

Grant, Robert M. *The Letter and the Spirit*. London: SPCK 1957.

Harrington, Daniel J., editor and translator. *The Hebrew Fragments of Pseudo-Philo's Liber Antiquitatum Biblicarum Preserved in the Chronicles of Jerahmeel*. SBL Texts and Translations, Pseudepigrapha Series 3. Missoula, MT: Scholars, 1974.

Kisch, Guido. *Pseudo-Philo's Liber Antiquitatum Biblicarum*. Publications in Mediaeval Studies 10. Notre Dame, IN: University of Notre Dame, 1949.

Koch, Klaus. "Spätisraelitisches Geschichtsdenken am Beispiel des Buches Daniel." *Historische Zeitschrift* 193 (1961) 1–32.

---

230. Herrmann, *History*; de Vaux, *Earliest History*.

The History of the Study of Israelite and Judean History

Kramer, Samuel Noah. "Sumerian Historiography." *Israel Exploration Journal* 3 (1953) 217–32.

Lindner, Helgo. *Die Geschichtsaufassung des Flavius Josephus im Bellum Judaicum: Gleichzeitig ein Beitrag zur Quellenfrage*. Arbeiten zur Geschichte des antiken Judentums und des Urchristentums 12. Leiden: Brill, 1972.

Meyer, Michael A., editor. *Ideas of Jewish History*. Library of Jewish Studies. New York: Behrman, 1974.

Milburn, R. L. P. *Early Christian Interpretations of History*. Bampton Lectures 1952. London: A. & C. Black, 1954.

Momigliano, A. "Pagan and Christian Historiography in the Fourth Century AD." In *The Conflict between Paganism and Christianity in the Fourth-Century*, 79–99. Oxford-Warburg Studies. Oxford: Clarendon, 1963.

———. "The Second Book of Maccabees." *Classical Philology* 70 (1975) 81–91.

Moscati, Sabatino. *Historical Art in the Ancient Near East*. Studi Semitici 8. Rome: Centro di Studi Semitici, 1963.

Mowinckel, Sigmund. "Israelite Historiography." *Annual of the Swedish Theological Institute* 11 (1963) 4–26.

Olmsted, A. T. E. *Assyrian Historiography: A Source Study*. University of Missouri Studies: Social Science Series III/1. Columbia: University of Missouri, 1916.

Otto, Eberhard. "Geschichtsbild und Geschichtsschreibung in Ägypten." *Die Welt des Orients* III/3 (1964/6) 161–76.

Pfeiffer, Robert H. *Introduction to the Old Testament*. New York: Harper, 1941.

Rad, Gerhard von. "Der Anfang der Geschichtsschreibung im alten Israel." *Archiv für Kulturgeschichte* 32 (1944) 1–42. Reprinted in *Gesammelte Studien zum Alten Testament*, 148–88. ThBü 8. Munich: Kaiser, 1958.

———. "The Beginnings of Historical Writing in Ancient Israel." In *The Problem of the Hexateuch and Other Essays*, 166–204. Translated by E. W. T. Dicken, Edinburgh: Oliver & Boyd, 1966.

Schulte, Hannelis. *Die Entstehung der Geschichtsschreibung im alten Israel*. BZAW 128. Berlin: de Gruyter, 1972.

Schürer, Emil. *Geschichte des jüdischen Volkes im Zeitalter Jesu Christi*. 3 vols. Leipzig: Hinrichs, 1886–90.

———. *A History of the Jewish People in the Time of Jesus Christ*. 4 vols. Edinburgh: T. & T. Clark, 1885–98. Rev. ed., by Geza Vermes and Fergus Millar. Edinburgh: T. & T. Clark, 1973.

Sevenster, J. N. *The Roots of Pagan Anti-Semitism in the Ancient World*. Novum Testamentum Supplements 41. Leiden: Brill, 1975.

Stern, Menahem. *Greek and Latin Authors on Jews and Judaism*. Vol. 1: *From Herodotus to Plutarch*. Jerusalem: Israel Academy of Sciences and Humanities, 1974.

Swain, J. W. "The Theory of Four Monarchies: Opposition History under the Roman Empire." *Classical Philology* 35 (1940) 1–21.

Tcherikover, Victor. "Jewish Apologetic Literature Reconsidered." *Eos* 48 (1956) 169–93.

Thackeray, H. St. J. *Josephus: The Man and the Historian*. New York: Jewish Institute of Religion Press, 1929.

Trieber, Conrad. "Die Idee der Vier Weltreiche." *Hermes* 27 (1892) 321–44.

Wacholder, Ben Zion. "Biblical Chronology in the Hellenistic World Chronicles." *HTR* 61 (1968) 451–81.

———. *Eupolemus: A Study of Judaeo-Greek Literature*. Monographs of the Hebrew Union College 3. Cincinnati: Hebrew Union College—Jewish Institute of Religion, 1974.
———. *Nicolaus of Damascus*. University of California Publications in History 75. Berkeley: University of California Press, 1962.
———. "'Pseudo-Eupolemus': Two Greek Fragments on the Life of Abraham." *HUCA* 34 (1963) 83–113.
Walter, Nikolaus. *Der Thoraausleger Aristobulos: Untersuchungen zu seinen Fragmenten und zu pseudepigraphischen Resten der jüdisch hellenistischen Literatur*. Texte und Untersuchungen zur Geschichte der altchristlichen Literatur 86. Berlin: Akademie, 1964.
———. "Zu Pseudo-Eupolemus." *Klio* 43–45 (1965) 282–90.
Winnett, F. V. "Re-examining the Foundations." *JBL* 84 (1965) 1–19.
Yoyotte, Jean. "L'Egypte ancienne et les origines de l'antijudaisme." *Revue d'Histoire des Religions* 163 (1963) 133–43.

Part 2: The Medieval Period

Baron, Salo W. *History and Jewish Historians*. Philadelphia: Jewish Publication Society of America 1964.
Brincken, Anna Dorothee von den. *Studien zur lateinischen Weltchronistik bis in das Zeitalter Otto von Freisings*. Düsseldorf: Triltsch, 1957.
Brooke, Christopher. *The Twelfth Century Renaissance*. Library of European Civilization. London: Thames & Hudson 1969.
Farmer, Hugh. "William of Malmesbury's Life and Works." *Journal of Ecclesiastical History* 13 (1962) 39–54.
Flusser, David. "Josippon." In *Encyclopaedia Judaica* 10 (1971) 296–98.
Fryde, E. B. "Historiography and Historical Methodology." In *The New Encyclopaedia Britannica*, 7:945–61. 15th ed. Chicago: Encyclopaedia Britannica, 1974.
Knowles, David. *The Evolution of Medieval Thought*. London: Longmans, Green, 1962.
———. *The Historian and Character and Other Essays*. London: Cambridge University Press 1963.
Kopf, Ulrich. *Die Anfänge der theologischen Wissenschaftstheorie im 13. Jahrhundert*. Beiträge zur Historischen Theologie 49. Tübingen: Mohr/Siebeck, 1974.
Lacroix, Benoit. *L'Historien an moyen age*. Conférence Albert-le-Grand. Montreal: Institut d'etudes medievales, 1971.
———. "The Notion of History in Early Medieval Historians." *Mediaeval Studies* 10 (1948) 219–23.
Loewe, Raphael. "Medieval History of the Latin Vulgate." In *Cambridge History of the Bible*, edited by G. W. H. Lampe, 2.102–54. Cambridge: Cambridge University Press, 1975.
Luneau, Auguste. *L' historie du salut chez les Pères de l'Eglise: La doctrine des ages du monde*. Théologie Historique 2. Paris: Beauchesne, 1964.
Markus, R. A. *Saeculum: History and Society in the Theology of St. Augustine*. London: Cambridge University Press, 1970. Rev. ed., 1988.
Meyer, Michael A. *Ideas of Jewish History*. New York: Behrman, 1974.
Morris, Colin. *The Discovery of the Individual, 1050–1200*. London: SPCK, 1972.

Reeves, Marjorie. *The Influence of Prophecy in the Later Middle Ages: A Study of Joachim-ism*. Oxford: Clarendon, 1969.
Rosenthal, Franz. *A History of Muslim Historiography*. Leiden: Brill, 1952. 2nd ed., 1968.
Schmidt, Roderich. "*Aelates Mundi*: Die Weltalter als Gliederungsprinzip der Geschichte." *Zeitschrift für Kirchengeschichte* 67 (1955–56) 288–317.
Smalley, Beryl. *Historians in the Middle Ages*. London: Thames & Hudson, 1974.
———. *The Study of the Bible in the Middle Ages*. Oxford: Basil Blackwell 1952. 3rd ed., 1983.
Southern, R. W. "Aspects of the European Tradition of Historical Writing. 1. The Classical Tradition from Einhard to Geoffrey of Monmouth." *Transactions of the Royal Historical Society*, 5th series, 20 (1970) 173–96.
———. "2. Hugh of St Victor and the Idea of Historical Development." *Transactions of the Royal Historical Society*, 5th series, 21 (1971) 159–79.
———. "3. History as Prophecy." *Transactions of the Royal Historical Society*, 5th series, 22 (1972) 159–80.
———. "4. The Sense of the Past." *Transactions of the Royal Historical Society*, 5th series, 23 (1973) 243–63.

Part 3: From the Renaissance to the Enlightenment

Allen, Don Cameron. *The Legend of Noah: Renaissance Rationalism in Art, Science, and Letters*. Illinois Studies in Language and Literature 33/3–4. Urbana: University of Illinois Press, 1949. 2nd ed., 1963.
Applegate, Kenneth W., translator and editor. *Voltaire on Religion: Selected Writings*. New York: Ungar 1974.
Barth, Karl. *Die Protestantische Theologie im 19. Jahrhundert: Ihre Vorgeschichte und Ihre Geschichte*. Zurich: Evangelischer, 1947
———. *Protestant Theology in the Nineteenth Century: Its Background and History*. London: SCM, 1972. 2nd ed., 2001.
Berlin, Isaiah. "Herder and the Enlightenment." In *Aspects of the Eighteenth Century*, edited by Earl R. Wasserman, 47–104. Baltimore: Johns Hopkins Press, 1965.
Burke, Peter. *The Renaissance Sense of the Past*. Documents of Modern History. London: Arnold 1969.
Butterfield, Herbert. *The Origins of Modern Science: 1300–1800*. New York: Macmillan, 1949. 2nd ed., 1957.
Cragg, Gerald R. *Reason and Authority in the Eighteenth Century*. London: Cambridge University Press 1964.
Diestel, Ludwig. *Geschichte des Alten Testamentes in der christlichen Kirche*. Jena: Mauke, 1869.
Frei, Hans W. *The Eclipse of Biblical Narrrative: A Study in Eighteenth and Nineteenth Century Hermeneutics*. New Haven: Yale University Press, 1974.
Fryde, Edmund B. "Historiography and Historical Methodology." In *The New Encyclopaedia Britannica*, 7:945–61. 15th ed. Chicago: Encyclopaedia Britannica, 1974.
Gay, Peter. *Deism: An Anthology*. Anvil Original 93. Princeton: Van Nostrand 1968.
Grant, Edward. "Late Medieval Thought, Copernicus, and the Scientific Revolution." *Journal of the History of Ideas* 23 (1962) 197–220.

Gray, Edward McQueen. *Old Testament Criticism: Its Rise and Progress from the Second Century to the End of the Eighteenth.* New York: Harper, 1923.

Hartlich, Christian, and Walter Sachs, *Der Ursprung des Mythosbegriffes in der modernen Bibelwissenschaft.* Schriften der Studiengemeinschaft der Evangelischen Akademien 2. Tübingen: Mohr/Siebeck, 1952.

Hazard, Paul. *La Crise de la Conscience Européene (1680–1715).* Paris: Boivin, 1935.

———. *The European Mind (1680–1715).* Translated by J. Lewis May. London: Hollis & Carter, 1953.

Headley, John M. *Luther's View of Church History.* Yale Publications in Religion 6. New Haven: Yale University Press, 1963.

Hooykaas, Reijer. "Science and Reformation." *Journal of World History* 3 (1956) 109–39.

Hornig, Gottfried. *Die Anfänge der historisch-kritischen Theologie: Johann Salomo Semlers Schrifiverständnis und seine Stellung zu Luther.* Forschungen zur Systematischen Theologie Religionsphilosophie 8. Göttingen: Vandenhoeck & Ruprecht, 1961.

Kelley, D. R. *Foundations of Modern Historical Scholarship: Language, Law, and History in the French Renaissance.* New York: Columbia University, 1970.

Knight, Douglas A. *Rediscovering the Traditions of Israel: The Development of the Traditio-historical Research of the Old Testament, with Special Consideration of Scandinavian Contributions.* SBLDS 9. Missoula, MT: Scholars, 1973. 2nd ed., 1975. 3rd ed., 2006.

Kraus, Hans-Joachim. *Geschichte der historisch-kritischen Erforschung des Alten Testaments.* Neukirchen-Vluyn: Neukirchener, 1956. 2nd ed., 1969.

Kümmel, Werner Georg. *Das Neue Testament: Geschichte der Erforschung seiner Probleme.* Orbis Academicus. Freiburg: Alber, 1958.

———. *The New Testament: The History of the Investigation of Its Problems.* Translated by S. McLean Gilmour and Howard C. Kee. Nashville: Abingdon, 1972.

Mason, S. F. "The Scientific Revolution and the Protestant Reformation." *Annals of Science* 8 (1952) 64–87; 154–75.

McKee, David Rice. "Isaac de la Peyrere, A Precursor of Eighteenth-Century Critical Deists." *Publications of the Modern Language Association of America* 59 (1944) 456–85.

Momigliano, Arnaldo. "Ancient History and the Antiquarian." *Journal of the Wartburg and Courtauld Institute* 13 (1950) 285–315. Reprinted in *Studies in Historiography*, 1–39. London: Weidenfeld & Nicolson, 1966.

Prideaux, Humphrey. *The Old and New Testament Connected: in the History of the Jews and Neighbouring Nations, from the Declension of the Kingdoms of Israel and Judah to the Time of Christ.* 2 vols. London: Knaplock, 1717–18.

Pullapilly, Cyriac K. *Caesar Baronius: Counter-Reformation Historian.* Notre Dame: University of Notre Dame Press 1975.

Rabil, Albert Jr. *Erasmus and the New Testament: The Mind of a Christian Humanist.* TUMSR 1. San Antonio: Trinity University Press, 1972.

Reventlow, H. Graf. "Die Auffassung von Alten Testament bei Hermann Samuel Reimarus und Gotthold Ephraim Lessing." *EvTh* 25 (1965) 429–48.

Reynolds, Beatrice R. "Latin Historiography: A Survey 1400–1600." *Studies in the Renaissance* 2 (1955) 7–66.

Rogerson, J. W. *Myth in Old Testament Interpretation.* BZAW 134. Berlin: de Gruyter, 1974.

Scholder, Klaus. "Herder und die Anrange der historischen Theologie." *EvTh* 21 (1962) 425–40.

———. *Ursprünge und Probleme die Bibelkritik im 17. Jahrhundert: Ein Beitrag zur Entstehung der historisch-kritischen Theologie*. Geschichte und Lehre des Protestantismus 10/33. Munich: Kaiser, 1966.

Shuckford, Samuel. *The Sacred and Profane History of the World Connected, From the Creation of the World to the Dissolution of the Assyrian Empire at the Death of Sardanapalus, and to the Declension of the Kingdom of Judah and Israel under the Reigns of Ahaz and Pekah*. 2 vols. London: Knaplock & Tonson, 1728–30.

Sonne, Isaiah. "Synagogue." In *IDB*, 4:476–91.

Stephen, Leslie. *History of English Thought in the Eighteenth Century*. 2 vols. London: Putnam, 1876. 2nd ed., 1881. 3rd ed., 1902. Reprinted, 1991.

Waring, E. Graham. *Deism and Natural Religion: A Source Book*. Milestones of Thought. New York: Ungar, 1967.

Weiss, Roberto. *The Renaissance Discovery of Classical Antiquity*. Oxford: Blackwell, 1969. 2nd ed., 1988.

Willi, Thomas. *Herders Beitrag zum Verstehendes Alten Testaments*. Beiträge zur Geschichte der Biblischen Hermeneutik 8. Tübingen: Mohr/Siebeck, 1971.

Part 4: The Nineteenth Century

Baron, Salo W. *History and Jewish Historians: Essays and Addresses*. Compiled with a foreword by Arthur Hertzberg and Leon A. Feldman. Philadelphia: Jewish Publication Society of America, 1964.

Bliss, Frederick Jones. *The Development of Palestine Exploration: Being the Ely Lectures for 1903*. New York: Scribner, 1906.

Bratton, F. Gladstone. *A History of Egyptian Archaeology*. London: Hale, 1967.

Briggs, Charles A. *The Higher Criticism of the Hexateuch*. New York: Scribner, 1893. Rev. ed., 1897. Reprinted, Eugene, OR: Wipf & Stock, 2008.

Bright, John. *A History of Israel*. 3rd ed. Philadelphia: Westminster, 1981.

Carpenter, J. Estlin. *The Bible in the Nineteenth Century: Eight Lectures*. London: Longmans, Green, 1903.

Cheyne, T. K. *Founders of Old Testament Criticism*. London: Methuen, 1893. Reprinted, Eugene, OR: Wipf & Stock, 2003.

Ewald, Heinrich. *Geschichte des Volkes Israel bis Christus*. 3 vols. in 5. Göttingen: Dieterich, 1843–52.

———. *The History of Israel*. Edited by Russell Martineau. 1871–86. Reprinted, Eugene, OR: Wipf & Stock, 2004.

Gooch, G. P. *History and Historians in the Nineteenth Century*. London: Longmans, Green, 1913. 2nd ed., 1952.

Graetz, Heinrich. *Geschichte der Juden von den ältesten Zeiten bis auf die Gegenwart*. 11 vols. Leipzig: Leiner, 1861–75.

———. *History of the Jews*. Abridged ed. Edited and translated by Bella Löwy. 6 vols. Philadelphia: Jewish Publication Society of America, 1891–98. Reprinted, 1956.

Herrmann, Siegfried. *A History of Israel in Old Testament Times*. Translated by John Bowden. Philadelphia: Fortress, 1975. 2nd ed., 1981.

Hilprecht, H. V. *Explorations in Bible Lands during the 19th Century*. Edinburgh: T. & T. Clark 1903.

Kraeling, Emil G. *The Old Testament since the Reformation*. 1955. Reprinted, New York: Schocken, 1969.

Kraus, Hans-Joachim. *Geschichte der historisch-kritischen Erforschung des Alten Testaments*. Neukirchen-Vluyn: Neukirchener, 1956. 2nd ed., 1969.

Lloyd, Seton. *Foundations in the Dust: A Story of Mesopotamian Exploration*. London: Oxford University Press, 1947.

Macalister, R. A. S. *A Century of Excavation in Palestine*. London: Religious Tract Society, 1925.

Milman, Henry Hart. *The History of the Jews*. 3 vols. Family Library 5, 6, 7. London: Murray, 1829.

Perlitt, Lothar. *Vatke und Wellhausen: Geschichtsphilosophische Voraussetzungen und historiographische Motive für die Darstellung der Religion und Geschichte Israels durch Wilhelm Vatke und Julius Wellhausen*. BZAW 94. Berlin: Töpelmann, 1965.

Thompson, R. J. *Moses and the Law in a Century of Criticism since Graf*. VTSup 19. Leiden: Brill, 1970.

Wellhausen, Julius. *Die Composition des Hexateuchs und die historischen Bücher des Alten Testaments*. Berlin: Reimer, 1899.

———. *Geschichte Israels*. Vol. 1. Berlin: Reimer, 1878.

———. "Heinrich Ewald." In *Festschrift zur Feier des 150jährigen Bestehens der Königlichen Akademie*. Berlin: Weidmann, 1901. Reprinted in *Grundrisse zum Allen Testament*, edited by Rudolf Smend, 120–38. ThBü 27. Munich: Kaiser, 1965.

———. "Israel." In *Encyclopaedia Britannica*, 13:396–420. 9th ed. Chicago: Encyclopaedia Britannica, 1880. Reprinted in *Prolegomena to the History of Israel*, 429–547.

———. *Prolegomena to the History of Israel*. Translated by J. Sutherland Black and Allan Menzies. 1885. Reprinted, Eugene, OR: Wipf & Stock, 2003.

———. *Prolegomena zur Geschichte Israels*. Berlin: Reimer, 1883.

Wilson, John A. *Signs and Wonders upon Pharaoh: A History of American Egyptology*. Chicago: University of Chicago Press, 1964.

Part 5: Current Approaches

Albright, W. F. "Archaeology Confronts Biblical Criticism." *American Scholar* 7 (1938) 176–88.

———. "The Ancient Near East and the Religion of Israel." *JBL* 59 (1940) 85–112.

Beegle, Dewey M. *The Inspiration of Scripture*. Philadelphia: Westminster, 1963.

Bright, John. *Early Israel in Recent History Writing: A Study in Method*. SBT 19. London: SCM, 1956.

Buss, Martin J. "The Study of Forms." In *Old Testament Form Criticism*, edited by John H. Hayes, 1–56. TUMSR 2. San Antonio: Trinity University Press, 1974.

Dus, Jan. "Mose oder Josua? (Zum Problem des Stifters der israelitischen Religion)." *Archiv Orientalni* 39 (1971) 16–45.

———. "Moses or Joshua? (On the Problem of the Founder of Israelite Religion)." *Radical Religion* 2 (1975) 26–41.

The History of the Study of Israelite and Judean History

Freedman, David Noel. "Archaeology and the Future of Biblical Studies 1. The Biblical Languages." In *The Bible in Modern Scholarship*, edited by J. Philip Hyatt, 294–312. Nashville: Abingdon, 1965.

Haupt, Paul. "Midian und Sinai." *Zeitschrift der Deutschen Morganländischen Gesellschaft* 63 (1909) 506–30.

Hayes, John H., and J. Maxwell Miller, editors. *Israelite and Judaean History*. OTL. Philadelphia: Westminster, 1977.

Keller, Werner. *The Bible as History: A Confirmation of the Book of Books*. Translated by William Neil. New York: Morrow, 1956.

———. *Und die Bibel hat doch recht: Forscher beweisen die historische Wahrheit*. Düsseldorf: Econ-Verlag, 1956.

Knight, Douglas A. *Rediscovering the Traditions of Israel: The Development of the Traditio-historical Research of the Old Testament, with Special Consideration of Scandinavian Contributions*. SBLDS 9. Missoula, MT: Scholars, 1973. 2nd ed., 1975. 3rd ed., 2006.

Lindsell, Harold. *The Battle for the Bible*. Grand Rapids: Zondervan, 1976.

Mendenhall, George E. "The Hebrew Conquest of Palestine." *Biblical Archaeologist* 25 (1962) 66–87. Reprinted in *Biblical Archaeologist Reader*, 3:100–126. Garden City, NY: Doubleday, 1970.

———. "The Monarchy." *Interpretation* 29 (1975) 155–70.

———. *The Tenth Generation: The Origins of the Biblical Tradition*. Baltimore: Johns Hopkins University Press, 1973.

Meyer, Eduard. *Geschichte der Alterthums*. 5 vols. Stuttgart: Cotta, 1884–1902. Reprinted, Basel: Schwabe, 1953.

Noth, Martin. *Die Gesetze im Pentateuch: Ihre Voraussetzungen und ihr Sinn*. Schriften der Königsberger Gelehrten Gesellschaft 17/2. Halle: Niemeyer, 1930. Reprinted as "Die Gesetze im Pentateuch." In *Gesammelte Studien zum Alten Testament*, 9–141. ThBü 6. Munich: Kaiser, 1957.

———. *Geschichte Israels*. Göttingen: Vandenhoeck & Ruprecht, 1950. 2nd ed., 1954.

———. *The History of Israel*. Rev. ed. Translated by P. R. Ackroyd. New York: Harper, 1960.

———. *A History of Pentateuchal Traditions*. Translated by Bernhard W. Anderson. Englewood Cliffs, NJ: Prentice Hall, 1972. Reprinted, Chico, CA: Scholars, 1981.

———. "The Laws in the Pentateuch: Their Assumptions and Meaning." In *Laws in the Pentateuch and Other Studies*, 1–107. Translated by D. R. Ap-Thomas. London: SCM, 1966.

———. *Das System der zwölf Stämme Israels*. BWANT IV/1. Stuttgart: Kohlhammer, 1930.

———. *Überlieferungsgeschichtliche Studien*. Schriften der Königsberger Gelehrten Gesellschaft 18/2. Halle: Niemeyer, 1943.

Rad, Gerhard von. "The Beginnings of Historical Writing in Ancient Israel." In *Problem of the Hexateuch and Other Essays*, 166–204. Translated by E. W. T. Dicken. New York: McGraw-Hill, 1966.

———. *Das formgeschichtliche Problem des Hexateuch*. BWANT IV/26. Stuttgart: Kohlhammer, 1938. Reprinted as "The Problem of the Hexateuch." In *The Problem of the Hexateuch and Other Essays*, 1–78. Translated by E. W. T. Dicken. New York: McGraw-Hill, 1966.

Thompson, R. J. *Moses and the Law in a Century of Criticism since Graf.* VTSup 19. Leiden: Brill, 1970.

Vaux, Roland de. *The Early History of Israel.* Translated by David Smith. Philadelphia: Westminster, 1978.

Weber, Max. *Gesammelte Aufsätze zur Religionssoziologie.* Vol. 3, *Das anlike Judentum.* Tübingen: Mohr/Siebeck, 1921. 2nd ed., 1923.

———. *Ancient Judaism.* Translated by Hans H. Gerth and Don Martindale. Glencoe: Free Press 1952.

Wilcoxen, J. A. "Narrative." In *Old Testament Form Criticism*, edited by John H. Hayes, 57–98. TUMSR 2. San Antonio: Trinity University Press, 1974.

Wood, Leon J. *A Survey of Israel's History.* Grand Rapids: Zondervan, 1970.

2

Wellhausen as a Historian of Israel

The Law and the Quest

THREE DEVELOPMENTS THAT WERE to have enormous consequences for the reconstruction of ancient Israelite history were reaching an advanced stage at the time Wellhausen entered the arena of Old Testament studies. These were: (a) the dating of the various strata of the Pentateuchal traditions, (b) the isolation and exposition of the theological tendencies and perspectives not only of the Pentateuchal traditions but also those of the historical books, and (c) the desire to produce a history of Israel that was neither theological nor apologetical in character.

(a) The dating of Deuteronomy to the time of Josiah and the dating of the Priestly document or the levitical tradition of the Pentateuch to the post-Deuteronomic period were the most radical results of nineteenth-century Pentateuchal studies. Such a late dating for these sources carried with it the general assumption of the sources' historical unreliability. These conclusions were first expounded by Wilhelm Martin Leberecht De Wette in 1805, Eduard Reuss in 1833, Wilhelm Vatke in 1835, Johann Friedrich Leopold George in 1835, Karl Heinrich Graf in 1866, Abraham Kuenen in 1869–70, and John William Colenso in 1862–65, among others.

As early as 1833, Reuss, Graf's teacher at Strasbourg, had formulated twelve theses that already provided the basic arguments for the lateness of the priestly laws and that pointed to the implications of such a late date for writing the history of Israel.[1] His theses were as follows:

1. The historical element in the Pentateuch can and must be examined apart from and not be confused with the legal element.
2. Both were able to exist without written documentary form. The mention, in some ancient writings, of certain patriarchal or Mosaic traditions does not prove the existence of the Pentateuch, and a nation can have customary law without a written code.
3. The national traditions of the Israelites appear earlier than the laws of the Pentateuch, and the writing down of the former is prior to that of the latter.
4. The principal interest of the historian should focus on the date of the laws because this is the area in which there is the best chance of arriving at certain results. Consequently, it is necessary to proceed through an interrogation of the evidence.
5. The narrated history, in the books of Judges and Samuel, and partially that which comprises the books of Kings, is in contradiction with the dictates of Mosaic law, thus the latter was unknown at the time of the composition of these books, a very strong argument that they did not exist at the time these books describe.
6. The prophets of the eighth and seventh centuries did not know anything of the Mosaic code.
7. Jeremiah is the first prophet who knew of the written law, and his quotations agree with Deuteronomy.
8. Deuteronomy (4:45—28:68) is the book that the priests pretended to have found in the temple at the time of King Josiah. This code is the oldest part of the edited legislation now comprising the Pentateuch.
9. Israelite history, insofar as it is a question of national development determined by the written law, may be divided into two periods, before and after Josiah.
10. Ezekiel is older than the composition of the ritual code and the law that definitely organized the hierocracy.

---

1. First published in Reuss, *L'histoire sainte*, 23–24. These are reprinted in Wellhausen, *Prolegomena* (1885), 4; and in his "Pentateuch and Joshua," 508–9.

11. The book of Joshua is not, as far as can be known, the most recent part of the entire work.

12. The author of the Pentateuch is to be clearly distinguished from the ancient prophet Moses.

The consequences of such perspectives were first developed in the area of the religion of ancient Israel by Kuenen and Bernhard Duhm. The task of delineating the consequences for the reconstruction of ancient Israelite history was left to Wellhausen.

(b) The recognition of the theological orientation and tendencies within the Pentateuchal sources and historical books meant, of course, that these materials could be used in reconstructing Israelite history only after a proper assessment of how their orientation and tendencies had influenced their presentation of the course of events. Gradually, it was becoming clear that the historical materials in the Hebrew Bible were as much products as portrayals of historical developments. The history of Israel and its religious institutions was slowly recognized as being as determinative for the history of the documents as the documents were depictive of the history of Israel. De Wette's critical essays on the credibility of the books of Chronicles and the Mosaic history (1806–7) were important harbingers of future developments in pre-Wellhausenian times.

(c) The nineteenth has been designated as the century of historical inquiry. The remarkable advances made in recovering and reconstructing the past—especially Greek and Roman history—could not but eventually influence the reconstruction of Israelite history. Writing as late as 1863, A. P. Stanley noted the following:

> The Jewish History has suffered from causes similar to those which still, within our own memory, obscured the history of Greece and of Rome. Till within the present century, the characters and institutions of those two great countries were so veiled from view in the conventional haze with which the enchantment of distance had invested them, that when the more graphic and critical historians of our time broke through this reserve, a kind of shock was felt through all the educated classes of the country. The same change was in a still higher degree needed with regard to the history of the Jews. Its sacred character had deepened the difficulty already occasioned by its extreme antiquity.[2]

2. Stanley, *Lectures*, VIII–IX.

On 10 February 1835, the classicist Thomas Arnold wrote the diplomat-theologian Christian Carl Josias von Bunsen that "what [Friedrich August] Wolf and [Barthold Georg] Niebuhr have done for Greece and Rome seems sadly wanted for Judaea."[3] The application of historiographic rigor to the history of Israel was not as easily done as its counterpart in classical study. The older histories of Humphrey Prideaux (1717–18, the Schürer of the eighteenth century) and Samuel Shuckford (1728–30), with their strong apologetic flavor and anti-deistic polemic, continued to be the standard English works into the nineteenth century. When Henry Hart Milman, in 1829, published his moderately critical *History of the Jews*, it met with widespread opposition. In his preface to the second edition (1830), he sought to defend his wish "to avoid the tone of a theological treatise" in his presentation of the history and his tendency to describe Jewish history in rather naturalistic terms as a gradual process of development. He wrote:

> Nothing is more curious, or more calculated to confirm the veracity of the Old Testament history, than the remarkable picture which it presents of the gradual development of human society: the ancestors of the Jews, and the Jews themselves, pass through every stage of comparative civilization. The Almighty Ruler of the world, who had chosen them as conservators of the knowledge of his Unity and Providence, and of his slowly brightening promises of Redemption, perpetually interferes, so as to keep alive the remembrance of these great truths, the object of their selection from mankind, and which nothing less, it should seem, could have preserved through so many ages. In other respects the chosen people appear to have been left to themselves to pass through the ordinary stages of the social state, and to that social state their hablts, opinions, and even their religious notions, were in some degree accommodated.[4]

When the history of Israel written by Heinrich Georg August Ewald began to appear in 1843, many felt that he had finally done for Israel what Wolf and Niebuhr had done for Greece and Rome. However, Ewald's verbose and passionate effort, which "closed rather than opened an epoch,"[5] was overly dominated by a theological program, viz. to demonstrate that the aim of Israelite history was the attainment of Perfect Religion:

3. Quoted in Stanley, *Life*, 355.
4. Milman, *History*, (1829/1834), V–VI.
5. J. W. Thompson, *History*, 578.

The beginning and end of the history of this people turn on this one high aim, and the manifold changes, and even confusions and perversities, which manifest themselves in the long course of the threads of its history, always ultimately tend to the solution of this great problem, which the human mind was to work out here. The aim was lofty enough to concentrate the highest efforts of a whole people for more than a thousand years, and to be reached at length as the prIze of the noblest struggles. And as, however the mode of the pursuit might vary, it was this single object that was always pursued, till finally attained only with the political death of the nation, there is hardly any history of equal compass that possesses, in all its phases and variations, so much intrinsic unity, and is so closely bound to a single thought pertinaciously held, but always developing itself to higher purity. The history of this ancient people is in reality the history of the growth of true religion, rising through all stages to perfection, pressing on through all conflicts to the highest victory, and finally revealing itself in full glory and power, in order to spread irresistibly from this centre, never again to be lost, but to become the eternal possession and blessing of all nations.[6]

Few works have received more back-handed praise than Ewald's history: "the present work, even in its introductory portions, claims to be a History of Israel, although no such lucid and connected narrative will be found in it as is generally associated with that term. We read Ewald, page after page, and seem to come across no clear and distinct event."[7] "I must confess that I read Ewald ever with increasing wonder at his unparalleled ingenuity, his surpassing learning, but usually with decreasing conviction. I should like an Ewald to criticise Ewald."[8]

The question of the place in history of the 'law of Moses' was a major concern for both Milman and Ewald just as it was the starting point for Wellhausen in the *Prolegomena*. For both, the question of whether the laws of the Pentateuch and the formation of the Israelites into a theocratic community were to be assigned to the wilderness or pre-settlement period had to receive an affirmative response. One can see Milman is struggling with this issue in the following passage:

> the Israelites wind along the defiles of this elevated region, till at length they come to the foot of the loftiest peak in the whole

---

6. Ewald, *History*, 1.4–5.
7. Russell, Martineau, in his preface to ibid., 1.viii–ix.
8. Milman, *History* (1829/1874), 1.30.

ridge, that of Sinai. Here after the most solemn preparations, and under the most terrific circumstances, the great lawgiver of the Jews delivered that singular constitution to his people, which presupposed their possession of a rich and fertile territory in which as yet they had not occupied an acre, but had hitherto been wandering in an opposite direction, and not even approached its borders. The laws of a settled and civilized community were enacted among a wandering and homeless horde who were traversing the wilderness, and more likely, under their existing circumstances, to sink below the pastoral life of their forefathers, than advance to the rank of an industrious agricultural community. Yet, at this time, judging solely from its internal evidence, the law must have been enacted. Who but Moses ever possessed such authority as to enforce submission to statutes so severe and uncompromising? yet, as Moses incontestibly died before the conquest of Canaan, his legislature must have taken place in the desert. To what other period can the Hebrew constitution be assigned? To that of the judges? a time of anarchy, warfare, or servitude! To that of the kings? when the republic had undergone a total change! To any time after Jerusalem became the metropolis? when the holy city, the pride and glory of the nation, is not even alluded to in the whole law! After the building of the temple? when it is equally silent as to any settled or durable edifice! After the separation of the kingdoms? when the close bond of brotherhood had given place to implacable hostility! Under Hilkiah? under Ezra? when a great number of the statutes had become a dead letter! The law depended on a stirct and equitable partition of the land. At a later period it could not have been put into practice without the forcible resumption of every individual property by the state, the difficulty, or rather impossiblity, of such a measure, may be estimated by any reader who is not entirely unacquainted with the history of the ancient republics. In other respects the law breathes the air of the desert. Enactments intended for a people with settled habitations, and dwelling in walled cities, are mingled up wlth temporary regulations, only suited to the Bedouin encampment of a nomad trlbe. There can be no doubt that the statute book of Moses, with all his particular enactments, still exists, and that it recites them in the same order, if it may be called order, in which they were promulgated.[9]

---

9. Milman, *History* (1829/1834), 78–79.

In later editions of his history, in which he shows thorough familiarity with Old Testament scholarship, Milman refused to budge from his position. As is well known, Ewald, who designated the main document of the Pentateuch (P) "The Book of Origins," argued that the theocratic community was founded in the wilderness period and that the literary deposit of the theocracy was composed in the tenth century BCE.

The reconstructed history of Israel in the works of Milman and Ewald, given the latter's reassignment of Deuteronomy to the seventh century and both's acceptance of the general non-historicity of Genesis 1–11, differed from the general flow of the Old Testament presentation itself only in degree and not in kind. Both, however, reflect the early nineteenth-century drive toward a quest for the historical Israel that would tell "what really happened"[10] rather than merely retell the Old Testament narrative with academic midrash.

Wellhausen and Literary Criticism

All three of the developments sketched above came to a focus in the work of Wellhausen. In the opening sentences of the *Geschichte Israels*, he stated the issue rather bluntly to demonstrate that literary conclusions about the Old Testament, especially the Pentateuch, have far-reaching consequences for understanding Israelite history. The literary history of the Pentateuch could not be rewritten (or written) without a simultaneous rewriting of the history of Israel. He stated: "Das vorliegende Buch unterscheidet sich von seinesgleichen dadurch, dass die Kritik der Quellen darin einen ebenso breiten Raum einnimmt als die Darstellung der Geschichte. Warum es so angelegt worden, wird es selber ausweisen, hier soll nur gesagt werden, um was es sich in diesem ersten, kritischen Teile handelt. Die Frage ist, ob das mosaische Gesetz der Ausgangspunkt sei für die Geschichte des alten Israel oder für die Geschichte des Judentums, d. h. der Sekte, welche das von Assyrern und Chaldaern vernichtete Volk überlebte."[11] Elsewhere, while describing the course of Pentateuchal criticism prior to the advent of "two Hegelian writers" (Vatke and George), Wellhausen made the same point in different terms: "Critical analysis made steady progress, but the work of synthesis did not hold even pace with it, this part of the problem was treated rather slightly, and merely by the way. Indeed the true scope of the

10. Ewald, *History*, 13.
11. Wellhausen, *Geschichte Israels* (1878), 1.

problem was not reallzed, it was not seen that most important historical questions were involved as well as questions merely literary, and that to assign the true order of the different strata of the Pentateuch was equivalent to a reconstruction of the history of Israel."[12]

His main criticism of Graf focused on the same issue. "He (Graf) brought forward his arguments somewhat unconnectedly, not seeking to change the general view that prevailed of the history of Israel For this reason he made no impression on the majority of those who study these subjects, they did not see into the root of the matter they could still regard the system as unshaken, and the numerous attacks on details of it as unimportant."[13]

For Wellhausen, literary criticism and historical reconstruction went hand in hand. The significance and impact of the former necessitated the latter, and for him the former was in service to and prerequisite to the latter. His Old Testament work moved primarily in three stages: from literary analysis, to the consequences of such analysis, to historical reconstruction demanded by the consequences of the literary analysis. His dissertation was a study in Chronicles (1870).[14] This was followed by an investigation of the text of Samuel (1871),[15] a study of the composition of the Hexateuch (1876–77),[16] and an analysis of the books of Judges, Ruth, Samuel, and Kings (1878).[17] His works of literary and textual analysis were never pedantic. He was primarily interested in the broader questions of source analysis and theological tendency rather than minute matters of detail. He was basically interested in what he called "the literary process." "Criticism has not done its work when it has completed the mechanical distribution [of the sources], it must aim further at bringing the different writings when thus arranged into relation wlth each other, must seek to render them intelllgible as phases of a living process, and thus to make it possible to trace a graduated development of the tradition."[18] Thus he was content to speak (following Theodor Nöldeke) of three main strata in the Pentateuch: Deuteronomy, the Jehovist (the Yahwist with extracts

12. "Pentateuch and Joshua," 508.
13. *Prolegomena*, 368.
14. "De gentibus."
15. *Der Text*.
16. "Die Composition."
17. "Die geschichtlichen Bucher."
18. *Prolegomena*, 295.

from the Elohist), and the Priestly Code.[19] Such a matter as the dating of the Jehovist was discussed in rather general terms: "the period of the kings and prophets which preceded the dissolution of the two Israelite kingdoms by the Assyrians."[20]

The Prolegomena

The *Prolegomena* provides not only a presentation of the results of Wellhausen's literary analyses of the Hexateuch and the historical books but also his description of the consequences of such analyses for the reconstruction of the history of Israel. The first part of this book is called "History of the Ordinances of Worship." His program in this section can be seen in his criticism of the earlier work of Friedrich Bleek and Ewald who had failed to undertake what Wellhausen pursued:

> [Bleek] never thought of instituting an exact comparison between them [the priestly laws] and the Deuteronomlc law, still less of examining their relation to the historical and prophetical books. [Ewald] too neglected the task of a careful comparison between the different strata of the Pentateuchal legislation and the equally necessary task of determining how the several laws agreed with or differed from such definite data of the history of religion as could be collected from the historical and prophetical books. He had therefore no fixed measure to apply to the criticism of the laws.[21]

Wellhausen described his own method of approaching the issue of the history of religious ordinances in the following way: "After laboriously collecting the data offered by the historical and prophetical books, we constructed a sketch of the Israelite history of worship, we then compared the Pentateuch with this sketch, and recognised that one element of the Pentateuch bore a definite relation to this phase of the history of

---

19. In ibid., 8 n. 2, Wellhausen describes his use of terminology in the following way: "In the following pages the Jehovistic history-book is denoted by the symbol JE, its Jehovistic part by J, and the Elohistic by E, the 'main stock' pure and simple, which is distinguished by its systematizing history and is seen unalloyed in Genesis is called the Book of the Four Covenants and is symbolised by Q [= *quatuor*]," see 1876a:392, and now also Silberman ("Whence Siglum Q?"), for the 'main stock' as a whole (as modified by an editorial process) the title of Priestly Code and the symbol RQ (Q and Revisers) are employed."

20. "Pentateuch and Joshua," 508.

21. Ibid.

worship, and another element of the Pentateuch to that phase of it."[22] The primary element of the Pentateuch that had not been associated with its proper phase of history and the historical consequences drawn therefrom was, according to Wellhausen, the Priestly Code.

> There are in the Pentateuch three strata of law and three strata of tradition, and the problem is to place them in their true historical order. So far as the Jehovist and Deuteronomy are concerned, the problem has found a solution which may be said to be accepted universally, and all that remains is to apply to the Priestly Code also the procedure by which the succession and the date of these two works has been determined—that procedure consisting in the comparison of them with the ascertained facts of Israelite history.[23]

The five chapters in the first section, on the place of worship, sacrifice, the sacred feasts, the priests and levites, and the endowment of the clergy, sought to demonstrate that the order of the documents was Jehovist, Deuteronomy, and Priestly Code and that the latter was post-Deuteronomic and thus the foundation of life in postexilic Judaism, not in preexilic Israel. For Wellhausen, the issue of the centralization of worship was the pivotal point in the history of the ordinances of worship.

> The turning-point in the history of worship in Israel is the centralization of the cultus in Jerusalem by Josiah (2 Kings XXII, XXIII).[24]

> I differ from Graf chiefly in this, that I always go back to the centralisation of the cultus, and deduce from it the particular divergences. My whole position is contained in my first chapter ["The Place of Worship"] there I have placed in a clear light that which is of such importance for Israelite history, namely, the part taken by the prophetical party. In the great metamorphosis of the worship, which by no means came about of itself. Again I attach much more weight than Graf did to the change of ruling ideas which runs parallel with the change in the institutions and usages of worship. Almost more important to me than the phenomena themselves, are the presuppositions which lie behind them.[25]

22. *Prolegomena*, 367.
23. Ibid., 366.
24. "Pentateuch and Joshua," 509.
25. *Prolegomena*, 368.

Wellhausen as a Historian of Israel

With methodological regularity, Wellhausen outlines the nature of the religious ordinances as these are reflected in the historical and prophetical books and compares these with the various legal strata to demonstrate how these legal strata reflect the conditions of three historical epochs: the period before Josiah (Jehovist), the transition period introduced by Josiah's reform (Deuteronomy), and the period after the exile (Priestly Code). The accompanying chart summarizes how Wellhausen viewed the development in five main areas of the history of the ordinances of worship.

In the second main section of the *Prolegomena*, "History of Tradition," Wellhausen set out to demonstrate that "the history of the tradition leads us to the same conclusion as the history of the cultus."[26] He discusses, first of all, Chronicles, then Judges, Samuel, and Kings, and finally the narrative of the Hexateuch. Chronicles (with Ezra–Nehemiah), whose composition Wellhausen placed in the early Hellenistic period,[27] embodies a history of the cultus that is very similar to that found in the Priestly Code. The unreliability of the historical portrait contained in Chronicles had to be demonstrated as a prerequisite for dating the priestly legislation in the post-Deuteronomic period. In his chapter on Chronicles, Wellhausen supported this position, which had first been systematically advocated by de Wette (1806).[28] Wellhausen argued for three basic conclusions about Chronicles: (1) The material and emphases found in Chronicles but not in the other canonical books are not the result of Chronicles' having possessed preexilic traditions, reliable nonbiblical sources, or a better text of Samuel and Kings. (2) Chronicles is the product of a particular historical epoch and the result of rewriting history viewed through the lens of the priestly tradition.

> When the narrative of Chronicles runs parallel with the older historical books of the canon, it makes no real additions, but the tradition is merely differently coloured, under the influence of contemporary motives. In the picture it gives the writer's own present is reflected, not antiquity. But neither is the case very different with the genealogical lists prefixed by way of introduction in I Chron I–IX, they also are in the main valid only for the period at which they were drawn up—whether for its actual condition or for its conceptions of the past.[29]

26. Ibid., 294.
27. Ibid., 171.
28. De Wette, *Beiträge*, vol. 1.
29. Wellhausen, *Prolegomena*, 211.

The alterations and additions of Chronicles are all traceable to the same fountainhead—the Judaising of the past, in which otherwise the people of that day would have been unable to recognise their ideal.[30]

Thus whether one says Chronlcles or *Midrash* of the Book of Kings is on the whole a matter of perfect indifference, they are children of the same mother, and indistinguishable in spirit and language, while on the other hand the portions which have been retained verbatim from the canonrcal Book of Kings at once betray themselves in both respects.[31]

	Place of Worship	**Sacrifice**	**Sacred Feasts**	**Priests & Levites**	**Endowment of the Clergy**
Jehovist	Multiplicity of altars, shrines, high places, and sacred sites	Assumed to be pre-Mosaic, spontaneous and related to ordinary life	Main form of worship, agricultural thanksgiving festivals, times of joyous gladness, three in number	No limitation of cultus to special class or family	Gifts presentd to Jehovah, priestly shares and dues not regulated
Deuteronomy	Single sanctuary commanded, other centers to be destroyed	Very similar to Jehovist, some regulation in light of centralization	Very similar to Jehovist, some historical dressing	Priests are organized class, all Levites have priestly functions	Some regulations and stipulation of priestly dues
Priestly Code	Limitation of worship to one sanctuary presupposed and assumed from the Mosaic period	Mosaic in origin, regulated by statute, sin and propitiation stressed	Fixed dates, denaturalization, additional feast days	Sharp division between priests and Levites, fully developed hierocracy under high priest	Sacred dues paid to priests, special possessions assigned priest, increased share of sacrifices

30. Ibid., 223.
31. Ibid., 227.

(3) Chronicles, therefore, cannot be used in reconstructing the history of Israel in preexilic times.

> With what show of justice can the Chronicler, after his statements have over and over again been shown to be incredible, be held at discretion to pass for an unimpeachable narrator? In those cases at least where its connection with his 'plan' is obvious, one ought surely to exercise some scepticism in regard to his testimony, but it ought at the same time to be considered that such connections may occur much oftener than is discernible by us, or at least by the less sharp-sighted of us. It is indeed possible that occasionally a gram of good corn may occur among the chaff, but to be conscientious one must neglect this possiblity of exceptions, and give due honour to the probability of the rule. For it is only too easy to deceive oneself in thinking that one has come upon some sound particular in a tainted whole.[32]

If the tradition in Chronicles has been recast in the form of *midrash* ("like ivy it overspreads the dead trunk with extraneous life, blending old and new in a strange combination"),[33] the situation is different in the case of Judges, Samuel, and Kings:

> In Judges, Samuel, and Kings even, we are not presented with tradtion purely in its original condition, already it is overgrown with later accretions. Alongside of an older narrative a new one has sprung up, formerly independent, and intelligible in itself, though in many instances of course adapting itself to the former. More frequently the new forces have not caused the old root to send forth a new stock, or even so much as a complete branch, they have only nourished parasitic growths, the earlier narratlve has become clothed with minor and dependent additions. To vary the metaphor, the whole area of tradition has finally been uniformly covered with an alluvial deposit by which the configuration of the surface has been determined. It is with this last that we have to deal in the first instance, to ascertain its character, to find out what the active forces were by which it was produced. Only afterwards are we in a position to attempt to discern in the earlier underlying formation the changing spirit of each successive period.[34]

---

32. Ibid., 224.
33. Ibid., 227.
34. Ibid., 228.

This "alluvial deposit" or the "uniform in which [the original contents of the tradition] is clothed" is the Deuteronomistic revision.[35] "This means no more than that it came into existence under the influence of Deuteronomy, which pervaded the whole century of the exile."[36] This Deuteronomistic (distinguishable from Deuteronomic) overlay, which preserved "only so much of the old tradition as those of a later age held to be of religious value,"[37] is characterized by a strong religious perspective, the idea of a central place of worship, a Judean point of view, and a chronological schematization. This Deuteronomistic redaction of the older material had also a very specific purpose:

> The writer looks back on the time of the kings as a period past and closed, on which judgment has already been declared. Even at the consecration of the temple the thought of its destruction is not to be restrained, and throughout the book the ruin of the nation and its two kingdoms is present in the writer's mind. This is the light in which the work is to be read, it shows why the catastrophe was unavoidable. It was so because of the unfaithfulness to Jehovah, because of the utterly perverted tendency obstinately followed by the people in spite of the Torah of Jehovah and His prophets. The narrative becomes as it were a great confession of sins of the exiled nation looking back on its history.[38]

The Deuteronomistic overlay is found from Judges, where it occurs with a monotonous beat reminding one of "Hegelian philosophy" in the scheme of "rebellion, affliction, conversion, peace, rebellion, affliction, conversion, peace,"[39] through the books of Samuel and Kings, where it appears most prominently in speeches and "at every important epoch in sermon-like discourses."[40]

Within the books, especially Judges, Wellhausen argued that between the original form of the tradition and the Deuteronomistic redaction an earlier effort at editorial redaction can be seen. The historian in him sought to move behind the Deuteronomistic redaction (and post-Deuteronomistic additions and retouching), through the earlier

---

35. Ibid., 231.
36. Ibid., 280.
37. Ibid., 281.
38. Ibid., 278.
39. Ibid., 231.
40. Ibid., 247, 274.

supplementation and additions, to the original form of the traditions. What emerged in the book of Judges was a number of individual narratives without the scheme of historical continuity or succession and without the peculiar theocratic emphasis.

> In these [original narratives] Israel is a people just like other people nor is even his relationship to Jehovah otherwise conceived of than is for example that of Moab to Chemosh (chap XI 24).[41]

> The period of the Judges presents itself to us as a confused chaos out of which order and coherence are gradually evolved under the pressure of external circumstances but perfectly naturally and without the faintest reminiscence of a sacred unifying constitution that had formerly existed.[42]

In the books of Samuel, Wellhausen isolates the double accounts of Saul's rise to kingship (1 Samuel 7; 8; 10:17ff; 12; and 9:1—10:16; 11), the narrative of David's rise to power (1 Sam 14:52—2 Sam 8:18), which now contains some interruptions and alterations; and the narrative of "occurrences at the court of Jerusalem" and how "Solomon reached the throne" (2 Samuel 9—2 Kings 2 [excluding 2 Samuel 21-24]). The latter "affords us a glance into the very heart of events, showing us the natural occasions and human motives which gave rise to the different actions."[43]

According to Wellhausen, in Kings one finds that the redaction "is essentially uniform with that of the two historical books which precede it"[44]—that is, its selection of materials, depiction of events, and evaluations are based on the perspectives of Deuteronomy and show no acquaintance with the Priestly Code. The main core of the original tradition of Kings is a secondary compilation made from annalistic records and provides evidence for reconstructing the history of Israel.

The final chapter in section two is an analysis of the narrative of the Hexateuch. Here he comments on the primitive world history, the history of the patriarchs, and the Mosaic history in the two strata of the Hexateuch and seeks to demonstrate their parallel structure and the priority of the Jehovist to the Priestly Code. Genesis 1–11 are treated as mythical. In his discussion of the patriarchal materials, Wellhausen

41. Ibid., 235.
42. Ibid., 5.
43. Ibid., 262.
44. Ibid., 277.

reaches a number of conclusions that are later reflected in his historical reconstructions: (1) The patriarchs are primarily ideal prototypes of the true Israelite-peace-loving shepherds. (2) The patriarchal stories do not provide us with the history of individuals but at best are representative of ethnological groups. (3) Of the partriarchal traditions, those of Abraham are the most enigmatic. "Abraham alone is certainly not the name of a people like Isaac and Lot: he is somewhat difficult to interpret. That is not to say that in such a connection as this we may regard him as a historical person, he might with more likelihood be regarded as a free creation of unconscious art. He is perhaps the youngest figure in the company, and it was probably at a comparatively late period that he was put before his son Isaac.[45]

(4) The patriarchal traditions are more informative of the age in which they developed than of the age they purport to describe. "The materials here are not mythical but national, and therefore more transparent, and in a certain sense more historical. It is true, we attain to no historical knowledge of the patriarchs, but only of the time when the stories about them arose in the Israelite people, this later age is here unconsciously projected, in its inner and outward features, into hoar antiquity, and is reflected there like a glorified mirage."[46] (5) In the stage of oral tradition, the narratives existed as separate and independent stories that could be understood in their individuality apart from the rest, were associated with and reflective of particular locales (many were cultus-myths), and were still plastic and living in the ninth and eighth centuries. The weaving together of the detached narratives wlth chronological and other connections was the work of the poetical or literary artist when being collected and reduced to writing.

In discussing the Mosaic tradition, Wellhausen again stresses the differences in perspective between the Jehovistic and Priestly materials. In doing so, he points to a number of factors of consequence for the writing of Israelite history. (1) Sinai played no role in the earliest form of the tradition in the Jehovist.

> In the Jehovist, one form of the tradltion may still be discerned, according to which the lsraelites on crossing the Red Sea at once proceeded towards Kadesh, without making the detour to Sinai. We only get to Sinai in Exod XIX, but in Exod XVII we are

---

45. Ibid., 320.
46. Ibid., 318–19.

already at Massah and Meribah, *i.e.*, on the ground of Kadesh. The story of the manna and the quails occurs not only in Exod XVI, but also in Num XI, and the rocky spring called forth by Moses at Massah and Meribah is both in Exod XVII and Num XX. In other words, the Israelites arrlved at Kadesh, the original object of their wanderings, not after the digression to Sinai but immediately after the Exodus and they spent there the forty years of their residence in the wilderness. Kadesh is also the original scene of the legislation [see Exod 15:25].[47]

(2) The Jehovist was originally a pure history-book, and it was only at a secondary stage that legal material was taken up into the history-book. (3) The original role of Moses is best seen in the earliest form of the Jehovist. (4) The "main stock" (*Grundschrift*) of the Priestly material (see note 19 above) ended with the death of Moses and cannot be traced in the book of Joshua although extensive sections in the second half of Joshua belong to the Priestly Code, that is to the final edited form of the "main stock" or Book of the Four Covenants. (5) There are three different accounts of the conquest in the Bible, and Judges 1 is vastly nearer the facts.

> The priestly narrator represents all Canaan as reduced to a *tabula rasa*, and then makes the masterless and unpeopled land be divided by lot The first lot falls to Judah, then come Manasseh and Ephraim, then Benjamin and Simeon, and lastly the five northerly tribes, Zebulon, Issachar, Asher, Naphtali, Dan. "These are the inheritances which Eleazar the priest and Joshua the son of Nun and the heads of the tribes of Israel apportioned by lot at Shiloh before Jehovah at the door of the tabernacle." According to the Jehovist (Josh xiv 6) Judah and Joseph seem to have had their portions assigned to them while the Israelite headquarters were still at Gilgal—but not by lot—and to have gone forth from Gilgal to take possession of them. A good deal later the rest of the land was divided by lot to the remaining tribes at Shiloh, or perhaps, in the original form of the narrative, at Shechem (Josh xviii 2–10). Joshua casts the lots and makes the assignments alone, Eleazar is not associated with him. The absolute uniformity in the method of the division of the land to all the tribes is in some degree given up in this account, it is still more strongly contradicted by the important chapter, Judges i. Fragments of this chapter are found also in the book of Joshua, and there is no doubt that it belongs to the Jehovistic group of narratives, in common with which it speaks of the Angel of

---

47. Ibid., 342–43.

> Jehovah. It is in truth not a continuation of but a parallel to the book of Joshua, presupposing the conquest of the lands east of the Jordan, but not of western Canaan.[48]

The third and final section of the *Prolegomena* contains three chapters: "Conclusion of the Criticism of the Law," "The Oral and the Written Torah," and "The Theocracy as Idea and as Institution." In this part of the volume, Wellhausen defends the literary-critical approach, notes some differences between himself and other scholars, and discusses the relationship of Jehovist, Deuteronomy, Ezekiel, Law of Holiness, and Priestly Code. His most significant comments are found in the chapter on oral and written torah. Here he is concerned to demonstrate that, in spite of the fact that "the law of Moses" is the starting-point for the history of Judaism, "ancient Israel was certainly not without God-given bases for the ordering of human life, only they were not fixed in writing."[49] This "God-given bases" was not only the unwritten laws of custom but also the torah, the "special Torah of Jehovah, which not only sets up laws of action of universal validity, but shows humankind the way in special cases of difficulty, where he is at a loss."[50] This torah was the product of priestly teaching and instruction, including the giving of oracles, "but it continued to be an oral decision and direction. There is no torah as a ready-made product, as a system existing independently of its originator and accessible to everyone: it becomes actual only in the various utterances, which naturally form by degrees the basis of a fixed tradition."[51] The prophets, in early Israel, were men of God who also gave torah or teaching: "the Torah of the priests was like a spring which runs always, that of the prophets like a spring which is intermittent, but when it does break forth, flows with all the greater force."[52]

> There is thus a close relation between priests and prophets, *i.e.*, seers, as with other peoples (1 Sam VI 2, 1 Kings XVIII 19, compare wlth 2 Kings 19), so also wlth the Hebrews. In the earliest time it was not knowing the technique of worship, which was still very simple and undeveloped, but being a man of God, standing on an intimate footing with God, that made a man a

---

48. Ibid., 512–13.
49. Ibid., 393.
50. Ibid., 394.
51. Ibid., 395.
52. Ibid., 397.

> priest, that is one who keeps up the communication with heaven for others, and the seer is better qualified than others for the office (1 Kings XVIII 30 seq). There is no fixed distinction in early times between the two offices, Samuel is in 1 Sam I–III an aspirant to the priesthood, in IX–X he is regarded as a seer.[53]

The writing down of the torah and its fixity as law developed as a process. The earliest deposit of such torah is found in the legal deposit (Exodus 19–24; 32–34) taken up into the Jehovist, which was originally "a pure history-book."[54] With the promulgation of Deuteronomy (Deuteronomy 12–27), a radically new dimension is introduced:

> Deuteronomy presupposes earlier attempts of this kind, and borrows its materials largely from them, but on the other hand it is distinguished from them not only by its greater compass but also by its much higher claims. It is written with the distinct intention not to remain a private memorandum, but to obtain public authority as a *book*. The idea of making a definite formulated written Torah the law of the land is the important point. It was a first attempt and succeeded at the outset beyond expectation.[55]

> After the solemn and far-reaching act by which Josiah introduced this law, the notion of covenant-making between Jehovah and Israel appears to have occupied the central position in religious thought. It prevails in Deuteronomy, in Jeremiah, Ezekiel, in Isaiah xl–lxvi, Lev xvii–xxvi, and most of all in the Book of the Four Covenants.[56]

Wellhausen saw the appearance of the law as the end of the old freedom, the creation of an objective authority, and the death of prophecy. Deuteronomy was primarily a program of reform that "took for granted the existence of the cultus, and only corrected it in certain general respects."[57] The later codes—Ezekiel, Holiness, and Priestly—were attempts at restoration.

> The temple was now destroyed and the worship interrupted, and the practice of past times had to be written down if it was

---

53. Ibid., 396–97.
54. Ibid., 345.
55. Ibid., 402.
56. Ibid., 418–19.
57. Ibid., 404.

not to be lost. Thus it came about that in the exile the conduct of worship became the subject of the Torah, and in this process reformation was naturally aimed at as well as restoration. Ezekiel was the first to take this step which the circumstances of the time indicated. In the last part of his work he made the first attempt to record the ritual which had been customary in the temple of Jerusalem. Other priests attached themselves to him (Lev xv 11–xxv l), and thus there grew up in the exile from among the members of this profession a kind of school of people who reduced to writing and to a system what they had formerly practised in the way of their calling. After the temple was restored this theoretical zeal still continued to work, and the ritual when renewed was still further developed by the action and reaction on each other of theory and practise, the priests who had stayed in Babylon took as great a part, from a distance, in the sacred services, as their brothers at Jerusalem who had actually to conduct them. The latter indeed lived in adverse circumstances and do not appear to have conformed with great strictness or accuracy to the observances which had been agreed upon. The last result of this labour of many years is the Priestly Code. It has indeed been said that we cannot ascribe the creation of such a work to an age which was bent on nothing but repristination. Granted that this is a correct description of it, such an age is peculiarly fitted for an artificial systematising of given materials, and this is what the originality of the Priestly Code in substance amounts to.

The Priestly Code, worked into the Pentateuch as the standard legislative element in it, became the definite "Mosaic law."[58]

It was Ezra who, in 444 BCE, introduced and published the Pentateuch in its final form as the authoritative law and norm of life in written code. "What distinguishes Judaism from ancient Israel *is the written Torah*. The water which in old times rose from a spring, the Epigoni stored up in cisterns."[59]

The theocratic ideas and goals of postexilic Judaism—the community as a church that "was merely a spiritualised survival of the nation"[60]—represented a religion and cultus that were estranged from their own roots. The older impulses were now replaced with a new

---

58. Ibid., 404–5.
59. Ibid., 410.
60. Ibid., 256.

emphasis—"exactly according to prescription, at the right place, at the right time, by the right individuals, in the right way."[61]

> In the Mosaic theocracy the cultus became a pedagogic instrument of discipline. It is estranged from the heart, its revival was due to old custom, it would never have blossomed again of itself. It no longer has its roots in childlike impulse, it is a dead work, in spite of all the importance attached to it, nay, just because of the anxious conscientiousness with which it was gone about. At the restoration of Judaism the old usages were patched together. In a new system, which, however, only served as the form to preserve something that was nobler in its nature, but could not have been saved otherwise than on a narrow shell that stoutly resisted all foreign influences.[62]

Reconstructing Early Israelite History

In his preface to the English edition of the *Prolegomena*, W. Robertson Smith wrote: "The Old Testament does not furnish a history of Israel, though it supplies the materials from which such a history can be constructed."[63] Wellhausen published four works demonstrating how "a history can be constructed" in light of the consequences of the issues raised and solutions proposed in his literary analyses. The foundation document (one is tempted to say *Grundschrift*) of these works was his article "Israel," first published in the *Encyclopaedia Britannica* (1881). This work, in a shorter German form, was distributed by Wellhausen at Christmastime in 1880.[64] An expanded form of the *EB* article was published in German in 1884.[65] His fullest treatment of Israelite and Judean

61. Ibid., 424.
62. Ibid., 425.
63. Ibid., vii.
64. This "Geschichte Israels," issued in manuscript form, contains sections 1–9 of "Israel" (1881:396–417), covering the period down to the exile, although with some passages omitted (on 1881:399–401, 403, 406, 414). This work has now been reissued in 1965:13–64.
65. The *Encyclopaedia Britannica* article of 1881 was reprinted as a separate work at least three times with the title *Sketch of the History of Israel and Judah* (3rd ed. 1891). The *Sketch* contains an appendix, "Judaism and Christianity," which is the translation of a section of the *Abriss* (1884), which was not in the original *Encyclopaedia Britannica* article. The *Encyclopaedia Britannica* article was reprinted in the English edition of *Prolegomena* (1885:427–548) wtth "Judaism and Christianity" as section

history was first published in 1894 with the title *Israelitische und jüdische Geschichte*.⁶⁶

In his treatment of "Die Anfange des Volkes," one finds no "Patriarchal Age" in the traditional sense, for "die Erzählungen über die Erzväter in der Genesis gehn von ethnologischen Verhältnissen und von Kultuseinrichtungen der Königszeit aus und leiten deren Ursprunge aus einer idealen Vorzeit her, auf die sie in Wahrheit nur abgespiegelt werden."⁶⁷ The origins of the people are located among the Hebrews, a group to which the ancestors of the Ammonites, Moabites, and Edomites belonged. Israelite ancestors also had connections with the Arameans as well as the nomadic and seminomadic Arabian tribes of the Sinai peninsula (Ishmaelites, Midianites, Kenites, Amalekites, and Kenizzites). From the steppes of southern Palestine, one of these Hebrew groups moved into the land of Goshen, a traditional "Besitz von Nomaden."⁶⁸ Here they continued their life as shepherds and goatherds, retaining their language and style of life.⁶⁹ This is about the extent of Wellhausen's utilization of the narrative material of Genesis, and practically all of this could have been derived or deduced from other Old Testament texts.

Wellhausen reconstructs the wilderness period or Mosaic epoch in the following manner. About 1250 BCE, the group of Hebrews fled Egypt, maybe undergoing some special event at the "sea" (Exod 14:31: "auf die der Natur der Sache nach kein Verlass ist").⁷⁰ The group made its way to Kadesh where it stayed for some time.⁷¹ Here the Rachel group (Joseph) and the Leah group (Reuben, Simeon, Levi, Judah, Issachar, and

---

11 (1885:499–513). Quotations and pagination from "Israel" in the present article are from the reissue of the *Prolegomena* (1885).

66. 1st ed., 342pp; 2nd ed. (1895) 378pp; 3nd ed. (1897) 388pp; 4th ed. (1901) 395pp; 5th ed. (1904) 395pp; 6th ed. (1907) 386pp; 7th ed. (1914) 372pp, with subsequent reprints. Quotations in the present article are from the 9th ed. (1958) a reprint of the 1914 edition.

67. *Israelitische und jüdische Geschichte*, 10.

68. Ibid., 10. In "Israel," 429, Wellhausen gives the general reference some fifteen centuries before our era, but in *Geschichte* he offers no date for the descent. One can see at many points where the positions taken in "Israel" have been modified in *Geschichte*.

69. *Israelitische und jüdische Geschichte*, 10–11. Cf. *Prolegomena*, 429, where he says that "forced labour was exacted of them for the construction of new public works in Goshen," which does not appear in *Geschichte*.

70. *Israelitische und jüdische Geschichte*, 11.

71. In "Israel" (*Prolegomena*, 430), he spoke of a visit to Sinai prior to arrival at Kadesh.

Zebulon, probably none of these had been in Egypt) came to a sense of tribal unity. This unity of the seven tribes was based on kinship ties ("Alle *legitime* Gemeinschaft ist Blutgemeinschaft die naturliche Gemeinschaft, die des Blutes, ist die heilige")[72] and religious community ("Yahve der Gott Israels, Israel das Volk Jahves.")[73] In this tribal relationship, warfare and military concepts played a significant role ("Der Krieg ist es, was die Volker macht das Kriegslager, die Wiege der Nation, war auch das alteste Heiligtum. Da war Israel und da war Jahve.")[74] Moses's role was that of priestly functionary and judicial authority at the sacred center of Kadesh and was viewed by Wellhausen in terms of his understanding of priesthood and torah in early Israel (see above).[75] Thus it is proper to speak, in a certain sense, of Moses as the originator of Israelite religion. The Israelites left Kadesh for the Transjordan in response to the need of their kinsmen, the Ammonites and Moabites whose territory was being overrun by the Amorite, King Sihon of Heshbon.

Wellhausen reconstructs the main features of this period without recourse to much of the narrative tradition of the Pentateuch; there is little if any uniqueness to the history of the Israelite ancestors, no desert theocracy, no monotheistic faith, no law set once and for all, no unified experience of all the tribes in Egypt, no covenant theology. "Die lsraeliten waren eine Nation wie andere Nationen."[76] "The religious starting-point

---

72. *Israelitische und jüdische Geschichte*, 221.

73. Ibid., 231.

74. Ibid., 23–24. In "Israel," he wrote "Jehovah is to be regarded as having originally been a family or tribal god, either of the family to which Moses belonged or of the tribe of Joseph, in the possession of which we find the ark of Jehovah, and within which occurs the earliest certain instance of a composite proper name with the word Jehovah for one of its elements (Jehoshua, Joshua). No essential distinction was felt to exist between Jehovah and El, any more than between Asshur and El, Jehovah was only a speclal name of El whlch had become current within a powerful circle, and which on that account was all the more fitted to become the designation of a national god" (*Prolegomena*, 433 n. 1). "Jehovah was the warrior El, after whom the nation styled itself" (ibid., 434). See *Israelitische und jüdische Geschichte*, 23 and also 25. "So ausserte sich Jahve vorzugsweise in den grossen Krisen der Geschichte, seine 'Tage' waren, wie die Tage der Araber, Schlachttage."

75. "If Moses did anything at all, he certainly founded the sanctuary at Kadesh and the torah there, which the priests of the ark carried on after him, thus continuing the thread of the history of Israel, which was taken up again in power by the monarchy" (*Prolegomena*, 397 n. 1). See also his article on Moses (1883).

76. *Israelitische und jüdische Geschichte*, 19.

of the history of Israel was remarkable, not for its novelty, but for its normal character."[77]

In the traditions about the settlement in Palestine and its immediate aftermath, Wellhausen found much to use in reconstructing the history of the ancient Israelites. According to him, there were two movements across the Jordan. The first, by Judah, Simeon, and Levi, was not overly successful. The second by Joseph and related groups under the leadership of Joshua moved into the area later occupied by the Benjaminites.[78] These movements across the Jordan and the settlement north and south led to a new division of the tribes—Israel and Judah—replacing the older Leah–Rachel division.[79] Many cities and much territory were captured although "Ai, Jericho und andere Städte scheinen allerdings nicht erst durch die Israeliten zerstort zu sein, sondern schon vor deren Einbruch in Trümmern gelegen zu haben."[80] The final act of Joshua was to lead the Israelites to victory over a coalition of forces under Jabin.

In addition to his emphasis on the military aspects of the settlement, Wellhausen also stressed the lack of wholesale conquest and the limited geographical occupation, which occurred in spite of the disintegrated state of the enemy. The effort led by Sisera was the last major attempt of Canaanites to stem the tide. The Israelite victory is celebrated in the song of Deborah, "dem frühesten Denkmal der hebräischen Literatur," in which, however, "Israel ist kein Organismus . . . ; Israel is nur eine Idee."[81] As a rule, however, the tribes operated on their own: "the period of the Judges presents itself to us as a confused chaos . . ."[82] Many of the individual stories in the book of Judges were seen as reflecting historical but not chronologically successive events: the migration of the tribe of Dan, the struggles with the Moabites under Eglon, the defeat of the Midianites, and the attempt of Abimelech the son of Jerubbaal to establish

77. *Prolegomena*, 437.

78. Reuben (and Gad?) remained behind in Transjordan (*Israelitische und jüdische Geschichte*, 34). "It is probable that Manasseh's migration to the teritory eastward of Jordan took place from the west, and later than the time of Moses" (*Prolegomena*, 455 n. 1).

79. Many of the tribes such as Ephraim and Benjamin were formed and acquired their names only after the settlement.

80. *Israelitische und jüdische Geschichte*, 25 n. 1.

81. Ibid., 37.

82. *Prolegomena*, 5. "Der kriegerische Bund der Stämme zerfiel unter den friedlichen Verhältnissen, die Ansiedlung zerstreute die durch das Lager- und Wanderleben Geeinigten" (*Israelitische und jüdische Geschichte*, 48).

himself as king over Israel (Ephraim and Manasseh). For Wellhausen, the most significant features of the period of the judges were the invaders' amalgamation with the indigenous population and their adaptation of an agricultural way of life. Religious practices, customs, and beliefs were not excluded from such amalgamation.

In Wellhausen's reconstruction of this period of Israelite history, one can see that he utilized what he considered to be the earliest stage of the traditions, after the various "alluvial deposits" with their religious coloration,[83] chronological cohesiveness, and all-Israel orientation have been removed, in order to describe what seemed to have the greatest probability of having happened.

For Wellhausen, the really pivotal period in the formation of Israel was the time of the early monarchy. Although he spoke of the community and commonality of the tribes ("kriegerischer Bund," "kriegerische Eidgenossenschaft") during the invasion and settlement, Wellhausen saw the establishment of kingship as the most decisive event in Israelite history since even postexilic and theocratic Judaism was a spiritualized survival of monarchical structures:

> Saul and David first made out of the Hebrew tribes a real people in the political sense (Deut XXXIII 5). David was in the eyes of later generations inseparable from the idea of Israel, he was the king par excellence. Saul was thrown onto the shade, but both together are the founders of the kingdom, and have thus a much wider importance than any of their successors. It was they who drew the life of the people together at a centre, and gave it an aim, to them the nation is indebted for its historical self-consciousness. All the order of after times is built up on the monarchy, it is the soil out of which all the other institutions of Israel grow up. In the time of the judges, we read, every man did that which was right in his own eyes, not because the Mosaic constitution was not in force, but because there was no king in those days. The consequences were very important in the sphere of religion as well since the political advance of the people brought the historic and national character of Jehovah to the front again. This was the result of Israel's becoming a kingdom, the kingship of Jehovah, in that precise sense which we associate

---

83. "It may stand as a general principle, that the nearer history is to its origin the more profane it is" (*Prolegomena*, 245).

with it, is the religious expression of the fact of the foundation of the kingdom by Saul and David.[84]

Wellhausen understood the establishment of the monarchy as the people's response to the threat of outside pressure, primarily from the Philistines from the west but also from the Ammonites from the east.[85] With Philistine pressure, there developed a "widespread exaltation of religious feeling," led by "troops of ecstatic enthusiasts."[86] The old seer Samuel, although himself not a *nabi'*, recognized from the neighboring peoples the advantages that could accrue from the consolidation of the tribes and families into a kingdom, utilized the spirit of the times, and discovered the humankind capable of meeting the needs of the hour. It was a time when "religion and patriotism were then identical."[87] The monarchy is thus described as a popular and natural development unattended by any immediate clash with the old orders. "What contributed more than anything else to David's elevation to the throne was the general recognition of the fact that he was the man best fitted on the whole to overtake the labour it brought with it, viz. the prosecution of the war with the Philistines, a war which was as it were the forge in which the kingdom of Israel was welded into one."[88] The above short discussion of Wellhausen's reconstruction of the history of ancient Israel—from the beginnings through the early monarchy—must suffice. At any rate, his methodology can best be seen in this area, and many aspects of the later period have been noted in the analysis of the *Prolegomena* above.

Evaluation and Critique

Three factors about Wellhausen's reconstruction of Israelite history cannot be overstressed. (1) He was the first to produce a history of Israel in which there was a thorough integration of literary criticism and historical reconstruction. The two movements were not viewed as two separate activities but as two aspects of a single activity. Regardless of the results

---

84. *Prolegomena*, 413–14.

85. "Aus freier Notwendigkeit war das Königtum erwachsen" (*Israelitische und jüdische Geschichte*, 52). (The monarchy arose from free necessity.)

86. *Prolegomena*, 449; *Israelitische und jüdische Geschichte*, 50–51.

87. *Prolegomena*, 449. Samuel was "der patriotische Prophet in Sonderheit" (*Israelitische und jüdische Geschichte*, 51).

88. *Prolegomena*, 453; see *Israelitische und jüdische Geschichte*, 59.

of Wellhausen's endeavor, or one's opinion of them, to disagree with his program and intent is difficult if not impossible. It was this aspect of his work that struck certain forms of Old Testament study such a devastating blow and put a generation of scholars on the defensive. (2) In his reconstruction as in his literary analysis, Wellhausen was interested in total perspectives, presuppositions, the larger meaning, the living process, and the interconnectedness of events, movements, and literary expressions. It was this aspect of his work that gave his writings their attractiveness and wide popularity. (3) Wellhausen sought to produce a secular or profane history of Israel that would sketch its developments in naturalistic terms. This does not mean that he disregarded the theological and religious interests of the Old Testament writings—in fact and in many ways these were the heart of his work—but that he did not utilize the theological perspectives of the Old Testament as elements in his historiographical methodology. It was this aspect of his work that frequently antagonized and sometimes traumatized religious believers of his and subsequent times.

Perhaps no scholar's work has been more scrutinized and criticized than his. Many of his critics, however, have confused denunciation with dialogue, repudiation with refutation, and malicious malignment with substantive argumentation.[89] Most are shots at targets in non-existent firing ranges. This, however, does not mean that his work is not open to criticism.

The following are offered as critiques of his reconstruction of Israelite history. (1) Wellhausen's own sentiments, personal character, and individualism led him to an idealization of early Israelite life and to an almost total disdain for religious structures and cultic institutions. His emphases on the freshness and naturalness of early Israelite impulses, the freedom of a less institutionalized culture, and the goodness of primitive forms led him not only to overplay these in his reconstruction but also to fail to see that the function of law (even written law) in a culture need not lead to oppressive and stifling forms of existence.[90] (2) Wellhausen's obsession with "the place in history of the 'law of Moses,'" although understandable in the context of nineteenth-century scholarship, not only created a certain tunnel vision that overlooked other matters but also

---

89. R. J. Thompson, *Moses and the Law*; and Perlitt, *Vatke und Wellhausen*.

90. Here one can see not only Wellhausen's personal disposition but also a tendency going back to Herder and the earlier deists and romantics. See Boschwitz, *Julius Wellhausen*; and Hahn, "Wellhausen's Interpretation."

led to an overemphasis on the importance of legal codes in Israelite history. (3) His radical distinction between preexilic Israel and postexilic Judaism, partially fed by his distinction between pre- and post-Deuteronomic traditions, led to his caricaturing of Judaism (see L. H. Silberman 1982). (4) Wellhausen overemphasized the importance and role of the prophets in the life of ancient Israel.[91] To see the preaching of the prophets as the impetus which eventually led to the complete reformation and centralization of religion—a movement that resulted in the tragic end of prophecy—is greatly to overstress the role of prophecy. Again Wellhausen shared in the nineteenth-century rediscovery of prophecy, and his overzealousness can be understood in this light. Further, however, one feels that the prophets were Wellhausen's heroes and that he sensed himself as a modern counterpart.[92] (5) Finally, Wellhausen did not sufficiently appreciate the importance of the monarchy and monarchial politics and interests for developments in Israelite life—even centralization of the cult. There is a certain naiveté about his treatment of royal politics and even the origin and nature of the monarchy. Surely the dominant Judean figures in the eighth and seventh centuries were the kings—not the prophets Isaiah and Jeremiah.

Bibliography

Boschwitz, Friedemann. *Julius Wellhuusen: Motive und Mass-Stabe seiner Geschichtsschreibung.* Darmstadt: Wissenschaftliche Buchgesellschaft, 1968.

Colenso, John Wllllam. *The Pentateuch and Book of Joshua Critically Examined.* 7 vols. London: Longmans, Green, 1862–79.

De Wette, Wilhelm Martin Leberecht. *Dissertatio critico-exegetica qua Deuteronomium a prioribus Pentateuchi libris diversum.* Jena: Etzdorf, 1805.

———. *Berträge zur Einleitung in das Alte Testament.* Vol. 1, *Kritischer Versuch über die Glaubwurdigkeit der Bücher der Chronik mit Hinsicht auf die Geschichte der mosaischen Bücher und Gesetzgebung.* Vol. 2, *Kritik der mosaischen Geschichte.* 2 vols. Halle: Schimmelpfennig, 1806–7.

Duhm, Bernhard. *Die Theologie der Propheten als Grundlage für die innere Entwicklungsgeschichte der israelitischen Religion.* Bonn: Marcus, 1875.

Ewald, Heinrich Georg August. *Geschichte des Volkes Israel bis Chrtstus.* 5 vols. Göttingen: Dieterich, 1843–55.

---

91. In his review of Duhm, *Die Theologie der Propheten*, Wellhausen (1876) criticized Duhm for overemphasizing the role of the prophets at the expense of the priests in the origin and formation of Old Testament law.

92. It is probably no accident that Thomas Carlyle's book on heroes could serve as a confirmation present from Wellhausen.

———. *The History of Israel*. Vol. 1. Edited by Russell Martineau. 2nd ed. 1869. Reprinted, Eugene, OR: Wipf & Stock, 2004.

George, Johann Friedrich Leopold. *Die alteren jüdische Feste, mit einer Kritik der Gesetzgebung des Pentateuch*. Berlin: Schroeder, 1835.

Graf, Karl Heinrich. *Die geschichtlichen Bücher des Alten Testaments: Zwei historisch-kritische Untersuchungen*. Leipzig: Weigel, 1866.

Hahn, Herbert F. "Wellhausen's Interpretation of Israel's Religious History: A Reappraisal of His Ruling Ideas." In *Essays on Jewish Life and Thought: Presented in Honor of Salo Wtttmayer Baron*, edited by Joseph L. Blau et a1., 299–308. New York: Columbia University Press, 1959.

Kuenen, Abraham. *De Godsdienst van Israel tot den Ondergang van den Joodschen Staat*. 2 vols. Haarlem: Kruseman, 1869–70.

———. *The Religion of Israel to the Fall of the Jewish State*. 3 vols. London: Williams & Norgate, 1874–75.

Milman, Henry Hart. *The History of the Jews: From the Earliest Period to the Present Time*. 3 vols. London: Murray, 1829. 2d ed., 1830. Harper's Family Library edition. New York: Harper & Brothers, 1834. New edition, New York: Widdleton, 1874.

Perlitt, Lothar. *Vatke und Wellhausen: Geschichtsphilosophische Voraussetzungen und historiographische Motive für die Darstellung der Religion und Geschichte Israels durch Wilhelm Vatke und Julius Wellhausen*. BZAW 94. Berlin: Töpelmann, 1965.

Prideaux, Humphrey. *The Old and New Testament Connected in the History of the Jews and Neighboring Nations, from the Declension of the Kingdoms of Israel and Judah to the Time of Christ*. 2 vols. London: Knaplock, 1717–18.

Reuss, Eduard. *L'histoire sainte et la loi (Pentateuque et Joshue)*. 2 vols. Paris: Sandoz & Fischbacher, 1879.

Shuckford, Samuel. *The Sacred and Profane History of the World Connected, from the Creation of the World to the Dissolution of the Assyrian Empire at the Death of Sandanapalus, and to the Declension of the Kingdoms of Judah and Israel under the Reigns of Ahaz and Pekah*. 2 vols. London: Knaplock & Tonson, 1728–30.

Silberman, Lou H. "Wellhausen and Judaism." *Semeia* 25 (1982) 75–82.

———. "Whence Siglum Q? A Conjecture." *JBL* 98 (1979) 287–88.

Stanley, Arthur Penrhyn. *Lectures on the History of the Jewish Church*. Part 1, *Abraham to Samuel*. New York: Scribner, 1863.

———, editor. *The Life and Correspondence of Thomas Arnold*. Vol. 1. New York: Scribner, 1844.

Thompson, James Westfall. *A History of Historical Writing*. 2 vols. New York: Macmillan, 1942.

Thompson, R. J. *Moses and the Law in a Century of Criticism since Graf*. VTSup 19. Leiden: Brill, 1970.

Vatke, Wilhelm. 1835. *Die biblische Theologie wissenschaftlich dargestellt*. Vol. 1, *Die Religion des Alten Testamentes nach den kanonischen Büchern entwickelt*. Berlin: Bethge.

Wellhausen, Julius. "Die Composition des Hexateuchs." *Jahrbuch für Deutsche Theologie* 21 (1876) 392–450, 531–602; 22 (1877) 407–79. Reissued separately in *Skizzen und Vorarbeiten*, vol. 2: *Die Composition des Hexateuchs*. Berlin: Reimer, 1885.

———. "De gentibus et familiis Judaeis quae 1. Chr. 2. 4. enurnerantur." Theol. Liz-Diss., Göttingen, 1870.

———. "Geschichte Israels." Privately published as manuscript at Christmastime, Greifswald, 1880. Reprinted in *Grundrisse* (1965), 13–64.

———. *Geschichte Israels in zwei Banden. Erster Band*. Berlin: Reimer, 1878. 2nd ed. and henceforth under the title *Prolegomena zur Geschichte Israels*. Berlin: Reimer, 1883.

———. "Die geschichtlichen Bücher [Richter, Ruth, Samuelis, Könige]." In *Einleitung in die Heilige Schrift*. Vol. 1, *Einleitung in das Alte Testament*, by Friedrich Bleek, 181–267. 4th ed. Berlin: Reimer, 1878. Reprinted, in *Die Composition des Hexateuchs und der historischen Bücher des Alten Testaments*, 208–301. 3rd ed. Berlin: Reimer, 1899.

———. *Grundrisse zum Alten Testament*. Edited by Rudolf Smend. ThBü 27. Munich: Kaiser, 1965.

———. "Israel." In *Encyclopaedia Britannica*, 13:396–431. 9th ed. 1881 (expansion of 1880) = 1885, 427–548 (with addition of section 11, "Judaism and Christianity," from 1884) = (with minor changes) *Sketch of the History of Israel and Judah*. 3rd ed. Edinburgh: A. & C. Black, 1891.

———. *Israelitische und jüdische Geschichte*. Berlin: Reimer, 1894. 7th ed., 1914 = 9th ed., Berlin: de Gruyter, 1958.

———. "Moses." In *Encyclopaedia Britannica*, 16:860–61. 9th ed. 1883.

———. "Pentateuch and Joshua." In *Encyclopaedia Britannica*, 18:505–14. 9th ed. 1885.

———. *Prolegomena to the History of Israel*. Translated from the 2nd ed. of 1878 by J. Sutherland Black and Allan Menzies. With Preface by W. Robertson Smith. Edinburgh: A. & C. Black, 1885. Reprinted, New York: Meridian, 1957.

———. Review of Bernhard Duhm, *Die Theologie der Propheten*. *Jahrbuch für Deutsche Theologie* 21 (1876) 152–58.

———. *Skizzen und Vorarbeiten*. Vol. 2, *Abriss der Geschichte Israels und Judas*. Berlin: Reimer, 1884. (Expansion of 1880 and 1881).

———. *Der Text der Bücher Samuels untersucht*. Göttingen: Vandenhoeck & Ruprecht, 1871.

3

The Twelve-Tribe Israelite Amphictyony

An Appraisal

IN 1930, MARTIN NOTH published his *Das System der zwölf Stämme Israëls*, a work that has been one of the most influential and epoch-making volumes in twentieth-century Old Testament study. This work gave not only a formative expression to, but also the classical expression of, premonarchical Israel as a twelve-tribe amphictyony.

Noth began his study with an analysis of the Old Testament traditions that speak of the twelve tribes and especially those texts that provide lists of the tribes (Gen 29:31—30:24; 35:16-20; 49:1-27; Num 1:5-15; 26:5-51; Deuteronomy 33; and Joshua 13-19). The oldest of these Noth considered to be, in chronological order, Genesis 49; Numbers 26; and Numbers 1. In these, the lists appear in two distinct forms. In the first and chronologically the oldest, Levi appears as a secular tribe (Genesis 49; cf. Genesis 34; and see Gen 25:23-26; 46:8-25; Exod 1:2-4; Deut 27:12-13; 1 Chron 2:1-2; and Ezek 48:31-35). In the second, and chronologicaliy later, Levi does not figure as a territory-holding tribe (Numbers 1; 26; see also Num 2:3-31; 10:14-28; 7:12-83). In all of these lists, Noth distinguished two recurring motifs: the constancy of the number twelve and the division and association of the tribes into two distinct sub-groups, viz. the so-called Leah-tribes (Reuben, Simeon, Levi, Judah, Issachar, and Zebulun) and Rachel-tribes (Joseph and Benjamin). The number twelve is preserved in those lists where Levi does not appear by the division of Joseph into the two tribes of Ephraim and Manasseh.[1]

This twelve-tribe tradition was accepted by Noth as an independent tradition reflective of a historical actuality. The origin of the twelve-tribe system and tradition was placed in the pre-monarchical period of the Judges. The terminus ad quem for such a system could not be placed any later than the time of David when a well organized state and empire system was the dominant government structure. The origin and existence of such a system was understandable only when the tribes were conscious of their individual existence and retained their individual political identity. By the time of David's reign, some of the twelve tribes had ceased to exist. The terminus a quo was considered to be the time of the settlement in the land of Canaan. The literary evidence suggested two stages in the twelve-tribe structure. The earliest is reflected in those lists in which Levi appears as a secular, land-holding tribe. Noth assigned this form of the system to the early period of the Judges, although he acknowledged that Gen 49:1–27 in its present form probably dates from the time of David or Solomon. A later or second stage in the tribal structure is reflected in the lists where Levi no longer appears as a landholding or secular tribe (esp. Numbers 26). This structure Noth dated to the second half of the Judges period when Levi's place was filled by the subdivision of the "house of Joseph." The "Song of Deborah" (Judges 5), upon which Noth places little emphasis because he claims it to be a free-formed composition that does not adhere to the divisions of Leah and Rachel groupings found elsewhere, does reflect a stage between the first system (with Levi) and the second system (without Levi). In the "Song of Deborah," the tribes of Machir (= Manasseh and Ephraim, which later appear as subdivisions of Joseph) already exist as independent tribal entities.

The historical period that saw the rise of this twelve-tribe system was the time immediately following the invasion of the "House of Joseph." Noth did not assume a full scale simultaneous invasion of all the tribes into Palestine and in this was following Alt's reconstruction of the settlement in Canaan.[2] Noth argued that the Leah-tribes and Benjamin[3]

---

1. *Das System*, 3–28. A more limited discussion by Noth of the material in *Das System* is found in his *The History of Israel*, 85–109.

2. See Alt, *Die Landnahme der Israeliten in Palistina* [reprinted in *Kleine Schriften zur Geschichte des Volkes Israel*, 1:89–125]; ET = "The Settlement of the Israelites in Palestine."

3. In his history of Israel, Noth considers Benjamin to have entered Palestine along

were already settled in the land at the time of the invasion of the house of Joseph.[4]

Noth compared the twelve-tribe structure of early Israel with similar tribal structures found elsewhere. Scholars prior to Noth had already referred to the biblical and some non-biblical references that mention special groupings of tribes somewhat analogous to the twelve tribes of Israel. Heinrich Ewald had pointed to the twelve Ishmaelite tribes in Gen 25:13–16, the enumeration of the twelve Edomite tribes in Gen 36:10–14, and the reference to a list of Horite tribes in Gen 36:20–28.[5] Ewald had suggested comparing these twelve-tribe groups to parallels of six- and twelve-tribe systems in Greek and Italian literature and even in some African and American tribal groupings. Ewald then postulated the existence of a twelve-tribe structure in the pre-Mosaic period of Israelite pre-history.

Hermann Gunkel, in discussing the stories of the birth of Jacob's children (Gen 29:31—30:24), drew upon these extra-biblical traditions in elucidating the biblical traditions.[6] Emil Szanto, in a study on the Greek tribes,[7] referred to the possible analogy between the Israelite and Greek tribal systems. Julius Wellhausen had described the early tribes as a "kriegerischen Eidgenossenschaft" ("military confederacy") and stressed the role of Yahweh as a "Kriegsmann" ("man of war") and as "Feldgeschrei" ("war-cry") of the confederacy.[8] Max Weber described early Israel as a war confederacy whose membership varied from time to time and who was led by the *shofetim*, the characteristic war heroes.[9] "The Israelite confederacy itself, according to unambiguous tradition, represented a war confederation under and with Yahweh as the war god of the union, guaranteeing its social order and creator of the material prosperity of the confederates, especially of the requisite rain. This is brought to expression by the name 'Israel' which was meant to designate directly 'the people of the fighting god.' . . . 'Israel' was no tribal name but the name

---

with the house of Joseph; see *History of Israel*, 89–90.

4. *Das System*, 28–39.
5. Ewald, *Einleitung in die Geschichte des Volkes Israels*, 1:519ff.
6. Gunkel, *Genesis*, 332; ET = *Genesis*, 321–22.
7. Szanto, *Die griechischen Phylen*.
8. Wellhausen, *Israelitische und jüdische Geschichte*, 23–24.
9. Weber, *Das Antike Judentum* = *Ancient Judaism*, 77–89.

of an association, at that, of a cult league."[10] Albrecht Alt pointed to the Greek and Italian tribal systems organized in a sacred union around a common sanctuary as an aid to understanding the pre- and early history of ancient Israel.[11] Noth acknowledged his indebtedness to these scholars and summarized most of their contributions. In some respects, Noth's work on the twelve-tribe system can be compared to Julius Wellhausen's work on pentateuchal criticism:[12] both took over ideas and concepts current in their day and expounded them in a convincing, definitive manner marshaling a great array of supporting evidence while utilizing the biblical materials with a systematic thoroughness and drawing the logical conclusions and consequences from their research.

Noth examined the structures and functions of the tribal systems in the Greco-Italian world[13] in order to make comparisons that would elucidate the existence of the twelve-tribe Israelite system that he had deduced from the biblical literary traditions. Such a tribal system was referred to in Greek as an "amphictyony," i.e. a "community of those who dwell around" (around a particular shrine). The most notable of the Greek amphictyonies was Pylae-Delphi which, as its double name implies, possessed two central sanctuaries, the temple of Demeter at Pylae and the temple of Apollo at Delphi. This amphictyony was composed of twelve tribes, not cities as in most other Greek amphictyonies, a factor that Noth took as a sign of the system's antiquity. Other Greek amphictyonies[14] to which Noth drew attention were:

- Delos with its temple of Apollo;

- Onchestus in Boeotia (Strabo 9.2.33) and Calauria (Strabo 8.6.14) each with its temple of Poseidon;

- the Panionium amphictyony of twelve Ionian cities on the Asia Minor coast with the temple of Poseidon at Myclae as a central cult-place;

10. Ibid., 81.

11. Alt, "Israel, politische Geschichte," 438–39.

12. Wellhausen, *Prolegomena zur Geschichte Israels*; ET = *Prolegomena to the History of Israel*.

13. On the European amphictyonies, see Freeman, *The History of Federal Government in Greece and Italy*; Cauer, "Amphiktyonia"; Busolt and Swoboda, *Griechische Staatskunde*, 1280–1309; Bürgel, *Die pylaeisch-delphische Amphiktyonie*; and Harland, "The Calaurian Amphictyony."

14. Most of these had already been referred to by Ewald, and on some the evidence is very scanty.

- the amphictyony of six Dorian cities with its temple of Apollo at Cnidus; and
- the amphictyony of six Triphylian cities with its temple of Poseidon.

Italian leagues similar to the Greek amphictyonies that had been noted by Ewald were utilized by Noth as comparative evidence. Livy (1.8.3) spoke of a league of *duodecim populi* among the Etruscans with its central sanctuary of the goddess Voltumna in the district of the city Volsinii, with its important spring cultic celebration, which seems to have had a chief official, a covenant administrator, who in one text (5.1.5) is called *sacerdos*. In addition, there was the Italian league, the Bruttian, which was also called a league of *duodecim populi* (Livy 25.1.2).

Several factors about these amphictyonies and leagues were stressed by Noth. (1) The numbers six and twelve occur with some frequency. (2) The tribal groupings were centered around and utilized a common sanctuary whose upkeep was a basic function of the league. (3) A council of official representatives from the members met at the central shrine and were responsible for its administration (in Greek the representative was called *hieromnemones*). (4) Periodic cultic festivals were held at the central sanctuary; the most important being the major yearly feast at which time the council of representatives met and expression was given to the treaty relationship of the members. (5) Union for common military protection was an element in the tribal association. (6) Amphictyonic law regulated various aspects of freedom. (7) Holy war could be carried out against members of the amphictyony for transgression of amphictyonic law.[15]

On the basis of the literary traditions concerning the twelve tribes, the biblical references to "twelve" among the neighbors of Israel, and the comparative material on Greek and Italian tribal and city leagues, Noth proceeded to reconstruct the origin, form, and functions of the pre-monarchical twelve-tribe amphictyony in ancient Israel.

Noth saw in the Yahwistic-Elohistic narrative of Joshua 24[16] the foundation story of the twelve-tribe amphictyony. According to him, the Leah and concubine tribes as well as the tribe of Benjamin[17] were already settled in Canaan before the invasion of the "house of Joseph." The

---

15. *Das System*, 39–60.

16. Noth provides an analysis of this chapter in *Das System*, 133–40; and in his commentary *Das Buch Josua*. See also Schmitt, *Der Landtag von Sichem*.

17. See n. 3 above.

twelve-tribe league came into existence after the settlement of the house of Joseph when the newcomers and the already settled tribes united. The role assigned to Joshua in Joshua 24 reflects an historical memory of his role in the establishment of the amphictyony. The location of the "Landtag von Sichem" also preserved a true historical reflection of the origin of the amphictyony at Shechem,[18] which was the first central sanctuary for the tribes. Joshua 24; Deut 11:29–30; 27; and Josh 8:30–35 reflect some of the elements in the covenant-making ceremony. Noth argued that the six Leah tribes (Reuben, Simeon, Levi, Judah, Issachar, and Zebulun) had formed a six-tribe amphictyony in the early part of the Judges era prior to the settlement of the house of Joseph. This six-tribe amphictyony had used Shechem as its central sanctuary. The tribes of Reuben, Simeon, and Levi had originally dwelt in the Samaritan mountains in the territory later occupied by the "house of Joseph" (see Genesis 34; 49:5–7).[19] This six-tribe confederation was therefore the forerunner and basis for the later twelve-tribe amphictyony. The numbers twelve and six should be seen as a reflection of the monthly and bimonthly rotation in the tribal responsibility for the upkeep of the common sanctuary and its worship.[20]

According to Noth, the Leah-amphictyony was not a Yahweh-amphictyony; neither had its members (or the tribes of Dan, Gad, Asher, and Naphtali) gone into Egypt and experienced the events of the exodus. Yahweh worship was first introduced into Palestine by the "house of Joseph" and under the latter's influence the newly created twelve-tribe alliance accepted Yahweh as the god of the amphictyony. Contact between the southern Leah-tribes and the "house of Joseph" at Kadesh prior to the latter's settlement in central Palestine was held open as a possibility by Noth.

The name "Israel" was the term used as the designation for the twelve-tribe amphictyony. Noth concluded that the older six-tribe amphictyony (the Leah-tribes) had gone under the name Israel and that this name was retained with the expansion to a twelve-tribe alliance and the

18. The importance of Shechem in the history of early Israel had figured prominently in the writings of Ernst Sellin. See his *Geschichte des israelitisch-jüdischen Volkes*, 1:98ff; "Seit welcher Zeit verehrten die nordisraelitischen Stäimme Jahwe?"; and "Wie wurde Sichern eine israelitische Stadt?"

19. Earlier references to a "smaller" than the twelve-tribe league had placed it in Hebron or Mamre. On the former, see Sayce, "Cuneiform Tablets of Tel El-Amarna," 347; and for the latter see Alt, *Der Gott der Väter*, 58–59 = *Kleine Schriften*, 1:54–55 (ET = "The God of the Fathers," 53–54).

20. *Das System*, 61–86.

The Twelve-Tribe Israelite Amphictyony

adoption of Yahwism. The reference to Israel in the famous stele inscription of the Egyptian pharaoh Merneptah referred to this six-tribe Israel and not the later constituted form.

The initial central sanctuary of Israel was Shechem (= *Tell Balatah*) located in the valley between Mt. Gerizim and Mt. Ebal.[21] Noth, however, claims that the central shrine was not so much a sanctuary as a sacred object—the ark. The ark was originally the portable or wandering sanctuary from the wilderness period that was attached to the house of Joseph. The formula "Yahweh, the god of Israel" was closely tied to the employment of the ark and to the Shechem sanctuary. The central sanctuary of the Israelite amphictyony was moved from Shechem to various other places. In his *History*,[22] Noth suggests that Bethel, Gilgal, and Shiloh functioned as the central sanctuary prior to the removal of the ark to Jerusalem by David. At the central sanctuary, a yearly festival or cultic celebration was held in which there was a public profession of faith in Yahweh, an act of covenant-making, and a proclamation of the statutes of the law.[23]

The official representatives of the tribes who met as a colloquium at the yearly festival at the central sanctuary were the twelve *nesi'im*. Several Old Testament passages speak of these representatives (Gen 25:16; Exod 22:28; Num 1:5–16; 13:4–15; 34:17–28) according to Noth. The *nasi'* was assumed by Noth to have performed in the Israelite amphictyony functions analogous to those of the *hieromnemones* in Greek amphictyonies. In an appendix to *Das System* (151–62), Noth recognized the problems involved in the use of the term *nasi'* within the Old Testament in so far as his amphictyonic theory was concerned. The usage of the term is limited almost entirely to the book of Ezekiel and the Priestly History, viz., to material from a period very late in Hebrew history. Nonetheless, Noth argued that the office was very old and that the priestly writer had taken over and incorporated in his work an old and independent list of the early tribal *nesi'im* now found in Num 1:5–16. The *nasi'* was not a priest but a tribal representative; and Exod 22:27, which prohibits the cursing of a *nasi'* suggests that the term was a *terminus technicus*.

Between the writing of *Das System* (1930) and his *Geschichte Israels* (1950), Noth developed his theory of the all-Israel office of "judge,"[24]

---

21. The sacred sanctuary was the very ancient tree shrine east of the city of Shechem; Noth, *History of Israel*, 91.
22. Ibid., 94–96.
23. Ibid., 92–93, 100–101.
24. See his "Das Amt des 'Richters Israels'"; ET = "The Office of 'Judge of Israel.'"

whose function was that of the central judicial official who publicly proclaimed the law and oversaw its observance.[25] The term "judge of Israel" (*shophet yisra'el*) is found only once in the Old Testament (Mic 4:14). Noth argued, however, that the "minor judges" mentioned in Judg 10:1–5 and 12:7–15 are to be distinguished from the "savior judges" who appear elsewhere in Judges. The so-called "major judges" were not all judges in the judicial sense but were incorporated as judges by the deuteronomistic editor because Jephthah appeared in both the list of judicial judges and that of the charismatic tribal leaders. Noth assumed that Judg 10:1–15 and 12:7–15 were based on official recollections of the period and that the minor judges noted there functioned as legal authorities over the amphictyony.

On the analogy of the Greek amphictyony, Noth argued that the Israelite tribal alliance possessed its divine or amphictyonic law, which regulated the common cult and perhaps ordered tribal conduct and the relationship between the members of the amphictyony. A deposit of this amphictyonic law is now found in parts of the Book of the Covenant. The codification or at least formulation of many of the Israelite laws could thus go back to the pre-monarchical period of the Judges or be developed from the early beginnings of this period.[26]

In addition to the accepted or "federal" law of the amphictyony, Noth argued that there also existed customary or unwritten law (*nomoi agrapoi*). The tribal association was committed to punish violation of the amphictyonic laws and if need be to call out the tribes to take punitive action against the transgressor. This capability to carry out a "holy war" against one of its own members lies behind the campaign against the tribe of Benjamin in Judges 19–21 because of the rape-murder of a Levite's concubine in Gibeah. After the failure of Benjamin to punish the crime, the tribes mustered in action against the Benjaminites.

Noth argued that at the time of the twelve-tribe amphictyony there existed a southern six-tribe amphictyony with a central sanctuary at Mamre near Hebron. This six-tribe league was composed of Simeon, Judah, Caleb, Othniel, Jerahmeel, and Kain (the Kenites). Judah and Simeon thus held membership in two tribal amphictyonies.[27]

---

25. *History of Israel*, 101–3.

26. Worked out more fully in his *Die Gesetze im Pentateuch* (1940); ET = *The Laws in the Pentateuch and Other Essays*, 1–107.

27. *Das System*, 86–108.

The Twelve-Tribe Israelite Amphictyony

Noth recognized that his theory of a tribal amphictyony during the period of the Judges carried consequential ramifications for the history and religion of ancient Israel. Only a few of these were mentioned in *Das System* although in later works Noth developed many of these concepts. A few of the consequences of his theory as noted in *Das System* may be referred to here. (1) The origin of kingship in Israel must be seen as an outgrowth of the amphictyonic structure. The amphictyonic organization laid the foundations for political structures and Saul, the first king of Israel, was primarily a charismatic leader of the amphictyonic tribes. (2) The amphictyonic concept supports the idea of a national Yahweh religion and a strong allegiance to Yahweh as the national god. (3) The prophetic movement in later times was strongly dependent upon the amphictyonic outlook and ideals. (4) The traditions of the patriarchs, Sinai, and the conquest of the land have their settings in the amphictyonic cult. (5) The amphictyonic structure stressed the prominence of one sanctuary. David sought to make Jerusalem into the central sanctuary by bringing the ark to Jerusalem, thus keeping operative the idea of Israel as the people of Yahweh as well as a national, political entity. (6) The concept of Israel as the people of Yahweh and the stress on the importance of the central sanctuary reasserted itself in the deuteronomic reformation under Josiah in the seventh century.[28]

In many of his later writings, Noth developed the themes and concepts already found in *Das System*. In his *Die Überlieferungsgeschichte des Pentateuch*,[29] Noth examined the growth of the pentateuchal themes out of the traditions of the amphictyony. His study *Die Gesetze im Pentateuch*,[30] developed the concept of the law as a constitutive feature of the amphictyonic system, which he argued was neither removed nor replaced by the development of the national state or the breakup of this state into the states of Israel and Judah.[31] In his *Geschichte Israels*, Noth accepted the consequences of his theory that the patriarchal, exodus, wilderness, Sinai, and settlement traditions were developed in the amphictyonic cult.

---

28. *Das System*, 109–21.

29. ET = *The History of the Pentateuchal Traditions*.

30. See n. 26 above.

31. "This institution (the tribal amphictyony) was neither replaced nor removed by the states later brought into being on the territory occupied by the people of Israel . . . neither did the regulations and functions of the state consciously displace that older institution." *The Laws in the Pentateuch*, 29.

That is, he began his history with the period of the Judges and treated the earlier traditions within the context of amphictyonic life.[32]

The Acceptance and Modifications of Noth's Amphictyonic Theory

George W. Anderson has remarked that "at least as many students of the Old Testament have accepted the amphictyonic theory without reading *Das System* . . . as have rejected Mowinckel's hypothesis of an enthronement festival without reading the second volume of *Psalmenstudien*."[33] What he is implying is the fact of almost universal acceptance. As a rule, Noth's theory has been accepted without question. Some scholars while accepting the general theory have sought to modify some of the details.

John Bright, as an example of enthusiastic acceptance and extension of the concept, has concluded that "the origins of the amphictyonic system, like those of Yahwism itself, reach back to Sinai. The amphictyony was a sacral league formed in covenant with Yahweh, perfectly expressive of primitive Yahwistic faith. If Yahwism originated in the desert (as it certainly did), we must conclude that the covenant society did also, for Yahwism and covenant are coterminus."[34] This statement also seeks to modify Noth's theory of the origin of the amphictyony by placing its origin in the wilderness period prior to the settlement of the tribes in Palestine. A similar modification is stressed by G. Ernest Wright. For Bright and Wright the terminus a quo for the origin of the Israelite amphictyony is not, as it was for Noth, the time of the settlement in Canaan but rather the period immediately after the exodus from Egypt.

An extensive attempt to re-create the history of Israel from the time of Moses until the establishment of the Davidic dynasty along the lines of Noth's amphictyonic theory has been made by Murray Newman.[35] He argues for the following amphictyonic units in early Israel: a six-tribe Leah amphictyony centered around Shechem in the fourteenth century, a period of association at Kadesh between the southern remnants of the Leah-amphictyony and the "house of Joseph" after the latter's exodus

---

32. See *History of Israel*, 110–38.

33. Anderson, "Israel: Amphictyony," 138–39.

34. Bright, *A History of Israel*, 1st ed., 145–46. In the 3rd ed. (p. 168), Bright changed "amphictyony" to "covenant league."

35. *The People of the Covenant*.

from Egypt in the mid-thirteenth century, a twelve-tribe league formed at Shechem, and a six-tribe league at Hebron.

Some scholars have modified Noth's theory in a different direction. Stressing the "Song of Deborah" with its reference to only ten tribes (Judges 5) at the expense of the twelve-tribe lists, Sigmund Mowinckel,[36] Artur Weiser,[37] and others[38] argue for a ten-tribe amphictyony during the period of the Judges. Mowinckel considers the twelve-tribe scheme to be post-Davidic in origin.

Many scholars have accepted Noth's theory of the amphictyony and proceeded to build interpretive systems on this basis, which seek to expound wide areas of Old Testament studies in light of the theory. Only a few of these may be mentioned here. Gerhard von Rad argued for the Holy War as a basic element in the tribal amphictyony and its ideology as a continuing influence in ancient Israel.[39] The convenant festival that Noth postulated as the basic annual amphictyonic ritual has provided scholars with an idea that in most Old Testament studies has become an overriding (overbearing?) concern. This covenant festival has been taken by Artur Weiser as the interpretive key to the book of Psalms.[40] H. Graf Reventlow has argued that some of the offices of the amphictyony continued in existence after the founding of the monarchy. One such was the tribal "prosecutor."[41] The function of the covenant-mediator in the amphictyonic cult has been used as the interpretive key to understanding the prophets. Hans-Joachim Kraus has argued that the prophets were successors to the mosaic and amphictyonic covenant mediator whose primary responsibility was the proclamation of the covenant law.[42] James Muilenberg has postulated the existence of a succession of prophets who filled the "office" of prophet in terms of the amphictyonic mediator.[43] Reventlow has taken this idea to its logical conclusion by arguing that the prophets were cultic functionaries within the covenant festival ritual whose task was interpretation, application, and proclamation of the cov-

---

36. Mowinckel, *Zur Frage nach dokumentarischen Quellen in Joshua 13–19*, esp. 20–23; and Mowinckel, "'Rahelstämme' und 'Leastämme.'"

37. Weiser, "Das Deborahlied."

38. Schunck, *Benjamin*, 48–57.

39. Von Rad, *Der Heilige Krieg im Alten Israel*; ET = *Holy War in Ancient Israel*.

40. Weiser, *Die Psalmen*; ET = *The Psalms*, esp. 35–52.

41. Reventlow, "Das Amt des *Mazkir*."

42. Kraus, *Die prophetische Verkündigung des Rechts in Israel*.

43. Muilenburg, "The 'Office' of the Prophet in Ancient Israel."

enant and its law.⁴⁴ Likewise, Old Testament law has been placed back within the covenant renewal festival and subsequently efforts have been made to trace the law materials back to the period of the Judges.⁴⁵ Noth's theory of the amphictyony and covenant law has been related to Near Eastern history and life through the comparison of the Hebrew covenant with ancient Near Eastern treaties. The first to do this was George E. Mendenhall⁴⁶ who compared the biblical materials to the Hittite state treaties. The fullest treatment of this subject is by Klaus Baltzer⁴⁷ who traces the theme of covenant and covenant renewal throughout the biblical traditions.⁴⁸

Recent Criticism of the Amphictyonic Theory

Some opposition to Noth's amphictyonic theory or to the idea of any amphictyony in the period of the Judges has on occasion been expressed. H. H. Rowley in his article on "Israel, history of" in the *Interpreter's Dictionary of the Bible* wrote the following:

> It has been suggested that the Israelite tribes formed an amphictyony, pledged by a religious oath to help one another, with an amphictyonic shrine as the center of their confederation. One may doubt whether there was any twelve-tribe amphictyony at this date, for one finds little evidence of it in the period of the judges. At the same time, the prominence of shrines in the narrative must be recognized, and it seems more likely that at various times there were alliances of groups of tribes, these alliances being sealed at sanctuaries. The variety of shrines mentioned

---

44. Reventlow, *Das Amt des Propheten bei Amos*; Reventlow, *Wächter über Israel*; and Reventlow, *Liturgie und prophetisches Ich bei Jermia*. For a similar but modified view, see Brueggemann, *Tradition for Crisis*.

45. See Stamm and Andrew, *The Ten Commandments in Recent Research*, esp. 35-75.

46. Mendenball, "Ancient Oriental and Biblical Law"; and Mendenhall, "Covenant Forms in Israelite Tradition."

47. Baltzer, *Das Bundesformular*; ET = *The Covenant Formulary*.

48. For a survey of the issues, see McCarthy, *Old Testament Covenant*. For a sharp criticism of the emphasis on covenant in Old Testament studies, see Perlitt, *Bundestheologie im Alten Testament*. For a restatement of the significance of the covenant concept, see Hillers, *Covenant*.

seems to tell against an amphictyony of all the tribes with a central amphictyonic shrine.[49]

A number of important studies have recently been published that are extremely critical of Noth's theory of a twelve-tribe amphityony.[50] Practically every element in the amphictyonic theory has been challenged.

The Greek Amphictyonies and Italian Leagues

The employment of evidence gathered from the Greek and Italian tribal groupings has been challenged on a number of points. Firstly, the Greek and Italian leagues were far more heterogeneous than Noth admitted. Part of his use of this comparative material was postulated on the supposed recurrence of the numbers six and twelve. However, these leagues were far from homogeneous entities and much of the supposed homogeneity has resulted from making comparisons with the twelve-tribe Delphic league and imposing the Delphic structure where it wasn't applicable. Apparently no set or particular number of tribes seems to have been a prerequisite for the leagues.[51] The Calaurian league had seven members; the Boeotian at various times had ten, eleven, or twelve members. The Boeotarchian league had eleven members while the second Achaean league began with two members and then went from four to seven to ten members within six years. The Lycian league had a membership of twenty-three cities. The numbers six and twelve are not therefore firmly fixed elements in the leagues reflecting monthly or bimonthly tribal responsibility for the care of a central sanctuary. Secondly, all the Greek amphictyonies and Italian leagues were Indo-European and not Semitic in background.[52] Tribal and city leagues were present in Norway, Denmark, and Sweden but all of these are ethnically and linguistically different from the early

---

49. Rowley, "Israel, History of," 753–54.

50. Herrmann, "Das Werden Israels"; Orlinsky, "The Tribal System of Israel and Related Groups in the Period of the Judges"; Smend, *Jahwekrieg und Stämmebund* (ET = *Yahweh War and Tribal Confederation*); Irwin, "Le sanctuaire central israelite avant l'establissement de la monarchie"; Rahtjen, "Philistine and Hebrew Amphictyonies"; Fohrer, "Alten Testament—'Amphiktyonie' und 'Bund'"; Mayes, "Amphictyony and Covenant"; Anderson, "Israel: Amphictyony"; and de Vaux, "La these de L'amphictyonie Israelite."

51. Rahtjen, "Philistine and Hebrew Amphictyonies," 103–4.

52. Fohrer, "Alten Testament—'Amphiktyonie' und 'Bund,'" 92; and de Vaux, "La these," 420.

Hebrew tribes. The closest contact with Indo-Europeans was experienced by the Phoenicians and Philistines. Nothing is ever heard among the former that would suggest the influence of Indo-European amphictyonic structures although Rahtjen[53] has argued for the existence of a five member Philistine amphictyony. Thirdly, the Greek city-state leagues reflect a culture radically different from the nomadic and semi-nomadic culture of the early Hebrew tribes.[54] Fourthly, most of the Greek amphictyonies date from the mid or late first millennium whereas the supposed Hebrew amphictyony would have belonged to the last quarter of the second millennium. This chronological difference raises serious questions about the possibility of comparison.[55]

The biblical references to non-Israelite groups of twelve noted by Ewald among the Ishmaelites (Gen 25:15–16), Edomites (Gen 36:10–14), and Horites (Gen 36:20–28) can no longer be classified as "the result of certain established organizations such as were customary in tribal societies which were still lacking settled political institutions."[56] Nothing is said in these texts about amphictyonic organization. Elsewhere in the Old Testament, there are references to groups of five-a coalition of five kings in Genesis 14, five Midianite kings (Num 31:8), five Amorite kings (Josh 10:5), or five Philistine city states but no one would assume that on the basis of these references, one should expound a theory of five tribe amphictyonies.

William W. Hallo has argued that the amphictyonic structure was current in early Sumerian times.[57] During the third dynasty of Ur at the end of the third millennium, the sanctuary at Nippur functioned as a 'national' shrine for the Sumerian and Akkadian cities that were required to contribute to the support of the national shrine. This example, however, does not parallel the type of conditions presupposed by Noth during the Hebrew amphictyonic period but rather reflects the type of provincial administration set up by Solomon in his division of Israel into twelve districts.[58]

53. See reference in note 45.
54. Fohrer, "Alten Testament—'Amphiktyonie' und 'Bund,'" 93.
55. De Vaux, "La these," 420–21.
56. Noth, *History of Israel*, 87.
57. Hallo, "A Sumerian Amphictyony"; Hallo, "Royal Hymns and Mesopotamian Unity"; and Hallo and Simpson, *The Ancient Near East*, 38–39; 2nd ed. (1998).
58. De Vaux, "La these," 421.

The Tribal Lists and the Number Twelve

In his discussion of the tribal lists and the employment of the number twelve, Noth says that the twelve-tribe references are "entweder einfache Wiedergabe einer naturgewachsenen historischen Situation oder reine Theorie."[59] This is obviously presenting the issue in an overdrawn manner to prejudice the case in his favor. The tribal lists in the Hexateuch are far less homogeneous and stylized than Noth admitted. In the story of the birth of the offspring of Jacob (Gen 29:31—30:25; 35:16–21), one actually has narrated the birth of thirteen offspring, not counting Ephraim and Manasseh. The thirteenth is the tribe of Dinah, which figures in the story of the assault on Shechem (Genesis 34). Deuteronomy 33 refers to twelve tribes with Joseph divided into Ephraim and Manasseh, with Levi retained but described as a religious tribe, but with no reference to Simeon. Judges 5, which Mowinckel has used to reconstruct a ten-tribe confederation, of course does not reflect Noth's twelve-tribe pattern. These passages therefore reflect schemes of tribal listings which Noth did not take into serious consideration.

The tribal lists found in Genesis 49, Numbers 1, 26, and Joshua 13–19 are in all probability not lists reflecting the historical reality of a twelve-tribe league from the period of the Judges. The individual songs of the tribes now found in Genesis 49 and Deuteronomy 3 have been shown to have existed originally as independent units and to date from various periods in early Hebrew history.[60] Their original purpose cannot therefore have been to enumerate the membership in a tribal amphictyony. Some other form than a collection of loosely associated tribal songs would surely have been a better means to depict the membership of a tribal amphictyony and a more natural one had such an amphictyony existed.

The tribal lists of Joshua 13–19, upon which Noth relied very little, are a collection of materials of various sorts, some boundary lists and some city lists, from various periods in Israelite history. The lists dealing with the tribal holdings of Benjamin, Manasseh, Ephraim, Zebulun, Asher, and Naphtali could come from the period prior to the monarchy.[61] The last editing of this material in Joshua could reflect the priestly con-

---

59. Noth, *Das System*, 41.

60. Zobel, *Stammesspruch und Geschichte*; and Gunneweg, "Über den Sitz im Leben der sog. Stammessprüche."

61. See Aharoni, *The Land of the Bible*, 227–39.

cept of the division of the land in the Priestly History written during the exile. Such a depiction would parallel Ezekiel's ideal allocation of the land in Ezek 47:13—48:35.[62] The tribal lists in the book of Numbers have traditionally been attributed to the priestly historian and Noth's arguments for their antiquity are dependent upon an acceptance of his amphictyonic theory.

The appearance of the number 12 in the tribal lists may be a reflection of the symbolic significance of the number. Twelve was a symbolic number among the Greeks and Italians and is frequently found in diverse cultures with a symbolic significance.[63] Many references in the Bible should be seen as reflection of the symbolism of the number (Gen 22:20–24; 25:12–16; 36:10–14; 1 Kgs 7:44; 10:20; 19:19, and elsewhere). The New Testament and later Jewish literature reflect this symbolic quality of the number.

The Central Sanctuary

Basic to the concept of the amphictyony is the existence of a central sanctuary. Noth hypothesized that the presence of the ark denoted the central sanctuary for the amphictyony. Where the ark was, there was the central sanctuary. Noth concluded that at least four sanctuaries served as the central amphictyonic sanctuary: Shechem, Bethel, Gilgal, and Shiloh.[64] There is no Old Testament reference to the ark at Shechem and even the foundation story of Noth's amphictyony (Joshua 24) contains not a single reference to the ark. Much of the material that Noth used (Deut 11:29–30; 27:4–8; 27:11–13) to reconstruct the Shechem ceremony was probably originally statements with reference to Gilgal.[65] W. F. Albright, while accepting the concept of an amphictyony, has denied that Shechem ever played the role of central sanctuary.[66]

The ark is mentioned as residing for a time at Bethel (Judges 20:27–28); however in the narrative complex in which this reference appears the

62. This is the position of Mowinckel, *Zur Frage*.

63. De Vaux, "La these," 422–23. See also Heiler, *Erscheinungformen*, 161–71; and Jaubert, "Le symbolisme des Douze."

64. Dus has argued that the ark was a wandering sanctuary even after the settlement of the tribes and he argues for a number of stations for the ark. See his "Der Brauch"; and "Noch zum Brauch."

65. See Eissfeldt, "Gilgal or Shechem?"

66. Albright, *Archaeology and the Religion of Israel*, 103–5.

The Twelve-Tribe Israelite Amphictyony

tribes are said to gather at Mizpah (Judg 20:1) which seems strange if one assumes that the presence of the ark was essential for the rallying of the tribes in amphictyonic assembly.

The presence of the ark at Gilgal is noted in Joshua 3–4; however there is no reference to the ark at Gilgal during the period of the Judges.[67] When Saul assembled the people at Gilgal (1 Sam 10:8; 11:14–15; 13; 15:12; 21–33), the ark was apparently still in the hands of the Philistines or at least at Kiriath-jearim not Gilgal.

Shiloh has far more claim to have been the central sanctuary if the presence of the ark constituted the decisive factor. The ark was at Shiloh under the care of the family of Eli at the end of the period of the Judges and was captured when taken into battle against the Philistines. Many scholars have denied that Shiloh even functioned as an amphictyonic center comparable to Noth's claim.[68] The texts make no reference to amphictyonic or tribal assemblies at Shiloh.

Rudolf Smend has recently argued that the ark was associated with the Rachel tribes and warfare but not with the amphictyonic element that he claims had its origin with the Leah group.[69] A recent and very attractive theory has been proposed which argues that the ark at Shiloh was associated with an anti-Philistine military league rather than with a cultic amphictyony.[70]

What is obvious from the biblical traditions is that there were a number of important shrines in use during the period of the Judges but one cannot prove a theory of a central amphictyonic shrine.

The Amphictyonic Law

Noth argued that the amphictyonic league in early Israel possessed its written and unwritten law, which regulated its common life, and that the office of judge in early Israel was an important and central amphictyonic office. If this be the case then there are some interesting lacuna in early Israelite law as this has been preserved. (1) There are no laws in the Old Testament that deal with the creation, organization, or structure of an

---

67. On Gilgal, see Kraus, "Gilgal."
68. Irwin, "Le sanctuaire," 176–78; de Vaux, "La these," 427–30.
69. Smend, *Jahwekrieg und Stämmebund*, 76–97.
70. Maier, *Das altisraelitische Ladeheiligtum*; see Smend, *Jahwekrieg und Stämmebund*, 43–75.

amphictyony or with the tribal responsibilities toward each other. (2) In fact, there is no word for amphictyony in the Hebrew Language. (3) There are no laws in the Old Testament that regulate and stipulate the functions of the central "judge of Israel." In fact, the term only occurs in the late passage of Mic 4:14. (4) Noth's case for the minor judges as central amphictyonic functionaries (Judg 10:1–5; 12:7–15) rests on the slightest of evidence. These lists contain some very legendary material that suggests that it does not derive from any official list of successive amphictyonic judges. In addition the years covered by these minor judges only totals 76, far too few to reflect the total list of judges for the so-called amphictyonic period.[71] This list of minor judges was probably added to the description of the major judges by the Deuteronomistic editor in order to bring the total number of judges to twelve.

Combined Amphictyonic Action

When one reads the book of Judges, there is little to suggest that the tribes rallied in amphictyonic fashion to their common defense. What one finds is concerted action occasionally by two or more tribes in the area threatened. "It is beyond every doubt that, apart from the battle of Deborah, only single alliances participated in the Yahweh wars of the time of Judges, and not Israel as a whole."[72] Even in the song of Deborah, only ten tribes are referred to and in the narrative account of the same battle in Judges 4 only the tribes of Naphtali and Zebulun are mentioned. Smend has argued that the concept of a joint Yahweh war was developed among the Rachel-tribes but was not amphictyonic in origin.[73]

In one episode, action is said to have been taken by all the tribes against one of its members (Judges 19–20). Noth made a great deal of this episode since one of the functions of an amphictyony was the policing of its members. However subsequent analysis has shown that this episode originally involved only a time of warfare between the two tribes of Ephraim and Benjamin.[74]

---

71. See Smend, *Jahwekrieg und Stämmebund*, 43–75.
72. Ibid., 19; see 13–25.
73. Ibid., 106.
74. Eissfeldt, "Der geschichtliche Hintergrundlicher."

The Amphictyonic Council

Noth argued that the individual tribes were represented at amphictyonic councils by delegated tribal representatives. This representative was the so-called *nasi'*. The passages which Noth utilized to support this theory came from Ezekiel and the priestly history.[75] No evidence exists in the early material for any such council. Orlinsky's comment is here to the point: "It is indeed noteworthy that nowhere in the book that is alleged to have sprung from an amphictyonic society, viz., the book of Judges, is the term *nasi'* found."[76]

Conclusion

The following paragraph written by de Vaux a few months before his death in the summer of 1971 summarizes the collapse of the amphictyonic theory and points to the need for a re-examination of the period of the Judges:

> All this research leads to the same conclusion: the proposed parallel between the grouping of the tribes of Israel and the Greek amphictyonies is not justified. The difference between their milieus is improbable from the outset. The essential features of an amphictyony are not found in Israel: one cannot prove the existence of a central sanctuary nor of a council of tribal delegates. There is no historical example of a joint action by all the tribes. Those follow common laws and habits, but there is no amphictyonic law. If it were proven that there was a central judge of the tribes, it would be an unknown function of the Greek amphictyonies. Employing the word "amphictyony" in connection with Israel can only generate confusion and give a false idea of the relations between the tribes. It must be abandoned.[77]

75. See Speiser, "Background and Function of the Biblical *Nasi.*"
76. Orlinsky, "The Tribal System" 14.
77. De Vaux, "La these," 436. "Toutes ces recherches conduisent à la même conclusion: le rapprochement qúon a proposé entre le groupement des tribus d'Israël et les amphictyonies grecques n'est pas justifié. La différence des milieux le rend dès l'abord improbable. Les traits essentiels d'une amphictyonie ne se retrouvent pas en Israël: on ne peut pas prouver l'existence d'un sanctuaire central ni d'un conseil des délégués des tribus. On n'a aucun exemple historique d'une action concertée de toutes les tribus. Celles-ci suivent des lois et des coutumes communes, mais il ne s'agit pas d'un droit amphictyonique. S'il était prouvé qu'il y a eu un juge central des tribus, ce serait une fonction inconnue des amphictyonies grecques. L'emploi du mot 'amphictyonie' à

Bibliography

Aharoni, Yohanan. *The Land of the Bible: A Historical Geography*. Translated by A. F. Rainey. Philadelphia: Westminster, 1967. 2nd ed., 1979.

Albright, W. F. *Archaeology and the Religion of Israel*. 1946. Reprinted with an Introduction by Theodore J. Lewis. OTL. Louisville: Westminster John Knox, 2006.

Alt, Albrcht. "The God of the Fathers." In *Essays on Old Testament History and Religion*, 3–86. Translated by R. A. Wilson. Oxford: Blackwell, 1966.

―――. *Der Gott der Väter*. Stuttgart: Kohlhammer, 1929. Reprinted as "Der Gott der Väter." In *Kleine Schriften zur Geschichte des Volkes Israel*, vol. 1, 1–78. Munich: Beck, 1953.

―――. "Israel, politische Geschichte." In *RGG²*, 3:438–39. Tübingen: Mohr/Siebeck, 1929.

―――. *Die Landnahme der Israeliten in Palästina: Territorialgeschichtliche Studien*. Sonderdruck aus dem Reformationsprogramm der Universität Leipzig, 1925. Reprinted as "Die Landnahme der Israeliten in Palästina." In *Kleine Schriften zur Geschichte des Volkes Israel*, vol. 1, 89–125. Munich: Beck, 1953.

―――. "The Settlement of the Israelites in Palestine." In *Essays on Old Testament History and Religion*, 133–69. Translated by R. A. Wilson. Oxford: Blackwell, 1966.

Anderson, George W. "Israel: Amphictyony: 'AM, KAHAL, 'EDAH." In *Translating and Understanding the Old Testament*, edited by H. F. Frank and W. L. Reed, 135–51. Nashville: Abingdon, 1970.

Baltzer, Klaus. *Das Bundesformular*. WMANT 4. Neukirchen-Vluyn: Neukirchener, 1960. (ET= *The Covenant Formulary*. Translated by David E. Green. Philadelphia: Fortress, 1970.)

Brueggemann, Walter. *Tradition for Crisis: A Study in Hosea*. Richmond: John Knox, 1968.

Bürgel, H. *Die pylaeisch-delphische Amphiktyonie*. Munich: Ackermann, 1877.

Busolt, Georg, and H. Swoboda. *Griechische Staatskunde*. Handbuch der Alterswissenschaft 4.1.1. Munich: Beck.

Cauer, G. "Amphiktyonia." In *Pauly's Real-Encyclopedia der classischen Altertumswissenschaft*, edited by Georg Wissowa, 1:1904–35. Stuttgart: Metzler, 1894.

Dus, Jan. "Der Brauch der Ladewanderung im alten Israel." *Theologische Zeitschrift* 17 (1961) 1–16.

―――. "Noch zum Brauch der 'Ladewanderung.'" *VT* 13 (1963) 126–32.

Eissfeldt, Otto. "Der geschichtliche Hintergrundlicher Erzählung von Gibeas Schandtat." In *Festschrift Georg Beer zum 70. Geburtstage*, edited by Artur Weiser, 19–40. Stuttgart: Kohlhammer, 1935. Reprinted in *Kleine Schriften*, 2:64–80. Tübingen: Mohr/Siebeck, 1963.

―――. "Gilgal or Shechem?" In *Proclamation and Presence*, edited by J. I. Durham and J. R. Porter, 90–101. London: SCM, 1970.

---

propos d'Israël ne peut qu'engendrer la confusion et donner une fausse idée des relations que les tribus avaient entre elles. Il doit être abandonné."

Ewald, Heinrich. *Geschichte des Volkes Israels.* Vol. 1, *Einleitung in die Geschichte des Volkes Israels.* 3rd ed. Göttingen: Dieterich, 1864.
———. *The History of the Israel.* Translated by Russell Martineau. 1869. Reprinted, Eugene, OR: Wipf & Stock, 2004.
Fohrer, Georg. "Alten Testament—'Amphiktyonie' und 'Bund.'" *TLZ* 91 (1966) 801–16; 893–904. Reprinted in *Studien zur alttestamentlichen Theologie und Geschichte (1949–1966)*, 84–119. BZAW 115. Berlin: de Gruyter, 1969.
Freeman, E. A. *The History of Federal Government in Greece and Italy.* 2nd ed. New York: Macmillan, 1893.
Gunkel, Hermann. *Genesis.* 3rd ed. HKAT. Göttingen: Vandenhoeck & Ruprecht, 1910.
Gunneweg, A. H. J. "Über den Sitz im Leben der sog. Stammessprüche." *ZAW* 76 (1964) 245–54.
Hallo, William W. "Royal Hymns and Mesopotamian Unity." *JCS* 17 (1963) 112–18.
———. "A Sumerian Amphictyony." *JCS* 14 (1960) 89–96.
Hallo, William W., and W. Kelly Simpson. *The Ancient Near East: A History.* New York: Harcourt, Brace, Jovanovich, 1971. 2nd ed., 1998.
Harland, J. Penrose. "The Calaurian Amphictyony." *American Journal of Archaeology* 29 (1925) 160–71.
Heiler, Friedrich. *Erscheinungformen und Wesen der Religion.* Die Religionen der Menschheit 1. Stuttgart: Kohlhammer, 1961.
Herrmann, Siegfried. "Das Werden Israels." *TLZ* 87 (1962) 561–74.
Hillers, Delbert R. *Covenant: The History of a Biblical Idea.* Baltimore: Johns Hopkins University Press, 1969.
Irwin, W. H. "Le sanctuaire central israelite avant l'establissement de la monarchie." *Revue Biblique* 72 (1965) 161–84.
Jaubert, Annie. "La symbolisme des Douze." In *Hommages à A. Dupont-Sommer*, edited by A. Caquot and M. Philonenko, 453–60. Paris: Adrien-Maisonneuve, 1971.
Kraus, Hans-Joachim. "Gilgal: Ein Beitrag zur Kultusgeschichte Israels." *VT* 1 (1951) 181–99.
———. *Die prophetische Verkündigung des Rechts in Israel.* Theologische Studien 51. Zollikon: Evangelischer, 1957.
Maier, Johann. *Das altisraelitische Ladeheiligtum.* BZAW 93. Berlin: Töpelmann, 1965.
Mayes, A. D. H. "Amphictyony and Covenant: A Study of Israel in the Pre-Monarchy Period." PhD diss., University of Edinburgh, 1969.
McCarthy, Dennis J. *Old Testament Covenant: A Survey of Current Opinions.* Growing Points in Theology. Oxford: Blackwell, 1971.
Mendenball, George E. "Ancient Oriental and Biblical Law." *BA* 17 (1954) 26–46.
———. "Covenant Forms in Israelite Tradition." *BA* 17 (1954) 50–76; reprinted in *The Biblical Archaeologist Reader III*, ed. by E. F. Campbell and D. N. Freedman, 3–53. Garden City, NY: Doubleday, 1970.
Mowinckel, Sigmund. "'Rahelstämme' und 'Leastämme.'" In *Von Ugarit nach Qumran: Beiträge zur alttestamentlichen und altorientalischen: Otto Eissfeldt zum 1. September 1957 dargebracht von Freunden und Schülern*, edited by Johannes Hempel and Leonhard Rost, 129–50. BZAW 77. Berlin: Töpelmann, 1958.
———. *Zur Frage nach dokumentarischen Quellen in Joshua 13–19.* Avhandlinger utgitt av det Norske Videnskaps-Akademi I Oslo. II. Hist.-filos. Klasse, 1946, no. 1. Oslo: Dybwad, 1946.

Muilenburg, James. "The 'Office' of the Prophet in Ancient Israel." In *The Bible in Modern Scholarship*, edited by J. Philip Hyatt, 74–97. Nashville: Abingdon, 1965.

Newman, Murray. *The People of the Covenant: A Study of Israel from Moses to the Monarchy*. Nashville: Abingdon, 1962.

Noth, Martin. "Das Amt des 'Richters Israels.'" In *Festschrift für Alfred Bertholet zum 80. Geburtstag gewidmet zum Kollegen und Freundens*, edited by Walter Baumgartner et al., 404–17. Tübingen: Mohr/Siebeck, 1959.

———. *Das Buch Josua*. 2nd ed. Handbuch zum Alten Testament 7. Tübingen: Mohr/Siebeck, 1953.

———. *The History of Israel*. 2nd ed. Translated by S. Godman and P. R. Ackroyd. New York: Harper & Brothers, 1960.

———. *The History of the Pentateuchal Traditions*. Translated by Bernhard W. Anderson. Englewood Cliffs, NJ: Prentice-Hall, 1971.

——— *The Laws in the Pentateuch and Other Essays*. Translated by D. R. Ap-Thomas. Edinburgh: Oliver & Boyd, 1966.

———. *Das System der zwölf Stämme Israels*. BWANT 4/1. Stuttgart: Kohlhammer, 1930.

———. *Die Überlieferungsgeschichte des Pentateuch*. Stuttgart: Kohlhammer, 1948.

Orlinsky, Harry M. "The Tribal System of Israel and Related Groups in the Period of the Judges." *Oriens Antiquus* 1 (1962) 11–20. Reprinted in *Studies and Essays in Honor of Abraham A. Neuman*, edited by Meir Ben-Horin et al., 375–87. Leiden: Brill, 1962.

Perlitt, Lothar. *Bundstheologie im Alten Testament*. WMANT 36. Neukirchen-Vluyn: Neukirchener, 1969.

Rad, Gerhard von. *Der Heilige Krieg im Alten Israel*. Abhandlungen zur Theologie des Alten und Neuen Testaments 20. Zurich: Zwingli, 1951.

———. *Holy War in Ancient Israel*. Translated and edited by Marva Dawn. 1991. Reprinted, Eugene, OR: Wipf & Stock, 2000.

Rahtjen, B. D. "Philistine and Hebrew Amphictyonies." *Journal of Near Eastern Studies* 24 (1965) 100–104.

Reventlow, H. Graf. "Das Amt des *Mazkir*." *Theologische Zeitschrift* 15 (1959) 161–75.

———. *Das Amt des Propheten bei Amos*. FRLANT 80. Göttingen: Vandenhoeck & Ruprecht, 1962.

———. *Liturgie und prophetisches Ich bei Jermia*. Gutersloh: Mohn, 1963.

———. *Wächter über Israel: Ezechiel und seine Tradition*. BZAW 82. Berlin: Töpelmann, 1962.

Rowley, H. H. "Israel, History of." In *IDB*, 2:750–65.

Sayce, A. H. "The Cuneiform Tablets of Tel El-Amarna . . ." *Proceedings of the Society of Bibiblical Archaeology* 11 (1888/89) 347.

Schmitt, Götz. *Der Landtag von Sichem*. Arbeiten zur Theologie 1/15. Stuttgart: Calwer, 1964.

Schunck, Klaus-Dietrich. *Benjamin: Untersuchungen zur Entstehung und Geschichte eines israelitischen Stammes*. BZAW 86. Berlin: Töpelmann, 1963.

Sellin, Ernst. *Geschichte des israelitisch-jüdischen Volkes*. Vol. 1. Leipzig: Quelle & Meyer, 1924.

———. "Seit welcher Zeit verehrten die nordisraelitischen Stäimme Jahwe?" In *Oriental Studies Published in Commemoration of the Fortieth Anniversary (1883–1923) of Paul Haupt as Director of the Oriental Seminary of the Johns Hopkins University*,

Baltimore, Md., edited by Cyrus Adler and Aaron Ember, 124–34. Baltimore: Johns Hopkins Press, 1926.

———. *Wie wurde Sichem eine israelitische Stadt?* Leipzig: Deichert, 1922.

Smend, Rudolf. *Jahwekrieg und Stämmebund: Erwägungen zur ältesten Geschichte Israels.* FRLANT 84. Göttingen: Vandenhoeck & Ruprecht, 1963.

———. *Yahweh War and Tribal Confederation: Reflections upon Israel's Earliest History.* Translated by Max Gray Rogers. Nashville: Abingdon, 1970.

Speiser, E. A. "Background and Function of the Biblical *Nasi.*" *CBQ* 25 (1963) 111–17. Reprinted in *Oriental and Biblical Studies*, 113–22. Philadelphia: University of Pennsylvania Press, 1967.

Stamm, J. J., and M. E. Andrew. *The Ten Commandments in Recent Research.* SBT 2/2. Naperville, IL: Allenson, 1967.

Szanto, Emil. *Die griechischen Phylen.* Sitzungsberichte Akademie der Wissenschaften in Wien 144. Vienna: Gerold, 1902.

Vaux, Roland de. "La these de L'amphictyonie Israelite." *HTR* 64 (1970) 415–36.

Weber, Max. *Ancient Judaism.* Translated by H. H. Gerth and D. Martindale. Glencoe, IL: Free Press, 1952.

———. *Gesammelte Aufsätze zur Religions-sozio*logie. Vol. 3, *Das Antike Judentum.* Tübingen: Mohr/Siebeck, 1923.

Weiser, Artur. "Das Deborahlied." *ZAW* 71 (1959) 67–97.

———. *Die Psalmen.* 2 vols. Das Alte Testament Deutsch 14–15. Göttingen: Vandenhoeck & Ruprecht, 1959.

———. *The Psalms: A Commentary.* Translated by Herbert Hartwell. OTL. Philadelphia: Westminster, 1962.)

Wellhausen, Julius. *Israelitische und jüdische Geschichte.* 7th ed. Berlin: Reimer, 1914.

———. *Prolegomena to the History of Israel.* Translated by J. Sutherland Black and Allan Menzies. Edinburgh: Adam & Charles Black, 1885.

———. *Prolegomena zur Geschichte Israels.* Berlin: Reimer, 1889.

Zobel, Hans-Jürgen. *Stammesspruch und Geschichte: Die Angaben der Stammessprüche von Gen 49, Dtn 33 und Jdc 5 über die politischen und kultischen Zustände in damaligen "Israel."* BZAW 95. Berlin: Töpelmann, 1965.

4

The Final Years of Samaria (730–720 BC)

(coauthored with Jeffrey K. Kuan)

UNCERTAINTY AND CONTROVERSY OVER the course of events during Samaria's final years continue in spite of extensive biblical and nonbiblical texts related to the topic.[1] The main disputed issues concern the date and nature of the Assyrian takeover of Samaria, whether the city was captured on only one or on more occasions and by which Assyrian ruler(s), when Samaria was provincialized, and the course of the reign of King Hoshea and the governing of Samaria following his arrest. In this paper, we shall argue (1) that the Israelites were forced to submit to the Assyrians on four different occasions in the 720s; (2) that Shalmaneser V ravaged Samaria in 725–724 BCE and at the same time arrested Hoshea, looted the temple at Bethel, and declared Samaria an Assyrian province; (3) that the Israelites subsequently rebelled, enthroned a new king (whose name remains unknown), and established a new sanctuary in Samaria before surrendering to the Assyrians just before Shalmaneser's death; and (4) that Sargon II had to retake the city during his second regnal year after Samaria had again revolted.

---

1. For recent general surveys of the issues see Tadmor, "The Campaign of Sargon II"; Becking, "De Ondergang van Samaria"; Hughes, *Secrets of the Times*, 203–9; Na'aman, "The Historical Background."

The Final Years of Samaria (730–720 BC)

The Appointment of Hoshea

Biblical texts date the Assyrian siege and capture of Samaria to the seventh and ninth years of King Hoshea's rule (2 Kgs 17:6; 18:9-10). If we knew the exact chronology of Hoshea's reign, this would make it possible to determine the years to which the biblical editors assigned the city's siege and capture. The chronology of Hoshea's reign, however, depends upon determining the time he assumed the throne and from when his regnal years were calculated. Both Assyrian and biblical texts refer to Hoshea's rise to the throne but there is scholarly disagreement concerning the chronology of Hoshea's reign.

Two of Tiglath-pileser III's inscriptions related to his 734-731 western campaigns refer to the Assyrian king's designation or recognition of Hoshea as king.[2] III R 10, 2:17-18 reports that "Pekah their king they (the Israelites) deposed and Hoshea [for king]ship over them I appointed."[3] Lines 10-11 (reverse) of ND4301 + 4305 may be reconstructed to read ". . . Hoshea as [ki]ng over them [I appointed] . . . to Sarrabanu before me . . ."[4] Borger and Tadmor have rightly assumed that line 11 refers to Hoshea's payment of tribute. III R 10, 2:17-18 and ND4301 + 4305: rev. 10-11 indicate that Tiglath-pileser recognized Hoshea as king during one of his three western campaigns conducted in 734-733 to 732-731. The recognition occurred probably before Tiglath-pileser left Syria-Palestine after his second campaign against Damascus, which occurred in 732-731 according to the Eponym Chronicle. Second Kings 16:10aα reports that King Ahaz of Judah met with the Assyrian ruler in Damascus after the Syrian King Rezin had been put to death. Ahaz may have attended a general meeting at which time Tiglath-pileser established political boundaries and made final arrangements for the vassal states and Assyrian provinces in Syria–Palestine. Hoshea was probably recognized as the new monarch over Beth Omri at the time, but did not yet posses his kingdom.

---

2. For a recent treatment of the Assyrian texts related to the period, see Irvine, *Isaiah, Ahaz*, 23–72.

3. The text was originally published in Rawlinson, *Cuneiform Inscriptions*, 3, pl. 10, no. 2; and a translation in Smith, *Assyrian Discoveries*, 284–85.

4. The text, discovered in the 1955 excavations at Nimrud, was published by Wiseman, "A Fragmentary Inscription of Tiglath-pileser III from Nimrud." The reading *Sarrabanu* was proposed by Borger and Tadmor, "Zwei Beiträge."

That Pekah still held Samaria at the time the Assyrian monarch withdrew from the region is indicated by four factors. First, in his annals, Tiglath-pileser notes that "Samaria alone I [le]ft . . . their king . . ." (Layard 66:228).[5] Although the text here reads URU *Samirina* ("the city of Samaria") more than the city itself may be involved. The Assyrian scribes were perhaps not consistent in their use of detenninatives. In Tiglath-pileser's inscriptions reference is made to both *Menihimme* URU *Samerina* ("Menahem of the city of Samaria") and to *Menihimme* KUR *Samerina* ("Menahem of the land of Samaria"). Pekah would have remained in power as long as he held Samaria securely, and Tiglath-pileser notes that Samaria was not attacked by the Assyrians. Second, that Hoshea sent tribute to Tiglath-pileser while the latter was away from the capital on campaign (ND4301 + 4305: rev.10–11) rather than delivering it personally while the Assyrian king was in Syria–Palestine or else sending it to the Assyrian capital indicates that Hoshea only gained control of Samaria after Tiglath-pileser had left the region and that he paid tribute in haste once he secured full control of the country. Third, Hiram of Tyre, Queen Samsi of Arabia, and Hannun of Gaza were all left on their thrones in spite of having joined the anti-Assyrian coalition but each offered at least token submission to Tiglath-pileser. Nothing is ever said in the Assyrian texts about Pekah's submission; this fact suggests that he remained unrepentant. Fourth, 2 Kgs 15:30, in agreement with III R 10, 2:17–18, notes it was Hoshea and his supporters, not the Assyrians, who attacked Pekah and executed him.[6]

Hoshea's payment of tribute to Tiglath-pileser at Sarrabanu probably occurred after Hoshea had gained control over Samaria and thus officially had replaced Pekah as king. Only with control of the capital city would he have gained access to the state and royal treasuries. Exactly when Hoshea paid tribute is somewhat uncertain. Although the exact location of Sarrabanu is unknown, the city lay somewhere in southern Mesopotamia.

---

5. Published in Rost, *Die Keilschrifttexte Tiglat-Pilesers III*, pls. XXII–XXIII, pp. 35–41.

6. Hos 2:2 probably refers to the co-operative effort of Hoshea and King Ahaz of Judah to overthrow Pekah. (Note the positive evaluation of Hoshea in 2 Kgs 17:2b.) Deuteronomy 32:1–43 was probably composed to encourage and justify the killing of Pekah and his supporters to purge the land; see Chong, "The Song of Moses." The wording of 2 Kgs 15:30, that Hoshea "attacked him and put him to death" (or "executed him") suggests an assault on Pekah followed by his being put to death. The terms used no more express the mere idea of a personal assassination than does the reference in 2 Kgs 16:9, which states that Tiglath-pileser "put Rezin to death."

Tiglath-pileser compaigned in this area in 731–730 (Eponymn Chronicle = "against Sapiya") and again in 729–728 (Babylonian Chronicle, I.i.19–23).[7] Thus Hoshea may have paid his initial tribute in either of these years. In all probability, the defeat of Pekah's forces and the capture of Samaria took some time to accomplish. Nonetheless, the earlier date seems the more likely.

In light of the chronological references given for Hoshea's reign, 729 appears too late a date. According to 2 Kgs 17:1, Hoshea began to rule in the twelfth year of Ahaz's reign (743–728), which would have been 732–731. This coincides with the year of Tiglath-pileser's third western campaign.[8] If the synchronism and the proposed dates for Ahaz are correct, then the biblical text suggest that Tiglath-pileser could have appointed Hoshea as ruler prior to departing the region. Since the regnal years of Israelite kings seem to have been counted from the fall (Marheshvan)[9] New Year Festival, subsequent synchronisms between Hoshea and Hezekiah (2 Kgs 18:9–10) imply that Hoshea had not deposed Pekah until after Marheshvan 731, that is, until Tiglath-pileser was already campaigning in Babylonia. Hoshea's first regnal year would have been calculated from Marheshvan 730.

Shalmaneser V and Samaria

Non-biblical texts regarding Shalmaneser's reign (726–722) are limited to statements in the Eponym Chronicle, a short section in the Babylonian Chronicles (I.i.27–30), and Josephus's reproduction of Menander's quotations from the Tyrian archives (*Ant.* 9.283–87).

The Eponym chronicle (K3203) reports the following for the years 728–723:[10]

(728–727)   Eponym Durassar governor of Tushhan, the king took the hand of Bel. The city Di . . .
(727–726)   Eponym Belharran-bel-usur governor of Guzana, to the city of . . .
            Shalmaneser sat on the throne.

---

7. See Grayson, *Assyrian and Babylonian Chronicles*, 72. No reference is made in the chronicles to Tiglath-pileser's 731–730 campaign.
8. See Hayes and Hooker, *A New Chronology*, 59–67.
9. See 1 Kgs 12:31 and Talmon, "The Cult and Calendar."
10. See Smith, "On a New Fragment."

(726–725)　Eponym Marduk-bel-usur governor of Ameda, in [the land].
(725–724)　Eponym Mahde governor of Nineveh, to the country of . . .
(724–723)　Eponym Assur-ishmeani governor of Kalzi, to . . .
(723–722)　Eponym Shalmaneser king of Assyria, to . . .

The Babylonian Chronicles (1.i.23–31) contain the following entries for the years 728–722:[11]

23　Tiglath-pileser ascended the throne in Babylon.
24　The second year: Tiglath-pileser died in the month Tebet.
25　For (*eighteen*) years Tiglath-pileser ruled Akkad and Assyria.
26　For two of these years he ruled in Akkad.
27　On the twenty-fifth day of the month Tebet,
28　Shalmaneser ascended the throne in Assyria (*and Akkad*). He ravaged the city of Samaria.[12]
29　The fifth year: Shalmaneser died in the month Tebet.
30　For five years Shalmaneser ruled Akkad and Assyria.
31　On the twelfth day of the month Tebet Sargon ascended the throne in Babylon.

In *Ant.* 9.283–287, Josephus reports the following concerning Shalmaneser's relationships to Phoenicia:

> And the king of Assyria came with an army and invaded Syria and all of Phoenicia. Now the name of this king is recorded in the Tyrian archives, for he marched upon Tyre in the reign of Elulaios. This is also attested by Menander, the author of a book of Annals and translator of the Tyrian archives into the Greek language, who has given the following account: "And Elulaios, to whom they gave the name of Pyas, reigned thirty-six years. This king, upon the revolt of the Kitieis (Cyprians), put out to sea and again reduced them to submission. During his reign Selampsas, the king of Assyria, came with an army and invaded all Phoenicia and, after making a treaty of peace with all (its cities), withdrew from the land. And Sidon and Arke and old Tyre and many other cities also revolted from Tyre and surrendered to the king of Assyria. But, as the Tyrians for that reason would not submit to him, the king turned back again and attacked them

---

11. See Grayson, *Assyrian and Babylonian Chronicles*, 72–73.

12. Doubts about reading Samaria (*Samara'in*) held by earlier scholars can no longer be taken seriously; see Tadmor, "Campaign of Sargon II," 39–40; and Na'aman, "Historical Background," 215–16.

The Final Years of Samaria (730–720 BC)

after the Phoenicians had furnished him with sixty ships and eight hundred oarsmen. Against these the Tyrians sailed with twelve ships and, after dispersing the ships of their adversaries, took five hundred of their men prisoners. On that account, in fact, the price of everything went up in Tyre. But the king of Assyria, on retiring, placed guards at the river and the aqueducts to prevent the Tyrians from drawing water, and this they endured for five years, and drank from wells which they had dug." This, then, is what is written in the Tyrian archives concerning Salmanasses, the king of Assyria. (LCL trans.)

Before attempting to integrate the evidence of these non-biblical texts and to correlate it with biblical texts, a special feature of the Babylonian Chronicles must be noted. In Babylonian Chronicle 1, horizontal lines in the text serve to organize the reported events chronologically. Most scholars have ignored the fact that the horizontal line between the statement on the destruction of Samaria and the statement about the fifth year of the king's reign indicates that Samaria was ravaged by Shalmaneser at some time prior to the final year of his rule (722–721). One scholar who has noted the importance of these transverse chronologcal markers is Na'aman but he wrongly interprets the evidence. He states that "the text of the chronicle is organized throughout in a chronological order, with each and every event accurately dated within a specific year of the king of Babylonia and a transverse line marked to separate the years of reign." He further concludes that "the 'ravaging' of Samara'in is included within the accession year of Shalmaneser and should accordingly be assigned to that year."[13] This makes the chronicle much more exact than is the case. The material between the horizontal markers following line 23 and preceding line 29 cover a period that includes the final year of Tiglath-pileser (727–726) as well as the accession year of Shalmaneser V

---

13. Na'aman, ibid., 210. Na'aman quotes Hugo Winckler, who argued that the assignment of the destruction to the accession year indicated that one should read *Sabara'in* rather than *Samara'in*; see Winckler's "Nachtrag," 351–52; and Winckler, *Geschichte und Geographie*, 62. Dalley argues exactly the opposite: "According to the Babylonian Chronicle, the capture of Samaria took place at the very end of Shalmaneser's reign" (S. Dalley, "Foreign Chariotry," 33). Decades ago, Olmstead pointed out that the capture of Samaria "is mentioned as the only event in Shalmaneser's reign, just before the account of his death and just after that of his accession. So far, then, as the Chronicle is concerned, we can only place it in his reign, that is, within the years 727–722" (Olmstead, "The Fall of Samaria," 181). Olmstead, however, failed to grasp the chronologcal significance of the horizontal line that places the ravaging of Samaria prior to the death year (722–721) of Shalmaneser.

(727–726) plus the first four years of his reign (726–725 to 723–722). The only event reported for Shalmaneser during these years is the ravaging of Samaria. Thus one can draw two and only two conclusions about the history of Samaria from this Babylonian chronicle: (1) the city was ravaged by Shalmaneser and (2) this occurred prior to his fifth year, that is, before 722–721.

The entries in the Eponym Chronicle for the last two years of Tiglath-pileser, unfortunately fragmentary, indicate rebellion in the west. The reference to "the city Di . . . ," in the entry for 728–727, no doubt refers to the city of Damascus (see the entries for 733–732 and 732–731). That this text probably referred to a revolt by Damascus receives indirect support from II R 67 (K3751): rev. 14–16 and ND4301 + 4305: rev. 27–29. The former text reports on Tiglathpileser's deposal of Uassurme of Tabal and his replacement by Hulli and the receipt of tribute exacted through the threat of force from Metenna of Tyre (in 728 or 727).[14] The latter text mentions a ruler who failed to pay proper homage to Tiglath-pileser, probably Hulli.[15] Thus Tiglath-pileser was having trouble with both Tabal and Tyre and probably Damascus by 728–727.

The expedition noted in the entry for 727–726 is probably best related to Assyrian troubles in the west. Although undertaken by Tiglath-pileser, the expedition may have been continued by Shalmaneser, who replaced his father on 25 Tebet, only a little over two months prior to the time he would have needed to be in the capital for the Nisan New Year Festival. Josephus reports that Shalmaneser "came with an army and invaded all Phoenicia and, after making peace with all (its cities), withdrew from the land" (*Ant.* 9.284). Certainly, Shalmaneser had no time to learn of the revolt, organize and carry out a western campaign, and defeat both Israel and Tyre after his father's death in the two months of his accession year, as is argued by Na'aman.[16] The new king may have completed a campaign already begun but Shalmaneser would have returned to the capital for his coronation in Nisan. The Eponym Chronicle reports that

---

14. The text appears in Rawlinson, *Cuneiform Inscriptions*, 2, pl. 67; and Rost, *Keilschrifttexte*, 55–77 and in translation in Smith, *Assyrian Discoveries*, 254–66; and Luckenbill, *Ancient Records of Assyria and Babylonia*, vol. 1, §§786–804. For a study of the text, see Olmstead, *Assyrian Historiography*, 32–35.

15. See Wiseman, "Fragmentary Inscription," 122.

16. Na'aman, "Historical Background," 212–16. Na'aman argues that the initial action of Shalmaneser against Hoshea (2 Kgs 17:3) and the general revolt in the west occurred at "the time of unrest that followed the death of Tiglath-pileser III," 213.

The Final Years of Samaria (730–720 BC)

no expedition occurred in 726–725, Shalmaneser's first regnal year, for the king was "in [the land]."

In the biblical account of the last years of the northern kingdom (2 Kgs 17:1–6; 18:9–11),[17] Shalmaneser is said to have come up against, that is, campaigned against Hoshea, who submitted and became his vassal paying tribute to the Assyrian monarch (17:3). The description of this campaign in the biblical text would not lead one to presume that much if any conflict occurred between the Israelites and the Assyrians. The text, however, clearly implies that Hoshea had revolted, that is, failed to pay tribute and that the Assyrian king marched against him. The text certainly does not depict any events that would imply the ravaging of Samaria as is presumed by Na'aman, whose conclusion is based on a misunderstanding of the Babylonian Chronicle.

The most plausible interpretation of both the biblical and non-biblical evidence appears to be the following scenario. Before the death of Tiglath-pileser in Tebet 727, rebellion had broken out in the west. Israel and Hoshea had joined this movement in which at least Damascus and Tyre were also involved. In 727–726, Tiglath-pileser began a campaign to suppress the rebellion, a campaign completed by Shalmaneser, who received the submission of the Phoenicians and Hoshea of Israel, at some time between 25 Tebet 727 when he assumed the kingship and the end of Adar 726 when he would have returned home for the New Year Festival.

Shalmaneser spent his first regnal year (726–725) "in [the land]," that is, the Assyrian king did not go on campaign that year. Shalmaneser's year of military inactivity witnessed renewed rebellion against Assyria in the west. To this period belongs the renewal of rebellion in Phoenicia led by Tyre (*Ant.* 9.285) and Hoshea's embassy to Egypt and withholding of tribute (2 Kgs 17:4a).[18] In 725–724, Shalmaneser, according to the Eponym Chronicle, again went on campaign, and although reference to the

---

17. Rather than reading 2 Kgs 17:3–6 as a continuous sequential narrative, several scholars assume the existence of two parallel accounts deriving from different archives. This one episode–two-source theory traces vv. 3–4 to northern archives and vv. 5–6 (plus 18:9–11) to Judean archives. First proposed by Winckler ("Beitrage zur Quellenscheidung der Königbücher"), the theory has been recently defended by Jones, *1 and 2 Kings*, 542–43; and Becking, "Ondergang van Samaria," 25–33. Such source division allows one to see the arrest of Hoshea as occurring simultaneously with the capture of Samaria after a three-year siege. There is nothing in the text, however, that would indicate different sources.

18. The issue of the identity of the much discussed "King So" of Egypt is of only indirect relevance to the present discussion and need not be pursued.

destination of the campaign has not survived in the broken text, the west was undoubtedly involved. The actions against Hoshea noted in 2 Kgs 17:4b and against Tyre described in *Ant.* 9.285–287 are best understood in the context of this 725–724 campaign.

With renewed Assyrian military action in the west, Phoenician cities that had temporarily joined Tyre in renewed rebellion capitulated and aided the Assyrians in an unsuccessful naval effort to subdue Tyre. The Assyrians, in spite of the assistance of a Phoenician fleet, had to abandon efforts to conquer Tyre. The island city was placed under a land blockade that endured for five years. If Tyre was blockaded for five years, this would indicate that Shalmaneser took action against the city in the first half of his second regnal year (Nisan 725—Nisan 724) since the siege was no doubt lifted with the death of Shalmaneser in Tebet 722/21 when trouble developed in Assyria over Sargon's accession to the throne. On the basis of a fall New Year calendar, the blockade, begun before the fall New Year Festival 725, lasted for five years (726–725 until 722–721), that is, from a time prior to the New Year Festival in 725 until after the New Year Festival in 722.

According to 2 Kgs 17:4b, Hoshea was seized and imprisoned by Shalmaneser. Unfortunately no details nor chronological information are provided by this text. If Shalmaneser took action against Hoshea in conjunction with putting Tyre under siege this would have been in 725. Exactly how Shalmaneser took possession of Hoshea also remains uncertain. That Hoshea surrendered voluntarily seems highly unlikely.[19] Hoshea could hardly have expected favorable treatment from Shalmaneser since he was guilty of two wrongdoings—conspiratorial negotiation with another major power and withholding of tribute—and Hoshea already had a past record of rebellion.

---

19. Many scholars argue that Hoshea surrendered voluntarily. See, most recently, Na'aman who concludes that "when Shalmaneser heard of the conspiracy he sent troops . . . and ordered the conspirator to appear before him. Hoshea did so" and was arrested ("Historical Background," 218), or Hughes, who sees all of 2 Kgs 17:3–6 as parts of a single sequence: "Hoshea had asserted Israelite independence from Assyria by withholding his yearly payment of tribute, and had also sought Egyptian support . . . Shalmaneser V reacted by launching a military campaign against Hoshea, at which point the latter apparently decided to abandon his revolt, and went to offer his submission and pay tribute. This belated offer of submission failed to satisfy Shalmaneser: Hoshea was arrested and Shalmaneser proceeded to lay siege to Samaria . . ." (*Secrets of the Times*, 205–6).

The Final Years of Samaria (730–720 BC)

If Hosea did not surrender voluntarily, then he must have been taken in the course of some military conflict. The reference to Shalmaneser's ravaging of Samaria in the Babylonian Chronicle was probably part of a complex of events during which Hoshea was seized and imprisoned. As noted earlier, Shalmaneser's taking of Samaria reported in the Babylonian Chronicle preceded his fifth year thus ruling out 722–721 as a potential date for his ravaging of Samaria. This leaves as the other known potential candidate one of two encounters with Hoshea, either that noted in 2 Kgs 17:3 or else that referred to in 2 Kgs 17:4b. As noted above, the first episode, in 2 Kgs 17:3, appears to have involved a voluntary submission since Hoshea is said to have resubmitted to Assyrian vassalage and paid tribute and no statement is made that clearly implies any major military encounter.

The arrest of Hoshea was probably part of a sequence of events in 725 that included not only Shalmaneser's ravaging of the Israelite capital but also the provincialization of Samaria and, from the Assyrian point of view, the termination of Israel's independence. The arrest and imprisonment, and perhaps actual or planned exile, of Hoshea was thus only one feature in a larger scenario that included the looting of the royal sanctuary at Bethel. If these events are to be placed in Shalmaneser's 725–724 campaign, then they probably occurred prior to the actions against Tyre. After his punitive actions against Samaria and Bethel, Hoshea was imprisoned probably awaiting exile once Shalmaneser had settled affairs with Tyre.

Obviously, all of these elements in Shalmaneser's treatment of Hoshea and Samaria are not discussed in either 2 Kings or in Assyrian texts. There do, however, appear to be allusions to these events in prophetic texts. In Hos 10:13b–15 the prophet warns his contemporaries of coming hostile action comparable to Shalmaneser's earlier exploits:

> 13 Because you have trusted in your way (or your chariotry),
>   in the strength of your warriors,
> 14 then the alarm of war will arise among your people,
>   and all your fortifications will be destroyed;

> like Shalman(eser)[20] destroyed Beth Arbel[21] on the day of battle,
> a mother with her children was bashed;
> 15 just as he did to you, O Bethel,[22]
> because of the wrongfulness of your crime;
> in the dawn (or suddenly) the king of Israel was silenced.

In depicting future conditions, the prophet alludes to three past events as analogies: Shalmaneser's vicious destruction of Beth Arbel, his actions against Bethel, and the silencing of the Israelite king. If the silencing of the king in v. 15b refers to Hosea's imprisonment, then the actions in vv. 14b–15a probably belong to the same complex of events. The destruction of Beth Arbel probably occurred in conjunction with either Shalmaneser's 727–726 or his 725–724 campaign in the west. The actions against Bethel are described in ambiguous terms but if they were carried out concurrently with the removal of Hoshea from office, they probably included the Assyrian confiscation of the cultic paraphernalia from the national sanctuary. Hosea 3:4 probably reflects the conditions alluded to in Hos 10:15 since it seems to presuppose both the arrest of Hoshea and the looting of the Bethel sanctuary: "Surely many days the children of Israel shall dwell without king and without prince and without sacrifice and without pillar and without ephod and teraphim."[23]

Shalmaneser's actions in Samaria in 725 may also be reflected in Isa 32:14:

20. Interpreters have identified this Shalman with Shalmaneser III (Astour, "841 B.C."), the usurper Shallum in 2 Kgs 15:1–15 (Ginsberg, "Hosea," 1018), or the Moabite king Salamanu who paid tribute to Tiglath-pileser in 734 according to II R 67 (K3751):10 (Wolff, *Hosea*, 187–88). Allusion to an event associated with Shalmaneser III, over a century in the past, hardly seems likely since the text seems to imply audience familiarity wth the event. Nothing is recorded or known about actions by Shallum or Salamanu, which would indicate the prophet was alluding to either of them. Given the historical context of the prophet Hosea, a reference to Shalmaneser V makes plausible sense (see below, n. 23)

21. Various proposals have been made regarding the identity of the site Beth-Arbel; see Donner, *Israel unter den Völkern*, 164–67.

22. There is no reason to read "O house of Israel" with the LXX. Bethel is textually the best authenticated reading and also the most difficult.

23. The book of Hosea is arranged in two panels: chaps. 1–3 and 4–14. Within each panel the materials are arranged chronologically. Chapters 1–3 cover a period from the last years of Jeroboam II (late 750s) until after the arrest of Hoshea (725). The second panel covers from the years of Shallum's coup until the capture of Samaria by Sargon. Chapters 4–7 derive from the time before King Hoshea's arrest; chaps. 8–9 from the time between Hoshea's arrest and the capture of Samaria in 722; and chaps. 10–14 from the time of Sargon's activity in the west.

> Surely, the palace lies unattended,
>> the noise of the city (or royal quarter) is left behind;
> the citadel (*'ophel*) and the watchtower have become,
>> according to the treaty,[24] denuded spots forever;
> a delightful place for wild asses,
>> pasture for flocks.

This text, which certainly cannot be understood as descriptive of Jerusalem at any period in Isaiah's ministry, is best seen as a description of Samaria.[25] The prophet's employment of perfect tense verbs indicates that the destruction is past not predicted. Such actions as the silencing of the city and palace and the destruction of the military quarters in the town would be expected in conjunction with the removal of a reigning, rebellious monarch.

The arrest of Hoshea, the looting of the state sanctuary at Bethel, and the demolition of the military headquarters in Samaria would point to one conclusion: Shalmaneser's actions represented the Assyrian termination of the state of Israel and the decreed provincialization of the area. To have arrested and imprisoned the reigning king, no doubt with the intention of exiling him, without making political arrangements for the state would have been contrary to general Assyrian policy. When rebellious kings were deposed by the Assyrians, they were either replaced with co-operative monarchs or the area provincialized. Samaria would certainly not have been left to be governed by its military leaders or city elders as is so often assumed. Shalmaneser's actions in 725 are thus best understood as initial steps in the provincialization of Samaria.

According to 2 Kgs 17:4-6 and 18:9-11, the arrest of Hoshea was not the end of Shalmaneser's dealings with Samaria. 2 Kgs 17:4-6[26] speak of a campaign against the whole land, of siege of the city before its capture

---

24. The enigmatic *b'd* is probably to be read *k'd* and *'d* associated with the Akkadian *adu/ade*, signifying treaty relations and obligations.

25. On the connections between Isaiah 28–33 and the reign of Hoshea and its aftermath, see Hayes and Irvine, *Isaiah*, 320-70.

26. Most recent interpretations assume that two Assyrian kings have been confused and events telescoped in 2 Kgs 17:5-6. According to Cogan and Tadmor, *II Kings*, 197, "two kings of Assyria oversaw the events referred to in v. 6; Shalmaneser V captured Samaria; Sargon II exiled Israel . . . The present telescoping of events might be as early as the Deuteronomic editing of Kings." Na'aman, "Historical Background," 219, is more drastic: "'the king of Assyria' in vv. 3-4 is Shalmaneser whereas the king in vv. 5-6 is Sargon, his successor." The straightforward sense of 2 Kgs 17:3-6 suggests that the same Assyrian king—Shalmaneser—is intended throughout.

in Hoshea's ninth year, and the deportation of Israelites. According to 2 Kgs 18:9–11[27] the siege of Samaria began in the fourth year of Hezekiah (Tishri 724—Tishri 723) or the seventh year of Hoshea (Marheshvan 724—Marheshvan 723) and the Assyrians captured or took possession of the city in the sixth year of Hezekiah (Tishri 722—Tishri 721) or the ninth year of Hoshea (Marheshvan 722—Marheshvan 721). Since Sargon began his rule on 12 Tebet in Shalmaneser's fifth year (Nisan 722—Nisan 721), Samaria must have fallen or surrendered to the Assyrians in the two-month period extending from the northern New Year Festival (15 Marheshvan) marking the beginning of Hoshea's ninth year to the 12th of Tebet when Sargon assumed the throne.

If Hoshea was arrested, Bethel looted, parts of Samaria demolished, and the region declared an Assyrian province in 725–724, and yet the city of Samaria had again to be taken by the Assyrians in 722/21 after a three-year siege, a number of questions present themselves. Did Israel reassert its independence in the face of the edict of provincialization? How were the people governed during this period? What compensation was made for the loss of the cultic paraphernalia from the royal sanctuary at Bethel? On these matters, 2 Kgs 17:5–6 and 18:9–11 offer no information. In the book of Hosea, however, the prophet provides a number of allusions whch make possible a general reconstruction of the course of events.

The Israelites apparently refused to submit to Assyrian provincialization and rose again in rebellion, probably while Shalmaneser was trying to subjugate Tyre in the summer or early fall of 725. They re-established a monarchy, set up a new government, and established a sanctuary with

---

27. There is no reason to assume that the chronologcal references in 2 Kgs 18:9–10 are secondary calculations. According to Cogan and Tadmor, *II Kings*, 216, the chronology here is as much as three years off; the inaccuracy "derives from the calculation made by the Judahite chronographer of Kings, who did not know that Hoshea's reign ended before the siege began . . ." According to Na'aman, the calculations in 2 Kgs 17:5b–6a are based on an earlier historical note stating "that Samana was besieged and conquered by the Assyrians three years after its rebellion and the imprisonment of its king." [The Deuteronomistic Historian] mistakenly interpreted the datum to mean that the city fell—after three years of siege—in Hoshea's last year, thus combining his last year with the fall of Samaria . . ." "The mistaken dates in vv. 5–6 were the basis for a later redactor (possibly DtrN) who composed 2 Kgs 18,9–12," which "is worthless for historical reconstruction . . ." ("Historical Background," 221–22). Tadmor's interpretation is based on his chronological conclusion that Hoshea's reign extended from 732/31 to 724/23. Na'aman's interpretation is used to buttress his theory that only Sargon captured Samaria after the arrest of Hoshea.

The Final Years of Samaria (730-720 BC)

refashioned cultic paraphernalia, including a golden calf, in the city or the environs of Samaria. These conditions are reflected in Hos 8:4-5a:

> They have enthroned a king,
> but not with my consent;
> they have set up a govermnent,
> but I have not recognized it.
> Their silver and their gold,
> they have fashioned for themselves cultic paraphernalia;
> in order that it might be cut down.
> It is rejected, your calf, O Samaria;
> my anger burns against them.

Although this text is almost universally understood as the prophet's condemnation of (northern) kingship in general and the Israelite fashioning of cultic artifacts for use in idolatrous worship, the text is best understood with reference to a very specific situation.[28] Practically all modern translations understand the opening of v. 5 to refer to the "setting up of kings" (see RSV), however, there is no term for "kings" in the text and the hiphil of the verb *mlk* simply means "to make someone king." Hosea was not opposed to kingship in principle nor to the use of cultic paraphernalia (see Hos 3:4 where loss of the king and cultic artifacts is considered a punishment). Only with strained exegesis can this text be seen as a condemnation of the Bethel cult. The golden calf of northern iconography was set up in Bethel (1 Kgs 12:28-33) and no Yahwistic sanctuary in Samaria is ever mentioned in the historical books. The calf of Samaria, mentioned by the prophet (Hos 8:5-6; 10:5), thus probably refers to a replacement image set up in a sanctuary in or near the city of Samaria after the looting of Bethel in 725. Two further factors support the existence of a sanctuary in Samaria in its final days of rebellion. First, in his Nimrud Prism, Sargon notes that he counted as spoil "the gods of their trust" when he captured Samaria (Fragment D, col. IV:32; see below). The presence of cultic paraphernalia (= "the gods") in Samaria when Sargon took the city indicates the presence of a sanctuary. Second, in a letter datable to this period, to be published by H. W. F. Saggs, an Assyrian official reports to the court that he saw a sanctuary in Samaria.

Rebellion in Ephraim and Samaria, accompanied by the establishment of a new monarchical government and the founding of a new cultic center in Samaria, forms the background of Shalmaneser's actions

---

28. On the general issues involved in Hosea's understanding of the monarchy, see Gelston, "Kingship."

reported in 2 Kgs 17:5–6 and 18:9–11. The Assyrian king is said to have campaigned against the whole country (2 Kgs 17:5a) and then moved against Samaria placing the city under siege (17:5b). The attack on Ephraim and Samaria occurred, as we have noted, after Tyre was placed under siege, a siege that began before the New Year Festival in 725. The prior siege of Tyre is reflected in Hos 9:13, where the prophet speaks of a coming time when Ephraim will suffer a similar fate to Tyre:

> Ephraim, just as I have seen Tyre
>   planted on an oasis,
> so Ephraim will lead his sons
>   to the slaughterer.

According to the Kings narrative, the siege of Samaria began in Hoshea's seventh year (Marheshvan 724—Marheshvan 723). The siege is also said to have begun in the fourth year of Hezekiah (Tishri 724—Tishri 723). If these references are correct the city could have been initially besieged at any time between Marheshvan 724 and Tishri 723. The siege thus may not have begun until Shalmaneser's fourth year (Nisan 723—Nisan 722). If Hoshea was taken prisoner in the spring or summer of 725, during his fifth year (Marheshvan 726— Marheshvan 725) and the second year of Shalmaneser (Nisan 725—Nisan 724), then the siege did not begin until at least a year and perhaps as much as two years after his imprisonment. This would have allowed sufficient time for the Samarians to rebel, re-establish a monarchical government, and open a sanctuary in Samaria.

Samaria was taken by, or surrendered to (the verb *lkd* used in 2 Kgs 17:6; 18:10 does not necessarily imply a destruction), the Assyrians in Hoshea's ninth year, that is, at some time after Marheshvan 722. The length of the siege—one full and parts of two additional regnal years at a minimum—would imply that the Assyrians did not push the attack very vigorously or else that the Israelites held out tenaciously. Probably the former is more likely. Three factors lend support to this argument. First, the Assyrians were also holding Tyre under siege simultaneously and this would have occupied part of the Assyrian forces. Second, Shalmaneser does not seem personally to have accompanied his troops into battle during his fifth and final year of reign. The eponym entry for this year does not note any campaign undertaken by the king but only mentions that "the foundation of the temple of Nabu was torn up for repairs." Third, when Sargon assumed the throne, he was confronted with serious dissension in the army (see below). Probably a portion of the Assyrian army without Shalmaneser presided over the capture/surrender of Samaria that occurred just prior to the death of Shalmaneser at which time the forces besieging Tyre and Samaria returned home to participate in the turmoil attendant upon Sargon's accession.

Second Kings 17:6 and 18:11 attribute the exiling of Israelites to Shalmaneser. Although practically all scholars assume that the Assyrian king who carried out the deportation mentioned in these verses was Sargon, this finds no support in the biblical text. Sargon almost certainly deported Samarians as he claims in various texts (see below) but this in no way precludes deportations by Shalmaneser. According to the 2 Kings account, the same king of Assyria who conquered Samaria in Hoshea's ninth year also deported "Israel." If the above-proposed reconstruction is correct, and Shalmaneser declared Israel an Assyrian province at the time of Hoshea's arrest in 725, then the deportation of Israelites may have occurred throughout the remainder of Shalmaneser's reign but especially during the years of Samaria's siege. The biblical text, however, contains no explicit reference to the deportation of people living in the city of Samaria itself.

Sargon II and Samaria

No explicit reference is made to Sargon II (721–705) in the historical books of the Bible (see Isa 20:1). The "king of Assyria" who settled foreigners in Samaria (2 Kgs 17:24), however, was probably Sargon. Shalmaneser certainly did not have sufficient time to resettle Samaria between its capture and his death nor had he carried out the military campaigns that would have produced foreign exiles to settle Samaria. For our knowledge of Sargon's relationship to Samaria, we are dependent primarily on the Assyrian king's inscriptions.

Although the Khorsabad annals appear to assign the capture of Samaria to Sargon's accession year,[29] it is now clear that his first western campaign did not occur before his second regnal year (720–719).[30] At the beginning of his reign, Sargon encountered both internal opposition and

29. Becking raises the possibility that . . . *i-na-a-a* in line 11 of the annals should not be restored to read *sa-me-ri-na-a-a* but to read the name of some other town ("Ondergang van Samaria," 44–47). Other possibilities, however, do not appear to be very likely candidates.

30. See Tadmor, "Campaigns of Sargon II," 22–32.

external rebellion. In the Borowski stela, he notes that he "pardoned and showed mercy on 6,300 guilty Assyrians, settling them in Hamath.[31] In the Assur Charter,[32] another document from early in his reign, granting or restoring special privileges to the citizens of Ashur, Sargon notes that in his second year he fought Humbanigash, king of Elam, and Yaubi'di of Hamath who headed a western coalition of rebellious powers. Although Sargon claims to have shattered the might of the Elamites, the Babylonian Chronicle reports a different story. At the accession of Sargon, Marduk-apla-iddina (Merodach-baladan) seized the throne in Babylon, occupied by Assyrians since 729, and was aided in his venture by the Elamite kingdom. The Babylonian version of Sargon's battle with the Elamite army backing Marduk-apla-iddina describes it as an Assyrian defeat:

> The second year of Marduk-apla-iddina [720–719],
> Humban-nikash, king of Elam, did
> battle against Sargon, king of Assyria, in
> the district of Der, effected an Assyrian
> retreat, and inflicted a major defeat
> upon them (1.i. 33–35).[33]

Sargon campaigned in the west, only after settling his domestic trouble and after his encounter with Elam. Since his battle with the king of Elam occurred in his second regnal year (720–719), Sargon probably did not get to the west before late in that year. The western ringleaders were apparently Hamath under the rule of the usurper Yaubi'di and Gaza ruled by Hannun and aided by an Egyptian force. Others joining in the rebellion were Arpad, Simirra, Damascus, Samaria, and probably Hadrach.[34] In several inscriptions, Sargon refers to the capture of Samaria as well as the land of Beth Omri.[35] The most interesting and important

---

31. A portion of the text with translation is provided by Lambert, *Ladders to Heaven*, 125.

32. See Saggs, "Historical Texts and Fragments." Sargon's reversal of policy toward Assur could suggest that Shalmaneser was already experiencing domestic trouble with his own people, a factor that could explain his failure to accompany his troops on campaign in 722–721.

33. Grayson, *Assyrian and Babylonian Chronicles*, 73.

34. Hadrach (Hatarikka) is indicated by the Asharna stela; see Thureau-Dangin, "La stèle d'Asharné."

35. In four texts, Sargon refers to capturing the land of *bit-humri* (Pavement Inscription IV:31–32, Display Inscription Salon XIV:15, Cylinder Inscription 19–20, and Bull Inscription 21).

The Final Years of Samaria (730–720 BC)

of the texts dealing with the capture of Samaria is the Calah or Nimrud Prism first published in 1954.[36] Lines 25–49 in column 4 of fragment D are demarcated as a separate unit by horizontal lines as is typical of the text. This section opens with a description of the capture of Samaria but unfortunately several signs are missing from the opening of each line. The following is preserved of the first four lines:

```
25 [ ]-me-ri-na-a-a Sa it-ti Sarri
26 [ ]-ia a-na la e-peg ar-du-ti
27 [ ]-se-e bil-ti
28 [ ] ig-me-lu-ma e-pu-su ta-ha-zu.
```

There is widespread agreement on the restoration of lines 25 and 27 to restore LU.URU sa- or LU. sa- in line 25 (to read "the Samarians") and *u la na-* at the beginning of line 27 (to read "not to deliver tribute"). The restoration of lines 26 and 28 is disputed with proposed restorations being dependent on one's understanding of the military and political conditions reflected in the text. Gadd suggested restoring *na-ki-ri* in line 26 and was followed by Tadmor (LU.KUR = LU *nakru*). Borger proposed reading IGI.DU-*ia* = *alik pani-ia*. Gadd declined offering a proposed reading at the beginning of line 28. Tadmor suggested reading *a-ha-mes*. The recent proposals of Dalley (to restore *ibbalkitu/ikpudu*)[37] and of Na'aman (to restore SA-su-nu or *lemutti*)[38] ignore the presence of a horizontal wedge following the break. This portion of the preceding sign makes their restorations impossible but provides the basis for Tadmor's restoration. The first full word in line 28 may be read as *ig-me-lu-ma* (from *gamalu* "to spare, be obliging, reach an agreement") or as *ik-me-lu-ma* (from *kamailu* "to become angry, wrathful").

Two main proposals have been made regarding the identity of the king mentioned in the text. One approach considers the king to be a non-Israelite anti-Assyrian monarch. The candidate most frequently suggested is Yaubi'di of Hamath[39] although the possibility has been proposed that the foreign ruler was an Egyptian, perhaps the notorious "King So"

---

36. Gadd, "Inscribed Prisms of Sargon II." For translations of the text, see Gadd, 180; Tadmor, "Campaigns of Sargon II," 34; Borger, *Textbuch zur Geschichte Israels*, 60; and Kaiser, ed., *Texte aus der Umwelt des Alten Testaments*, 1/4:382; and Spieckermann, *Juda unter Assur*, 348–50.

37. Dalley, "Foreign Chariotry," 36 n. 30.

38. Na'aman, "Historical Background," 209–10.

39. Gadd, "Inscribed Prisms of Sargon II," 181–82; and Tadmor, "Campaigns of Sargon II," 37.

mentioned in 2 Kgs 17:4.⁴⁰ The second, alternative is to understand Sargon to be referring to his predecessor Shalmaneser V.⁴¹ The first interpretation restores the beginning of line 26 to read *sarri* [*na-kiri*]-*ia* or [LU.KUR]-*ia* "a king [hostile to] me." The second interpretation is based on the restoration *sarri* [IGI.DU = *alik pani*]*ia* " the king [my predecessor]."

It seems highly unlikely that the king referred to in the text was an Egyptian. The leader of the Egyptian force defeated by Sargon near Raphia is called *re'e* the *turtan* of Egypt and no reference is made to an Egyptian king in any of the Assyrian descriptions of the events of 720–719.

The association of the king with Yaubi'di of Hamath is based on the prominence given him in other texts concerned with the western uprising. A usurper, he is mentioned in a dozen of Sargon's texts and blamed with enticing Arpad, Sirnirra, Damascus, and Samaria to revolt (see the so-called Display Inscription). Dalley has argued against identifying the king with Yaubi'di based on the conclusion that "Sargon is elsewhere so derogatory about him that it is out of the question that he would ever allow him such a prestigious title as LUGAL 'king.'" Such an argument, however, is based on presuppositions about the character of a situation rather than on the text. At any rate, Dalley's argument is negated since, in his Cyprus Stela, Sargon does refer to Yaubi'di as "king."⁴² Nonetheless, there are reasons for not assuming that Sargon is here referring to the king of Hamath. First, the struggle with Hamath does not fall within the purview of this particular text. Thus such an elliptical allusion to Yaubi'di would have made no sense in this context. Second, elsewhere when Sargon wishes to cast disparagement on Yaubi'di, he does so in clear and very uncomplimentary terms, not in such an indirect fashion as here.

The proposal to understand "the king" referred to as a reference to Shalmaneser V was first made by Borger and has been defended by Dalley and Na'aman. Dalley accepts the restoration on the assumption that reading "hostile" is out of the question since the text cannot refer to Yaubi'di. Na'aman's acceptance of this proposal is based on his larger argument that

---

40. Redford, "Sais and the Kushite Invasion": "there can be little doubt that in the 'hostile king' we must see Tefnakhte" (15).

41. So Borger, *Textbuch zur Geschichte Israels*, 60; and Spieckermann, *Juda unter Assur*, 348–50; Dalley, "Foreign Chariotry," 36; and Na'aman, "Historical Background," 209–10.

42. Dalley, "Foreign Chariotry," 36. In addition to the Cyprus Stela, a text published by Thompson refers to Yaubi'di as LUGAL: Thompson, "A Selection"; the text is 122614 line 18.

Shalmaneser took Samaria in his accession year (727–726) but that only Sargon took the city subsequently. According to him, Sargon "suppressed a rebellion that had already broken out in the time of Shalmaneser."[43] Two basic factors argue against understanding the text as Sargon's reference to hostilities and rebellion begun under Shalmaneser. First, in his fullest descriptions of the general western rebellion, Sargon always associates this with the usurpation of the throne of Hamath by Yaubi'di and his influence on the co-conspirators. None of the texts that offer an explanation of the revolt associate it in any way with Shalmaneser. Second, in his texts, Sargon glorifies his own deeds and stresses his own initiation of actions. One of these actions was the capture of Samaria, which, in his annals, is given special prominence and placed in his accession year. It is thus highly unlikely that he would have described his own activity as bringing to conclusion something begun under his predecessor.

Instead of some non-Israelite monarch, "a king" in line 25 of the Nimrud Prism could simply refer to a native Israelite king. This would appear to be the plain sense of the text particularly if one follows a restoration that reads "a king [hostile] to me." Only Tadmor has seriously raised the question of whether Israel was ruled at the time by a native king. In discussing how Samaria may have been governed after the arrest of Hoshea and during its prolonged warfare with Assyria, Tadmor raised two possibilities: "(a) that there was no king in Samaria . . . and that the besieged city was governed by the generals of the army or by the city elders; (b) that a king whose name was recorded neither in the Bible nor in the Assyrian Inscriptions reigned until 722 or 720." As argument against the latter proposal, he offered the following: "the probable reference to the 'Samarians' rather than to the 'King of the Samarians' in the Nimrud Prism—while Hannun of Gaza and Yaubi'di of Hamath are usually mentioned by name—seems to favour the first assumption."[44] However, if Samaria had already been declared an Assyrian province by Shalmaneser in 725, a reference to "the Samarians" is exactly what one would expect. The references to Hannun king of Gaza and Yaubi'di the usurper of the throne of Hamath is also what one would expect since both of these states still held the status of vassal kingdoms rather than that of provinces. The other regions—Arpad, Simirra, and Damascus—mentioned as participants in the revolt spearheaded by Yaubi'di have nothing said about their

---

43. Na'aman, "Historical Background," 210.
44. Tadmor, "Campaigns of Sargon II," 37.

leadership. They too, like Samaria, had been provincialized. These cities thus belonged to a totally different political category than did Hamath and Gaza. For Sargon to have referred to "King X of Samaria" (or Arpad, Simirra, or Damascus) would have implied political conditions contrary to reality as viewed by the Assyrians since Arpad, Simirra, Damascus, and Samaria were provinces not states.

On the basis of the preceding discussion, the following restoration and translation of the opening lines of the Nimrud Prism may be proposed:

> 25 [LU.*sa*]-*me-ri-na-ai-a sa it-ti* LUGAL
> 26 [LU.KUR]-*ia a-na la e-pes ar-du-ti*
> 27 [*u la-na*]-*se-e bil-ti*
> 28 [*a-ha-me*]*s ig-me-lu-ma e-pu-su ta-ha-zu*

> The Samarians, who with a king hostile to me, not to offer servitude and not to deliver tribute, came to an agreement and they offered battle.

The Samarians, the inhabitants of the province of Samaria proclaimed by Shalmaneser in 725, covenanted together under a king to join in rebellion against Sargon who had assumed the throne in Tebet 722–721. The domestic strife within Assyria, the rebellion of Babylon under Marduk-apla-iddina, and the defeat of Sargon at Der by the Elamites may have contributed to Samaria's hopes of continuing to forestall the full consequences of provicialization. The outbreak of a rebellion under conditions very comparable to those following the death of Shalmaneser is reflected in Hos 10:1–8:

> 1. A luxuriant vine was Israel,
>   his fruit was like him;
> when his fruit increased,
>   so he increased altars;
> according to the bounty of his land,
>   so he made bountiful cultic pillars.
> 2. Their heart became deceitful;
>   now they will bear their guilt.
> He will break their altars;
>   he will destroy their cult pillars.
> 3. Surely they will now say,
>   "There is no king over us.
> Surely, do we not fear Yahweh?
>   And what can this king do to us?"

4. They have exchanged words,
    vain oaths, making a covenant;
and judgment spreads like poison weeds
    along the furrows of a field.
5. Over the calf of the house of iniquity
    they have been agitated,
    the one set up in Samaria.
Surely its people mourned over it,
    and its priests concerning it.
They wailed over its glory,
    because it has departed from them;
6. for it has been carried to Assyria
    as tribute to the great king.
Within the year, Ephraim will be taken,
    and Israel will be dismayed over his plan;
7. silenced will be the king of Samaria,
    like a chip on the surface of the water;
8. and the high places of iniquity will be destroyed, the sin of Israel;
    thorns and thistles shall grow up on their altars;
    and they will say to mountains, "Cover us!" and to the hills, "Fall upon us!"

Several factors are presupposed in the rhetorical circumstances addressed by this text. (1) Widespread Israelite rebellion has broken out and the rebels have united under oath in a covenant pact (vv. 2, 4, 6b). (2) Monarchical authority over the people in the form of a particular king, probably Sargon during his accession year, has weakened and the people see this as a time for action in the name of Yahweh (v. 3). (3) The calf of Samaria has been taken into exile to the Assyrian ruler (vv. 5–6a). The reference is probably to the fact that when Samaria earlier surrendered to or was captured by the Assyrian army (between 15 Marheshvan and 12 Tebet 722) the sanctuary in the city or in the vicinity of Samaria was looted and the recently fashioned golden calf was carried as booty to Shalmaneser. (4) A king is ruling in Samaria, and Ephraim as a whole seems to be in rebellion (vv. 6b, 7). In light of these circumstances, the prophet proclaims future disaster, which he envisions coming within the year (vv.6a–8). The parallels between the historical circumstances presupposed by this text and those of the early days of Sargon are striking. The involvement in the rebellion of Ephraim/Israel and not just the city of Samaria (v. 6b) explains why Sargon in four texts refers to his capture of not only the city of Samaria but also of the land of Omri.

If Sargon in 720–719 was opposed by the Samarians led by a native king, two questions arise in light of the preceding discussion. First, was the Israelite king at the time of Sargon the same person elevated to kingship after the arrest of Hoshea (Hos 8:4)? Second, if one or two kings reigned over Samaria/Ephraim after the arrest of Hoshea, why do 2 Kgs 17:3–6 and 18:9–11 make no reference to this fact? To these questions, no satisfactory answers can be given.

Hosea 13:1–14:1, which probably derives from very close to the time of Sargon's assault on Samaria (see 14:1), contains references to the people's request for a king (v. 10) as well as Yahweh's declaration that a king had both been given and taken away in divine wrath (v. 11). This, however, is most likely a reference to King Hoshea, placed over the people as a consequence of Pekah's rebellion against Assyria and then himself taken away because of rebellion against Assyria. The anger of Yahweh in both cases was the consequence of the breaking of a treaty sworn in the name of Yahweh. Whether Hoshea's replacement avoided capture in 722–721 and continued to rule until Sargon took the city some two years later or was deposed by Shalmaneser's forces and subsequently replaced by a second "anonymous" ruler cannot be determined.[45]

The lack of any reference in 2 Kings to any Israelite king following Hoshea may be due to either of two reasons. First, those who produced the sources used by the editors of the Kings material may have possessed no knowledge of the internal affairs prevailing in Israel because of the unsettled conditions of the time and Judah's isolation from the events. That is, the Judean court may not have known the name of such a monarch. Although this would appear to be a highly unlikely situation, it must be noted that the Kings material does not report the conquest of Samaria by Sargon either. Second, the failure to record this information may have been based on ideologcal reasons, namely, the Judeans considered Hoshea to have been the last legitimate king in the north. Hoshea was placed in power by Tiglath-pileser and would have begun his rule with proper credentials according to a pro-Assyrian Judean court. Hoshea was probably still alive, though perhaps in exile, when the last reported event regarding the northern kingdom occurred, namely the capture of the region in 722–721. The southerners may have chosen not

---

45. How destructive the Assyrian capture was in 722–721 cannot be determined. The archaeological remains from the site do not clearly indicate a massive destruction. On the archaeological data, see Becking, "Ondergang van Samaria," 64–68; and Na'aman, "Historical Background," 209.

The Final Years of Samaria (730–720 BC)

to dignify the claims of a rival claimant to the throne and condemned him by non-mention. That the Judean court was favorably disposed to Hoshea is indicated by the assessment of his reign: "He did the evil in the eyes of Yahweh though not like the kings of Israel who preceded him" (2 Kgs 17:2).[46] This positive attitude toward Hoshea was probably based on Israel and Judah's pro-Assyrian policy at the time of Hoshea's rise to power and on the fact that Ahaz and Hoshea shared in the overthrow of Pekah (Hos 2:2).[47]

Other issues regarding Sargon's relationship to Samaria are less controversial than the question of Samaria's leadership at the time. Sargon makes no reference to any prolonged siege of Samaria nor does he describe the nature of its capture; thus how much destruction of the city occurred cannot be determined. Only chariots and the gods in which they trust (= their cultic paraphernalia) are listed as spoil taken by the Assyrians. If Sargon's western campaign saw him first defeating Yaubi'di at Qarqar and then moving down the coast where he subdued Hannun of Gaza, defeated the Egyptian army, and destroyed Raphia taking 9,033 inhabitants as spoil before returning to deal with the Samarians, as seems most likely, the latter may have offered little resistance. This might explain the moderate punishment imposed on Samaria. Sargon appointed one of his officers as the governor. Some chariot crews (50 or 200; cf. Large Display Inscription: 24 with Nimrud prism, Fragment D, col. N: 33) were incorporated into the royal forces. No special penalties were imposed on the people and no reference is made to any special booty taken. Sargon claims to have set the tribute at the rate of the former king (Large Display Inscription: 24) (Hoshea? Shalmaneser?) or to have required of the Samarians the same duties and tax as of Assyrians (Khorsabad Annals: 17). Apparently the city of Samaria did not require rebuilding, as Dalley

---

46. This "positive" assessment of Hoshea suggests that at least some of the editorial evaluative judgments made about the monarchs in the Books of Kings may not derive from a late deuteronomistic editor. No one in the late pre-exilic or exilic periods would have had knowledge of events in Hoshea's day that would have suggested this "positive" assessment unless it was preserved in written sources.

Rabbinic interpreters noted the positive evaluation of Hoshea and attributed it to Hoshea's willingness to allow northerners to worship in Jerusalem (see b. Baba Batra 121a; Gittin 88a; and Taanit 30b). Van der Kooij, "Zur Exegese von II Reg. 17, 2," sees the positive assessment to be the result of the Assyrian capture of Dan, which removed one of the northern golden calves. Hoshea ruled over a kingdom with only one calf!

47. Scribes at the pro-Sargonid Jerusalem court may have deliberately omitted reference to Sargon's destruction of Samaria for political reasons.

has recently argued. Instead of the widely accepted reading *Sa-me-ri-na u-tir-ma eli sa pa-ni u-se-me* ("Samaria I resettled and made it greater than before"), in lines 37–38 of the Nimrud Prism, she proposed reading the verb *ataru* rather than *taru* and *u-se-sib* instead of *u-se-me* and understanding the verbs as a hendiadys: "I repopulated Samaria more than before."[48] Sargon further claims to have deported over 27,000 people from the area and to have imported to the region foreigners whom he had captured. The settlement of foreigners in the north, noted in 2 Kgs 17:24, probably occurred in several waves and extended over several years.[49]

Conclusion

In light of the previous discussion the following conclusions may be drawn about the final days of Samaria.

(1) Hoshea began the organization of an anti-Pekah movement probably during Tiglath-pileser's second campaign against Damascus in 732–731 (2 Kgs 15:30aα) and was designated the new king over Israel (or *bit Humria*) by Tiglath-pileser (III R 10, 2:17–18; ND4301 + 4305: rev. 10–11) before he left the region in 731 or during the twelfth year of Ahaz (Tishri 732—Tishri 731) (2 Kgs 17:1).

(2) Hoshea, aided by the pro-Assyrian Ahaz (Hos 2:2), had to overcome the unrepentant Pekah and his forces who remained in control of Samaria (Layard 66:228) and the Ephraimite hill country at the time of Tiglath-pileser's withdrawal. Samaria was not taken (2 Kgs 17:30aβ) until after Marheshvan 731. In his accession year (ending Marheshvan 730), Hoshea sent tribute to Tiglath-pileser encamped at Sarrabanu (ND4301 + 4305: rev. 10–11) in southern Babylonia.

(3) Hoshea paid annual tribute to Assyria during his first two regnal years (Marheshvan 730—Marheshvan 728) but joined the western revolt participated in by Damascus and Tyre that broke out in Tiglath-pileser's seventeenth year (Nisan 728—Nisan 727).

(4) Shalmaneser, in his accession year (25 Tebet—Nisan 726), completed a western campaign begun by Tiglath-pileser (Eponym Chronicle).

---

48. Dalley, "Foreign Chariotry," 36. If the city was not heavily damaged rebuilding would not have been necessary.

49. Tadmor, "Some Aspects of the History of Samaria"; Cogan and Tadmor, *II Kings*, 209; and Na'aman and Zadok, "Sargon II's Deportations."

The Final Years of Samaria (730–720 BC)

When he campaigned against Hoshea, the latter submitted and paid tribute (2 Kgs 17:3).

(5) When Shalmaneser remained in Assyria during his first year (Nisan 726–Nisan 725) (Eponym Chronicle), revolt erupted again in the west and Hoshea joined the movement sending to Egypt to negotiate for assistance (2 Kgs 17:4a).

(6) Shalmaneser marched to the west probably early in his second regnal year (Nisan 725–Nisan 724) attacked Hoshea for the second time, demolished parts of Samaria, looted the royal temple in Bethel, arrested Hoshea, and decreed provincial status for Samaria (2 Kgs 17:4b; Hos 10:14–15; Isa 32:14; Babylonian Chronicle I.i.28). After subduing Samaria, Shalmaneser moved against Tyre, placing it under siege before the autumn New Year Festival in 725 (Hos 9:13; *Ant.* 9.285–286).

(7) In response to the decree of Shalmaneser, Samaria and Ephraim rose up in rebellion, placed a new king on the throne, and established a state sanctuary within the city or in the environs of Samaria (Hos 8:4–5a). In his third regnal year (Nisan 724–Nisan 723), Shalmaneser campaigned in the west again. He had to attack the whole of Ephraim (2 Kgs 17:5a) eventually placing Samaria under siege after Marheshvan 724 in the seventh year of Hoshea (Marheshvan 724–Marheshvan 723) and the fourth year of Hezekiah (Tishri 724–Tishri 723) (2 Kgs 18:9). The deportation of Israelites (2 Kgs 17:6aβ) began in Shalmaneser's third year during the course of this campaign.

(8) Samaria was captured by or surrendered to the Assyrians for the third time in Shalmaneser's fifth year (Nisan 722–Nisan 721) during which the king was not on campaign (Eponym Chronicle). The city fell to the Assyrian army at some time between 15 Marheshvan and the death of Shalmaneser in Tebet 722, in Hezekiah's sixth year (Tishri 722–Tishri 721) and Hoshea's ninth year (Marheshvan 722–Marheshvan 721) (2 Kgs 17:6aα; 18:9).

(9) With Sargon's accession marked by domestic strife (Borowski Stela) and by troubles with Elam and Babylon (Babylonian Chronicle I.i.33–35; Assur Charter: 16–18), the Assyrian army withdrew from the west, lifting the siege of Tyre and leaving matters unsettled in Samaria. Rebellion again broke out, involving the province of Samaria and its capital (Nimrud Prism, Fragment D, col. IV:25–28), co-ordinated with revolt by the states of Hamath and Gaza and the provinces of Arpad, Simirra, Damascus, and Hadrach (Khorsabad Annals; Asharna Stela). The

rebellion probably coincided with the death of Shalmaneser or the early days of Sargon's troubles.

(10) Late in his second regnal year (Nisan 720—Nisan 719), Sargon campaigned in the west defeating Yaubi'di of Hamath, Hannun of Gaza, and the *turtan* of Egypt before quickly suppressing the revolt in the province of Samaria. Sargon presided over the fourth submission of Samaria, finally implemented the full provincialization of the region, deporting Samarians, carrying off their cultic paraphernalia, placing one of his officers as governor over the region, repopulating the city, and importing foreigners into the region.

Bibliography

Astour, Michael C. "841 B.C.: The First Assyrian Invasion of Israel." *Journal of the American Oriental Society* 91 (1971) 383–89.
Becking, E. J. H. "De Ondergang van Samaria." PhD diss., University of Utrecht 1985.
Borger, Riekele. *Textbuch zur Geschichte Israels*. Edited by Kurt Galling. 2nd ed. Tübingen: Mohr/Siebeck, 1968.
Borger, Rikele, and Hayim Tadmor. "Zwei Beiträge zur alttestamentliche Wissenschaft aufgrund der Inschriften Tiglathpilesers III." *ZAW* 94 (1982) 244–51.
Chong, Joong Ho. "The Song of Moses (Deuteronomy 32:1–43) and the Hoshea–Pekah Conflict." PhD diss., Emory University, 1990.
Cogan, Mordechai, and Hayim Tadmor. *II Kings*. AB 11. Garden City, NY: Doubleday, 1988.
Dalley, Stephanie. "Foreign Chariotry and Cavalry in the Armies of Tiglath-pileser III and Sargon II." *Iraq* 47 (1985) 31–48.
Donner, Herbert. *Israel unter den Völkern*. VTSup 11. Leiden: Brill, 1964.
Gadd, C. J. "Inscribed Prisms of Sargon II from Nimrud." *Iraq* 16 (1954) 173–201.
Gelston, A. "Kingship in the Book of Hosea." *OTS* 19 (1974) 71–85.
Ginsberg, H. L. "Hosea." In *EncJud* 8 (1971) 1010–24.
Grayson, A. Kirk. *Assyrian and Babylonian Chronicles*. Texts from Cuneiform Sources 5. 1975. Reprinted, Winona Lake, IN: Eisenbrauns, 2000.
Hayes, John, and Paul K. Hooker. *A New Chronology for the Kings of Israel and Judah*. 1988. Reprinted, Eugene, OR: Wipf & Stock, 2007.
Hayes, John H., and Stuart A. Irvine. *Isaiah, the Eighth-century Prophet: His Times and His Preaching*. Nashville: Abingdon, 1987.
Hughes, J. *Secrets of the Times: Myth and History in Biblical Chronology*. JSOTSup 66. Sheffield: JSOT Press, 1990.
Irvine, Stuart A. *Isaiah, Ahaz, and the Syro-Ephraimitic Crisis*. SBLDS 123. Atlanta: Society of Biblical Literature, 1990.
Jones, G. H. *1 and 2 Kings*. NCB. Grand Rapids: Eerdmans, 1984.
Kaiser, Otto. *Texte aus der Umwelt des Alten Testaments*. 1/4. Gütersloh: Mohn, 1984.
Kooij, A. van der. "Zur Exegese von II Reg. 17, 2." *ZAW* 96 (1984) 109–12.
Lambert, W. G. *Ladders to Heaven: Art Treasures from Lands of the Bible*. Edited by Oscar White Muscarella. Toronto: McClelland & Stewart, 1981.

The Final Years of Samaria (730–720 BC)

Luckenbill, D. D. *Ancient Records of Assyria and Babylonia.* 2 vols. Chicago: University of Chicago Press, 1926–27.

Na'aman, Nadav. "The Historical Background to the Conquest of Samaria (720 BC)." *Bib* 71 (1990) 206–25.

Na'aman, Nadav, and Ran Zadok. "Sargon II's Deportations to Israel and Philistia (716–708 BC)." *JCS* 40 (1988) 36–46.

Olmstead, A. T. *Assyrian Historiography: A Source Study.* University of Missouri Studies, Social Science Series 3/1. Columbia: University of Missouri, 1916.

———. "The Fall of Samaria." *American Journal of Semitic Languages and Literatures* 21 (1904–1905) 181.

Rawlinson, H. C. *Cuneiform Inscriptions of Western Asia.* 5 vols. London: Bowler, 1861–1909.

Redford, Donald B. "Sais and the Kushite Invasion of the Eighth Century B.C." *Journal of the American Research Center in Egypt* 22 (1985) 5–15.

Rost, Paul. *Die Keilschrifttexte Tiglat-Pilesers III nach den Papierabklatschen und Originalen des Britischen Museums.* Leipzig: Pfeiffer, 1893.

Saggs, H. W. F. "Historical Texts and Fragments of Sargon II of Assyria, 1. The 'Assur Charter.'" *Iraq* 37 (1975) 11–20.

Smith, George. *Assyrian Discoveries.* 1876. Reprinted. ANECS. Eugene, OR: Wipf & Stock, 2006.

———. "On a New Fragment of the Assyrian Canon Belonging to the Reigns of Tiglath-Pileser and Shalmaneser." *Transactions of the Society of Biblical Archaeology* 2 (1873) 321–32.

Spieckermann, Hermann. *Juda unter Assur in der Sargonidenzeit.* FRLANT 129. Göttingen: Vandenhoeck & Ruprecht, 1982.

Tadmor, Hayim. "The Campaigns of Sargon II of Assur: A Chronological-historical Study." *JCS* 12 (1958) 22–40, 77–100.

———. "Some Aspects of the History of Samaria during the Biblical Period." *Jerusalem Cathedra* 3 (1983) 1–11.

Talmon, Shemaryahu. "The Cult and Calendar Reform of Jeroboam I." In *King, Cult and Calendar in Ancient Israel: Collected Studies,* 113–39. Aspects of the Hebrew Bible. Jerusalem: Magnes, 1986.

Thompson, R. C. "A Selection from the Cuneiform Historical Texts from Nineveh (1927–32)." *Iraq* 7 (1940) 85–111.

Thureau-Dangin, F. "La stele d'Asharne." *Revue d'Assyriologie et d'Archéologie Orientale* 30 (1933) 53–56.

Winckler, Hugo. "Beiträge zur Quellenscheidung der Königbücher." In *Alttestamentliche Untersuchungen,* 16–25. Leipzig: Pfeiffer, 1892.

———. *Geschichte und Geographie.* Keilinschriften und das Alte Testament 1. Edited by Eberhard Schrader. 3rd ed. Berlin: Reuther & Reichard, 1903.

———. "Nachtrag." *Zeitschrift für Assyriologie* 2 (1887) 351–52.

Wiseman, D. J. "A Fragmentary Inscription of Tiglath-pileser III from Nimrud." *Iraq* 18 (1956) 117–29.

Wolff, Hans Walter. *Hosea: A Commentary on the Book of the Prophet Hosea.* Translated by Gary Stansell. Hermeneia. Philadelphia: Fortress, 1974.

5

The History of the Form-Critical Study of Prophecy

IN 1881, EDUARD REUSS wrote that "the prophets are older than the law and the Psalms are later than both."[1] Subsequent decades witnessed the wide acceptance of this position and then its gradual erosion. Speaking very broadly, one can say that the history of prophetical studies during the last dacades of the nineteenth century and the whole of the twentieth century is the history of this proposition; its meteoric ascendancy to almost canonical status, its time of siege and defense, its final capitulation, and its subsequent amplification. The exuberance characteristic of the nineteenth century's discovery of prophecy as a unique religious phenomenon and the recognition that the prophets were flesh and bone representatives of historically conditioned humanity speaking face to face with their contemporaries has dimmed. In spite of prophecy's loss of its triumphalism in Old Testament studies, prophetical research has retained its vibrant and exciting qualities; perhaps not in spite of this loss but because of it. In Old Testament research, prophecy has now had its *bar mitzvah*, prophecy too has had its pilgrimage to the cult, and prophecy has even been instructed by the teachers of ancient Israel.

---

1. Reuss, *Die Geschichte*, VII.

The History of the Form-Critical Study of Prophecy

The First Generation

Hermann Gunkel

As a genre, histories of form-critical research seem to adhere to a law that requires that all such surveys begin with an analysis of the contributions of Hermann Gunkel (1862–1932).[2] This is as it should be since his writings and influence have left an indelible impression upon all areas of Old Testament form-critical studies either directly, in the case of the psalms, narratives, and prophecy or indirectly, in the case of law and wisdom. Gunkel shared in the original thrusts of two distinct but closely related developments in biblical studies: the history of religions approach[3] and form-critical analysis.[4] The two developnents had their origin in a common intellectual, historical, and cultural milieu and have, since their origin, been related in lesser or greater degree although on occasions somewhat ambivalently.

Gunkel spoke of four movements of his day that he understood as advancement leading to altered perspectives and new approaches in Old Testament study.[5] In relating these directly to Old Testament prophecy, he argued that they challenged both the orthodox interpretation of the prophets as implements in the hands of a supernatural revelation and the rationalistic assessment of the prophets as devout teachers and

---

2. For studies of Gunkel, see Baumgartner, "Hermann Gunkel"; Baumgartner, *Zum Alten Testament*, 31–38; Baumgartner, "Zum 100. Geburtstag von Hermann Gunkel"; Galling, "Hermann Gunkel"; Hubert, "Hermann Gunkel"; Schmidt, "In Memoriam Hermann Gunkel"; Kraus, *Geschichte*, 341–67; von Rabenau, "Hermann Gunkel"; von Rabenau, "Hermann Gunkel auf rauhen Phaden"; Klatt, *Hermann Gunkel*; and Buss, "The Study of Forms." Bibliographies of Gunkel's publications have been compiled by Hempel, "Hermann Gunkels Bücher"; and Klatt, *Hermann Gunkel*, 272–74.

3. See Gressmann, *Albert Eichhorn*; Gunkel, *Die Religionsgeschichte* (ET = *The History of Religion*); Hahn, *The Old Testament*, 2nd ed., 83–118; Klatt, *Hermann Gunkel*, 15–103; Kraus, *Geschichte*, 315–40.

4. See Hahn, *The Old Testament*, 119–56; and Klatt, *Hermann Gunkel*, 104–16.

5. See Gunkel, "Einleitungen," XX. In assessing the shift in Old Testament studies that took place at the turn of the century, Obermann wrote: Gressmann's "work bears witness to the fact that the profundity of the Nineteenth has given way to the versatility of the Twentieth century: that, for better or worse, philological penetration, textual criticism, and source-analysis have been replaced by historio-comparative speculation, literary-aesthetic appraisal, psychological appreciation; that the Old Testament, as indeed all mental, science has come to deal not so much with dates, persons and phenomena as with epochs, milieus, movements" (Obermann, "Preface," XII–XIII).

respectable preachers.⁶ These four movements were neo-Romanticism, comparative religion (*Erforschung fremder Religionen*), history of literature with its stress on form analysis and history, and psychology. According to Gunkel, the neo-romantic or impressionistic⁷ movement saw new colors and heard new sounds that manifested the inner life of humankind. Comparative religion provided a wealth of valuable material for comparison with the Old Testament. *Literaturgeschichte*⁸ offered the means to analyze the literary forms, which themselves provided a means of access to the inner life of the user. Psychology as a science allowed the investigator to seek for and appreciate an immediate perception of the ancient person that had not been the concern of the orthodox and rationalistic approaches.

These four movements that Gunkel saw as bringing a deeper understanding of the Old Testament were supported by a general widespread negative attitude toward, even a certain exhaustion with, the results of purely literary-critical study of the scriptures. Literary criticism, it was claimed, with its obsession with external problems about dates, documents, and authors did not penetrate aesthetically to the essence of the materials.⁹

Gunkel belonged to a circle of scholars with strong interests in the history of religions approach and who saw great weaknesses in literary criticism. Hugo Gresmnann expressed the feelings of this group when he said: "We are fed up with being treated with literary criticism only."¹⁰ Such

---

6. For nineteenth-century conceptions of Hebrew prophecy, see Baumgartner, "Die Auffassungen."

7. On the interpretation of the Old Testament by Romantics and especially Herder, see Kraus, *Geschichte*, 114–32; Scholder, "Herder"; Willi, *Herders Beitrag*; and Herder, *The Spirit of Hebrew Poetry*.

8. On this, see Gunkel's programmatic essay, "Die israelitische Literatur," with its stress on what today would be called both diachronic and synchronic issues. The literary history of Old Testament literature was of course an issue prior to Gunkel's time, and he acknowledged the importance of the works of Meier, Ehrt, Cassel, Kautzsch, Wünsche, Reuss, Kuenen, and others. In "Neue Ziele," Gunkel spoke of the difference between historical criticism or a purely literary history of the Old Testament as a *Vorarbeit* and an aesthetic approach as a true history.

9. Gunkel, *Die Propheten*, 106.

10. See Klatt, *Hermann Gunkel*, 74. Gunkel's positions led him quite early in his career into controversy with Julius Wellhausen, the greatest representative of Old Testament literary criticism. In several respects, Gunkel shared many of the positions and ideas of Wellhausen, some of which were later to influence his form-critical work. The basic point of disagreement between Wellhausen and Gunkel centered on the

sentiments, revealing a deep dissatisfaction with literary criticism, found expression in the English-speaking world in similar forms largely independent of the continental disquietude.[11] This negative attitude toward the products of literary critical investigations was in reality a positive desire for a greater appreciation of the biblical materials, for an aesthetic, empathetic understanding of the very life and soul of the ancient authors and their literature.

Gunkel considered form criticim (a term that he does not seem to have used), or *Gattungsforschung*, or *Literaturgeschichte*, as one of the tools for acquiring this greater and deeper understanding and appreciation of the biblical traditions. The overall goal of such an endeavor was the ability to see the literature of ancient Israel in its totality, that is, in its functional relationship to the whole of the people's life and history. The study of literary genres would allow the interpreter, Gunkel believed, to relate the individual fonns to their context and usage in human life, that is, to their *Sitz im Leben*. Gunkel felt that form-critical analysis of the Old Testment would yield categories into which the whole of the Old Testament would fall.[12] Such categories could then be studied in their interrelatedness and individuality. The analyzed types of Old Testament traditions would provide the means for developing an aesthetic appreciation of the material. This stress on the aesthetic appreciation of the biblical materials occurs frequently in Gunkel's writings and on this point he recognized his kinship with Herder.[13] Form-critical analysis was seen as the means for discovering the inner life of the writer. Here again, the theme of the inner life of the writer—the desire to discover and explore the inner thoughts of the ancients—with its romantic, idealistic expectations appears as a recurring goal in Gunkel's work,[14] a goal that led him to preserve a strong individualistic and spiritualized interpretation in many areas, often to the detriment of his form-critical analysis, particularly in his study of the psalms.[15] A form-critical emphasis, Gunkel believed, would allow one to trace the evolution of the individual, at least

---

employment of comparative religious phenomena to elucidate the Old Testament. For the controversy, see Klatt, *Hermann Gunkel*, 70–74.

11. See Buss, "The Study of Forms," 39–52.
12. See Gunkel, *What Remains*, 115.
13. Gunkel, "Die israelitische Literatur," 99.
14. Gunkel, *What Remains*, 72; and "Einleitungen," XX.
15. See Gerstenberger, "Psalms," 198–207.

negatively, revealing the extent of the individual's divergence from the traditional.[16]

What Gunkel meant by a literary genre or a form-critical unit was best expressed in writings published toward the close of his career.[17] He wrote:

> Every genre shows its individuality in defined characteristics:
> (1) In a common store of thoughts and moods, which is carefully transmitted from generation to generation, despite the sundry changes in the customary spiritual quality that can be carried out at the hands of outstanding individual authors.
> (2) In a traditional linguistic form, i.e., definite phrases, sentence structures, images, and so forth; that is the customary form that usually preserves the thoughts and can endure sometimes for many centuries; on this linguistic form we lay a special value because it is just this that is the easiest to recognize.
> (3) A third characteristic of a genre is a definite *Sitz im Leben* of the people, in which it originally had its special place, out of which just these thoughts and their forms of expression have arisen and in which they are therefore also to be understood, even if it is true that the genres in a more developed time, when writing came to dominance in the cultural life, had given up this oldest situation in favor of the written book.
> Only where we have all three criteria preserved together, only where we can ascertain that definite thoughts in a definite form on a definite occasion were expressed have we the right to speak of a genre.[18]

According to Gunkel then, every genre has a specific content and mood, a formal language of expression, and a setting in life.

Gunkel's interest in the prophets spanned the whole of his career.[19] His first publication in the area was a study of the opening chapter of the book of Nahum published in 1893,[20] and his last writings on the prophets were published in the second edition of *Die Religion in Geschichte und Gegenwart* (1927–1931). Unfortunately, Gunkel never devoted a systematic and extensive study to the form criticism of the prophets comparable

---

16. Gunkel, *Die Propheten*, 108.

17. Gunkel, "Der Micha-Schluss" (ET = "The Close of Micah"); "Jesaia 33"; and *Einleitung in die Psalmen*, 22–23.

18. "Jesaia 33," 182–83.

19. See Klatt, *Hermann Gunkel*, 192–203.

20. Gunkel, "Nahum 1."

to his introduction to the psalms, which would have given his insights free reign nor did he prepare a form-critical commentary on any prophet comparable to his work on the narratives in Genesis, which would have revealed his methodology at work. Three of his longer publications on the prophets contain form-critical discussions but in the general context of an overall study of the prophets.[21]

Before examining in some detail Gunkel's particular observations on prophetical form criticism, it should be pointed out that Gunkel shared with many of his contemporaries four basic and important concepts concerning the prophets that greatly influenced his form-critical analysis. Three of these were concepts inherited from earlier literary critical studies and the fourth was a concept that had risen to prominence through the writings of Duhm,[22] Hölscher,[23] and Gunkel himself. The first of these was the acceptance of the idea of a unilinear evolution of phenomena, an opinion shared in Gunkel's day by many Old Testament literary critics. The idea of the development from the primitive, the simple, the pure, and the ordinary to the sophisticated, the complex, the complicated, and the spiritual pervades much of Gunkel's Old Testament research and was an unrecognized hindrance in many respects. (Similar verdicts will rightly be pronounced on contemporary Old Testament studies someday!) The prophets developed from ecstatics, to orators, to poets, preachers, teachers, and thinkers. The prophetic oracles developed from a single saying, to several lines, to long sermons. The prophetic tradition developed from oracle sayings, to small collections, to pamphlets, to books. Prophetic oracles developed from a set rhythmic form, to a freer style, to prose.[24]

A second important concept for Gunkel was the assumption that the prophets represent the culmination and pinnacle of ancient Israelite religion. The excessive enthusiasm attendant upon the nineteenth century's rediscovery of the prophets lived on in the work of Gunkel. Nonetheless, in many respects, Gunkel interpreted the prophets within the context of the traditional religion of Israel. He claimed that they did not seek to proclaim something new; they represented the old religion, especially in

---

21. Gunkel, "Propheten II seit Amos" (ET = "The Israelite Prophecy from the Time of Amos"); "Einleitungen," XI–LXXII; and *Die Propheten*.

22. Duhm, *Das Buch Jesaia*, 41–46

23. Hölscher, *Die Propheten*.

24. See throughout "Einleitungen" and "Propheten Israels seit Amos"; Gunkel assumed that these developments eventually led to deviations and mixtures, that is, to the dissolution of pure forms. See Gunkel, *What Remains*, 65.

their ethics, and they preached in the name of the ancient Israelite deity. They challenged the new developments associated with the monarchy and in so doing were spokesmen of older Israelite concepts of freedom and values.[25] The prophets harked back to the historical traditions of Israel, especially those associated with Moses and Sinai and David and the Israelite empire. Nonetheless Gunkel could talk about the newness and originality of the prophets expecially in their combination of religious and ethical concerns and their consistent monotheistic outlook.[26]

A third dominating hypothesis that Gunkel shared with much of the prophetic research of his time was the emphasis on the priority of the future and prediction in prophetic proclamation.[27] Gunkel could describe the prophets as future-oriented men, foretellers, men who lived in the future, and the revelation received in the revelatory state as a word concerning the future.[28] As will be noted below, this concept possessed numerous ramifications for Gunkel's form-critical analysis of prophetical preaching.

A fourth important emphasis in Gunkel's prophetic studies was his stress on the personal experience of the prophets and in particular the ecstatic experience in which they received their revelatory words concerning the future. This emphasis on the person and personal experience of the prophets was a natural outgrowth of the nineteenth century's stress upon the prophet as a creative individual. For Gunkel, Duhm, Hölscher, and others, however, the new emphasis was on the irrational, the extraordinary experiences of the prophets. Gunkel was apparently the first of modern scholars to emphasize this aspect of prophecy, and he first did so in his dissertation on the Holy Spirit.[29]

In his subsequent publications the ecastatic character of prophecy and ecstacy as an important element in all aspects of prophecy received a

---

25. On some of these issues, Gunkel like Max Weber, seems to have been influenced directly or indirectly by the social and political thought and interest of his day. See Buss, "The Study of Forms," 39–52.

26. See Gunkel's chapter on the religion of the prophets in *Die Propheten*, 68–103.

27. For similar views, see Wellhausen, *Israelitische und jüdische Geschichte*, 110; W. R. Smith, *The Old Testament in the Jewish Church*, 278.

28. See, for example, Gunkel, *Die Propheten*, 125.

29. Gunkel, *Die Wirkungen* (ET = *The Influence*); earlier, the term ecstasy had been used in describing the prophets but with reference to the inner rapture of their spirits. See, for example, Knobel, *Der Prophetismus*, 1.155–56. See Duhm, *Die Theologie*, 87–88, who does speak of vision and ecstasy.

particular stress.[30] Numerous works published contemporaneously with Gunkel's research also stressed this aspect of prophecy,[31] an element already noted as early as Philo.[32] The important role assigned to ecstasy by Gunkel influenced his form-critical analysis in a direct manner as shall be seen below.

Gunkel was the first modern biblical scholar to stress the indispensibility of genre study and analysis for an adequate interpretation of the Scriptures. This in itself is not an overly significant fact since *Gattungsforschung* in several disciplines and in its relationship to religious literature were in the air near the end of the last centry.[33] Gunkel declared

30. See Gunkel, "Die geheimen Erfahrungen" (ET = "Israelite Prophecy," 48–55).

31. See notes 22 and 23 above; and Duhm, *Das Geheimnis*; Duhm, *Die Gottgeweihten*. For similar emphasis in English works, see W. R. Smith, *The Old Testament*, 278–94; and Davidson, *Old Testament Prophecy*, 115–43. Hölscher's work, *Die Profeten*, with its use of Wundt's psychology, was, in actuality, a frontal assault on the rationalistic interpretation of prophecy represented in such works as Kuenen's *De Profeten* (ET = *The Prophets*).

32. Philo wrote: "For no pronouncement of a prophet is ever his own; he is an interpreter prompted by Another in all his utterances, when knowing not what he does is filled with inspiration, as the reason withdraws and surrenders the citadel of the soul to a new visitor and tenant, the Divine Spirit which plays upon the vocal organism and dictates words which clearly express its prophetic message" (*Laws* 4.49). Philo is here comparing prophecy and divination. Elsewhere he writes: "When the light of God shines, the human light sets; when the divine light sets, the human dawns and rises. This is what regularly befalls the fellowship of the prophets. The mind is evicted at the arrival of the divine Spirit, but when that departs the mind returns to its tenancy. Mortal and immortal may not share the same home. And therefore the setting of reason and the darkness which surrounds it produce ecstasy and inspired frenzy" (*Who Is the Heir* 53). Plato wrote similarly of inspiration associating the mantic faculty with that part of the soul located in the liver: "For inspired and true divination is not attained to by anyone when in his full *senses*, but only when the power of thought is fettered by sleep or disease or some paroxyxm of frenzy" (*Timaeus* 32). These descriptions are similar to what Gunkel says about ecstasy and may suggest an acquaintance with them, although Gunkel, so far as I know, does not refer to them. (Both Gunkel and Duhm, however, do refer to Greek ecstatisicm as a parallel to Old Testament prophetism.) Note Gunkel's remarks that "the prophet demanded a belief in his person, in his *divine inspiration*. And this inspiration was so conceived that it excluded all human cooperation" ("Israelite Prophecy," 48). The similarity between Gunkel's and Philo's descriptions of ecstasy suggests Gunkel's familiarity with Philo, but I have found no direct proof. It should be remembered, however, that Gunkel's primary field of specialization in his graduate training was the Hellenistic and New Testament era, an area in which one could assume his familiarity with Philo.

33. Form-critical studies in the classics predating Gunkel were undertaken by such scholars as Nietzsche, Reitzenstein, Wendland, Bethe, Norden, and others. For bibliographical references, see Gercke and Norden, eds., *Einleitung in die*

that the first question in *literaturgeschichtliche* study is the question of the *Gattung*.[34] "Whoever would investigate an author without an acquaintance with the genre used by him begins the building of the house with the roof."[35] Form-critical study for Gunkel, therefore, is a basic and foundational requirement, an intellectual and aesthetic requirement for the interpreter. Such an assumption implies that one must ask form-critical questions before asking interpretive, content, and theological questions, although in actuality and in theory Gunkel emphasized the role of content even at the level of asking form-critical questions. The necessity of form-critical study was threefold: (1) many genres used by the ancients are completely unknown or foreign to the modern reader; (2) genres in the literature of ancient people were far more important than for moderns; and (3) the function of the literature within the ancient folk-life of Israel must be the beginning point of one's understanding, and this is attainable only through form criticism. Gunkel considered one of the particularities of the spiritual life of ancient culture to be that the individual was bound to the speech and literary forms by social custom and every new thought was expressed in customary thought forms.[36]

In discussing the prophetical materials form critically,[37] Gunkel stressed that the prophets were originally speakers and not authors. They began their messages with a call "to hear," not "to read."[38] These speakers functioned as oracle givers, counsellors, and intercessors.[39] Enquiry addressed to the divine and the response in an oracle, Gunkel saw as one of the basic aspects of early prophecy. When man reached his wits' end, he

---

Altertumswissenschaft, 1.585; and Bethe and Wendland, "Quellen und Materialien," 427. Some of the interests of these scholars are reflected in the titles of two works by Norden: *Die antike Kunstprosa* and *Agnostos Theos*. The first extensively form-critically oriented volume on the prophets was Wilhelm Erbt's *Jeremia und seine Zeit*, but his work was apparently influenced by Gunkel; see Baumgartner, *Die Klagegedichte*, 4, and below, note 95.

34. "Einleitungen," XXXVII.
35. Ibid., XXXVIII; and similarly, *Die Propheten*, 108–10.
36. Ibid., XXXVII–XXXVIII.
37. For Gunkel's specific contributions to prophetical form-critical research, see Klatt, *Hermann Gunkel*, 210–18; and Westermann, *Grundformen*, 15–21 (ET=*Basic Forms*, 23–31). Westermann's treatment of Gunkel is, as a whole, extremely poor, and, in places, omission of elements in Gunkel's presentations does a great disservice to Gunkel.
38. Gunkel, "Einleitungen," XXXVIII.
39. Ibid., XXVIII–XXIX.

The History of the Form-Critical Study of Prophecy

turned to God with questions about everyday life: dreams (Genesis 41), sickness (2 Kings 1), siege (2 Kgs 7:1), journeys (Judg 10:5), battle (1 Sam 14:18, 37). Appeal in such cases were directed to "men of God" of whom the prophets were one type. Questions about the future were addressed to the prophet who in the form of prophecies and predictions foretold the future. In his counsel and intercession the prophet moved beyond the "prediction of" to a "control over" the future. The word of the prophet spoken in the name of God possessed the power to control the future and to control the powers of the world (Isa 55:10–11; Hos 6:5; 2 Kings 1; Jer 1:10; 25:15ff; 28:16). From these considerations, Gunkel arrived at what he considered to be one of the basic characteristic of the earliest form of prophetic address: it was a future-oriented word.[40] The certainty of the coming events in the immediate future came to the prophet in ecstatic experiences.

The ecstasy of the prophets Gunkel spoke of in terms of the "psychically abnormal," the "second self," "mental illness and nervous derangements."[41] This ecstatic experience had its influence on the earliest form of prophetic address. "Men who acted in such special ways cannot have spoken calmly and discreetly."[42] They screamed, cried out, and slavered.[43] Thus the "Original prophetic genre was an ecstatic description of the future."[44] Some oracles even in the classical prophets, Gunkel suggested, appear to be directly related to and spoken out of ecstasy (Jer 4:19–20; Isa 21:1ff; 63:1ff; and the Balaam oracles). The oracle was, however, most commonly spoken in the more dispassionate situation after the demise of the ecstatic experience; in a calmer condition the prophet introduced his oracle with: "Thus has Yahweh spoken to me."[45] As a result of the revelations and in his calmer state "the prophet regards himelf as the 'messenger' of Yahweh—a favorite and characteristic image from an early period—and just as the messenger reports the words of his master exactly as he has heard them from him, so the prophet also has the right to speak in the first person in the name of Yahweh himself. "Thus has Yahweh spoken," his oracle begins, and at certain points at the end of the

---

40. Ibid., XXXIX; *Die Propheten*, 125.
41. "Israelite Prophecy," 48–54.
42. "Einleitungen," XXXIX.
43. Ibid., XXIV.
44. *Die Propheten*, 125.
45. "Einleitungen," XXXIX; "Israelite Prophecy," 62.

sections he adds "says the Lord" (*ne'um yhwh*). This can alternate at will with another form, in which he speaks about Yahweh's thoughts in his own name, and so speaks of Yahweh in the third person."[46]

In discussing the ecstatic future word as the earliest form of prophetic utterance, Gunkel cited as examples of this form two widely different specimens. In emphasizing sayings in the classical prophets in which he said one could still see the "cries" of the ecstatic, he wrote:

> The short enigmatic words and combinations of words such as Jezreel, Lo-ammi, Lo-ruhamah (Hosea), Emmanuel, Shear-jashub (Isaiah), Maher-shalal-hash-baz "the spoils speed, the prey hastes" (Isa 8:1), Rahabhamoshbath ("Rehab who sits still," the bound dragon of chaos; Isa 30:7) are examples of the very earliest prophetic style. In such mysterious words the literary prophets, imitating the cries of the ancient ecstatics summed up their ideas.[47]

In emphasizing the future aspect, Gunkel wrote as follows:

> There never arose a prophet in Israel whose first saying was not the foretelling of an event of the immediate future. Consequently, we may accept that the earliest prophetic style is to be found in passages in which the future is described. It is characteristic that particularly clear examples of this style are found in the *oracles concerning foreign nations* (Isa. 13–21; Jer. 46–51; Ezek. 25–32) . . . however, the passages aimed at foreign nations represent a category which at the time they wrote was completely dead, but which reveals to us the concerns of an earlier period.[48]

It is difficult to see how Gunkel could understand the oldest prophetical style reflected in both the short, enigmatic words and the oracles against foreign nations. No reference is made to the possibility that oracles against foreign nations may have originally been only short, enigmatic words nor is any attempt made to explain the length and form of the foreign oracles except to say that only late examples have survived.

---

46. "Israelite Prophecy," 67–68. Gunkel spoke of the prophet as Yahweh's messenger to his people and compared the function and speech of the prophetic messenger with royal messengers and messages with references to the negotiations between David and Abner (2 Sam 3:12–16) and David's message sent to Zadah and Abiathar (2 Sam 19:12). See "Einleitungen," XLVIII, LVII.

47. "Israelite Prophecy," 64–65; more fully, "Einleitungen," XXIV–XXV.

48. "Israelite Prophecy," 69; see also "Einleitungen," IL.

Nonetheless, Gunkel's three main publications on the prophets[49] contain almost identical pargraphs on these two items; the only difference is that the oracles against foreign nations as genuinely prophetic descriptions of the future are said in one place to be "the clearest examples of the genuinely prophetic form of revelation,"[50] whereas in two places the word "ekstatische" is added to read "genuinely-prophetic, ecstatic form of revelation."[51] I suggest that the use of these two examples (short, enigmatic words and oracles against foreign nations) reflect two unreconciled emphases in Gunkel's thought regarding the style of the earliest prophetic genre, namely the ecstatic and the futuristic. This seems to be the case in spite of his use of the term 'ecstatic' with reference to oracles against the nations in two of his writings.

In addition to its ecstatic and futuristic character, the earliest prophetic style was characterized by brevity. "The oldest units of prophetic style are likewise the shortest . . ."[52] Speaking in short oracles was a practice of the early prophets that was taken over by the later classical prophets who, however, developed the ability to deliver longer forms of address. This tendency to shortness in the address demands that the exegete isolate and distinguish between the units in a prophetical work.

> Since it is characteristic of every literary category, that the units within the category are of a specific form and extent, and since if these units are not identified, it is impossible to understand the style in question, the study of the style of the prophets must begin with the units in which their utterances were made. This study is all the more vaulable, in that in general they are not indicated in the tradition of the text we possess, and many scholars, who have not yet realized the necessity of this task, and following modern ideas of style, still think in terms of units which are much too large and display great uncertainty in the distinguishing and identification of the passages.[53]

---

49. "Israelite Prophecy," 64–65, 69; "Einleitungen," XXIV–XXV, IL; *Die Propheten*, 116, 125.

50. "Israelite Prophecy, 69.

51. "Einleitungen," IL; *Die Propheten*, 125.

52. "Einleitungen," XLII. See also *Die Propheten*, 116; and "Israelite Prophecy," 64–65. The division of the prophetical texts into short units is reflected in the commentaries on Isaiah by Duhm (1892) and Gray (1912) who divided the tradition into short units but not on the basis of form-critical considerations. See Robinson, "Higher Criticism."

53. "Israelite Prophecy," 64.

Gunkel insisted that one of the innate laws of a *Gattung* was the fact that as a unit it possessed a thoroughly customary and conditioned extent. The discovery of the true limits of the individual, originally independent passage, not necessarily reflective of the present chapter and verse division, was of signal importance. When the prophetical unit extends to two, three, or more lines (as in Amos 1:2; 3:1–2; 5:1–3; 9:7; Isa 1:2–3; 3:12–15; 14:24–27; 17:12–14; 49:1–2, 3–5, 6–8, 9–11; Jer 2:1–3, 4–9, 10–13, 14–19), one is already dealing with a developed form and stage in the history of prophecy and the prophetic form of address.[54]

Associated with the brevity of the original prophetic oracle is Gunkel's emphasis on the poetical and metrical character of the earliest prophetic speech. For him, poetry took precedence over prose. "Of its nature, enthusiastic inspiration speaks in poetic form, and rational reflection in the form of prose. Consequently, in form the prophetic speech was originally a poem. People like the prophets, who received their ideas in times of exalted inspiration, and uttered them under the impulse of an overflowing emotion, could only speak in poetic rhythms."[55] As an antecedent and parallel to the poetic form of the prophetic oracle, Gunkel pointed to the verse form of the divine response at the sanctuary ("die Antwort Jahwes am Heiligtum"; see Gen 25:23) and to the words of the Delphic Apollo. This poetic verse form was characterized by a rhythmic meter.[56]

> As far as the metrical form is concerned, two categories can be distinguished in the poems of the prophets: a stricter style, in set rhythms, and a more free style which, depending upon the fluctuation of the prophet's mood, used a mixture of different verse forms. Examples of the first category are Isa. 1.10ff; 3.12–15; Jer. 2.1–3; Mic 4:1–3, and of the second such passages as Isa. 1.28 and 29.1–8. From the aesthetic point of view, these poetic compositions of the prophets reach extraordinarily high standards, and represent the most sublime element in the Old Testament, which is full of the sublime.[57]

---

54. "Einleitungen," XLII–XLIII.

55. "Israelite Prophecy," 66. See also "Einleitungen," XLIV–XLV.

56. Gunkel had already utilized metrical structure in his treatment of Nahum 1 in reaching his verdict that "the poem in Nahum I is no prophetic vision but a post-prophetic psalm" ("Nahum 1," 242).

57. "Israelite Prophecy," 66. See also "Einleitungen," XLIV.

The History of the Form-Critical Study of Prophecy

The rhythmic meter of the early prophetic style suggested to Gunkel that some of these oracles were sung, a practice still reflected in Isaiah.[58] The "stricter style" (noted in the above quote) appears to have been utilized in song form while the "freer style" belonged more to the cateory of recited poetry.[59] The movement away from purely poetic, rhythmic address to a much freer form that ultimately turned into prose or led to the utilization of such forms as torah or historical narrative, which naturally made use of prose, was associated by Gunkel with the development of the prophets from ecstatics into preachers and religious thinkers.[60]

A further characteristic of early prophetic style of address in addition to its brevity, predictive content, ecstatic quality, and rhythmic and metrical form was its "mysteriousness," a reflection of the fact that "revelations were received in mysterious times of ecstasy; they appeared obscure and shadowy before the soul of the prophet. This is faithfully reflected in the style of the visions of the future, and explains the strange demonic and enigmatic tones of these passages."[61] The mood of mystery in the prophecies is reflected in the avoidance of specific names, the use of approximate or generalized numbers, the employment of indirect expressions, the utilizations of concrete but imprecise imagery, the use of allegorical and mythological references, and the coining and application of special names.[62] This secretive mysteriousness in the prophetic prediction was traced by Gunkel to both the nature of the ecstatic revelation and conscious concealment on the part of the prophets. In interpreting the prophets Gunkel noted that "we ought to recognize that mysteries are being presented to us, and take care not to destroy with our own overhasty explanations the impression that the prophet is trying to achieve.[63]

"Another characteristic of the prophetic prediction is its particularly jumpy style."[64] What Gunkel is referring to is the abruptness, incoherence, and discontinuity found in many oracles in which the prophet jumps into a subject with both feet, without introduction, and without regard for

---

58. Gunkel, "Einleitungen," XXV.
59. Ibid., XLIV.
60. "Israelite Prophecy," 66.
61. Ibid., 69; see "Einleitungen," IL; and *Die Propheten*, 125–29.
62. "Israelite Prophecy," 69–71; and "Einleitungen," IL–LII.
63. "Israelite Prophecy," 71; and "Einleitungen," LII, where the same idea appears and the "mysterious quality" of prophetic speech is related to the category of "mood."
64. "Einleitungen," LII; misleadingly translated in "Israelite Prophecy," 71. In *Die Propheten*, 129, he uses the term *impressionistische* with regard to this jumpy style.

his hearers' understanding, or changes subject, especially from doom to salvation (Isa 6:13; 29:5), or heaps up "isolated individual elements, uprooted from their context." The reading of such magnificent passages as Jer. 64, 3ff. (sic! so also *RGG*²); Joel 4:9ff.; and Nah 3:1ff. is sufficient to show that this very heaping up of apparently incoherent elements is a genuinely prophetic trait."[65]

A further characteristic of prophetic prediction is the use of extraordinarily concrete descriptions and visual imagery.[66] Such concreteness reflects both the manner of the revelation and a characteristic of Hebrew thought. As examples of this employment of concrete imagery, Gunkel refers to Isa 2:13, 16, 20; 6:12; 7:21, 23; 14:9ff, 22, 23; 16:14; Jer 2:1; Amos 6:9–10; Mic 3:12; Zeph 1:8.

Prophetic speech is, according to Gunkel, passionate address. "No characteristic is so evident as the profound and passionate intensity of the prophets. No word is too terrible or too cruel for the prophets of doom, and nothing too extravagant for the prophets of good fortune."[67] The prophet had sensed the significance of what was approaching and it had set his soul on fire; in his passion and vehemence, the prophet sought to kindle a glow in the hearts of his hearers. The passion and intensity of the prophet vented itself in a spate of puns, reminiscences, allusions, ironic, and satirical expressions, and mythological illusions especially in contrasting the present with the future.

A final characteristic of the distinctly prophetic manner of speaking are certain elements related to syntactical style.[68] In discussing this point, Gunkel reiterated his major premise concerning the relationship of genre to syntactical forms: "It is characteristic of the peculiarity of fixed genres that they favor (*lieben*) certain syntactical constructions."[69] Characteristic of prophetic address is the use of the future tense or prophetic perfect in which the predicted is treated as already having happened, of address in the second person reflecting the prophet's function as messenger coming face to face with those to whom Yahweh had sent him, of the imperative that is genuinely prophetic and through whose usage the prophet feels justified in giving commands to the whole world in the name of Yahweh,

---

65. "Israelite Prophecy," 71.
66. Ibid., 71–72; "Einleitungen," LIV; *Die Propheten*, 130–31.
67. "Israelite Prophecy," 72; "Einleitungen," LIV; *Die Propheten*, 130–31.
68. "Einleitungen," LVI–LVIII; "Israelite Prophecy," 72–73; *Die Propheten*, 132–33.
69. "Einleitungen," LVI–LVII.

and of questions that reflect the use of inquiries as the prophets' means of understanding the initial revelation.

To summarize Gunkel's characterization of the oldest prophetic style and prediction, one might say that the original prophetic addresses were short, future-oriented, ecstatically colored, poetic, metrical, mysterious, sometimes jumpy, passionate, and dominated by certain syntactical constructions. Gunkel would surely not have argued that all of these features are to be found in any one prophetic passage, and he certainly did not attempt to suggest any single passage as a specimen of the earliest style. However, he did write: "All the characteristics which we have described, and to which it would be an easy matter to add many other similar features, show the considerable degree to which the prophets' revelations of the future display the original and genuine prophetic style."[70]

The oldest prophetic style could take the form of either a promise (*Verheissung*) or a threat (*Droh*) depending on whether the word about the future was of good or evil omen.[71] Corresponding to these were of course the two types of Israelite prophecy—salvation and judgment prophecy—which at almost every period existed side by side.[72] Gunkel does not devote much space in his writings to the discussion of promise and threat, he simply notes their existence as two means of preaching about the future and then proceeds to expound the characteristics of the early prophetic style, which have been discussed above.

Before proceeding to examine what Gunkel referred to as the more developed prophetic style, it is necessary to comment on his classification of prophetic oracles into two groups: visions and auditions.[73] His discussion of this division appears in the context of his comments on the infinite variety of genres in the prophetical books and the insurmountable difficulty involved in arranging the material according to genre. He writes:

---

70. "Israelite Prophecy," 73.

71. "Einleitungen," IL.

72. Gunkel gave an appreciative evaluation of the prophets of good fortune ("Einleitungen," XXXII; "Israelite Prophecy," 55–59; *Die Propheten*, 32–36) who had much in common with the prophets of doom and whose words are now to be found here and there in the Scriptures and not least in the form of additions and accretions to the prophetical books, some of which may be quite early (*Die Propheten*, 35–36).

73. Westermann writes: "In this division of the prophetic speeches into visions and auditions lies the basically erroneous starting point of Gunkel's and Gressmann's genre investigation" (*Basic Forms*, 24).

> There we find narratives about the deeds and events of the prophets, reported by contemporary or later disciples, and beside them passages which originated from the prophets themselves, among which are those written for themselves and their God and in addition to those others which were produced for the people. We will examine first of all the last of these because they comprise the essential, basic stock of the prophetical writings. These prophetical "oracles" fall according to type, just as the revelation was received, into two classes: visions and auditions, the seen and the heard, the appearance and the "words," with the characteristic beginnings: "Thus has Yahweh shown me" and "Thus has Yahweh spoken to me."[74]

From this statement, it is obvious that Gunkel, in dividing this public material into visions and auditions, is attempting to accomplish three objectives: (1) to treat some of the narrative material in the prophetic books as distinctly narrative material; (2) to integrate this material with what he has written about the prophetic experience with its accompanying phenomena of seeing and hearing—vision and verbal revelations; and (3) to insist that most of the tradition was preaching material.[75] Commenting on visions, Gunkel discusses their extent, content, narrative and prose form, their quality of mystery, and their tendency to stress the spoken word rather than the vision per se. In his discussion of auditions, he is concerned with the message given the prophets as divine messengers, their speaking of Yahweh in the first person, and the prophets' dialogue with Yahweh. Only passages in which intercession appears are referred to (Amos 7:2,4; Hab 1:11ff; Jer 11:14; 12:5; 14:10; 15:1, 19.) As is obvious, Gunkel, in speaking of visions and auditions, is not primarily concerned with forms of address but rather with forms of revelation and how these experiences were then used. Nowhere in his specifically form-critical analyses does he rely on this division into visions and auditions; nonetheless his use of the word 'oracles' for these two classes of material was unfortunate. The point he was pursuing is understandable. A discussion of visions and auditions, however, could have been more properly assigned to his section on the prophetic experience, although such an arrangement could have led to a loss of the sense of these traditions as preaching material.

74. "Einleitungen," XLV; the following section (3.9) about three pages in length, has no counterpart in the *RGG* article that Westermann used as the basic statement of Gunkel.

75. "Israelite Prophecy," 50–51; "Einleitungen," XXII–XXIII; *Die Propheten*, 14–19.

The History of the Form-Critical Study of Prophecy

"The earliest prophetic style never completely disappeared";[76] but in proclaiming their message the prophets adopted a wide range of foreign genres and added new developments to the older style.[77] On the basis of content, Gunkel spoke of the incalculable variety of prophetic words: "promise and threats, descriptions of sins, exhortations, priestly injunctions, historical review, disputes, songs of every kind, religious poems and imitation of secular poems, songs of lamentation and rejoicing, short lyrical passages and complete liturgies, parables, allegories, etc."[78] This borrowing of genres and the more developed prophetic style were discussed by Gunkel in terms of the prophets having developed into, on the one hand, poets and, on the other hand, into preachers, teachers, and thinkers. The reason for this prophetic development and the prophets' adoption of foreign forms was "their burning desire to gain power over the minds of their people. The fact that they mastered such an extraordinary number of literary categories is a sign of the zeal with which they struggled with the hearts of their people."[79]

First, Gunkel discussed the prophets as poets and here he primarily emphasized the prophets' appropriation of forms from Israel's rich and ancient lyrical traditions. Among the borrowed forms utilized by the prophets in the ornamentation of their proclamations were such secular types as victory songs (Isa 37:22–29; 47), wedding songs (Jer 33:11), drinking songs (Isa 22:13; 56:12), watchman's songs (Isa 21:11), mocking songs (Isa 23:16) and funeral songs (Amos 5:2; Isa 14:4–21; Jer 9:16–21 [ET = 17–22]; Ezek 26:17–18; 27:3–11; 28:11–19; 32:2–16).[80] Among the religious lyrics borrowed and imitated by the prophets, Gunkel noted the thanksgiving song (Jer 33:11), pilgrim songs (Isa 2:3; 26:2; 30:29; Mic 4:1ff.), hymns (Isa 25:1–2; 40:22–23; 42:5, 10–13; 43:16–17; 44:23ff; 46:13: 52:9; Jer 31:35; 51:15; Amos 4:13; 5:8; 9:5–6), communal laments (Isa 16:9, 11; 63:7ff; Jer 4:10; 14:1–6, 7–9, 13, 19–22; 15:5–9;

---

76. "Israelite Prophecy," 73.

77. Ibid., 68–69, 73–75; "Einleitungen," XLVII–IL, LVIII–LXXII.

78. "Israelite Prophecy," 68; "Einleitungen," XLVIII–IL. See *Die Propheten*, 124, for a slightly different terminology. Duhm, in his *Die Theologie*, had already used some of the terminology employed by Gunkel, such as *Mahnrede* and *Geschichtebetrachtung*.

79. "Israelite Prophecy," 68–69.

80. Gunkel acknowledged the work of Budde on the funeral song and attributed to him the discovery of the first of Israelite genres. See Budde, "Das hebräische Klagelied"; and "Ein althebräisches Klagelied." This genre was given detailed study under Gunkel's direction by Jahnow, *Das hebräische Leichenlied*.

Ezek 9:8; 21:11–12; Hos 9:14; Amos 7:2, 5; Joel), penitential songs (Hos 6:1–3; 14:3–4; Jer 3:21–25; Zech 12:10–14), the response of Yahweh (Hos 14:4–6; Jer 15:1), liturgies (Isa 33:14–16; Mic 6:6–8),[81] and individual laments (Jer 11:18–23; 12:1–6; 15:11, 15–20; 17:12–18;18:18–23; 20:7–13, 14–18).[82] Gunkel also distinguished a mixture of prophetic and lyrical styles in examples of prophetic communal laments with associated oracles (Jer 3:22—4:2; 14:1–11; 14:19–15:2; Isa 26:16–21; 63:7—65:25; Hab 1:12—2:1ff; Mic 7:7–13; 7:14–20).

The prophets also developed into preachers, teachers, and thinkers and correspondingly altered the old form of prophetic address. For Gunkel, this was demonstrated in several ways but especially in speaking of the sins of Israel and the wickedness of the people by the prophets of doom.

> The earlier prophets prophesied individual events in the immediate future; the later literary prophets certainly did not cease to speak in the first instance of the future, but they were able to do more than this: they were capable of giving the reasons why Yahweh was sending the event they prophesied; they knew his thoughts and they felt his moods.[83]

> They were not satisfied merely with foretelling the future, although this always remained their principal purpose; but they also began to give the *ethical reason* why what they had prophesied had come to pass.[84]

In explicating the reasons for the proclaimed threat, the prophets utilized the reproach (*Scheltwort*).[85] The threat and reproach (*Drohung* and

---

81. See Gunkel, "Jesaia 33"; and "Der Micha-Schluss" (ET = "The Close of Micah").

82. Baumgartner (*Die Klagegedichte*) demonstrated that the material in Jeremiah was dependent upon traditional lamentation forms and thus countered the widely held view that Jeremiah was the originator of psalmody.

83. Gunkel, "Israelite Prophecy," 53.

84. Ibid., 74.

85. Westermann (*Basic Forms*, 29–30) seems to me to have completely misrepresented Gunkel's treatment of the threat and reproach. He claims that Gunkel considered the reproach a borrowed form. Gunkel did not; he considered it instead as an inner prophetical development utilized to undergird or explain the threat. Westermann claims that Gunkel considered the two as independent and separate genres. Gunkel did not; he considered them closely bound together. Westermann in attempting to reproach Gunkel writes: "This lack of clarity has produced after effects in most of the investigations down to this day. It has caused the evidence that is clear in the texts to remain hidden. This evidence shows that, in actuality, the "threat" and the

Scheltwort) belong together in the same passage, the former proclaims the coming doom (*Unheil*) and the latter, following "because," adds the exposition of the sins (classical examples are Amos 1:3, 6, 9, 11, etc.) or the reproach precedes the threat, which is introduced by "therefore" (Amos 4:11; 5:11; 6:7; Isa 5:13; 10:16; 29:14; Jer 2:8; 5:7, etc.). Gunkel assumed that this close association was the ordinary usage of the threat and reproach although sometimes the prophets "in their carelessness toward the fixed arrangement" would move from reproach to threat and back again (Amos 2:6–16).[86] When the reproach appears first, it is sometimes introduced by *hoy* ("woe") with a following participle or something similar (Isa 1:4, 5, 8, 11, 18, 20, 21, 22; 29:11; 30:1; Amos 5:16; 6:1; Jer 22:13, etc.) or with "hear" (Amos 4:1; 8:4). Whole books, such as Amos, could consist essentially of these two categories: the threat and the reproach.[87]

The prophets' desire to expose the sins of the people led "to a new, uniquely prophetic genre, the independently appearing reproach" (Isa 1:2–3, 4–9; 58:1; Jer 2:10–13).[88] For Gunkel then, the independent status of the reproach was a development subsequent to the use of the reproach in support of the threat. The independent reproach could be expressed in the form of a judgment speech (*Gerichtsrede*)[89] of Yahweh to Israel (Isa 1:18–20; 3:13–15; Mic 6:1ff.; Jer 2:4–9; Hos 2:4ff). Sometimes such judgment speeches were introduced with an indignant question (Isa 3:15; Mic 6:3; Jer 2:5). Later prophets proclaimed their message in eschatological judgment speeches (Joel 4:1–8).

In addition to threats and reproaches,[90] the prophets also uttered exhortations (*Mahnen* or *Mahnrede*) and preached repentance since there steals into every humandkind's heart a little "perhaps" and because every legitimate prophet had as his final goal the conversion of the people from its evil ways. The prophetic exhortation developed out of

---

"reproach" are found in a great majority of the prophetic texts, not as two separate genres, but as one speech form, i.e., as two constituent parts or members of one speech form the prophetic judgment-speech" (30). The last sentence could easily have been written by Gunkel; in fact, the first paragraph on p. LXV of Gunkel's "Einleitungen" says it just as well.

86. "Einleitungen," LXV.
87. Ibid.
88. Ibid.
89. In *RGG*², 1553 (see "Israelite Prophecy," 74) he spoke of a *Rede vor Gericht* ("speech before a court").
90. For the following paragraphs see "Einleitungen," LXVI–LXXI; and "Israelite Prophecy," 74–75.

the ancient prophetic practice of answering questions and giving advice (Jer 42:1–17; Zech 7:1–10; Mic 6:6–8). The exhortation might be employed ironically (Amos 4:4; Jer 7:21) or legitimately (Amos 5:15; Hos 2:4; 4:15; Isa 1:10–14, 19–20; 7:9; 28:16; 29:5ff: 30:15 etc.). Isaiah offered political advice throughout his career (Isa 7:13; 28:12; 30:15), and Jeremiah made extensive use of exhortations (Jer 3:13; 14ff; 4:1, 3, 14; 5:20ff; 6:8; 7:1–7; 11:1ff; 13:15–16; 18:11; 21:11–12; 22:3ff; 23:16; 26:13; 27:12). The exhortation might be associated with promise (Jer 3:13, 14ff; 4:1–2, etc.) or with threat (Jer 4:3–4; 7:1–15; 13:15ff; 21:11ff etc.) or the two combined (Jeremiah 18; Ezekiel 18; Amos 5:4–6). The prophetic oracle was proclaimed as Yahweh's revelation; the exhortation appears to have frequently represented the prophet's own good advice (Jer 26:13; 27:13). The style of the prophetic speech of exhortation was mainly poetic but in the case of Jeremiah often prose.

Closely allied with prophetic exhortation is the prophetic imitation of priestly torah that the priests had employed for instruction in worship and ethics and in liturgical exercises. The prophets utilized this method of instruction (Jer 3:1; Hag 2:12–13; Amos 5:21–24; Isa 1:10–17; Hos 6:6; Jer 6:20; 7:21ff; Isa 58:6–7; 66:3; Ezekiel 18; Zech 7:4ff.) as well as the liturgical torah with its question and answer character (Isa 33:14–16; Mic 6:6–8). The use of the torah form allowed the prophets to expound on the will of God or express their exhortations. Thus they moved toward being philosophers.

In order to express their abstract thought, the prophets utilized a new genre, the historical narrative (*Geschichtserzählung*) or historical review (*Geschichtsbetrachtung*). This form was used to relate the past to the present, making special use of the exodus and conquest traditions (Amos 2:9–10; 5:25; 9:7; Hos 9:10; 11:1; 12:14; Jer 2:1ff; 7:22 etc.). With Ezekiel, this usage reached its apogee (Ezekiel 16; 20; 23) where it tended toward allegory, a factor already present in Hosea 1–3.

Arising out of the prophets' dialogue and conversation with their audience and prophetic opponents are the controversy speeches (*Streitgespräche*) or disputations (Amos 5:14; Isa 22:12; 28:9ff; 30:16; Zeph 1:12; Jer 2:20, 25, 27, 35; 3:4–5; 7–10; Ezek 11:3, 15; 12:22–23; 18:2; 21:5; Isa 40:27; 58:1ff; Hag 1:2; 2:3; almost all of Malachi, etc.). Sometimes the words of the opponents are recorded but in most cases they are omitted although entire passages in the prophets, Gunkel argued, read like the answers of the prophets to objections raised by their audiences. Many of these disputations reflect the efforts of the prophets to convince their audiences of the rightness of their proclamation and to justify the work of God. Such efforts attempting to convince led the prophets to the use of parables (Amos 3:3-8; 5:19; Isa 5:1-7; 28:23-29) and proverbs (Hos 4:11; Ezek 12:21; 16:44).

Hugo Gressmann

Hugo Gressmann (1877-1929) stands with Gunkel as a pioneer in the history of form-critical work on the prophets. Several of his writings dealt in systematic fashion with a form-critical eludication of the prophetical preaching.[91] Except for Gunkel's brief discussion of form criticism on the prophets in his contribution to Hinneberg's *Kultur der Gegenwart*,[92] Gressmann's form-critical analysis in SAT,[93] written as a part of the introduction to his exegesis of Amos, constitutes the first systematic presentation in this area. The parallels between Gunkel's and Gressmann's treatments are striking and often too similar to be coincidental. It is difficult, however, to ascertain the lines of influence since the two men carried on extensive oral and written communications.[94] The main issues that characterize both men's subsequent work on form criticism of the prophetic material are already outlined in Gunkel's "Die israelitische Literatur." Nonetheless, Gressmann's study published in SAT in 1910 goes far beyond this early contribution of Gunkel and has its closest parallels in Gunkel's 1913 article in *RGG*.[95] Gressmann's priority may be only a

---

91. Gressmann, *Die älteste Geschichtsschreibung*, 322-29; "Die literarische Analyse Deuterojesajas"; *Der Messias*, 64-148. His earlier important work on the prophets, *Der Ursprung*, contains no form-critical discussion per se but does display what can be called, speaking broadly, form-critical interests such as his focus on the influence of court style on the prophets and the relationship of salvation and doom proclamations. For a complete list of Gressmann's writings, see Sprondel, "Bibliographie Hugo Gressmann."

92. Gunkel, "Die israelitische Literatur," 80-90 (= *Die israelitische Literatur*, 28-38).

93. This section was subsequently omitted in the second edition of SAT II/1 published in 1921 since Gunkel, in the meantime, had written his more extensive treatment in his "Einleitungen" to Schmidt's volume in the series.

94. See Klatt, *Hermann Gunkel*, 136.

95. See note 21 above. Parallels between the early presentations of Gunkel and Gressmann are noted in subsequent footnotes. Whether the material in Gressmann's presentation which is without parallel in Gunkel's early publications can be considered uninfluenced by Gunkel and thus the creative work of Gressmann is a difficult question to answer. If Erbt's work on Jeremiah was dependent on Gunkel (see note 33 above), perhaps through Gunkel's class lectures, then it suggests that Gunkel's remarks

priority of publication rather than of conception and personal communication may have provided opportunity for the exchange of ideas. In several of his works, Gressmann admits his general dependency upon the published works of Gunkel.[96] In a 1908 letter,[97] however, Gressmann spoke of a new and better understanding of prophecy that he had developed in his study of Amos through the use of *Stilgeschichte*, which he says only Gunkel had previously taken into consideration. Such a statement implies both a dependence upon Gunkel and a creative independence on the part of Gressmann. At least, the emotional independence of Gressmann is suggested by two further factors. Among Gunkel's close circle of friends and associates, Gressmann seems to have been least willing to accept Gunkel's role as teacher and father.[98] In addition, Gunkel was initially hesitant about Gressmann's participation in the SAT project although he later praised his "brilliant work."[99] Such initial hesitancy and subsequent praise suggest Gressmann's independence of thought and a certain lack of familiarity with and confidence in him by Gunkel.

Gressmann began his discussion of prophecy and the prophetical *Gattungen* in SAT II/1 with a statement about the individual personality of the prophet and a short general comment about the nature of the prophetic word.[100] In discussing the general character of the prophetical word,[101] he noted its enigmatic quality, the influence of the ecstatic experience, its futuristic orientation, its extreme brevity, and its poetical and rhythmic form.[102] He stressed the necessity of isolating the individual and independent unit of address through the aid of introductory and concluding formulas although he stated that, in importance, it is the content that is most decisive in such an understanding.

---

on the prophets in "Die israelitische Literatur" were only "the tip of the iceberg" insofar as his early analysis was concerned. Erbt spoke of *Mahnwörte* and *Drohwörte* as if these were commonly understood designations that needed no explanation.

96. Gressmann, *Ursprung der israelitish-judischen Eschatologie*, 327; and "Die literarische Analyse Deuterojesajas," 258–59.

97. See Klatt, *Hermann Gunkel*, 195–97.

98. See ibid., 197 n. 18; and Gressmann's letter in the same volume, 223–66.

99. See ibid., 195–97.

100. As had Gunkel, *Die israelitische Literatur*, 28.

101. He argued that "prophetical sayings" or "prophetical words" was a more adequate terminology than "prophetical speeches" (*Die älteste Geschichtschreibung*, 323). Gunkel had spoken of prophetische "Rede" (*Die israelitische Literatur*, 33).

102. See Gunkel, *Die israelitische Literatur*, 30–33.

Gressmann divided specifically prophetical *Gattungen* into two broad categories: visions (or appearances) and auditions (or words).[103] Visions, with their characteristic formulas ("So the Lord Yahweh showed me" or "I saw the Lord"), do appear in the prophets, but Gressmann considered these of slight importance. The call visions of many of the prophets reflect their experience of being carried away to the "heavenly parliament" where they participated in the deliberations about the future.[104] The words (or oracles, as he subsequently refers to them) are recognizable by their introductory formulas, "Thus says Yahweh" or "In those days" and by their concluding or intermediate formula, "Yahweh whispered."

According to their content, prophetical words or oracles may be broken down into the categories of promise and threat.[105] The scarcity of promises in the preexilic canonical prophets is noted by Gressmann. Although he recognized a preponderance of promises in post-exilic and non-canonical prophecy, Gressmann refused to deny the proclamation of promises to the canonical pre-exilic prophets. He claimed that salvation and judgment could co-exist in the message of the same prophet and even in the same prophetic oracle.[106]

The counterpart to the promise was the threat that had been employed by the early prophets against Israel's enemies. From the time of

---

103. As had Gunkel; ibid., 33.

104. See further Gressmann's discussion of Micaiah ben Imlah (1 Kgs 22:1-28) in *Die älteste Geschichtschreibung*, 278-80. Gunkel had spoken of the prophetic transference, in his vision, to "Yahweh's Council" (Die israelitische Literatur, 34).

105. Gunkel's discussion of the prophetical genres in *Die israelitische Literatur* (35-37) contains nothing really comparable to Gressmann's analysis of promises, threats, exhortations, reproaches, and judgment speeches (*Die älteste Geschichtschreibung*, 324-26). Gunkel simply refers to the diversity of prophetical words ("These prophetical words reflect an amazing diversity: there are promises and threats, descriptions of sins, exhortations, historical reviews, disputations, songs of all sorts, not only religious, but also imitations of profane songs, songs of lament and jubilation, short lyrical pieces and complete liturgies, parables allegories, and so forth," 35) and then proceeds to discuss what he called the earliest and then the more developed style. The closest parallels to Gressmann's discussion are found in Gunkel's 1913 *RGG* article.

106. This was a consistent emphasis in Gressmann's writings on the prophets. This emphasis derived from his assumption that the prophets inherited a mythological eschatology that embodied the concepts of both a world judgment or catastrophe and a world renewal. See *Die älteste Geschichtschreibung*, 327-28; and his "Foreign Influences."

Amos, the threat came to be directed against Israel and became the dominant form of prophetic address.

The exhortation, according to Gressmann, occurs infrequently in the prophets (see Isa 1:10–17; Jer 7:1–15). In the whole of the book of Amos, only two examples appear (Amos 5:4ff, 14–15). Originally the words of exhortation were the condition on the basis of which salvation could be proclaimed and were thus associated in proclamation with promise. Later, the exhortation was loosed from this connection and became independent.

Reproaches were used in conjunction with threats where they served as the reason (*Begründung*) for the proclamation of judgment. Like the exhortation, the threat was developed, on occasion, into an independent genre (Isa 1:2–3; 3:13–15; Jer 2:10–13). The reproach was the product of prophetic reflection on the oracle of threat and was developed in an attempt to elucidate the reason for the act of God.[107] The threat, and the exhortation as well, was considered by Gressmann as the prophet's word expounding the divine oracle (the threat or the promise). "Characteristically, the exhortation and reproach words were not, in general, introduced as the words of God as were the threats and promises. The prophet distinguished between the oracle that he had received from Yahweh and his own observations thereon, through which he hoped to make the oracle understandable.[108] On the secondary use of the reproach as an independent genre, Gressmann wrote: "It is of special interest to pursue how the words of reproach assumed an ever greater importance for the prophets, how these reproaches which in scope and inner importance ought to have prepared for the threat sometimes came to predominate and how they finally appear as an independent genre."[109] According to Gressmann, the customary introductory formula for the reproach was "woe."

---

107. So also Gunkel in his brief remark on the reproach (*Die israelitische Literatur*, 37). Gressmann wrote ("Die literarische Analyse"): "The threats of the preexilic prophets are almost always accompanied by a shorter or longer introduction which reflects upon the following oracle. The form is generally a reason (*Bergründung*), the content accordingly a reproach (*Scheltwort*). The union of threats with reproaches can be explained very simply because the prophets had to make understandable on the basis of the sins of Israel the doom which they preached. In doing so, they pointed to the sins which they dealt with. Frequently, then, the reproach became a special *Gattung* and became completely detached from the threat."

108. Gressmann, *Die älteste Geschichtschreibung*, 326.

109. Ibid.

The History of the Form-Critical Study of Prophecy

In addition to the promise, threat, exhortation, and reproach, Gressmann discussed the judgment-speech as a genre of prophetical oracle. The judgment-speech, which rarely appears in the prophets (see Isa 1:18ff; 3:13ff; Jer 2:4ff), was taken over by the prophets from Israelite legal proceedings. In conjunction with his comments on the judgment-speech, Gressmann spoke of the prophetic development of "historical reviews" (*Geschichtsbetrachtungen*)[110] found in such passages as Amos 2:9ff; Jer 3:6ff; 25:1ff., and he noted that certain passages originate from the prophetical discussion with their contemporaries (Isa 23:7ff; Jeremiah 28).

Finally, in the SAT article, Gressmann discussed the prophetical use of lyrical *Gattungen*,[111] which the prophets took over and imprinted with their spirit. Among these, Gressmann noted victory songs, funeral songs, drinking songs, watchman's songs, hymns, laments, liturgies, and monologues (the latter a literary creation of prophecy). In all of these, the prophets poured new wine into old skins.

The most comprehensive and detailed form-critical study of prophecy undertaken by Gressmann was his analysis of Deutero-Isaiah published in 1914.[112] In many respects, it is an outstanding example of a rigorous application of form-critical methodology.[113] The article is particularly significant because of Gressmann's attempt to divide the material into independent units primarily on the basis of introductory and concluding formulas. The 333 verses of Deutero-Isaiah were divided by Gressmann into 49 independent prophetical units, which were then categorized on the basis of their particular *Gattungen*.

Gressmann operated on the assumption that introductory and/or concluding formulas provided an important clue for distinguishing the independent units. "The customary introduction to prophetical speeches[114] is: 'Thus said Yahweh'; for a word of the prophets is a word of God; it is an oracle. Therefore where we find this formula we must first of all be inclined to recognize the beginning of a prophetical saying."[115] As an

---

110. These form the beginning of a philosophy of history that exercised a strong influence on Israelite historians. "The deuteronomistic edition of the historical books would not have been possible without prophecy" (ibid.).

111. See *Die israelitische Literatur*, 36–37, for a very similar discussion.

112. Gressmann, "Die literarische Analyse."

113. In this essay, Gressmann acknowledges his indebtedness to Gunkel and refers to the latter's articles in KdG and *RGG* (see footnotes 21 and 92).

114. See note 101 above.

115. Gressmann, "Die literarische Analyse," 260.

introductory formula, "Thus said Yahweh" (*koh 'amar yahweh*) appears at the beginning of a unit or as the introduction to an exhortation or reproach within a unit on eighteen occasions (42:5, 43:1, 14, 16; 44:2, 6, 24; 45:1, 11, 14, 18; 48:17; 49:5, 7, 8, 22; 50:1; 51:22).[116] "Yahweh says" (*yo'mar yahweh*) or similar, appears at or near the beginning of three units (40:1, 25; 41:21). *Ne'um yahweh* introduces a divine word in four places (41:14; 43:10; 49:18; 55:8). "A voice crying" (*qol kore'*) or "a voice saying" (*qol 'omer*)[117] introduces two oracles (40:3, 6).

Concluding formulas, he argues, appear at or near the end of seven oracles: "Says Yahweh: (*'amar yahweh* or similar) in 45:13; 54:1, 8, 9;[118] *ne'um yahweh* in 43:12; 54:17; and "for the mouth of Yahweh has spoken" (*ki pi yahweh dibber*) in 40:5. Four of these (54:1, 8, 10, 17) appear with units lacking an introductory formula so that the concluding formula serves to mark off the unit.

In addition to the strictly prophetical introductory and concluding formulas, Gressmann noted the secondary (that is, borrowed) prophetical introductory formula, "Woe" (*hoy*), which occurs in only two passages (45:9, 10) introducing a double-woe reproach.

Gressmann distinguished lyrical introductory formulas that the prophet utilized in 41:1; 42:18; 44:1; 46:3, 12; 48:1, 12; 49:1; 51:1, 4, 7, 21, as well as hymnic introductory formulas in 42:10; 52:9; 54:1.

Gressmann's division of Deutero-Isaiah into forty-nine independent units does not coincide identically with the results of his analysis of the use of introductory and concluding formulas. Ten of his units contain no formula and in some units more than one formula appears.

After his "literary analysis" of the formula usage, Gressmann examined the prophetical *Gattungen* used by Deutero-Isaiah dividing these into visions (represented only in the form of the after effects of ecstatic experience, 40:3–5, 6–8), threats (none against Israel), promises (43 out of the 49 units contain direct promises), reproaches[119] (42:18–25; 43:22–

---

116. Gressmann did not take Isa 52:4–6 into consideration since he considered this passage a redactional gloss. The formula in 49:25, he felt was a secondary development within a unit rather than the beginning of a new unit.

117. Both of these formulas Gressmann recognized as unique to Deutero-Isaiah, and he noted that they introduce not a divine but an angelic word ("Die literarische Analyse," 262).

118. An error on Gressmann's part, read 54:10.

119. On the reproach in Deutero-Isaiah he wrote: "Since no threats are encountered in Deutero-Isaiah, one also expects no reproaches. But the expectation is disappointed" ("Die literarische Analyse," 270). The reproach, he discovered, was related in

28; 45:9–13; 48:1–11; 50:1–2a) that are associated with promises rather than threats, exhortations (44:21–22; 48:18a; 50:10; 55:6–7), consolations (*Trostwörte*: 40:1–2a, 27–31; 46:12–13; 49:15–17; 51:7–8, 12–13, 17–20; 54:1–6; 55:1–3) that had their origin in the exhortation and their parallel in the divine answer to the communal lament, judgment words (41:1–13; 41:21–29; 43:8–13; 44:6–20; 45:20–21, 48:12–16; see also 43:26), words of assurance (45:18–25; see also 40:6–8; 43:17; 45:17; 55:8–11), and historical review (51:1–3; historical allusions occur throughout the book).

Foreign *Gattungen* were employed by the prophet: the victory song (40:9; 52:7–8), the mocking song or lampoon (47:1–15), and the hymn. Gressmann devotes considerable space to the use of the hymn and hymnic elements by Deutero-Isaiah.[120] He considered hymnic style to be more characteristic of Deutero-Isaiah than for any other prophet. Gressmann distinguished between the prophet's employment of hymnic elements and motifs to expand existing standard formulas and his use of hymns proper. He spoke of the hymnic expansion of the prophetic introductory (41:14; 42:5; 43:1, 14, 16; 44:2, 6, 24; 45:11; 48:17; 49:5, 6; 51:22) and concluding (43:12–13; 47:4) formulas as well as the use of hymnic elements to expand the introductory and concluding formulas of divine address. In discussing the latter, Gressmann commented on two types of revelatory-address formulas encountered in Deutero-Isaiah: the divine self-predication (41:4, 10, 13, 15, 17; 42:8–9; 43:11ff; 44:3ff., 12, 18–19, 21; 46:9; 48:11ff., 17; 49:26; 50:2–3; 51:15–16) and the command not to fear (41:10, 13, 14; 43:1, 5; 44:2, 8; 51:12). He placed the origin of the self-prediction formula within the sphere of polytheism where it served to identify the deity, but in Deutero-Isaiah he recognized the influence of Babylonian oracle style and compared the self-predication and "Fearnot" formulas to the Esarhaddon and Assurbanipal oracle texts.[121] The use of hymns and hymnic elements that went beyond the expansion of existing formulas was noted by Gressmann (*Schlusshymnen*: 44:23; 45:1–8, 15–17; 48:20–21; 49:13; 50:2b–3; 51:3; 52:9–10 and *grossere Hymnen*: 40:12–26; 42:10–13).

Deutero-Isaiah to the promise.

120. Ibid., 283–95.

121. Gressmann referred to the work of Jastrow (*Die Religion Babyloniens and Assyriens*, vol. 2), which contains a discussion of these texts. In addition, the influence of Norden's discussion of these texts in *Agnostos Theos* (see footnote 33) is acknowledged on several occasions by Gressmann.

The importance of Gressmann's study of Deutero-Isaiah in the history of form-critical study of the prophets is manifold.[122] (1) The attempt to subject a large body of material to form-critical analysis goes beyond anything undertaken in the published works of Gunkel. (2) His utilization of formulas as the key for determining the literary units anticipates many subsequent developments (and problems!) in form-critical study.[123] On the use of formulas, Gressmann wrote:

> The indispensable precondition for interpretation rests in the determination of literary units. The last conclusive recourse about whether a connection exists or whether something new begins lies however with logic. But logical considerations ... are supported by the investigation of *Gattungen*, and indeed partly replaced. Whoever pays attention to style will frequently be able to say for superficial reasons, such as the occurrence of particular formulas, whether there is a connection or not. Since the prophetical *Gattungen* have not been handed on in tradition, they must first be recovered and reconstructed. A methodological investigation must begin with the introductory and concluding formulas since they formed the germ cells of every *Gattung* and in the course of later development they have also always remained characteristic signs. Where one encounters introductory and concluding formulas, no doubt can exist about the divisions of literary elements ... The prophetical sayings are usually very simply constructed. Beginnings and conclusions are almost always recognizable to the trained eye at first glance because of the constantly recurring introductory and concluding formula.[124]

Gressmann's division of Deutero-Isaiah into 49 independent units was frequently based on logical rather than formula considerations since these formulas were sometimes missing. In this regard, it should be noted that Gressmann elsewhere allowed logic to overrule formula considerations in determining the limits of a unit: he treats Amos 1:3—2:16 as a unit of seven strophes although each strophe contains clear introductory and

---

122. For a critique of Gressmann's study, see Sidney Smith, *Isaiah Chapters XL–LV*, 6–9.

123. See Westermann, *Basic Forms*, 35. Some of the weaknesses involved in the division of prophetical material into independent units on the basis of formula analysis are already reflected in Gressmann's study and become more obvious in later attempts at isolating the independent units in Deutero-Isaiah. See Sydney Smith, *Isaiah Chapters XL–LV*, 7–11, 90–96.

124. Gressmann, "Die literarische Analyse," 259–60.

The History of the Form-Critical Study of Prophecy

concluding formulas.[125] (3) Gressmann concluded that the basic forms of prophetic address could be modified and expanded in diverse ways but that in Deutero-Isaiah one witnesses the onset of the disintegration of these forms.

> If one assigns a place to Deutero-Isaiah in the literary history of Israelite prophecy, it must be stated as characteristic that with him the dissolution of the prophetic *Gattungen* begins. The fixed forms that had prevailed till then break up. While the types of speech which the pre-exilic prophets had employed are mostly quite sharply distinguished from one another, with Deutero-Isaiah exact separation is often impossible; the reflective supplements, with which the oracles are entwined, have overgrown everything, so that the dividing lines between divine word and prophetic word cannot always be clearly recognized. Thus the promises and the consolations coalesce. Further, the distinctions between the exhortations and the reproaches have lost their meaning. Individual motifs have become independent and have found their expression in poems which can nowhere be rightly classified. Finally, hymnic components, which were originally foreign to prophecy, have been included and have burst the old framework.[126]

Before leaving Gressmann, a word should be said about his discussion of prophetical genres in *Der Messias*.[127] Although Gressmann devoted a large section of this work to a discussion of prophetic genres,[128] his treatment is augumentative and specific rather than descriptive and comprehensive. His form-critical assessments of the material are primarily expounded as a service to his eschatological contentions. As is well-known, Gressmann believed in the existence of a pre-Israelite and a pre-prophetic Israelite eschatology, whose focus of concern was a great world catastrophe and

---

125. Gressmann, *Die älteste Geschichtschreibung*, 333–37.

126. Gressmann, "Die literarische Analyse Deuterojesajas," 295.

127. It is unfortunate that this was the only work of Gressmann discussed by Westermann in his survey of the history of form-critical study of the prophets (*Basic Forms of Prophetic Speech*, 31–34). Gressmann's work was published posthumously; it does not represent a final polished product but contains gaps and certain incompletely developed ideas that have contributed to some of the inconsistencies noted by Westermann. See the introduction to Gressmann's *Der Messias* by Hans Schmidt (3*–7*) and his notes throughout the work.

128. *Der Messias*, "Zweites Buch: Prophetische Gattungen," 65–148.

world renewal. This eschatology was taken over and employed by early Israel and is reflected in the preaching of the classical prophets.

In *Der Messias*, Gressmann is, first of all, anxious to defend the authenticity of numerous[129] prophetic promises or oracles of salvation that have been and still are assigned to the exilic or post-exilic periods.[130]

Secondly, he argued for a close connection, in fact an original unity, between the prophecies of salvation and the prophecies of doom. In addition to a utilization of psychological,[131] religio-historical,[132] and chronological[133] considerations, Gressmann sought to establish the antiquity of the prophecies of salvation or eschatological oracles on form-critical grounds. He argued that one finds, in the threats and promises, identical introductory and concluding formulas, identical phrases ("in that day," "in those days," "in that time," "behold the days are coming"), and that statistically the distinct phraseology is more characteristic of the promise than the threat. The promise found in the classical prophetical preaching, he argued, had close parallels to the blessings of Jacob and the songs of Balaam (from the time of Saul and David), in the prose and conventional promises to the patriarchs (Gen 12:2–3; 13:14–17; 15:4–5; 16:10; 18:17–19; and so on, from the early monarchy), in the promises to David and his descendants (2 Sam 7:8ff; Psalm 89), and in the royal psalms.[134]

---

129. He admitted that some of the salvation prophecies now attached to prophetical sayings and books date from the exilic and later times (*Der Messias*, 75).

130. Gressmann, "Die Echtheit der Verheissungen," 69–74.

131. Gressmann spoke of the temperament, the inner life, and the changing moods of the prophets as explanations of the movement between doom and salvation (see especially 67–72). Gunkel had spoken in somewhat similar terms in his explanation of the prophetic exhortation (see "Einleitungen," LXVI).

132. Gressmann pointed to Egyptian parallels as support for his contentions; see *Der Messias*, 72–73, 82, 415–45, and in English, see his "Foreign Influences." Gressmann's extensive (and excessive?) comparisons with Egyptian texts should be read in light of a statement he published in 1924 within a context focusing on the similarities and differences between Old Testament and ancient Near Eastern materials: "The problem of all problems remains prophecy, which forms the high point of Israelite religious history and which, in the final analysis, can be understood only in its own terms" ("Der Aufgaben der alttestamentliche Forschung").

133. The prophets, like Amos, already presuppose the existence of a developed eschatological perspective and the proclamation of promise; see *Der Messias*, 74–77, 144. In addition, throughout Israelite history "prophets of salvation" and "prophets of doom" existed side by side with the latter a decided minority (77–82).

134. Ibid., 82–87. Gressmann outlined the chronological development of the promise in the following stages: (1) the absolute promise, (2) the combination of promise with exhortation, and (3) the absolute exhortation; but he argued that the oldest

The History of the Form-Critical Study of Prophecy

Gressmann not only argued for the antiquity of the promise but also contended that "originally threats and promises were bound together in a literary unit" as attested in ancient Egyptian oracles.[135] This original connection between threat and promise—doom and salvation—is illustrated, according to Gressmann, in prophetical speeches which contain conditional predictions (Isa 1:18-20; 7:9; Jer 4:1-2; 7:1-11; 12:14-17; 17:24-27; 22:1-5; 26:1-6; 38:17-18; 42:7-22),[136] by speeches that proclaim both threat and promise, often successive (Hos 1:1—2:3; 3:4-5; Mic 4:9-10; Isa 1:21-26; 28:1-6),[137] and by the speeches on foreign nations. According to Gressmann, "salvation and judgment were regularly combined in the oracles on foreign nations,"[138] and he devoted over fifty pages to a discussion of these foreign oracles. Gressmann divided oracles on foreign nations into two classes: *Heidenorakel* and *Völkerorakel*. *Völkerorakel* referred to a complex of peoples, most often unnamed and unspecified, who stand in hostility over against Israel or Jerusalem, while *Heidenorakel* referred to a specific, individual known people who may not necessarily be in opposition to Israel. The proclamation of doom upon the foreign nation in the *Heidenorakel* was always indirectly a promise or salvation oracle to Israel.[139] Gressmann claimed that the *Völkerorakel* (such as Isa 8:5-10; 10:5-19, 20-26, 28-34; 28:14-22; 29:1-8; 30:27-33; Zeph 3:8-10; Joel 4:9-17; Zechariah 12-14)[140] always combined doom and salvation: doom (*Unheil*) against Zion, judgment against (destruction of) the peoples, salvation for Zion. Thus they contained both threat and promise addressed to Israel or Zion. The development of the threat or doom against Zion in strongly ethical and religious terms, Gressmann considered a contribution of the prophets of doom—the classical proph-

---

form was never completely lost but continued to be used in later times (92–93).

135. Ibid., 82; see 72, 436, 440–45.

136. Ibid., 70–72.

137. Ibid., 72–73.

138. Ibid., 72.

139. Ibid., 94. The section on the *Heidenorakel* was apparently being rewritten or written by Gressmann at the time of his death. The manuscript edited by Schmidt contained no discussion but only a list of individual oracles belonging to this class. Nonetheless, Gressmann's discussion does not suffer from the "lack of clarity" ascribed to it by Westermann (*Basic Forms*, 33), who makes no reference to Gressmann's lengthy discussion of these two types of oracles on foreign nations. For Gressmann's treatment of the *Völkerorakel*, see *Der Messias*, 97–148.

140. Gressmann compared the elements in some of these oracles to the Zion psalms, especially Psalms 46 and 76.

ets—although he considered the *Völkerorakel* without the ethically-religiously oriented character of the threat or doom against the prophet's own people to be the best representative of the prophetical preaching prior to Amos.¹⁴¹ Gressmann, of course, correlated the *Völkerorakel*, which he considered to be "pre-prophetical" (pre-classical), with his ideas about the nature-oriented, eschatological world catastrophe and world renewal.

In light of Gressmann's discussion of the oracles on foreign nations, it is now possible to summarize his reconstruction of the history of the eschatological oracle in his own words.

> Originally, threats and promises were combined in one literary unit; this postulate which can be inferred from the Israelite traditions can actually be proven on the basis of the Egyptian oracles. The oracles on foreign nations have preserved this oldest form . . . With Amos . . . the great shift begins.¹⁴² The threat which had been previously directed against the peoples is now directed against Israel . . . Threats against Israel were something so new and unheard of that they could develop into an independent genre, indeed they must so develop; all new genres originate in this fashion. New ideas require new forms; one does not put new wine into old skins . . . Thereafter each genre had its independent existence and its individual history.¹⁴³

Sigmund Mowinckel

The history of religions approach in general and form-critical studies in particular experienced a sympathetic response in much Scandinavian Old Testament study. The work of Sigmund Mowinckel (1884–1965) represents an admirable and creative combination of these two interests. Two impulses contributed enormously to his unique combination of interests. On the one hand, Mowinckel was a post-doctoral student of Gunkel and adopted his form-critical perspectives.¹⁴⁴ On the other hand, he was indebted to his two outstanding Danish professors, Vihelm Grøn-

---

141. See esp. *Der Messias*, 139–41, 148.

142. In a discussion of 1 Kings 22 (*Der Messias*, 77–78), Gressmann had argued that the separation of the threat and promise was already evident in the preaching of Micaiah.

143. Ibid., 82.

144. See his tribute to Gunkel in Mowinckel, *Zur Komposition des Buches Jeremia*, 67.

The History of the Form-Critical Study of Prophecy

beck and Johannes Pedersen, who stressed the social, psychological, and institutional—especially the cultic—forms of primitive religion and the creative and mysterious powers of the individual and communal primitive mentality.[145] For Mowinckel, form, content, and social setting were always important elements in interpreting Old Testament literature.[146]

Broadly speaking, it can be said that Gunkel's decisive contribution to form-critical study consists in his division of the prophetic material into genres and his aesthetic and stylistic analysis and appreciation of these genres. Gressmann's decisive contributions lie in his attempts to relate promise and threat—salvation and judgment—to one another, to a general scheme of Near Eastern eschatological thought, and to comparative material, especially the Egyptian,[147] Near Eastern texts. Mowinckel's distinctive contribution was his emphasis on the function and usage of genres within the institutional, especially the cultic, life of ancient Israel.[148] Mowinckel posed, in an unavoidable fashion, the question of the relationship between the prophets and prophetical genres and the cult.[149] These three elements—the formal and stylistic analysis of the genres, the comparison of Old Testament and Near Eastern texts, and the institutional association of prophetic address—have dominated subsequent form-critical study of the prophets.

---

145. Note the influence of these two men in his chapter on "The Psalms and the Cult" in Mowinckel, *The Psalms in Israel's Worship*, 1.1–22.

146. See ibid., 1.24–29.

147. Gressman of course was not the first to suggest analogies between Old Testament prophetical texts and Near Eastern materials. See Meyer, *Geschichte des Altertums*, 1/2, 274–75; Meyer, *Die Israeliten and ihre Nachbarstamme*, 451–55; and Norden, *Agnostos Theos*.

148. Gunkel had of course recognized the similarity between certain royal and "eschatological" psalms and certain prophetic oracles. Gressman had spoken of the court style and its influence on the prophets and in his projected revision of his work on the messiah had planned to incorporate a section on court prophecy (see Schmidt's introduction to *Der Messias*). Both Gunkel and Gressmann had pointed to the influence of the legal institutions in their descriptions of the "word or speech of judgment" that the prophets had used to "clothe" some of their reproaches against Israel. Weber, in 1921, pointed to the association of prophets with warfare and the importance of this for understanding the prophetical movement (see his *Ancient Judaism*, 90–117).

149. Both Gunkel and Gressmann, of course, had drawn analogies between prophetical speeches and certain cultic forms of address, especially the divine response and words of assurance to the worshipping parties, the use of lyrical materials, and the employment of torah.

Mowinckel's first published work on the prophets[150] was an investigation of the relationship between the various types of prophets and seers in ancient Israel and the relationship of these to Near Eastern phenomena in general[151] and to the priesthood in particular. According to Mowinckel, the early seer and the ecstatic prophet derived from two distinctly different social and institutional backgrounds. The seer belonged to the earliest stratum of Israelite society and was related to the priest who "was not originally in the first instance a sacrificer, but as with the old Arabs, custodian of the sanctuary, oracle priest, 'seer' and holder of the effectual future-creating and future-interpreting word of power, the blessing and the curse."[152] Ecstatic prophecy—*nebiism*—and temple priests were indigenous to Canaanite culture and represented elements adopted by the Israelites. With the fusion of the functions of the seer-priest with the functions of the temple-sacrificial priests and ecstatic prophets, two main groups developed: the priests occupied with cult and sacrifice but in control of the "technical system of oracles, '*urim and thummim*' and so on, dispensing 'guidance' on cultic, ritual, moral and spiritual questions, and mediating Yahweh's 'laws' (*toroth*) and 'judicial decisions' and "judgments" (*mishpatim*) and "the prophets" who "continued the more 'pneumatic' aspect of the character and work of the old 'seers'" and "were mediums of the divinely inspired 'word' which was 'whispered to' them, or 'came to them.'"[153] The prophets retained, in guild fashion, the old seer relationship to the cult so that one can legitimately speak of the institution of cultic prophecy and is required to see a close relationship between cult and prophecy,[154]

Before proceeding to outline Mowinckel's theories on the relationship of prophecy, prophetic speech forms, and the cult, it should be noted that he pursued form-critical investigations along lines very similar to the work of Gunkel and Gressmann. In a work published in 1914, Mowinckel utilized stylistic, form-critical, and traditio-historical considerations in order to elucidate the origin and composition of the

150. Mowinckel, "Om nebiisme og profetie," 185ff; 330ff.

151. Ibid., 217-24; 358-60. Mowinckel utilized much of the material that figures prominently in the reconstruction of early prophecy in the later and independent work of Holscher, *Die Profeten*, 79-142.

152. *The Psalms*, 2.53. See also *Psalmstudien III*, 9-14 and cf. Hölscher, *Die Profeten*, 100-107.

153. *The Psalms*, 2.55.

154. *Psalmenstudien III*, 16-17.

book of Jeremiah. In Jeremiah 1–45, he distinguished four types of material in addition to editorial redactional notations. Class A consisted of genuine poetic oracles,[155] B of historical narratives influenced by the style of legendary narratives,[156] C of prose first-person speeches in deuteronomistic style,[157] and D of later originally anonymous interpolations.[158] In addition to this study of Jeremiah, Mowinckel published a purely form-critical analysis of Jeremiah in 1926, a work that has received little or no attention in form-critical studies.[159] In this work he commented on the general characteristics of prophetic speech stressing its poetic and oral form and its close association with the seer's vision, the *nabi*'s oracle, and the *nabi*'s symbolic-magical actions of power. In general, Mowinckel's formal analysis of the prophetic speech genres parallels Gunkel's work. He stressed the cultic influence more strongly than Gunkel, not only with regards to the lament material but also in his association of the "woe" sayings with cultic curse and his comparison of the prophetic call to the royal ritual of anointment and ascenion to the throne. In discussing the reproach, Mowinckel pointed to the diversity in the motivations for the coming doom—in addition to sin-registers, he noted the employment of references to Yahweh's earlier saving deeds and judgments. Mowinckel stressed the exhortation or warning function of the doom oracle and took due note of prophetic symbolic actions and the accounts reporting such actions.

The clearest and most concise summary of Mowinckel's formal analysis of the earliest form of prophetic address is found in his work *Prophecy and Tradition*.[160] Relying upon prophetic oracles in prophetic narratives and the Psalms, Mowinckel argued that the self-contained prophetic message was very brief, poetic, and metric and introduced by the messenger, or some corresponding formula of introduction. The simplest content of the saying was "either a prediction of what is to happen . . . or an instruction (guidance as to the right behavior in the concrete situation), a command, or a task . . . or a combination of both . . . The second

155. *Zur Komposition des Buches Jeremia*, 17–23.
156. Ibid., 24–30.
157. Ibid., 31–45.
158. Ibid., 45–48.
159. "Stilformer og motiver."
160. *Prophecy and Tradition*, 45–47 (= *The Spirit and the Word*, 40–45). See also his introduction to the prophets in *Det Gamle Testament* (edited by Michelet, Mowinckel and Messel).

type contains two elements: the prediction and the motivation . . . The order of the two elements may vary. An extension of the basic type may occur because of both elements being further developed . . . Ultimately all forms and elements of the prophetic message may be derived from these two basic elements."

Just as Mowinckel saw a close relationship between the seer-prophet and the priest, between prophecy and the cult, so he also believed that a close relationship existed between the oracle of the seer-prophet and the torah or oracle of the priest.[161] Behind much of Mowinckel's association of prophecy and prophetic speech forms with the cult lies his theory of an autumn New Year festival with its celebration of Yahweh's enthronement and the reestablishment and recreation of cosmic order.[162] Working with much of the "eschatological" material investigated by Gunkel and Gressmann, Mowinckel differed from them in his anchoring of the material within a concrete cultic observance (through the use of Near Eastern analogies) rather than in some nebulous Near Eastern eschatological perspective. In addition, Mowinckel assigned a far greater role to cultic considerations and to the importance of the king in Israelite culture than was the case with either Gunkel or Gressmann.[163] In his study on cultic prophecy and prophetical psalms, Mowinckel placed prophetic oracles within the *Sitz im Leben* of the great New Year festival, royal rituals, and communal and private services of lamentation.

Mowinckel contended that the oracles in the psalms in which there is direct divine address were spoken by prophets during cultic observances as responses to the worshipper or worshipping community. The content of these oracles, as a rule, were promises or oracles of salvation. Mowinckel distinguished prophetic oracles from priestly instruction or oracles in the following manner:

> The guidance of the priest from the very first had a characteristic style of its own: the more or less apodictic instruction or

---

161. See ibid., 101, n. 13.

162. See Mowinckel, *Psalmenstudien II*; and Mowinckel, *The Psalms*, 1.106–92.

163. In his *Einleitung in die Psalmen*, Gunkel accepted, somewhat begrudgingly, many of the insights of Mowinckel. Gunkel had, of course, stressed the importance of the royal psalms (see his "Königspsalmen") and in the projected revision of his work on Israelite and Judean eschatology, Gressmann had assigned a significant role to court prophecy (see notes 127 and 148 above). In his analysis of Old Testament eschatology, Gressmann had come very close to Mowinckel's concept of the annual enthronement festival; see Mowinckel, *Psalmenstudien II*, 16–18.

order: "thou shalt do (not do)such and such a thing"; or with an introductory sentence stating the particulars of the case: "when such and such a thing shall happen, or if such be the case, thou shalt do so and so." As far as the psalms are concerned, neither the promises ('oracles') of Yahweh that have been handed down to us, nor those that may be inferred from different allusions, have this form; they are all of them clearly and distinctly kept in the usual prophetic style. This seems to show a likelihood that they arose within the prophetic circles on the basis of prophetic style and traditional ideas, consequently that they were also announced by one of the temple prophets in the cult liturgy. The occasional statements of the Chronicler point in the same direction; the promises of Yahweh at the cultic festivals are always put into the mouth of a singer or a Levite. But this in nowise implies that in earlier times priest and temple prophet may not on occasion have been one and the same person . . . It is therefore quite possible that in the time of the monarchy Yahweh's promise in the cult would be announced by one of the priests on duty. But even in this case it shows how extraordinarily strong was the influence of the prophetic movement: the priest speaks like a prophet and in the traditional style of the prophetic speech.[164]

Prophetic oracles of promise were generally expressed as direct oracles of salvation to the worshipper but might also assume the form of an indirect promise expressed as an oracle directed against the worshipper's enemy or foe. The cultic prophet not only proclaimed oracles to the worshipping congregation or individual but also offered intercessory addresses to the deity on their behalf. "Not only the cult oracle but also the cultic prayer was the responsibility of the prophet."[165]

Mowinckel not only related the oracles of promise and the prayers of intercession to cultic prophecy, but also saw the cultic prophets as proclaimers of admonitory oracles and judgment preaching. The New Year festival, according to Mowinckel, contained elements stressing Yahweh's judgment over the nations and powers of the world,[166] and in its

---

164. *The Psalms*, 2.58. See also *Psalmenstudien III*, 12–14, 23–24. The problem of the cultic oracle—whether priestly or prophetic—still remains a debateable issue. Küchler and the Gunkel circle attributed these oracles to the priests. See Oehler, "Das priesterliche Orakel"; Gunkel, *Einleitung in die Psalmen*, 367–75 (ET = *Introduction*, 282–87); and Begrich, "Das priesterliche Heilsorakel."

165. *The Psalms*, 2.63.

166. See *Psalmenstudien II*, 38–43, 65–74, 126–28, 263–76; and *The Psalms*, 1.146–54.

stress on the covenant contained elements exhorting the people to obedience and condemning them for transgression of the covenant.[167] In the proclamation of the judgment of Yahweh against the nations, one finds the background—the original *Sitz im Leben*—for the prophetic oracles against foreign nations. "In the oracles of doom against the enemies of Israel, these latter are always referred to in general terms, not mentioning any particular people—unlike the casual oracles in the psalms of lamentation. It is, however, very possible that a custom of pronouncing a series of oracles against different peoples may have developed out of the general oracles at the epiphany feast, and that we have here the 'cultic' background of such oracles as we find in Am 1–2."[168] The prophetic admonition to obedience and the prophetic speech of judgment (as evidenced especially in Psalms 50, 81 and 95) condemning the people for transgression were considered basic elements in the New Year festival.[169]

> In this cultic admonition and rebuke of the transgressions of the people lies the root of the prophetic speech of rebuke and doom. Yahweh's claim to the complete surrender of the people to him as their one and only God, and the inherent ethical approach of the Yahweh religion, resulted in picturing the just judgment of his coming as a judgment not only of their demonic and historical enemies and of the sinners within Israel, but as judgment of his own people as well . . . The differences between the ordinary cult prophets and the classic 'great prophets' are not to be blurred; but the first creative impulse came from the ideas of the cult prophets.[170]

Mowinckel's form-critical work on the prophets deserves to be set alongside that of Gunkel and Gressmann as representative of a major an innovative approach to the problems. This is especially the case with his discussions of the *Sitz im Leben* of prophetic speech forms. Mowinckel studied under Gunkel and of course was heavily dependent upon him; but many of his concepts about the role, functions, and *Sitz im Leben* of

---

167. See *Psalmenstudien II*, 288–90; *Le Decalogue*, 114–141; and *The Psalms*, 1.157–61.

168. *The Psalms*, 1.154. So already in *Psalmenstudien II*, 337–38. Oracles against foreign nations were also related by Mowinckel to the prophetic response in general lamentation rituals and to preparation for warfare (see *The Psalms*, 1.196–200).

169. See *Psalmenstudien II*, 152–57; *Psalmenstudien III*, 38–45; *Le Decalogue*, 124–33; and *The Psalms*, 1.155–61.

170. *The Psalms*, 1.160–61 and n. 149.

prophecy were developed prior to his student days with Gunkel.[171] This was apparently also the case with regard to the cultic use of the psalms and the central role of the New Year festival.[172] With Mowinckel, the problem of prophecy and cult became the issue of the prophet in the cult. Unfortunately, in his discussion of the prophetic oracle in the cult and the form of that oracle, Mowinckel is less precise than one would prefer. Any oracle utilizing divine address but not characterized by very specific priestly address style he designated as prophetic.

The Second Generation

Gunkel, Gressmann, and Mowinckel laid the foundations, defined the issues, and, in many respects, set the boundaries for subsequent form-critical study of the prophets. Refinements, modification, more detailed analysis, the introduction of new evidence and perspectives, and controversies over earlier conclusions have characterized form-critical study executed in the shadow of these three giants. Some important work has been done apparently uninfluenced by these three. The second generation in the title to this section refers to those scholars who worked in the period following the trailblazing innovations of Gunkel, Gressmann, and Mowinckel but prior to the dominance of neo-orthodoxy or theology of the word in systematic theology and biblical studies and the later but concomitant perspective designated covenant theology.

Several of Gunkel's students made significant contributions to the form-critical study of the prophets. Along lines already laid down by Budde, to whom Gunkel was deeply indebted,[173] Hedwig Jahnow investigated the form of the funeral song and its influence on many prophetical passages.[174] Earlier than her work, Walter Baumgartner had studied the lamentations of Jeremiah along lines laid down by Gunkel.[175] The two most important of Gunkel's students, in so far as form-critical study of

---

171. See the article in footnote 150. Mowinckel's employment of Near Eastern comparative material to reconstruct the early history of prophecy predated Hölscher's utilization of this material; see note 151 above.

172. See *Psalmenstudien II*, XI.

173. See note 80 above.

174. *Das hebräische Leichenlied*.

175. *Die Klagegedichte*.

the prophets is concerned, were Emil Balla (1885–1956)[176] and Joachim Begrich (1900–1945).[177]

Emil Balla

Balla's study of the threats and reproaches in Amos[178] attempts to subject the entire content of a prophetical book to a rigid form-critical analysis along the lines laid down by Gunkel. Balla gives due regard to the questions of mood[179] and meter[180] in prophetic address (both issues having already been discussed by Gunkel) as well as to the issue of introductory and concluding formulas[181] (an important emphasis in the work of Gressmann). Balla divided the words of Amos into "pure threats" (5:16–17; 6:11; 7:11; 8:2b-c, 9–10; 9:1–4), "threats with short motivations" (*Begründungen*) (1:3–5, 6–8, 13–15; 2:1–3; 3:1–2, 12, 13, 13–15; 5:5b, 18–20, 26–27; 6:8–10; 7:8b–9; 8:11–14), "threats with developed motivations" (2:6–16; 3:9–11; 4:1–3; 5:7+10–11; 6:1–7, 13–14; 7:16–17; 8:4–5+7), which, because of the motivations, developed a rather independent character he designated as "reproaches," and "pure reproaches" (5:12; 6:12).[182] Like Gunkel, Balla saw the close association that existed between threat and motivation and designated the reproach as simply a developed form of the motivation. He explored the linguistic and syntactical relationship between the threat and reproach and recognized the preponderance of divine address in the threat (but see 5:5b, 18–20; 6:11; 7:11) and the preponderance of the prophetic word in the developed motivations or reproaches (but see 2:6–11; 4:6–11; 5:12; 6:13): Balla attempted to relate the material in Amos to the history of the prophetic threat[183] and concluded that:

---

176. Balla's inaugural work, *Das Ich der Psalmen*, was undertaken under the direction of Gunkel.

177. Begrich's dissertation, *Der Psalm der Hiskia*, was directed by Gunkel, and he was Gunkel's son-in-law and assistant for several years, completing Gunkel's *Einleitung in die Psalmen*.

178. *Die Droh- und Scheltwörte des Amos*.

179. Ibid., 3–5.

180. Ibid., 10–22.

181. Ibid., 7–10.

182. For the preceding and what follows, see ibid., 22–34.

183. Ibid., 40–46.

The History of the Form-Critical Study of Prophecy

The development which the genre has undergone is extremely important. Originally it existed only in the form of pure threats or threats with short motivations. The utterance was the repetition of a vision or an audition. With Amos, the strong association with this mysterious inner experience is already broken. Even though he, for the most part, only reports what Yahweh has allowed him to see or what Yahweh has said to him, nonetheless he still threatened and reproached occasionally himself and in so doing was certain of his conviction that he was speaking completely in accord with Yahweh. In the background, there lies here the certainty, although for Amos still fully unconscious, that God speaks to man not only in visions and voices. Also the deepest thoughts which man himself thinks are finally of divine origin. Likewise, the reproaches which Amos himself speaks demonstrates a further development of the genre. Originally, the emphasis lay fully on the threat. It is still there indeed in most of the examples in Amos. In the reproaches which he himself speaks, a slight shifting of emphasis takes place. This can be seen most clearly in 6:1, 3–7. The reproach is here seven lines long; the threat only one line long. The exposure of sin has begun to be a more important part of the prophetical task.[184]

In something of an appendix to his analysis of Amos, Balla discussed what he called the "doom oracle" (*Unheilsorakel*), a genre he considered to be originally independent of the threat and reproach.[185] Examples of this genre he saw in 1 Kgs 22:17; Isa 21:1–10; and Jer 46:2–6. The characteristics of this genre, unattested in Amos, were, according to Balla: (1) The genre is prophetic address rather than divine address, although divine address may be quoted in the oracle.[186] (2) The prophet speaks of the future as if it had already occurred by use of the prophetic perfect in contrast to the use of the imperfect in the threats.[187] (3) The prophet speaks of the coming events in a demonic-enigmatic tone. (4)

---

184. Ibid., 45–46. Misquoted by Westermann (*Grundformen*, 29 = *Basic Forms*, 41–42), who omits the reference to "pure threats" in line two of the quotation and thus radically distorts Balla's description.

185. *Die Droh- und Scheltwörte*, 46–52.

186. The question of the speaker's identity was recognized by Gunkel as an important element in form-critical study, although he did not develop this interest very extensively in his study of the prophets. See his "Fundamental Problems of Hebrew Literary History," in *What Remains*, 57–68, especially 62.

187. The use of the perfect tense in many prophetic passages was already noted by Keil, *Manual*, 1.275, and frequently since.

The style of the oracle is particularly disjointed, abrupt, and jumpy. Balla attributed the threats to the prophetic experience of visions and auditions; the doom oracle he related to the immediate experience of ecstacy. He claimed that many prophetic passages reflect a mixed style in which the threat genre and the oracle genre have been combined. In some texts, the style of the oracle has penetrated the reproach-threat (Isa 5:11–13), whereas in other examples the reverse is true (Isa 17:12–14). Balla did not explore the historical relationship of these two genres, nor examine questions related to their origin, employment, and *Sitz im Leben*.

Joachim Begrich

Joachim Begrich, Gunkel's close associate during his last years, published a number of works relevant to the form-critical study of the prophets.[188] Begrich provided a detailed analysis of the "oracle of salvation" or "oracle of assurance (of a hearing),"[189] which Gressmann had discussed in his study of Deutero-Isaiah.[190] Begrich saw in the prophetic use of this form an imitation of the cultic priestly oracle spoken as a response to the lamenting community and individual in which the oracle alludes to the description of distress and promises redemption from the distress.[191] The elements in the typical oracle as described by Begrich were: (1) an exhortation to fearlessness, (2) a declaration of Yahweh that speaks of his intervention, (3) a description of the change in the distress situation, and (4) a statement of the purpose of Yahweh's intervention or hearing. Begrich discussed in detail the so-called "judgment speech" or "judicial speech," which Gunkel and Gressmann had noted as being sometimes used by the prophet to clothe his speech.[192] The importance of the legal process that

---

188. Gunkel, "Das prophetische in den Psalmen," in *Einleitung in die Psalmen*, 329–81 (in part); Begrich "Das priesterliche Heilsorakel"; "Die priesterliche Tora"; and *Studien zu Deuterojesaja*. On Begrich and for a bibliography of his writings, see Bardtke, *TLZ 75* (1950) 441–46.

189. "Das priesterliche Heilsorakel"; and *Studien zu Deuterojesaja*, 16, 18 (ThBü 20, 14–26).

190. See above.

191. See Gunkel, *Einleitung in die Psalmen*, 136–38 (ET = *Introduction*, 96–98). Contrast Mowinkel's analysis of the oracle as prophetic; see note 164 above.

192. See above; Begrich, *Studien zu Deuterojesaja*, 18–48 (=ThBü, 26–41). The form was analyzed earlier by Köhler, who will be discussed later. For a history of research on the form, see Harvey, *Le plaidoyer*, 9–22.

The History of the Form-Critical Study of Prophecy

Begrich saw as the background of the judicial speech was first fully outlined by Ludwig Köhler.[193] Begrich classified the various forms of judicial speech according to their place in the legal proceeding. He distinguished the following forms: (1) The speech of the accused (Isa 43:22–28; see Gen 31:32, 37, 41–42; 1 Sam 24:10–16), (2) the speech of the accuser (Isa 41:1–5; 48:3, 6, 11; see Gen 16:5; Isa 1:18–20), (3) the speech of the plaintiff before the court (Isa 44:6–8; see Isa 1:2–3; 3:13–15; 5:3–6; Psalm 50), (4) the speech of the defendant before the court (Isa 50:1–2a; see Jer 2: 4–13, 29–30; Mic 6:3–5; Joel 4:4–8), (5) the speech of the judge (Isa 41:21–29; Ps 82:1–7) and (6) judicial pleading (Isa 43:8–13).

Begrich isolated the disputation words in Deutero-Isaiah (Isa 40:12–17; 18–20=25–26, 21–24, 27–31; 44:24–28; 45:9–13, 18–25; 46:5–11, 12–15; 50:1–3) and subjected the genre to a more detailed analysis than had Gunkel.[194] The elements in his analysis of the genre are question and answer, assertion and counter-assertion. He noted that in Deutero-Isaiah, the disputation or controversy genre, like the judicial speech, contained hymnic elements and forms. Begrich's description of the lyrical genres in Deutero-Isaiah[195] shows no appreciable variation from the treatment by Gunkel and Gressmann although he did compare Isa 52:13—53:12 with the narrative of redemption, a constitutive element in the thanksgiving hymn.[196] In addition to these genres, Begrich spoke of "brief directives" (Isa 48:20–21; 52:1–2, 11–12) in imitation of some such address to a city's population, of exhortations that he related in form to priestly torah, of the herald's message, wisdom teaching, and call oracle.[197] In his discussion of priestly torah, Begrich pointed to prophetic imitation in Amos 4:4–5; 5:4b-5b, 21–22; Isa 1:10–17.

Ludwig Köhler

Not associated with Gunkel's circle was Ludwig Köhler who made several significant contributions to prophetic form-critical study.[198] In many

---

193. "Die hebräische Rechtsgemeinde" (ET = "Justice in the Gate").

194. *Studien zu Deuterojesaja*, 41–46 (=ThBü 20, 48–53).

195. Ibid., 47–49 (=ThBü 20, 54–56).

196. Ibid., 56–60 (=ThBü 20, 62–66).

197. Ibid., 50–54 (=ThBü 20, 57–61).

198. *Deuterojesaja*, 1–2, 27; and "Der Botenspruch," in *Kleiner Lichte* (Zurich: Zwingli, 1945) 11–17. See footnote 193.

respects, Köhler stood worlds apart from Gunkel, Gressmann, Mowinckel, and Begrich,[199] but he shared their concern for genre research and social setting. His most significant contribution, or at least the one most frequently noted, was his analysis of the messenger speech in Deutero-Isaiah. In this regard, he was developing an insight of Gunkel and was strongly dependent upon Gressmann's work on the introductory and concluding formulas in Deutero-Isaiah.[200] Köhler compared passages from the prophets (Isa 40:1-2; Amos 1:6-8; Jer 2:1-2) and the Pentateuch (Gen 32:4-6; Exod 4:21-36) with Near Eastern epistolary style, which he argued reflected the style of oral transmission.[201] The usages of the messenger formula ("Thus says the Lord" and variations) in Deutero-Isaiah were described by Köhler as *Einleitung*, *Weiterleitung*, and *Ausleitung* depending upon the location in the pericope.

Utilizing the insights of his research on the legal institution or 'justice in the gate' process, Köhler distinguished nine judicial speeches in Deutero-Isaiah (Isa 40:12-16, 17-20, 21-26; 41:1-5, 21-24; 42:18-25; 43:8-13; 48:14-16; 49:14-21), which he designated *Streitgespräche* and which corresponds to Gunkel's designation *Gerichtsrede*.[202] According to Köhler, the participant in the trial brought against his opponent his legal dispute (Hebrew *rib*) in which he called upon the witnesses in the form of a *Zweizeugenruf*, delivered his accusation, presented his arguments, invited refutation, and ended with a statement of the offence and a declaration of the punishment. This form of address Köhler saw in its literary form in the prophets and especially in Deutero-Isaiah. Köhler noted that the controversy or judicial speech in Deutero-Isaiah, in some passages, focuses on the dispute between Yahweh and the gods, in others, on the dispute between Yahweh and his own people. In the former, Yahweh is the accuser, in the latter he is the accused. Although Köhler related the controversy speeches to the dialogue situation of the trial, he argued that in Deutero-Isaiah, the manner of the dialogue appears but the speech is in reality a monologue.

---

199. In his Old Testament theology, originally published in 1935, Köhler wrote: "In the Old Testament the cult is almost identical with the sacrifices; there is little more to it than that, above all there is hardly any proclamation of the word" (*Old Testament Theology*, 181).

200. See above.

201. See also Pfeiffer, "Assyrian Epistolary Formulae."

202. Köhler, *Deuterojesaja*, 110–20.

The self-predication and "Do not fear" formulas, which occur frequently in Deutero-Isaiah and had been discussed by Gressmann, were related by Köhler to the theophany.[203]

Johannes Hempel

In one of the first form-critically oriented introductions to the Old Testament, Johannes Hempel[204] built upon the work of previous scholars, especially Gunkel, and compared Israelite prophetic address with numerous Near Eastern parallels. Hempel argued for various stages in the development of the prophetic oracle.[205] The basic oracle was a short oracle received in ecstatic experience and expressed in the form of divine address. This short oracle was then subjected by the prophet to a "primary rationalization" in which a motivation (*Begründung*) was associated with the divine saying. A "secondary reworking" in light of the prophet's experience came to expression in warning, exhortation, and woe-cry. The subjective developments by the prophet utilizing foreign forms could produce extensive units and compositions such as prophetical liturgies. Hempel divided the prophetical sayings into epic genres (visions, salvation, and historical descriptions) and predicative genres. The latter he divided into conditional (exhortation, repentance-speech, and conditional promise) and unconditional (threat, salvation-speech, and reproach) forms. The prophetic reflection and confession he considered to be secondary to the divine oracle. Like Gunkel, Hempel placed particular stress upon the prophetic experience and influence in both the receipt of revelation and in the formulation and expression of that revelation. In the development of prophetic address, Amos does not represent a beginning but rather a high point.

Additional German Contributions

Konrad Beyer devoted his 1933 Erlangen dissertation to the development of the prophetic sermon.[206] Beyer considered the basic prophetic saying

---

203. Ibid., 120–27; and "Die Offenbarungsformel."

204. Hempel, *Die althebräische Literatur*, 56–69. See also his "The Forms of Oral Tradition," esp. 43–44.

205. Hempel, *Die althebräische Literatur*, 66–67.

206. Beyer, *Spruch und Predigt*. His work was strongly dependent upon the 1929

to be the prediction announcing weal or woe.[207] This basic saying could be and was expanded with reproaches or exhortations.[208] The budding sermon was built around a divinely expressed threat and elaborated with either a reproach or exhortation with divine address sometimes found in the latter.[209] The full-fledged sermon contained a far more complicated and developed structure and reflected the incorporation of other genres.[210]

The primary focus of continental research on the prophets during what I have called the first and second generations concentrated overwhelmingly on the address and poetic forms. Two studies that contain a different focus should be noted since they were precursors of subsequent studies. The visions in the prophetic books were subjected to a typological study by Moses Sister, who stressed the striking similarity in structure to be found in the visions from Amos to Daniel.[211] Otto Plöger investigated the prophetical narratives in the books of Samuel and Kings.[212] He categorized these narratives into three divisions depending upon the emphasis of the account as: "Prophetenwort" Geschichte, "Prophetentat" Geschichten, and Propheten-geschichten.

Johannes Lindblom

During this period, numerous form-critical studies on the prophets were undertaken by Scandinavian scholars of whom the most important are Johannes Lindblom and Gunnar Hylmö. Lindblom[213] stood firmly within the history of religions approach and sought to relate prophetic experiences and prophetic preaching to the activity of medieval mystics.[214] He

---

study by Gunnar Hylmö. See also Mowinckel's examination of the sermon in Jeremiah: *Zur Komposition*, 31–45.

207. Beyer, *Spruch und Predigt*, 25–36.
208. Ibid., 36–42.
209. Ibid., 42–51.
210. Ibid., 52–97.
211. Sister, "Die Typen."
212. Plöger, *Die Prophetengeschichten*. See, already, Mowinckel's interest in prophetic narratives in *Zur Komposition*, 24–30.
213. Lindblom, *Die literarische Gattung*; *Hosea*; *Micha*; and "Die Gesichte der Propheten." See also his *Prophecy in Ancient Israel*.
214. This was especially the case in Lindblom, *Die literarische Gattung*, 19–66. See the breadth of his comparisons drawn from various religions and backgrounds in

The History of the Form-Critical Study of Prophecy

classified both the words of medieval mystics and the words of the prophets as "revelation literature." The material in Amos, he divided into fifteen revelation units.[215] These he described as *die grosse Volkerrevelation in Orakelform* (Amos 1–2); four *Predigtrevelationen* (3:1–11, 4:1–13; 5:1–6; 8:4–14), three *Weherevelationen* (5:7–17; 5:18–27; 6:1–7), *eine Schwurrevelation* (6:8–14), five *Gesichtsrevelationen* (7:1–3, 4–6, 7–9; 8:1–3, 9:1–8a), and *die biographische Bethelrevelation* (7:10–17).[216] Such a division suggests extensive rather than short units as the form of prophetical address. Throughout his *Die literarische Gattung*, Lindblom argued against dividing the prophetical traditions into minute units.[217] For him, the prophetic speeches were not in the first instance speeches but revelations or auditions that became speeches when they were given public expression.[218] In an appendix to *Die literarische Gattung*, Lindblom discussed what he called the "prophetic oracle formula."[219] He detected three forms in which the oracle formula appeared: *koh 'amar yahweh*, *'amar yahweh*, and *we'amarta* (or *'emor*) *koh 'amar yahweh*. The second of these he considered to be a fragmented form of the first. The other two forms he considered quite ancient and argued that *koh 'amar yahweh* was a formula unique to the prophets in the Old Testament.

This formula can be compared with similar expressions in other Near Eastern texts. In addition, he compared *koh 'amar yahweh* to similar formulas used in Near Eastern epistolary documents, public proclamations and edicts, and the introductory statements to messages brought from one person to another. Epistolary parallels to *we'amarta koh 'amar yahweh* were also noted. Lindblom considered the formula to have been borrowed by the prophets from its usage in one of these areas, but from which area he considered of little significance.[220] Lindblom pointed to the absence or infrequent occurence of these formulas in large portions

---

Prophecy in Ancient Israel, 1–46.

215. *Die literarische Gattung*, 66–97.

216. Ibid., 95–96.

217. Ibid., 14, 63–66.

218. Ibid., 56.

219. Ibid., 97–115. Lindblom's analysis of this formula is very similar to that of Köhler in his *Deuterojesaja*, a work with which Lindblom was familiar and which he quotes.

220. See his summary in *Prophecy in Ancient Israel*, 103–4.

of the prophetical books (especially Hosea and Isaiah),[221] a factor often bypassed in subsequent research.

Gunnar Hylmö

Gunnar Hylmö published several significant studies on form criticism of the prophets, which one seldom sees referred to, perhaps because of the language barrier.[222] Hylmö's study on prophecy was the most extensive form-critical study of the prophets published to its date. He was heavily dependent upon Gunkel and Gressmann and provided his readers with a synopsis of their work and approach.[223] Hylmö divided the prophetical sayings into the distinctly prophetic, the lyrical, and the didactic forms.[224] The distinctly prophetic speech he classified into future-sayings or oracles (which could be divided psychologically into visions and auditions or according to content into doom or salvation oracles), rebukes or reproaches (which might appear with an oracle or independently), exhortations (which might appear in conjunction with other forms or independently), and the prophetic legal decisions or torah. Hylmö considered the reproach to be a categorical judgment and the exhortation, since it proclaimed the conditions for salvation, to be a hypothetical judgment. In his introduction, Hylmö pointed to 1 Kgs 21:17-27 to illustrate the use of the reproach, to Isa 7:1-9 to demonstrate the use of exhortation, and to Isa 56:1-8 and Zech 7:1-7 to suggest the situational usage of the torah.[225] Lyrical types he divided into secular (victory songs, drinking songs, watchmen's songs, reviling songs, and lamentations or *qinah*) and religious (hymns or public praises, public lamentations, liturgical torahs, individual laments or prayer songs, and pilgrim songs). Didactic types he divided into historical reflections, prophetic contention or controversy speeches, prophetical trial speeches, and proverbs.

---

221. *Die literarische Gattung*, 98-100.

222. Hylmö, *Studier över stilen*; *De s.k. profetiska*; and *Gamla Testamentets*, 72-99, 151-56. For some reason, Scandinavian scholars like Lindblom and Mowinckel make little or no reference to Hylmö. Bentzen's *Introduction* was, however, heavily indebted to Hylmö. Neither Eissfeldt nor Fohrer refer to Hylmö's introduction.

223. *Studier över stilen*, 8-12.

224. See his synopsis in ibid., 16-19.

225. *Gamla Testamentels*, 85, 91-92, 95-97.

The History of the Form-Critical Study of Prophecy
Postscript

Time and space do not permit the completion of this survey to bring it up to the present. At this stage, only some of the main lines of research can be noted, hopefully to be explored in more detail later. Several important developments in Old Testament study, beginning in the 1930s, have introduced new perspectives that have greatly influenced form-critical research on the prophets. The following ten developments seem to me to have been of major consequence.

1. Neo-orthodox theology of the word with its stress on the radical character of divine revelation and its antipathy toward human experiences and prophetic ecstacy has intensified the search for the divine word within prophetic address, has stressed the prophet as merely the mediator of revelation, and has played down the hortatory role earlier assigned to the prophets (Wolff, Wildberger, Westermann, and others).

2. The comparison of early Hebrew tribal structures and institutions with the amphictyonic Greek and Italian leagues (first by Paul Karge in 1910, then others, and in its most developed form by Noth).

3. The idea of the covenant as a dominant institutional concept in Hebrew life and thought from the earliest times (Noth, Eichrodt, von Rad, and others).

4. The idea of a covenant renewal festival with structures and forms of address within which the prophetic office and prophetic speech could be placed (von Rad, Weiser, Würthwein, Reventlow, Hillers, Fensham, Muilenberg, and others).

5. The comparison of the covenant with international treaties (already Paul Karge, Mendenhall, and Baltzer).

6. Developments in the study of Hebrew law (Alt) and the association of law with amphictyonic cult, the covenant festival, and prophecy (Kraus, Bach, Zimmerli, Reventlow, and others).

7. The association of law with international treaty agreements and the placing of the legal dispute (*rib*) within the arena of international and covenant relations (Huffman, Harvey, Wright, Limburg, and others).

8. The assignment of a significant role to the military institutions in ancient Israel (already Schwally, Fredriksson, and Weber) and the

association of the prophets with warfare (von Rad, Bach, Rendtorff, and Ramlot).

9. The recognition of wisdom influence upon the prophets (already Rankin and Gressmann, Fichtner, Terrien, Lindblom, Wolff, and Whedbee).

10. The discovery of the Mari prophetical texts and their comparison with Old Testament prophetic address (Malamat, Westermann, Ellermeier and others).

In addition to these general impulses related to the form-critical study of the prophets, numerous investigations have been made of particular prophetically employed genres: the threat and promise (Wolff, Westermann, von Waldow, Koch, Dion, and others), the disputation (Pfeiffer and Crenshaw), the lament (Bright, Gerstenberger, Reventlow, Long, and Berridge), the *rib* (Huffman, Harvey, Limburg, and North), the woe-speech (Westermann, Gerstenberger, Clifford, Williams, Wanke, Janzen, and Kraus), prophetic narratives (Fohrer, Steck, Rofe, and Nicholson), and vision and call accounts (Horst, Zimmerli, Habel, Reventlow, Richter, and Long).

Bibliography

Bach, Robert. *Die Aufforderungen zur Flucht und zum Kampf im alttestamentlichen Prophetenspruch*. WMANT 9. Neukirchen: Neukirchener, 1962.

Balla, Emil. *Die Droh- und Scheltwörte des Amos*. Leipzig: Edelmann, 1926.

———. *Das Ich der Psalmen*. FRLANT 16. Göttingen: Vandenhoeck & Ruprecht, 1912.

Bardtke, Hans. *TLZ* 75 (1950) 441–46.

Baumgartner, Walter. "Die Auffassungen des 19. Jahrhunderts vom israelitischen Prophetismus." *Archiv für Kulturgeschichte* 15 (1922) 21–35. Reprinted in *Zum Alten Testament und siener Umwelt: Ausgewählte Aufsätze*, 27–41.

———. "Hermann Gunkel." *NZZ* (1932) 489–99.

———. *Jeremiah's Poems of Lament*. Translated by David E. Orton. Historic Texts and Interpreters in Biblical Scholarship 7. Sheffield, UK: Almond, 1987.

———. *Die Klagegedichte des Jeremia*. BZAW 32. Giessen: Töpelmann, 1917.

———. *Zum Alten Testament und seiner Umwelt*. Leiden: Brill, 1959.

———. "Zum 100. Geburtstag von Hermann Gunkel." In *Congress Volume: Bonn, 1962*, 1–18. VTSup 9. Leiden: Brill, 1963. Reprinted in Hermann Gunkel, *Genesis*, CV–CXXII. 6th ed. Göttingen: Vandenhoeck & Ruprecht, 1964.

Begrich, Joachim. *Gesammelte Studien zum Alten Testament*. Edited by Walther Zimmerli. ThBü 21. Munich: Kaiser, 1964.

———. "Das priesterliche Heilsorakel." *ZAW* 52 (1934) 81–92. Reprinted in *Gesammelte Studien zum Alten Testament*, 217–31.

The History of the Form-Critical Study of Prophecy

———. "Die priesterliche Tora." In *Werden und Wesen des Alten Testament*, edited by Paul Volz et al., 68-88. BZAW 66. Berlin: Töpelmann, 1936. Reprinted in *Gesammelte Studien*, 232-60.

———. *Der Psalm der Hiskia*. FRLANT 42. Göttingen: Vandenhoeck & Ruprecht, 1926.

———. *Studien zu Deuterojesaja*. BWANT 4/25. 1938. Reprinted, ThBü 20, Munich: Kaiser, 1963.

Bentzen, Aage. *Introduction to the Old Testament*. 2 vols. 2nd ed. Copenhagen: Gad, 1952.

Bethe, Erich, and Paul Wendland. "Quellen und Materialien, Gesichtspunkte und Probleme zur Erforschung der griechischen Literaturgeschichte." In *Einleitung in die Altertumswissenschaft*, edited by Alfred Gercke and Eduard Norden, vol. 1, 399-450. Leipzig: Teubner, 1910.

Beyer, Konrad. *Spruch und Predigt bei den vorexilischen Schriftpropheten: Eine Untersuchungen der Gestalt der prophetischen mündlichen Verkündigung*. Erlangen: Gutenburg, 1933.

Budde, Karl. "Das hebräische Klagelied." *ZAW* 2 (1882) 1-52.

———. "Ein althebräisches Klagelied." *ZAW* 3 (1883) 299-306.

Buss, Martin. "The Study of Forms." In *Old Testament Form Criticism*, edited by John H. Hayes, 1-56. TUMSR 2. San Antonio: Trinity University Press, 1973.

Davidson, A. B. *Old Testament Prophecy*. Edited by J. A. Paterson. Edinburgh: T. & T. Clark, 1903.

Duhm, Bernhard. *Das Buch Jesaia*. HKAT. Göttingen: Vandenhoeck & Ruprecht, 1892. 2nd ed., 1902. 3rd ed., 1914.

———. *Das Geheimnis in der Religion*. Tübingen: Mohr/Siebeck, 1896. 2nd ed., 1927.

———. *Die Gottgeweihten in der alttestamentlichen Religion: Vortrag*. Tübingen: Mohr/Siebeck, 1905.

———. *Die Theologie der Propheten als Grundlage für die innere Entwicklungsgeschichte der israelitischen Religion*. Bonn: Marcus, 1875.

Erbt, Wilhelm. *Jeremia und seine Zeit: Die Geschichte der letzten fünfzig Jahre des vorexilischen Juda*. Göttingen: Vandenhoeck & Ruprecht, 1902.

Galling, Kurt. "Hermann Gunkel." *Zeitschrift für Mission und Religionswissenschaft* 42 (1932) 257-74.

Gercke, Alfred, and Eduard Norden, editors. *Einleitung in die Altestumswissenschaft*. Vol. 1. Leipzig: Teubner, 1910.

Gerstenberger, Erhard S. "Psalms." In *Old Testament Form Criticism*, edited by John H. Hayes, 198-221. TUMSR 2. San Antonio: Trinity University Press, 1973.

Gray, George Buchanan. *A Critical and Exegetical Commentary on the Book of Isaiah, I-XXXIX*. ICC. Edinburgh: T. & T. Clark, 1912.

Gressmann, Hugo. *Albert Eichhorn und die religionsgeschichtliche Schule*. Göttingen: Vandenhoeck & Ruprecht, 1914.

———. *Die älteste Geschichtsschreibung and Prophetie Israels*. SAT 2/1. Göttingen: Vandenhoeck & Ruprecht, 1910.

———. "Der Aufgaben der alttestamentliche Forschung." *ZAW* 42 (1924) 1-33.

———. "Foreign Influences in Hebrew Prophecy." *Journal of Theological Studies* 27 (1926) 241-54.

———. "Die literarische Analyse Deuterojesajas." *ZAW* 34 (1914) 254-97.

———. *Der Messias*. FRLANT 43. Göttingen: Vandenhoeck & Ruprecht, 1929.

———. *Der Ursprung der israelitisch-jüdischen Eschatologie.* FRLANT 6. Göttingen: Vandenhoeck & Ruprecht, 1905.
Gunkel, Hermann. "The Close of Micah." In *What Remains of the Old Testament and Other Essays*, 115–49.
———. *Einleitung in die Psalmen: Die Gattungen der religiösen Lyrik Israels.* Completed by Joachim Begrich. HKAT. Göttingen: Vandenhoeck & Ruprecht, 1933.
———. "Einleitungen." In *Die grossen Propheten*, edited by Hans Schmidt. SAT 2/2. Göttingen: Vandenhoeck & Ruprecht, 1915.
———. "Fundamental Problems of Hebrew Literary History." In *What Remains of the Old Testament and Other Essays*, 57–68.
———. *The History of Religion and Old Testament Criticism.* London: Williams & Norgate, 1919.
———. *The Influence of the Holy Spirit: According to the Popular View of the Apostolic Age and the Teaching of the Apostle Paul: A Biblical-Theological Study.* Translated by Roy A. Harrisville and Philip A. Quanbeck II. Philadelphia: Fortress, 1979.
———. *Introduction to Psalms: The Genres of the Religious Lyric of Israel.* Completed by Joachim Begrich. Translated by James D. Nogalski. Macon, GA: Mercer University Press, 1998.
———. "The Israelite Prophecy from the Time of Amos." In *Twentieth-Century Theology in the Making.* Vol. 1, *Themes of Biblical Theology*, edited by Jaroslav Pelikan, 48–75. Translated by R. A. Wilson. New York: Harper & Row, 1969.
———. "Die israelitische Literatur." In *Kultur der Gegenwart* 1/7, edited by P. Hinneberg, 51–102. Berlin: Teubner, 1906.
———. "Jesaia 33: Eine prophetische Liturgie." *ZAW* 42 (1924) 177–208.
———. "Die Königspsalmen." *Preussische-Jahrbuch* 158 (1914) 42–68.
———. "Der Micha-Schluss: Zur Einführung in die literaturgeschichtliche Arbeit am Alten Testament." *Zeitschrift für Semitistik und verwandte Gebiete* 2 (1923/24) 145–83.
———. "Nahum 1." *ZAW* 13 (1893) 223–44.
———. "Neue Ziele der alttestamentlichen Forschung." *Christliche Welt* 21 (1907) 78–84.
———. *Die Propheten.* Göttingen: Vandenhoeck & Ruprecht, 1917.
———. "Propheten II seit Amos." In *RGG* 4 (1913) 1866–86 = "Propheten Israels seit Amos." In *RGG*² 4 (1930) 1538–54.
———. *Die Religionsgeschichte und die alttestamentliche Wissenschaft.* Berlin-Schöneberg: Protestantischer Schriftenvertrieb, 1910.
———. *What Remains of the Old Testament and Other Essays.* Translated by A. K. Dallas. New York: Macmillan, 1928.
———. *Die Wirkungen des heiligen Geistes nach der populären Anschauung der apostlischen Zeit und der Lehre des Apostels Paulus.* Göttingen: Vandenhoeck & Ruprecht, 1888.
Hahn, Herbert F. *The Old Testament in Modern Research.* 2nd ed. With a survey of recent literature by Horace D. Hummel. Philadelphia: Fortress, 1966.
Harvey, Julien. *Le plaidoyer prophetique contre Israel apre la rupture de l'alliance.* Bruges: Desclée deBrouwer, 1967.
Hempel, Johannes. *Die althebräische Literatur und ihr hellenistisch-jüdisches Nachleben.* 6 parts. Handbuch der Literaturwissenschaft. Wildpark-Potsdam: Akademische Verlagsgesellschaft Athenaion, 1930–1934.

The History of the Form-Critical Study of Prophecy

———. "The Forms of Oral Tradition." In *Record and Revelation*, edited by H. Wheeler Robinson, 28–44. London: Oxford University Press, 1938.

———. "Hermann Gunkels Bücher, Schriften und Aufsätze." In *Eucharisterion*, edited by Hans Schmidt, 2.214–25. FRLANT 37. Göttingen: Vandenhoeck & Ruprecht, 1923.

Herder, Johann Gottfried von. *The Spirit of Hebrew Poetry*. Translated by James Marsh. Burlington, VT: Smith, 1933.

Hölscher, Gustav. *Die Propheten: Untersuchungen zur Religionsgeschichte Israels*. Leipzig: Hinrichs, 1914.

Humbert, Paul. "Hermann Gunkel, un maitre des etude hébraiques." *Revue de Théologie et Philosophie* 11 (1932) 5–19.

Hylmö, Gunnar. *Gamla Testamentets litteraturhistoria*. Lund: Gleerup, 1938.

———. *De s.k. profetiska liturgiernas rytm, stil och komposition*. LUA, NF, 1/25/5. Lund: Gleerup, 1929.

———. *Studier över stilen i de gammaltestamentliga profetbackema I: De egentliga profetiska diktarterna*. Lunds Universitet Arsskrift, NF, 1/25/4. Lund: Gleerup, 1929.

Jahnow, Hedwig. *Das hebräische Leichenlied im Rahmen der Volkerdichtung*. BZAW 36. Giessen: Töpelmann, 1923.

Jastrow, Morris. *Die Religion Babyloniens und Assyriens*. Vol. 2. Giessen: Töpelmann, 1912.

Keil, K. *Manual of Historico-Critical Introduction*. Translated by G. C. M. Douglas. Edinburgh: T. & T. Clark, 1869.

Klatt, Werner. *Hermann Gunkel: Zu seiner Theologie der Religionsgeschichte und zur Entstehung der formgeschichtlichen Methode*. FRLANT 100. Göttingen: Vandenhoek & Ruprecht, 1969.

Knobel, August W. *Der Prophetismus der Hebräer*. Vol. 1. Breslau: Max, 1837.

Köhler, Ludwig. "Der Botenspruch." In *Kleiner Lichte: Fünfzig Bibelstellen Erklärt*, 11–17. Zwingli Bücherei 47. Zurich: Zwingli, 1945.

———. *Deuterojesaja (Jesaja 40–55) stilkritisch untersucht*. BZAW 37. Giessen: Töpelmann, 1923.

———. "Die hebräische Rechtsgemeinde." In *Festrede des Rektors* (April 29, 1931) = his *Der hebräische Mensch*, 143–71. Tübingen: Mohr/Siebeck, 1953.

———. "Justice in the Gate." In *Hebrew Man*, 127–50. Translated by P. R. Ackroyd. Nashville: Abingdon, 1956.

———. "Die Offenbarungsformel 'Fürchte dich nicht' in Alten Testament." *Theologische Zeitschrift* 36 (1919) 33–39.

———. *Old Testament Theology*. Translated by A. S. Todd. Philadelphia: Westminster, 1957.

Kraus, Hans-Joachim. *Geschichte der historisch-kritischen Erforschung des Alten Testaments*. 2nd ed. Neukirchen-Vlyun: Neukirchener, 1969.

Kuenen, Abraham. *De Profeten en de Profetie onder Israel*. Leiden: Engels, 1875.

———. *The Prophets and Prophecy in Israel: An Historical and Critical Enquiry*. Translated by Adam Milroy. London: Longmans, Green, 1877.

Lindblom, Johannes. "Die Gesichte der Propheten." *Studia Theologica* 1 (1935) 7–28.

———. *Hosea literarisch untersucht*. Acta Academia Aboensis 5/2. Abo: Abo Akademi, 1928.

---. *Die literarische Gattung der prophetischen Literatur: Eine literargeschichte Untersuchung zum Alten Testament*. Uppsala Universitet Arsskrift, 1924, Teologi 1. Uppsala: Lundequistska, 1924.

---. *Micha literarisch untersucht*. Acta Academia Aboensis 6/2. Abo: Abo Akademi, 1929.

---. *Prophecy in Ancient Israel*. Philadelphia: Muhlenberg, 1962.

Meyer, Eduard. *Geschichte des Altertums*. Vol. 1/2. 2nd ed. Stuttgart: Cotta, 1909.

---. *Die Israeliten und ihre Nachbarstamme: Alttestamentliche Untersuchungen*. Halle: Niemeyer, 1906.

Mowinckel, Sigmund. *Le Decalogue*. Etudes d'Histoire et de Philosophie Religieuses 16. Paris: Alcan, 1927.

---. *Zur Komposition des Buches Jeremia*. Videnskapsselskapets skrifter: Hist.-filos. klasse, 1913, 5. Kristiania [Oslo]: Dybwad, 1914.

---. "Om nebiisme og profetie." *Norsk Teologisk Tidsskrift* 10 (1909) 185ff; 330ff.

---. *Prophecy and Tradition: The Prophetic Books in the Light of the Study of the Growth and History of Tradition*. Avhandlinger utgitt av det Norske Videnskaps-Akademi I Oslo, Hist. Filo. Klasse, 1946, 3. Oslo: Dybwad, 1946.

---. *Psalmenstudien II: Das Thronbesteigungsfest Jahwäs und der Ursprung der Eschatologie*. Kristiania [Oslo]: Dybwad, 1923.

---. *Psalmenstudien III: Kultprophetie und prophetische Psalmen*. Kristiania [Oslo]: Dybwad, 1924.

---. *The Psalms in Israel's Worship*. 2 vols. Translated by D. R. Ap-Thomas. 1962. Reprinted with a new foreword by James L. Crenshaw. Grand Rapids: Eerdmans, 2004.

---. *The Spirit and the Word: Prophecy and Tradition in Ancient Israel*. Edited by K. C. Hanson. Fortress Classics in Biblical Studies. Minneapolis: Fortress, 2002.

---. "Stilformer og motiver i profeten Jeremias diktning." *Edda* 26 (1926) 233–320.

Michelet, S., Sigmund Mowinckel, and Nils Messel. *Det Gamle Testament*. Oslo: Aschenhoug, 1929–.

Norden, Eduard. *Agnostos Theos: Untersuchungen zur Formengeschichte religiöser Rede*. Leipzig: Teubner, 1913.

---. *Die antike Kunstprosa vom VI. Jahrhundert v. chr. bis in die Zeit der Renaissance*. 2 vols. Leipzig: Teubner, 1898.

Obermann, Julian. "Preface." In Hugo Gressmann, *The Tower of Babel*, XII–XIII. Edited by Julian Obermann. New York: Jewish Institute of Religion Press, 1928.

Oehler, Friedrick. "Das priesterliche Orakel in Israel und Juda." In *Abhandlungen zur semitischen Religionskunde und Sprachwissenschaft*, edited by Wilh. Frankenberg and Friedr. Küchler, 285–301. BZAW 33. Giessen: Töpelmann, 1918.

Pfeiffer, Robert H. "Assyrian Epistolary Formulae." *Journal of the American Oriental Society* 43 (1923) 26–40.

Plöger, Otto. *Die Prophetengeschichten der Samuel- und Königsbücher*. Greifswald: Adler, 1937.

Rabenau, K. von. "Hermann Gunkel." In *Tendenzen der Theologie im 20. Jahrhundert: Eine Geschichte in Porträts*, edited by Hans Jürgen Schultz, 80–87. Stuttgart: Kreus, 1966.

---. "Hermann Gunkel auf rauhen Phaden nach Halle." *EvTh* 30 (1970) 433–44.

Reuss, Eduard. *Die Geschichte der heiligen Schriften des Alten Testaments*. Braunschweig: Schwetschke, 1881.

Robinson, T. H. "Higher Criticism and the Prophetic Literature." *Expository Times* 50 (1938/39) 198-202.
Schmidt, Hans. "In Memoriam Hermann Gunkel." *Theologische Blätter* 11 (1932) 97-103.
Scholder, Klaus. "Herder und die Anfänge der Theologie." *EvTh* 22 (1962) 425-40.
Sister, M. "Die Typen der prophetischen Visionen in der Bibel." *Monatschrift für Geschichte und Wissenschaft des Judentums* 78 (1934) 399-430.
Smith, Sydney. *Isaiah Chapters XL-LV: Literary Criticism and History*. Schweich Lectures 1940. London: Oxford University Press, 1944.
Smith, W. Robertson. *The Old Testament in the Jewish Church*. Edinburgh: A. & C. Black, 1881; 2nd ed., 1895.
Sprondel, Gottfried. "Bibliographie Hugo Gressmann." *ZAW* 69 (1957) 211-28.
Wellhausen, Julius. *Israelitische und jüdische Geschichte*. Berlin: Reimer, 1894.
Westermann, Claus. *Basic Forms of Prophetic Speech*. Translated by Hugh Clayton White. Philadelphia: Westminster, 1967. Reprinted, 1991.
———. *Grundformen prophetischer Rede*. BevTh 31. Munich: Kaiser, 1960; 2nd ed., 1964.
Willi, Thomas. *Herders Beitrag zum Verstehen des Alten Testaments*. Beiträge zur Geschichte der Biblischen Hermeneutik 8. Tübingen: Mohr/Siebeck, 1971.

6

The Usage of Oracles against Foreign Nations in Ancient Israel

EVERY PROPHETICAL BOOK IN the Old Testament, with the exception of Hosea, contains oracles against non-Israelite nations (e.g., Amos 1:1—2:3; Isaiah 13–23; Jeremiah 46–51; and Ezekiel 25–32). These speeches against foreign powers represent a major problem-area for exegetes and commentators since they sit like extraneous literary and theological blocks within the prophetical books.

It is obvious that these speeches were not primarily spoken or written to be heard or acted upon by the nations mentioned in the texts. Their function and importance were not dependent on the foreign powers' knowledge of or response to them. The importance of the speeches must not be sought, therefore, in what they "said" to the enemy but rather in the function that they performed within the context of Israelite society.

The usage of such nation oracles by the classical prophets and their employment at the beginning of the classical period in the eighth century would suggest that the practice of delivering such oracles had a long history within ancient Israel. An investigation into the usage of these oracles within the institutional life of Israel should contribute to our understanding of the function of the oracles within the prophetical literature.

The Usage of Oracles against Foreign Nations in Ancient Israel

The Context of War

The usage of oracles against and denunciations of one's enemies is found in the Old Testament as part of the preparation and execution of warfare.[1] On occasion, these speeches in a warfare context took the form of curses. The Balaam traditions (Numbers 22–24) depict the role of the seer-prophet who issued curses and oracles against an enemy to weaken him and to assist in the accomplishment of victory.[2] Balak the king of Moab, when confronted by the invading host of Israel, acquired the assistance of a 'diviner'[3] from Pethor on the Euphrates to "curse Jacob and execrate Israel" (Num 23:7b). On the basis of the Balaam traditions, Mowinckel has concluded that "before the battle a curse was flung against the enemy to break his 'luck,' put 'bane' and evil 'charms' into his soul, to enable them to stand up to him and drive him away."[4] Although Balaam was no Israelite and in the narrative is unable to curse Israel, these traditions do suggest that Israel was familiar with the practice of cursing the enemy before warfare.

In the story of David's battle with Goliath (1 Samuel 17), one can envision a type of situation in which the curses would have been heard by the combatants on both sides. The reference to Goliath's cursing David by his god (1 Sam 17:43)[5] does not give the content of the imprecation and thus limits what can be said about this type of cursing procedure. Similarly, 2 Kgs 2:23–25, which is not however concerned with warfare, shows that cursing one's antagonists in the name of Yahweh was a practice, but again, the content of the curse is not given.

As a general rule in the Old Testament, speeches made against the enemy before battle do not take the form of curses but rather appear as

---

1. The possible similarity between the prophetical speeches against the nations and the use of curses and oracles against the enemy employed by other Semites during warfare has been suggested by Guillaume (*Prophecy and Divination*, 171, 255, 281–82) and Haldar (*Associations of Cult Prophets*, 195, 200–201).

2. The nature and function of the curse in the Old Testament are discussed by Hempel, "Die israelitischen Anschauungen"; Blank, "The Curse"; and Brichto, *The Problem of "Curse."*

3. Daiches, "Balaam." Reference is made in the Mari letters to the presence of a diviner (*barum*) as part of the military force, see *ANET*, 482. On the functions of the diviner, see Oppenheim, *Ancient Mesopotamia*, 206–27 and Largement, "Les oracles de Bile'am."

4. Mowinckel, *The Psalms*, 1.27.

5. On this text, see Scharbert, "'Fluchen' und 'Segen,'" esp. 10.

speeches of judgment denouncing the enemy or as oracles announcing the defeat of the opponent. During Ahab's Aramean wars, a man of God came to the encamped Israelite troops and delivered an oracle from Yahweh (1 Kgs 20:26–30).[6] This oracle contains three elements: a condemnation of the Arameans, a promise of victory over the enemy, and a declaration concerning divine recognition. The condemnation of the enemy in the speech forms the motivational foundation for the promise of victory made to the Israelite king. The judgment of the Arameans is made as a word of Yahweh (v. 28). On the basis of this condemnation, the Israelite king is granted the divine assurance of victory (v. 28b).

Another statement of judgment against an enemy is contained in 1 Sam 15:2–3. In this material, Samuel delivers an oracle from Yahweh to Saul that contains two statements: a condemnation of Amalek and a command to battle, with the former as the justification of the latter. In spite of the fact that this chapter represents a paradigmatic account of the conflict between prophet and king and, therefore, cannot be used as a genuine source for the historical relationship between Samuel and Saul, it does show that in Israel the usage of judgment speeches against the enemy was part of the preparation for and justification of warfare.

This usage of judgment speeches within the context of warfare is further illustrated by Isaiah's speech to Ahaz during the Aramean–Israelite coalition against Judah (Isa 7:3–9). The judgment against Aram (vv. 5–6) is part of the promise of victory addressed to the Judean king (v. 7).

In all three of these judgment speeches (1 Kings 20:26–30; 1 Sam 15:2–3; Isa 7:5–7), the enemy is referred to in the third person, the address is spoken to the Israelite leader and not the enemy, and the enemy's condemnation is used in conjunction with the command to battle or with the divine assurance of victory.

The utterance of oracles against an enemy could be accompanied by symbolical or divinatory acts associated with the attempt to gain victory.[7] In 2 Kgs 13:14–19, the prophet Elisha is shown co-operating with king Joash of Israel in the performance of certain omen-producing activities against Aram. At this time, Elisha was an old man at the point of death, a

---

6. For a study of this passage, see Zimmerli, "Erkenntnis Gottes," esp. 54–56 [ET = "The Knowledge of God," 39–42]. It is probable that the material in 1 Kings 20 and much of the Elisha cycle, which has been dated to the Omride period, belongs in fact to the time of the Jehu dynasty; see Miller, "The Elisha Cycle."

7. For the possible connection of such acts with the world of magic, see Fohrer, "Prophetie und Magie."

The Usage of Oracles against Foreign Nations in Ancient Israel

time especially suited for the utterance of future-creating words. With the prophet's hands resting upon those of the king, the monarch shot an arrow through an open window toward the east, in the direction of Aram. With the arrow in flight, the prophet declared:

> Yahweh's arrow of victory,
>   the arrow of victory over Aram;
> So you shall smite Aram[8]
>   until he is destroyed. (2 Kgs 13:17b)

This Elisha tradition contains no speech of judgment but is merely an oracle announcing the defeat of Aram. Like the judgment speech, it forms part of the assurance of victory addressed to the Israelite monarch. The materials surveyed so far place the usage of oracles against the nations within the context of warfare. Further evidence for the usage of such denunciations of the enemy in Israelite tradition is found in Josephus and the Dead Sea Scrolls. Josephus tells of a certain righteous man named Onias who was taken to the battle area during the conflict of Aretas and Hyrcanus with Aristobulus and ordered to curse Aristobulus and his followers. Onias had assisted previously in an intercession for rain during a drought, but he refused this cursing task and was stoned.[9]

In the Qumran War Scroll,[10] a part of the ritual of warfare was to include the cursing of Belial and his followers. This cursing of the enemy was to occur during battle[11] and be performed by the high priest along with the other priests and the elders of the *serekh* as a chorus (13:2–6).

The recognition of warfare as an original *Sitz im Leben* for Israelite oracles against foreign nations is supported by the use of oracles and curses against the enemy during military undertakings in other Near Eastern cultures. One of the oldest of such speeches is the Sumerian "Curse of Agade,"[12] which, however, lends only indirect support since it is a *post eventum* interpretation of the fall of Agade as the result of a curse pronounced upon the city. The oracle, which is too lengthy for inclusion

---

8. "In Aphek" in the MT is either an insertion from 1 Kgs 20:26 or should be read "as in Aphek."

9. *Ant.* 14.2.1. For a discussion of this incident, see Zeitlin, *The Rise and Fall*, 1:347; and Driver, *The Judaean Scrolls*, 151–52.

10. The text is found in Yadin, *The Scroll of the War*.

11. This is also the view of Dupont-Sommer, *The Essene Writings*, 188. Yadin places the cursing after the battle when the enemy has been slain (*The Scroll of the War*, 210).

12. Translated and discussed by Kramer, *The Sumerians*, 62–66.

in this paper, is of interest for the prehistory of the Israelite oracle for a number of reasons. (1) The curse is related as the pronouncement of the deities themselves, which agrees with the biblical oracles delivered as the word of Yahweh, but disagrees with the common tomb, boundary, and treaty inscriptions that invoke the curse of the deity or deities.[13] (2) The speech is a statement of judgment spoken against the city because of its leader's desecration of the temple in Nippur. (3) The punishment pronounced is destruction, desolation, and loss of identity.

Among numerous documents discovered at the site of ancient Mari, there are ten letters that have been published[14] that refer to persons of a prophetical type who pronounced oracles to be written to the Mari king Zimrilim. These letters written by royal officials incorporate the prophetical oracles, generally giving the conditions under which they were spoken. One of these documents is of special importance for the prehistory of the Israelite oracles against the nations. It is a letter from an official in the court of Mari that, after the customary introduction, states:

> After I had offered sacrifice
> to the god Dagan for the well-being of my Lord,
> the *aplum*-prophet of the god Dagan of Tuttul
> arose and thus spoke as follows: "O Babylon! Why
>   dost thou ever (evil)? I will gather thee
>   in the net! Thy god is a *wild ox* (?).
>   The houses of the seven confederates
>   and all their possessions
>   I shall place
>   in Zimrilim's hand!"[15]

A number of factors in this document are noteworthy. (1) The giving of the oracle is closely associated with the cult and the offering of a sacrifice. (2) The judgment against Babylon is given as the direct address of Dagan to Babylon though it is obvious that the statement was to be transmitted to the king of Mari and not to the Babylonians. This indirect usage of direct address is characteristic of the Old Testament oracles against foreign powers. (3) The oracle proclaiming Babylon's doom forms part of an oracle of salvation addressed to the ruler of Mari.

---

13. For the form and content of the latter, see Gevirtz, "West-Semitic Curses"; and Hillers, *Treaty-Curses*, esp. 12–29.

14. Full bibliographical references are given in Malamat, "Prophetic Revelations."

15. The translation is that of Malamat, ibid., 214–15. The original is published in Bottero, ed., *Textes divers*, text no. 23.

The Usage of Oracles against Foreign Nations in Ancient Israel

One further letter from Mari probably contained a pronouncement upon the enemy.[16] This document gives an oracle spoken by the wife of a freeman to be transmitted to Zimrilim, but unfortunately most of the text is illegible. The part of the oracle preserved states:

> The god Dagan hath sent me.
> Send (a message) to thy Lord.
> Let him not be anxious and . . .
> Let him not be anxious.
> Hammurapi
> [King] of Babylon.

Along the edge of this text are the words *ana bkrqishu* ("for his loss"). If this text contained, as is likely, a denunciation of Hammurapi for his warfare against Mari, then this oracle is very similar to that of Isa 7:3–9 containing an oracle of assurance and a denunciation of the enemy as part of the assurance.

Among the Hittites, accusations against the enemy and his gods were a part of the ritual preparation for battle. A Hittite text discusses the preparatory ceremony conducted at the boundary of the enemy country.[17] Sacrifice was offered and the Hittite god and other friendly deities were summoned to battle and implored for assistance. The charge against the enemy was stated:

> But now the Kashkeans have taken them [i.e., sanctuaries].
> The Kashkeans have begun war. They boast of their power
> (and) strength. They have made light of you, O Gods!

The gods of the enemy were summoned to appear before the tribunal of Hittite gods to hear accusations against them.

> The gods of the Hatti land have done nothing against
> you, the gods of the Kashkean country. They have
> not put you under constraint. But ye, the gods of
> the Kashkean country, began war. Ye drove the gods
> of the Hatti land out of their realm and took over
> their realm for yourselves. The Kashkean people
> also began war. From the Hittites ye took away
> their cities and ye drove them out of their field (and)
> fallow and out of their vineyards.

---

16. Bottero, ed., *Textes divers*, 114. The text is translated by Malamat, "Prophetic Revelations," 221.

17. Translated by Goetze in *ANET*, 354–55.

These accusations form the motivation for the announcement of warfare and the pronouncement of doom upon the enemy.

Among the ancient Egyptians[18] and early Arabs[19] execrations and oracles were used against the enemy during warfare and in preparation for battle. But since this material has been commented on by others, it is not necessary to go into further detail here.

The biblical texts, later Jewish traditions, and comparative Near Eastern material all suggest that speeches against foreign and enemy powers were utilized within the context of warfare.[20] In Israel this was primarily a prophetical function,[21] which would substantiate Jeremiah's statement that "the prophets who preceded you [sc. Hananiah] and me from ancient times prophesied war, famine, and pestilence against many countries and great kingdoms" (Jer 28:8).

Cultic Setting

The Old Testament evidence also points to the employment of nation oracles within cultic services of lamentation. Such services were the *Sitz im Leben* for the national psalms of lament. The structure of these psalms generally consists of an invocation to the deity, a lament describing the

---

18. The Egyptian execration texts were oracular curses against real or potential enemies written on pottery vessels or figurines that were ritually smashed. These texts from the nineteenth–eighteenth centuries BCE, however, were probably not employed in an actual military undertaking but were used in hopes of preventing actual warfare. The texts were published by Sethe, *Die Ächtung*; and Posener, *Princes et pays d'Asie et de Nubie*. Some of these texts are translated by Wilson in *ANET*, 328–29. Recently, a new find of execration texts has been made, see Vila, "Un dépôt de textes." Further bibliography is given by Fohrer, "Prophetie und Magie," 33, n. 25

19. On the Arabic material, see Guillaume, *Prophecy and Divination*, 171; Pedersen, "The Role"; and Hayes, "The Oracles against the Nations," 89–90, with further bibliography.

20. The influence of the victory song sung in commemoration of the nation's triumph or in celebration of the enemy's downfall should also be mentioned as a possible source of nation oracles. See Exod 15:21; Num 21:27–28; Judges 5; and Eissfeldt, *The Old Testament*, 92–94, 99–101. Jeremias, *Theophanie*, associates these victory songs with early prophetical activity and considers them to be the original *Sitz im Leben* of the theophany formula; see ibid., esp. 150–64.

21. Both Gunkel and Gressmann considered the oracles against the nations to be the oldest form of prophetical oracle. See the references and discussion in Westermann, *Basic Forms*, 23–34; and for a similar opinion see Gottwald, *All the Kingdoms*, 47–49.

state of distress, a confession of confidence in the deity, a petition containing specific entreaties, and a statement concerning the outcome should God act on behalf of the community.[22] Joachim Begrich has shown that responses were often spoken to the supplicant as a divine answer to the lament.[23] References to such oracles spoken by the officiating priest or some other cultic official are found frequently in the Old Testament (1 Sam 1:17; Pss 35:1–3; 85:8; Lam 3:55–57). The relevant question is: were nation oracles used in the cult as *Heilsorakel* spoken to the worshiping community or king? Several considerations would suggest that they were.

The distress of the nation is often described in the psalms as the result of the activity of other nations who have defeated and plagued Israel (Pss 44:8–19; 74:4–8; 79:1–4; 83:1–8; Lam 1:10–11; 2:15–16). Similarly, prayers and entreaties for the destruction of the enemy were an important part of the national psalms of lamentation (Pss 79:5–7; 83:9–18; Lam 1:21–22). These laments of distress and the prayers for destruction of the enemy center on foreign non-Israelite nations.

Psalm 21, although not a psalm of lamentation, suggests that oracles of assurance were addressed to the king promising him victory over his enemies. The role of this psalm in a cultic ritual is substantiated by its structure. The elements of the psalm consist in a hymn of thanksgiving (vv. 1–7), an oracle (vv. 8–12), and a prayer of adoration (v. 18). Similarly, Psalm 20 contains an oracle of assurance addressed to the king in vv. 1–5 with a response spoken by or on behalf of the king in vv. 6–8 introduced by, "Now I know that Yahweh will help his anointed."

To return to the question of whether or not these divine responses ever assumed the form of a pronouncement of judgment upon or the announcement of the destruction of Israel's enemies, the answer must be affirmative. Oracles referring to the nations within the context of the cult are illustrated by Psalm 60. The opening section of this psalm includes a lament to Yahweh concerning the nation's distress (vv. 1–5). In response to the lament, Yahweh spoke through his representative to the complaining community:

> God has spoken in his sanctuary:
> "I will triumph, I will portion out Shechem,
>   and the valley of Succoth I will divide up.

---

22. Not all of these elements are found in every psalm of this type. For the form of the lamentation psalm, see Westermann, *The Praise of God*, 52–64.

23. Begrich, "Die priesterliche *Heilsorakel*."

> To me belongs Gilead; Manasseh is mine;
>   Ephraim is my helmet;
>   Judah is my scepter.
> Moab is my washbasin;
>   upon Edom I will cast my shoe;
> over Philistia I will triumph." (Ps 60:6–8)[24]

Several points should be noted regarding this oracle. (1) It is given as a Yahweh oracle with the deity speaking in the first person. (2) The setting of the speech locates it within the cultic life of the nation. (3) Reference by name is made to non-Israelite nations that are referred to in the third person.

The function of a nation oracle as *Heilsorakel* within the context of a lamentation setting is further illustrated in the book of Lamentations. Lamentations 4:21–22 combines an oracle of salvation to Zion with a condemnation addressed to Edom. In light of the alphabetic arrangement of the chapter, these strophes are clearly an integral part of the material. These oracles are the immediate response to the collective lament of Lam 4:17–20. Two elements should be noted in this passage. (1) The Edom oracle is spoken as if addressed directly to the nation and is not merely a speech in which the nation is mentioned. (2) The judgment of Edom and the salvation of Zion are so closely joined that the two appear as simply two phrasings of the same idea.

Further evidence to support the use of nation oracles as *Heilsorakel* within the context of a lamentation ritual is found in 2 Kings in the account of Sennacherib's siege of Jerusalem (2 Kgs 18:13—19:37).[25] In the narrative of 2 Kgs 19:14–28, Hezekiah is shown confronted with the power of the Assyrian army demanding his capitulation. The Judean king receives and reads the Assyrian dispatch, perhaps to be envisioned as containing the terms of surrender, after which he carries the document to the temple where he spreads it out before Yahweh. There follows in the text a prayer of lamentation by the king. The prayer contains an address to the deity (v. 15), an entreaty (v. 16), a lament (vv. 17–18), and a request for deliverance (v. 19). In response to the lamentation, Isaiah

---

24. Reading the last word of v. 8 with the MT of Ps 108:9 and several of the versions.

25. The varied arguments against the historicity and authenticity of this material do not affect the argument of this paper since the conclusions assume that the content reflects a typical situation though not necessarily a particular one. On the historical problem see the summary of viewpoints in Rowley, "Hezekiah's Reform"; and Childs, *Isaiah and the Assyrian Crisis*, 69–103.

The Usage of Oracles against Foreign Nations in Ancient Israel

delivered an oracle against the king of Assyria (vv. 21–23). This oracle is placed in the text as a statement of assurance to Hezekiah (v. 20).[26] The oracle against the Assyrian king occupies the same position in this passage as does the prophetical word of consolation in 19:5–7, which is a response to the lament and action of the king that took place within the temple (vv. 1–4). The oracle against the Assyrian king and the word of assurance to the Judean monarch serve identical functions. Both are *Heilsorakel* addressed to the lamenting king. The oracle against the Assyrian in 19:21–28, however, is not simply a curse or denunciation but a genuine speech of judgment condemning Assyria for its haughtiness and self-confidence in its actions against Jerusalem and its god.

A Recurring Israelite Ritual?

The use of oracles against foreign nations within the context of military situations and lamentation services would perhaps have been associated with the existence of actual periods of national crisis and calamity. Is it possible that this type of oracle was a standard part of a recurring Israelite ritual?

H. Graf Reventlow has argued that the employment of oracles against foreign nations formed part of the ritual of the covenant festival.[27] His conclusion is summarized: "There is absolutely no difference between the speeches against foreign peoples and those against one's own people so that both belonged in the covenant festival."[28] Reventlow's arguments, however, rest upon two basic but unproved assumptions. On the one hand, he concludes that the prophets were the direct descendants of the covenant festival spokesmen who in the course of the ritual recited the blessings and the curses. On the other hand, he argues that the judgment ritual of the covenant festival involved not only Israel but the nations of the world. The absence of oracles against foreign nations within passages that might be assigned to the covenant festival argues against Reventlow's conclusions.

---

26. The method used in transmitting this oracle is not stated, but could it not have been in written form as were the prophetic oracles in the Mari letters?

27. Reventlow, *Das Amt des Propheten*, esp. 56–75; and Reventlow, *Wächter über Israel*, esp. 134–57.

28. "Zwischen den Sprüchen gegen die Fremdvölker und denen gegen das eigene Volk besteht dabei gar kein Unterschied, da beide in das eine Bundesfest hineingehören." Reventlow, *Das Amt des Propheten*, 65.

Aage Bentzen sought to interpret the oracles against foreign nations in the light of the Egyptian execration texts and concluded that such speeches were part of the purgatory rites associated with the judgment portion of the ascension festival in the Israelite celebration of the New Year.[29] With such an opinion, Mowinckel was in substantial agreement when he traced the oracles against different individual peoples back to the general oracles at the epiphany feast. He did not, however, locate such oracles within the ritual proper but suggested that they represented the "extempore inspirations and improvisations of the cult prophet, only loosely connected with the festival..."[30]

A number of indications suggest that oracles against foreign nations were employed within the context of the royal court as part of the ritual associated with the king. The studies of Mowinckel, Widengren, Johnson, Kraus, and von Rad relative to the theology of the royal psalms have shown that an emphasis on the universal dominion of the Jerusalemite king was a constitutive factor in the royal ideology. This conception seems to have been dependent upon three basic influences. (1) The influence of the court style of royal predications in Mesopotamian and Egyptian royal theology contributed immensely.[31] (2) The royal theology assimilated many features from the Jerusalem cult with its affirmation of Yahweh's kingship.[32] (3) The empire of David and Solomon provided Israel with an international perspective and a sense of international importance. This royal theology was given special expression in the coronation ritual.[33] If Psalms 2 and 110 reflect this coronation ritual, as is assumed by most scholars, then we possess some clues regarding the use of foreign oracles within the royal cult. In the royal recitation of the divine decree in Psalm 2, two elements are dominant: the divine adoption (v. 7b) and the promise of universal dominion (v. 8). There follows a reference to the king's shattering of the nations (v. 9) and an address to the rulers of

---

29. Bentzen, "The Ritual Background."

30. Mowinckel, *The Psalms*, 1.154

31. See Gressmann, *Der Messias*, 1–63; and Mowinckel, *He That Cometh*, 56–58.

32. See Kraus, *Psalmen* I, 197–201 (ET = *Psalms 1–59*, 81–86). Part of the Jerusalem cult was a celebration of Yahweh's triumph over the hostile powers; see Mowinckel, *The Psalms*, 1.140–82. The association of these powers with the nations represents a historicizing of the myth.

33. See Kraus, *Worship in Israel*, 222–24. If the coronation took place at the New Year festival, then Bentzen and Mowinckel's arguments support the following conclusions.

The Usage of Oracles against Foreign Nations in Ancient Israel

the earth (vv. 10–11). Does this not reflect a symbolic enactment of the destruction of the nations in which pottery vessels were representative of the foreign powers? Is there not reflected in the address to the kings of the world the practice of oracles addressed to foreign powers? Parallels to such practices are found in 2 Kgs 13:14–19, Jeremiah 19, the Egyptian execration texts, and the Egyptian rituals at the pharaoh's coronation and in the anniversary *sed* festival.[34] Similarly, Ps 110:1 probably reflects a symbolical action in the coronation ritual which gave expression to the king's power over the nations. This verse contains a Yahweh oracle spoken by some cultic official to the king promising to make the national enemies his footstool.[35] One cannot avoid connecting this reference and the act reflected with the Egyptian practice of depicting the traditional enemies in bound condition on the royal footstool.[36]

Further confirmation of the connection between the royal theology and nation oracles is offered by an addition to the book of Amos (9:11–12). In this passage, reference is made to the restoration of the house of David and the subsequent possession of Edom and the other nations. The significance of this passage may have been overlooked due to a poor translation of the phrase *'asher-niqra' shimi 'alehem*.[37] The RSV translates this, "who are called by my name," but a better translation might be, "over whom my name is called." Does this not reflect a ritual of addressing oracles over the nations in the name of Yahweh in conjunction with the royal theology?

A further line of argument supports the usage of oracles against the nations as part of the royal court procedure. This is based on the use of, and the presence of curses in, international treaties.[38] Ancient Israel and Judah were familiar with such treaties not only from their vassalage to the Assyrians and Babylonians but also from parity and vassal treaties with their neighbors. Several references are made to nations becoming David's servants (2 Sam 8:2, 6, 14; 10:15–19) implying a state of servitude and vassalage. Solomon and Hiram negotiated a treaty (1 Kgs 5:12;

---

34. See Frankfort, *Kingship and the Gods*, 79–88, 105–9; Nielsen, "The Burial of the Foreign Gods"; and Uphill, "The Egyptian Sed-Festival Rites."

35. The Hebrew word for footstool (*chadom*) is probably of non-Semitic origin; in Ugaritic and Hebrew it is probably a word borrowed from Egypt.

36. The footstools from the tomb of Tut-ankh-Amon were so decorated: one with a portrayal of Egypt's nine traditional enemies, another with six.

37. On this expression, see Galling, "Die Ausrufung des Namens."

38. See McCarthy, *Treaty and Covenant*; and Hillers, *Treaty-Curses*.

MT 5:26)[39] as did Asa and Ben-Hadad (1 Kgs 15:19). The stipulations of such treaties, penalties involved, and curses announced must have been known and proclaimed at the royal court. Possibly some type of formal prosecution and condemnation of the violators of a treaty may have taken place at the royal court.[40] Such condemnations would probably have been made in terms drawn from the content of the treaty.[41] The biblical traditions contain two intimations about such condemnations, both related to Zedekiah's violation of his treaty with Nebuchadnezzar (Ezek 17:12–13). After Zedekiah's capture, he was taken to Riblah before Nebuchadnezzar. Prior to the slaying of his sons and his subsequent blinding, Zedekiah was forced to appear before the Babylonian king. What took place in this encounter is referred to in 2 Kgs 25:6b, which the RSV translates, "passed sentence upon him." The phrase *wayidabru 'ito mishpat* used in this passage is generally assumed by commentators to mean something like "pass sentence" or "take process" in the sense of a trial or hearing.[42] But in light of the Jeremiah parallels (39:5; 52:9) where the singular form of the verb occurs with the plural (*mishpatim*), would it not be better to translate, "he spoke to him the stipulations"? Nebuchadnezzar simply condemned Zedekiah; no trial was necessary, in the terms of the treaty agreement that stipulated slaughter of the sons and blindness as penalties for disobedience. In Ezekiel's preaching on this treaty violation (17:11–22), Zedekiah was condemned for his lack of loyalty and in terms of his having broken an oath sworn in the name of Yahweh.[43]

Conclusion

In summary, what conclusions may be drawn from the above discussion relative to the employment of oracles against the nations by the classical prophets and the presence of such oracles in the prophetical books? The following seem to be pertinent: (1) The presence of such oracles in the prophetical books should not surprise us since such oracles were used in

---

39. On the use of *shalom* and *salimun* as treaty terminology, Noth, "Old Testament Covenant-Making."

40. Harvey, "Le '*rib*-Pattern,'" esp. 182–88.

41. On the possibility that Isa 34:11–17 preserves such a condemnation, see Hayes, "The Oracles against the Nations," 167–70; and Hillers, *Treaty-Curses*, 43–53.

42. See, for example, Montgomery, *Kings*; or Gray, *I & II Kings*.

43. See Tsevat, "The Neo-Assyrian and Neo-Babylonian Vassal Oaths."

multiple contexts in ancient Israel. (2) The element of judgment within these speeches was not the special creation of a "prophetical perspective." (3) The oracles in the prophetical books should not be evaluated on the basis of any one particular *Gattung*. Diversity in form and usage should be expected. (4) The primary motifs in many of the prophetical oracles reflect the interests of the institutional employment of similar oracles. Amos apparently was influenced by the cultic usage whereas in Jeremiah the dominant influence seems to have been the military employment. (5) The institutional usage of foreign nation oracles was no doubt the source of many of the inauthentic oracles in the prophetical books. (6) The organization of the prophetical materials into a scheme of judgment upon the Israelites—judgment upon the nations; salvation for Israel—is perhaps dependent upon the structure of the lamentation ritual in which the scheme of lamentation—judgment upon the enemy; salvation for Israel—predominated.

Bibliography

Begrich, Joachim. "Die priesterliche Heilsorakel." *ZAW* 52 (1934) 81–92. Reprinted in *Gesammelte Studien zum Alten Testament*, 217–31. ThBü 21. Munich: Kaiser, 1964.

Bentzen, Aage. "The Ritual Background of Amos i 2—ii 16." *OTS* 8 (1950) 85–99.

Blank, Sheldon H. "The Curse, the Blasphemy, the Spell, and the Oath." *HUCA* 23 (1950/51) 73–95.

Bottero, Jean, editor. *Textes divers*. Archives royales de Mari 13. Paris: Geuthner, 1964.

Brichto, H. C. *The Problem of "Curse" in the Hebrew Bible*. JBL Monograph Series 13. Philadelphia: Society of Biblical Literature and Exegesis, 1963.

Childs, Brevard S. *Isaiah and the Assyrian Crisis*. SBT 2/3. Naperville, IL: Allenson, 1967.

Daiches, Samuel. "Balaam—A Babylonian Baru." In *Hilprecht Anniversary Volume: Studies in Assyriology and Archaeology Dedicated to Hermann V. Hilprecht upon the Twenty-fifth Anniversary of His Doctorate and His Fiftieth Birthday (July 28)*, 60–70. Leipzig: Hinrichs, 1909. Reprinted in *Bible Studies*, 110–18. London: Goldston, 1950.

Driver, G. R. *The Judaean Scrolls: The Problem and a Solution*. New York: Schocken, 1965.

Dupont-Sommer, A. *The Essene Writings from Qumran*. Translated by G. Vermes. Oxford: Blackwell, 1961.

Eissfeldt, Otto. *The Old Testament: An Introduction*. Translated by Peter R. Ackroyd. Oxford: Blackwell, 1965.

Fohrer, Georg. "Prophetie und Magie." *ZAW* 78 (1966) 25–47. Reprinted in *Studien zur alttestamentlichen Prophetie (1949–1965)*, 242–64. BZAW 99. Berlin: Töpelmann, 1967.

Frankfort, Henri. *Kingship and the Gods: A Study of Ancient Near Eastern Religion as the Integration of Society and Nature*. Chicago: University of Chicago Press, 1948. Reprinted, 1978.

Galling, Kurt. "Die Ausrufung des Namens als Rechtsakt in Israel." *TLZ* 81 (1956) 65–70.

Gevirtz, Stanley. "West-Semitic Curses and the Problem of the Origins of Hebrew Law." *VT* 11 (1961) 137–58.

Gottwald, Norman K. *All the Kingdoms of the Earth: Israelite Prophecy and International Relations in the Ancient Near East*. New York: Harper & Row, 1964.

Gray, John. *I & II Kings*. 2nd ed. OTL. Philadelphia: Westminster, 1976.

Gressmann, Hugo. *Der Messias*. FRLANT 43. Göttingen: Vandenhoeck & Ruprecht, 1929.

Guillaume, Alfred. *Prophecy and Divination among the Hebrews and Other Semites*. Bampton Lectures 1938. London: Hodder & Stoughton, 1938.

Haldar, Alfred. *Associations of Cult Prophets among the Ancient Semites*. Uppsala: Almqvist & Wiksells, 1945.

Harvey, J. "Le 'rib-Pattern,' requisitoire prophétique sur la rupture de l'alliance." *Bib* 43 (1962) 172–96.

Hayes, John H. "The Oracles against the Nations in the Old Testament." PhD diss., Princeton Theological Seminary, 1964.

Hempel, Johannes. "Die israelitischen Anschauungen von Segen und Fluch im Lichte altorientalischer Parallelen." *Zeitschrift der Deutsche Morganländischen Gesellschaft* N.F. 4 (1925) 20–110. Reprinted in *Apoxysmata: Vorarbeiten zu einer Religionsgeschichte und Theologie des Alten Testaments: Festgabe zum 30. Juli 1961*, 30–113. BZAW 81. Berlin: Töpelmann, 1961.

Hillers, Delbert R. *Treaty-Curses and the Old Testament Prophets*. Biblica et Orientalia 16. Rome: Pontifical Biblical Institute Press, 1964.

Jeremias, Jörg. *Theophanie: Die Geschichte einer alttestamentlichen Gattung*. WMANT 10. Neukirchen-Vluyn: Neukirchener, 1965.

Kramer, Samuel Noah. *The Sumerians: Their History, Culture, and Character*. Chicago: University of Chicago Press, 1963.

Kraus, Hans-Joachim. *Psalmen*. Vol. 1. Biblischer Kommentar: Altes Testament 15. Neukirchen-Vluyn: Neukirchener, 1961.

———. *Psalms 1–59*. Translated by Hilton C. Oswald. Continental Commentaries. Minneapolis: Augsburg, 1988.

———. *Worship in Israel: A Cultic History of the Old Testament*. Translated by Geoffrey Buswell. Richmond: John Knox, 1966.

Largement, R. "Les oracles de Bile'am et la mantique suméro-akkadienne." *Travaux de l'Institut Catholique de Paris* 10 (1964) 37–50.

Malamat, Abraham. "Prophetic Revelations in New Documents from Mari and the Bible." In *Volume du Congrès: Genève 1965*, 206–27. VTSup 15. Leiden: Brill, 1966. Reprinted in *Mari and the Bible*, 83–101. Studies in the History and Culture of the Ancient Near East 12. Leiden: Brill, 1998.

McCarthy, Dennis J. *Treaty and Covenant: A Study in Form in the Ancient Oriental Documents and in the Old Testament*. Analecta Biblica 21. Rome: Pontifical Biblical Institute Press, 1963. 2nd ed., 1978.

Miller, J. Maxwell. "The Elisha Cycle and the Accounts of the Omride Wars." *JBL* 85 (1966) 441–54.

Montgomery, James A. *A Critical and Exegetical Commentary on the Book of Kings*. Edited by Henry Snyder Gehman. ICC. Edinburgh: T. & T. Clark, 1951.

Mowinckel, Sigmund. *He That Cometh: The Messiah Concept in the Old Testament and Later Judaism*. Translated by G. W. Anderson. 1956. Reprinted with a new Foreword by John J. Collins. Grand Rapids: Eerdmans, 2005.

———. *The Psalms in Israel's Worship*. 2 vols. Translated by D. R. Ap-Thomas. 1962. Reprinted with a new Foreword by James L. Crenshaw. Grand Rapids: Eerdmans, 2004.

Nielsen, Eduard. "The Burial of the Foreign Gods." *Studia Theologica* 8 (1955) 103–22.

Noth, Martin. "Old Testament Covenant-Making in the Light of a Text from Mari." In *The Laws of the Pentateuch and Other Studies*, 108–17. Translated by D. R. Ap-Thomas. London: SCM, 1966. Reprinted, 1984.

Oppenheim, A. Leo. *Ancient Mesopotamia: Portrait of a Dead Civilization*. Chicago: University of Chicago Press, 1964.

Pedersen, Johannes. "The Role Played by Inspired Persons among the Israelites and the Arabs," in *Studies in Old Testament Prophecy: Presented to Professor Theodore H. Robinson by the Society of Old Testament Study on His Sixty-fifth Birthday, August 9th, 1946*, edited by H. H. Rowley, 127–42. Edinburgh: T. & T. Clark, 1957.

Posener, Georges. *Princes et pays d'Asie et de Nubie: Textes hiératiques sur les figurines d'envoutement du Moyen Empire*. Brussels: Fondation égyptologique reine Elisabeth, 1940.

Reventlow, H. Graf. *Das Amt des Propheten bei Amos*. FRLANT 80. Göttingen: Vandenhoeck & Ruprecht, 1962.

———. *Wächter über Israel: Ezechiel und seine Tradition*. BZAW 82. Berlin: Töpelmann, 1962.

Rowley, H. H. "Hezekiah's Reform and Rebellion." In *Men of God: Studies in Old Testament History and Prophecy*, 98–132. London: Nelson, 1963.

Scharbert, Josef. "'Fluchen' und 'Segen' in Alten Testament." *Bib* 39 (1958) 1–26.

Sethe, Kurt. *Die Ächtung feindlicher Fürsten, Völker und Dinge auf altägyptischen Tongefässscherben des mittleren Reiches*. Abhandlungen der Preussischen Akademie der Wissenschaften, 1926.

Tsevat, Matitiahu. "The Neo-Assyrian and Neo-Babylonian Vassal Oaths and the Prophet Ezekiel." *JBL* 78 (1959) 199–204.

Uphill, Eric. "The Egyptian Sed-Festival Rites." *Journal of Near Eastern Studies* 24 (1965) 365–82.

Vila, E. "Un dépôt de textes d'envoutement au Moyen Empire." *Journal des Savants* (1963) 135–60.

Westermann, Claus. *Basic Forms of Prophetic Speech*. Translated by Hugh Clayton White. 1967. Reprinted with a new Foreword by Gene M. Tucker. Louisville: Westminster John Knox, 1991.

———. *The Praise of God in the Psalms*. Translated by Keith R. Crim. Richmond: John Knox, 1965.

Yadin, Yigal. *The Scroll of the War of the Sons of Light against the Sons of Darkness*. London: Oxford University Press, 1962.

Zeitlin, Solomon. *The Rise and Fall of the Judaean State: A Political, Social and Religious History of the Second Commonwealth*. 3 vols. 2nd ed. Philadelphia: Jewish Publication Society of America, 1968.

Zimmerli, Walter. "Erkenntnis Gottes nach dem Buch Ezechiel." In *Gottes Offenbarung: Gesammelte Aufsätze zum Alten Testament*, 41–119. ThBü 19. Munich: Kaiser, 1963.

———. "Knowledge of God according to the Book of Ezekiel." In *I Am Yahweh*, edited by Walter Brueggemann, 2–98. Translated by Douglas W. Stott. Atlanta: John Knox, 1982.

7

Amos's Oracles against the Nations (1:2—2:16)

THE BOOK OF AMOS opens with a long section containing charges against and pronouncements of judgment upon eight Syro-Palestinian states: Damascus, Gaza, Tyre, Edom, Ammon, Moab, Judah, and Israel.

Genre and Structure of the Material

The individual "oracles on the nations" (or "prophecies against foreign kingdoms") in this material are developed with a repetitive regularity. After an attributive formula designating the following declaration as a divine word ("thus says [or "has said"] Yahweh"), the individual subunits are introduced with a formulaic expression, "For three transgressions of ... and for four, I will not recall it, because ..." The only variation in this opening formula is the name of the people being denounced.

Two other components are characteristic of these nation oracles. (1) Following a "because," the wrongdoings of each of the individual peoples are noted. (2) The statement of the offense or wrongdoing is followed by a pronouncement of coming punishment or disaster.

Within this general structure, the nation oracles manifest considerable diversity. Four of the initial seven oracles—those concerning Damascus (1:3–5), Gaza (1:6–8), Ammon (1:13–15), and Moab (2:1–3)—fall into one group and contain very brief statements of the offenses (see 1:3b, 6b, 13b; 2:1b) followed by somewhat lengthier pronouncements of coming disaster (1:4–5, 7–8, 14–15; 2:2–3). All four oracles also contain concluding attributive formulas ("says the LORD [God]") at the end (see 1:5, 8, 15; 2:3). The other three oracles comprising a second group—concerning Tyre (1:9–10), Edom (1:11–12), and Judah (2:4–5)—contain statements of the offenses (1:9b, 11b; 2:5). None of these latter three oracles contains a final attributive formula.

The Israel section (2:6–16) differs from all seven preceding oracles, possessing both a lengthy statement of offenses (2:6b–12) and a lengthy pronouncement of coming disasters (2:13–16) as well as two attributive formulas ("says Yahweh" or "declares Yahweh," *ne'um YHWH*).

In addition to these two major sub-groups, all of the oracles contain various stylistic features that give each a slightly unique character.

Recently, Steinmann[1] has shown that the pattern of the nations addressed not only shows geographical orientation moving from the northeast (Damascus) to southwest (Gaza and Philistia) to northwest (Tyre) and then to the southeast (Edom, Ammon, and Moab) before Judah and Israel, but it also shows that the nature of the state addressed and their proximity to Israel and Judah comprise part of the pattern. He outlines the scheme of presentation as follows:

TEXT	NATION	PRESENTED AS	NEIGHBOR OF	GROUP
1:3–5	Damascus	City-State	Israel	1
1:6–8	Gaza	City-State	Judah	1
1:9–10	Tyre	City-State	Israel	2
1:11–12	Edom	Nation	Judah	2
1:13–15	Ammon	Nation	Israel	1
2:1–3	Moab	Nation	Judah	1
2:4–5	Judah	Special Nation	Israel	2
2:6–16	Israel	Special Nation	Judah	2

One can thus conclude that the entire section appears to be a well-structured, artistic unit with sufficient framing to provide repetition and regularity, allowing the hearer/reader to anticipate, and yet with sufficiently varied structural blocks, to stimulate interest and appeal to the intellect. On the basis of the interwoven and interlocking patterns presented in the text, Steinmann has concluded:

---

1. Steinmann, "The Order of Amos's Oracles," 687.

Amos's Oracles against the Nations (1:2—2:16)

Thus, the patterns in the order of the oracles, although not decisive in determining whether all of the oracles are authentic to the original author of Amos 1–2, demonstrate that these are a coherent presentation. Thus, the recognition of these patterns shifts the burden of proof off of those who maintain that oracles originate from one author and places it on those who maintain that some of them are redactional additions.[2]

The Relationship of 1:2 to 1:3—2:16

Throughout the history of interpretation, most translators and commentators have considered 1:2 as either a part of the superscription, as a motto of the book, or a late redactional addition (perhaps borrowed from Joel 3:16). The verse, however, should be seen as the introduction to the oracles on the nations. If one understands *ne'oth* as "oases" rather than "pastures" and Carmel as "woodland"[3] then the verse may be translated as:

> Yahweh from Zion shall roar,
>   and from Jerusalem give forth his voice;
> and the oases of the shepherds shall dry up,
> and the height of the woodlands shall wither.

The two geographic references in lines 3 and 4 express polar opposites—the low waterholes and the mountaintops—thus indicating totality, signifying everywhere.

The close association of 1:2 with 1:3 following is indicated by the syntax of the expression "For three transgressions... and for four, I will not revoke (or recall) it." What does the "it," a third masculine singular pronominal suffix, refer to (see Knierim)? An examination of the difficulties in translating this form is indicated in the diversity of readings suggested. The Geneva Bible of 1560 translates "I will not turn to it"; the KJV reads "I will not turn away the punishment thereof," with the italics indicating that "the punishment" does not occur in the Hebrew. The following readings are found in recent translations: "the punishment" (NRSV), "grant them reprieve" (NEB), "revoke it (the decree of punishment)" (NJPS), "revoke my word" (NAB), "I have made my decree and will not relent" (JB). Early and medieval Jewish commentators read

---

2. Ibid., 689.
3. On the latter, see Isa 10:18; 16:10; Amos 9:2; 2 Kgs 19:23.

"forgive them" (Targum), "let the deported population return" (Rashi, Ibn Ezra, Kimchi).

In his *Harmony, Chronicle, and Order of the Old Testament* published in 1647, John Lightfoot (1602–75) offered what could be understood as the correct interpretation, but one followed by practically no modern commentators or translators. He wrote:

> For the sense lieth thus; "The Lord will roar from Zion, and utter his voice from Jerusalem: and thus saith the Lord, For three transgressions of Damascus, and for four, I will not revoke it," that is, 'I will not revoke that voice . . .' for the masculine affix in *'shybnw* cannot possibly be referred to anything that went before, but only to *qwlw* 'his voice,' in ver. 2; and to something that went before it, it must of necessity be referred.[4]

Thus if one sees v. 2 as integrally related to what follows then two factors become evident. First, in 1:2 the prophet sets the stage, creates the emotion, and introduces the deity and the divine action, which will be explicated in first-person address in the verses that follow. Second, the "it" that Yahweh will not recall in 1:3—2:16 is his "voice" that will blast forth from Zion with withering force. That 1:2 envisions Yahweh roaring over the entire area constitutes a further basis for seeing all the subsequent nation oracles as integral to Amos's preaching. Since Yahweh's roar affects the entire region, no major power could fail to be mentioned.

The Individual Nation Oracles

The addresses to each of the eight nations begins with a repeated expression. What "for three transgressions and for four" signified to Amos's audience remains uncertain. Graduated numerical sayings (x, x + 1) are common in the Hebrew Scriptures[5] and are also found in non-biblical literature. The numbers most frequently employed in sequential enumeration are one and two (Ps 62:11; Job 33:14–15), two and three (Hos 6:2; Sir 26:28), three and four (Prov 30:15–33; Sir 26:5–6), six and seven (Job 5:19), and seven and eight (Mic 5:5; Eccl 11:2). Frequently, the elements in the numerical schemes are listed, with the last representing the climax of the series. Amos 1:3—2:5, however, repeatedly uses a stylized formula ("for three and for four") but generally specifies only one component.

---

4. Lightfoot, *Whole Works*, vol. 2.

5. See for example Prov 6:16–19; 30:15–16, 18–19, 21–23, 29–31.

Amos's Oracles against the Nations (1:2—2:16)

Various proposals for understanding the prophet's point have been made. A number of these are worth noting. (1) "For three and for four" is regarded as a way of referring to "the innumerable crimes" committed by the nations condemned. In such an interpretation, the emphasis is understood to fall on the quantity of wrongdoing. (2) The paraphrastic translation "again and again" (Good News Bible) stresses the persistence of the wrongdoers. (3) "Three" and "four" may be seen as a way of alluding to the number seven, signifying completion or fullness (so already, Luther and Calvin). (4) Ancient rabbinic interpreters concluded that three transgressions might be forgiven but not a fourth.[6] (5) Probably the numerical reference with its staircase gradation (3 and 4) was a way of saying that a limit had been passed. Three was enough but four was beyond what could be endured; four was the last straw.

Whether Amos and his audience were aware of four crimes committed by the peoples condemned or whether the last was considered climactic remains unknown. The numerical expression was probably intended to function formulaically rather than realistically in any case. Amos has God declare that for the transgression, God will not recall his voice that will roar in judgment out of Zion.

Against Damascus (1:3–5)

The wrongdoing attributed to Damascus consisted of "threshing Gilead with iron threshing sledges," which appears to refer to brutal and cruel treatment of the region during or following military activity. The term *dwsh* "to thresh" refers to the process of separating grain and seeds from the stalks. When not done by hand, this was usually performed by moving animal-drawn carts (Deut 25:4) or flat-bottomed sledges over the heaped-up grain. To increase the efficiency of the sledge, metal studs could be driven through the floor, with the protruding points aiding in dislodging the heads of grain. Whether Amos is speaking realistically or metaphorically about the threshing is uncertain, although the latter seems more likely (2 Kgs 13:7). Although the Old Testament speaks of post-battle atrocities (Judg 8:7, 16), these are always realistic depictions, whereas threshing captives or bodies with sledges hardly seems a task one could perform. The imagery of threshing one's opponents (still sometimes employed in modern speech) occurs in a statement of the Assyrian

---

6. *b. Yoma* 86b and *Sanhedrin* 7a.

king, Tiglath-Pileser I (1114–1076 BCE), who claimed: "the land Bit-Amukkani I threshed as with a threshing instrument; all its people and its possessions I brought to Assyria."

The land of Gilead, which was "threshed," lay east of the Jordan. In its broadest limits, the name denoted the territory between the Arnon Gorge in the south and the Yarmuk River in the north. Through this region passed a caravan route between Damascus and the Red Sea, providing access to Arabian and African trade. Gilead was also an important source of iron ore.[7] Claimed by the Israelites, this region was almost constantly a source of contention between Israel and its neighbors (Damascus, Moab, and Ammon).

The general means of judgment on the first seven nations is always said to be by fire, no doubt a reference to destruction through warfare. In the Damascus section, the objects of Yahweh's fiery attacks are to be "the house of Hazael" and "the fortresses of Ben-hadad." Whether the "house" here denotes the territory of Damascus, the reigning house, a political alliance headed by Rezin, the king of Damascus, or merely the royal palace in Damascus, remains uncertain. The ambiguity of the expression may have allowed the audience to understand the referent in various ways.

Hazael and Ben-hadad were kings who had ruled in Damascus in the latter half of the ninth and the first part of the eighth century. The reigning king in Damascus, contemporary with Amos, was Rezin, who may or may not have been a direct descendant of Hazael and his son Ben-hadad II. An inscription of Tiglath-Pileser III refers to Hadara rather than Damascus as the birthplace of Rezin,[8] which could imply that he was a usurper. A usurper, however, could be linked by outsiders with the previous ruling family. Assyrian texts, for example, associate the Israelite usurper Jehu with the previous ruling family of Omri.[9]

In addition to Damascus and its reigning king, v. 5 refers to two other rulers and kingdoms. Verse 5 should be translated:

> And I will break the gate bar of Damascus,
>   and I will cut off the one ruling (*yosheb*) in the Valley of Awen,
>   and the one wielding the scepter in Beth-eden;
>   and the people of Aram should be exiled to Kir.

---

7. Josephus, *War* 4.454; *m. Succoth* 3:1.
8. Luckenbill, *ARAB*, vol. 1, sec. 777; *ANET*, 283.
9. Luckenbill, *ARAB*, vol. 1, sec. 590; *ANET*, 281.

Amos's Oracles against the Nations (1:2—2:16)

The singular masculine participle *yosheb* means the "one sitting" but is frequently used of the sitting in authority, i.e., the ruler. The Akkadian cognate verb *washab* is used to refer to the monarch's ascendency to the throne. The term parallels "the one wielding the scepter" in the following line. Thus in addition to the present king of Damascus—Rezin—this verse refers to two other rulers, one associated with the Valley of Awen and the other with Beth-eden.

Beth-eden is the well known region, Bit-Adini, frequently referred to in Assyrian royal inscriptions. Bit-Adini, which lay east of the western bend of the Euphrates River, was part of the Assyrian kingdom and was ruled from about 806 to 752 BCE by the Assyrian general Shamshi-ilu, the most powerful figure in the Assyrian empire at the time. Shamshi-ilu was almost the virtual ruler of the Assyrian empire in the west during the reigns of several weak Assyrian kings. In some inscriptions, he makes no consession to and no mention of his overlord, the Assyrian king. In one inscription he refers to himself as "viceroy, chief herald, overseer of temples, chief of a vast army, ruler of the land of Hatti (Syria–Palestine), the highlands, and all the land of Namri."[10] Amos 1:5 probably refers to his successor who apparently had joined with Rezin of Damascus in a western alliance against Assyria.

The one ruling in the Valley of Awen is probably a reference to the Israelite king Pekah who seems to have served part of his twenty-year reign (2 Kgs 15:27) as a rival king to the Samarian monarch. We know from the Assyrian king Tiglath-Pileser III's inscriptions that Pekah was killed after the Assyrian king left Syria–Palestine in 731. This means that Pekah had claimed the throne of Israel as a rival ruler about 751, about the time of Amos's ministry, but was unable to take Samaria the capital city until the reign of Pekahiah or in about 734 BCE (2 Kgs 15:23–26).

The term *'awen* in 1:5b is not to be taken as either a play on the name Beth-el or as a pun employing the term "iniquity" or "evil." References to Awen in place names occur in Josh 7:2; 18:12; 1 Sam 13:5; 14:23; Hos 4:15; 5:8. In Josh 7:2, Joshua is said to have sent men "from Jericho to Ai which is near Beth-awen, east of Bethel." The northern boundary of Benjamin is described in Josh 18:12 as extending from the Jordan River up through the hill country to the wilderness of Beth-awen. In the account of Saul's battle with the Philistines, Beth-awen is spoken of as lying west of Michmash (1 Sam 13:5; see 14:23). In Hos. 5:8, Beth-awen is placed in

---

10. *ANET*, 659–61.

the vicinity of Gibeah (probably modern *jeba'*) and Ramah (modern *er-ram*). All of these texts locate Awen and Beth-awen in the upper reaches of the Wadi es-Suweinit. This wadi forms, along with Wadi el-Qelt, the valley running up into the central hill country from the region of Jericho. Along with Wadi Farah, which cuts into the hill country in the vicinity of Tirzah and just north of Shechem, this valley was one of the main avenues of entry into the central hill country from the Jordan Valley. In all probability, the Valley of Awen was the Suweinit-Qelt valley. Gilgal lay in the lower reaches of this valley (Amos 4:4; 5:5) and was probably the religious center for the Pekah faction as Bethel was the royal sanctuary for Jeroboam II (787–748 BCE).

The Damascus oracle thus condemns a coalition of rulers, perhaps headed by Rezin the king in Damascus, which also included the ruler of Bit-Adini, and Pekah the rival Israelite king, who throughout his career was associated with Rezin (2 Kgs 15:37; 16:5; Isa 7:1). Amos declares that the "people of Aram" will be exiled to Kir. In all probability, "Aram" here refers to a larger political entity than the kingdom of Rezin. Assyrian texts never use the term "Aram" to refer to the kingdom of Damascus but rather employ it with reference to northern Syria. The Aramaic treaty texts from Sefire speak of "all Aram" as well as "upper and lower Aram" and the so-called Bar-Hadad stela refers to an Aram in northern Syria. The "people of Aram" in v. 5 thus should be seen as an inclusive term referring to the people of the region extending from the River Euphrates to the Transjordan. The location of Kir is unknown although probably in southern Babylonia. The area is mentioned three other times in the Old Testament (Isa 2:26; Amos 9:7; 2 Kgs 16:9). Amos probably envisioned the Assyrians moving westward and putting down this coalition of states headed by Damascus, as they did once Tiglath-Pileser III ascended the throne in 745 BCE.

Against Gaza (1:6–8)

This section, like vv. 3–5, begins with a focus on a specific city but expands to include other principalities as well. The four cities mentioned—Gaza, Ashdod, Ashkelon, and Ekron—were Philistine towns in southwestern Palestine. The first three were port cities located just inland from the Mediterranean coast. Ekron, like Gath, was located inland, on the plain.

Gaza is condemned for sending "into exile entire communities" (NRSV). Amos here appears to be condemning Gaza for engaging in the wholesale removal of local populations and their sale in international slave trade although nothing is said specifically about the actual selling or commercial transaction. The taking of captives in warfare was standard practice in the ancient world (Deut 21:10; 2 Sam 12:31), and the fact that the consequences of warfare could be inflicted on a total population is illustrated by the stories of David's activities (1 Sam 27:8-12). Amos obviously believed such practices to be inhumane and contrary to acceptable international behavior.

Against Tyre (1:9-10)

With v. 9, Amos turns to a denunciation of Tyre, the prosperous Phoenician maritime power to the northwest of Israel proper. Tyre, with its rocky island fortress, was located about thirty miles north of Mt. Carmel. In the mid-eighth century, Tyre was by far the strongest of the Phoenician cities. Amos condemns Tyre for two wrongs: (1) the handing over of entire communities to Edom; and (2) the failure to remember a covenant of brothers.

(1) Unlike Gaza in v. 6, Tyre is not unequivocally condemned for the actual seizure and deportation of captives but only for handing them over, that is, engagement in slave trade. The difference between what is being described in vv. 6 and 9, however, may be more apparent than real. The statement in v. 9 may simply be an abbreviated form of what is said more fully in v. 6. Edom is again said to be the destination of this trade in humans although Phoenicia's geographical proximity to Aram and Damascus would make Aram a more logical trading partner than Edom. No textual evidence, however, reads "Aram" instead of "Edom" in either verse. Tyre's involvement in slave trade is noted in other Old Testament texts (Joel 3:4-8 [MT 4:4-8]; Ezek 27:13).

(2) The expression "covenant (or "treaty") of brothers" is not only unique to the Bible but also apparently to the literature of the Near East. A treaty or covenant agreement between states establishing a legal relationship with recognized obligations had been common in the Near East for centuries before Amos. The content of such covenants varied depending upon whether the relationship was imposed, as in vassal treaties, or entered into by equals, as in parity treaties. Although the expression

"covenant of brothers" is without parallel, the idea it expresses was common in Near Eastern diplomacy. A covenant/treaty between two independent states created a relationship that could be described in terms of "brotherhood" between the participants (1 Kgs 9:13; 20:32). Vassal kingdoms subordinate to a common overlord could speak of themselves as "brothers."

Against Edom (1:11–12)

The fourth nation denounced by the prophet was Edom, a kingdom lying south and southeast of Judah, spanning both sides of the Arabah depression south of the Dead Sea. The close kinship of Israelites and Edomites is reflected in the patriarchal narratives of Genesis where Jacob (= Israel) and Esau (= Edom) are described as twins (Gen 25:19–34). Their hostilities and animosities conjoined with their brotherhood were prefigured, according to legend, in the twins' prenatal struggle in their mother's womb (Gen 25:22–23).

Second Samuel 8:13–14 and 1 Kings 11:15–16 indicate that David brought Edom under Israelite control. During Solomon's rule, the Edomites apparently asserted their freedom and harassed Israel (1 Kings 11:14–25). During the reigns of Ahab of Israel (868–854) and Jehoshaphat of Judah (877–853) when Israel/Judah again exercised control over the port of Elath, the Edomites were again subjected to vassal status (1 Kgs 22:47; 2 Kgs 3:9). After the death of Jehoshaphat, the Edomites reasserted their independence (2 Kgs 8:16–22). We next hear of Edom in the days of King Amaziah (802–786) who attacked the Edomites in the Valley of Salt (Wadi el-Milh east of Beer-sheba), slaying great numbers of them (2 Kgs 14:7).

The wrongdoings of Edom, noted in v. 11b, are expressed in terms whose exact meanings allude us. The general sense, however, seems clear: Edom's harsh treatment of Israelites/Judeans, which the prophet understood as hideously extravagant. The specific events alluded to remain uncertain but should probably be seen against the background of the episodes noted in 2 Kgs 16:6 and 2 Chr 28:17 although both of these texts place the events in the reign of King Ahaz (743–728), a few years after the time of Amos.

Amos's Oracles against the Nations (1:2—2:16)

Against Ammon (1:13-15)

The land of Ammon skirted the Arabian Desert east and south of Gilead. The usual biblical designation, as here, speaks of the "children of Ammon" and Akkadian texts of the "house of Ammon" (*bit-Ammon*)[11] rather than just of "Ammon," but for reasons unknown. The Israelites viewed themselves as rather close relatives to the Ammonites. The rather coarse story in Gen. 19:30-38 ascribes the latter's (and the Moabites') origin to a drunken, incestuous relationship between Lot, Abraham's nephew, and one of his daughters after the destruction of Sodom. The biblical texts frequently note the hostile relations between the Ammonites and Israelites. Jephthah, Saul and David are described as fighting Amrnonites.[12]

The Ammonites are condemned for war atrocities carried out in expanding their territory into Gilead. The practice of slaughtering the unborn during warfare is mentioned in Akkadian and Arabic literature. In the *Iliad*, Agamemnon pleaded with Menelaus to slaughter a Trojan captive: "Let us not spare a single one of them—not even the child unborn and in its mother's womb; let not a man of them be left alive, but let all in Ilius perish, unheeded and forgotten" (6.57-58). Three biblical texts refer to this practice (2 Kgs 8:12; 15:16; Hos 13:16). Second Kings 15:16 reports that when Menahem took over the throne in Israel, he had to force a region or city to submit to his authority: "Because they did not open it to him, he attacked it and ripped open all its pregnant women." In describing the overthrow of reigning families, several biblical texts note that all the males of the line were killed (1 Kgs 14:10; 16:11; 21:21; 2 Kgs 9:8). No reference is made in these texts to the slaughter of the unborn but this may have been the case, especially when the goal was to exterminate all the royal line. (Such a situation is the background to Isaiah's promise to Ahaz that the unborn child, Immanuel, will not be killed; Isaiah 7.)

Against Moab (2:1-3)

Amos concluded his denunciations of the nations to Israel's southeast and east with Moab, the "brother-nation" to Ammon (Gen 19:30-38). The heartland of Moabite territory was the lofty tableland directly east of the Dead Sea. Bounded on the south by the River Zered, the east by the

---

11. *ANET*, 282, 287.
12. See Judg 10:7—11:33; 1 Samuel 11; 2 Sam 8:12; 10:1—11:1; 12:26-31.

Arabian Desert, and the west by the Dead Sea, Moab struggled throughout much of its history to extend and control its northern border, often in conflict with Israel (note the anti-Moabite sentiment in Deut 23:3–6; Isa 16:12–14).

Moab is not condemned for any anti-Israelite activity but for the desecration of an Edomite monarch's remains. The exhuming of human bones and the desecration of tombs were condemned in biblical times as they have been throughout human history. Something of the sentiments involved in the official desecration of tombs are illustrated in the actions the Babylonian king Ashurbanipal (668–627) took after defeating his treacherous enemies the Elamites.

> The rest of the sons, . . . his family, the seed of his father's house, . . . and the bones of the father who begot them, . . . I carried off from Gambulu to Assyria.[13]
>
> The sepulchers of their earlier and later kings, who did not fear [the Assyrian gods] Assur and Ishtar, my lords, and who had plagued the kings, my fathers, I destroyed, I devastated, I exposed to the sun. Their bones I carried off to Assyria. I laid restlessness upon their shades. I deprived them of food offerings and libations of water.[14]
>
> The bones of Nabu-shum-eresh, which they had brought from Gambulu to Assyria, these bones I had his sons crush in front of the gate inside Nineveh.[15]

The dead rulers were deprived of their resting places—cut off from their ancestors in the realm of the dead—were denied the benefits of the cult for the dead (food-offerings and water libations), and were symbolically eradicated from memory in the crushing of their bones by their own descendants, which removed the final traces of their existence.

Against Judah (2:4–5)

Many scholars during the past century have concluded that this Judah section is a late addition to the authentic words of Amos. The main arguments for this conclusion are as follows. (1) Outside of this section,

---

13. Luckenbill, *ARAB*, vol. 2, sec. 788.
14. Ibid., sec. 810.
15. Ibid., sec. 866.

Amos's Oracles against the Nations (1:2—2:16)

the prophet shows no special interest in Judah and makes only passing references to the southern kingdom (only in 6:1; 7:12; 9:11). (2) The accusations against Judah are not only couched in theological terms that sharply contrast with the ethical and moral aspects of the other national denunciations but also are expressed in insipid generalities rather than in the concrete and vivid language used about the other nations. (3) The material contains internal inconsistencies since it begins as a divine speech but in v. 4b utilizes third-person references to God. (4) Elimination of the Judah section would leave speeches against seven nations, a more likely pattern than a sequence of eight nations. (5) The ideas and terminology of the section reflect special Deuteronomic nomenclature and therefore must derive from a time after the appearance of the book of Deuteronomy, a period considerably later than Amos. (6) Like the Tyre and Edom oracles, this section contains a longer description of the wrongs than of the coming judgment. Since this pattern breaks with the remainder of the units, the Judah, Tyre, and Edom oracles are considered inauthentic (see above for arguments that rule out this view).

None of these arguments is very strong. For all the nations in the region to have been treated and Judah omitted seems unlikely. The expressions used in the text—"torah of Yahweh" and "to be led away by lies"—are not expressions found in Deuteronomy and "to keep his statutes" is found in diverse Old Testament texts. Since Judah was a part of the chosen worshipers of Yahweh, one would expect Amos to speak of the people's wrongdoing in theological terms.

The general character of the accusations against Judah make it difficult to determine with any manner of certainty to what the prophet was referring.

Against Israel (2:6–16)

After having noted the wrongs of and described the judgment coming upon seven nations, Amos completes his survey of the kingdoms in the region by focusing on the central object of his proclamation—Israel. In his preaching, Amos has moved from the northeast (Damascus), to the southwest (Philistia), to the northwest (Tyre), to the southeast (Edom, Ammon, Moab), to the south (Judah), and, after this rhetorical and geographical circumambulation, hones in on the center, his actual audience.

This Israel section differs from those on the other nations in several ways. (1) Both the general description of the wrongs (vv. 6-8, 12) and the depiction of the coming judgment (vv. 13-16) are generally expanded. (2) The accusations no longer concern matters of international relations but instead address domestic matters. (3) Reference is made to specific events of the people's past. (4) Second-person, direct address to the audience becomes interspersed with third-person, indirect address. (5) The stylized announcement of judgment—"I will send (set on) fire the fortresses (wall)"—is dropped.

The enumeration of Israel's wrongdoings in vv. 6-8 can be understood as stipulating either four or seven depending on how the text is divided. One way of reading the text is to see the two statements in v. 7a as parallel to and a repetition of the charge in v. 6b, which is already spelled out in two parallel statements. Verses 7b, 8a, and 8b would then contain the second, third, and fourth charges. Such an interpretation assumes that the prophet was listing the four transgressions alluded to in the opening formula.

Another approach is to read each of the elements in vv. 6b-8 as an independent accusation. This provides a total of seven charges, giving the three plus four noted in the opening formula. This seems to be the better line of approach since the various elements are not identical and therefore no two are quite parallel. None of the charges in vv. 7b-8 is stated in parallelism; perhaps those in vv. 6b-7a were also to be heard as separate accusations. If this be the case, then the prophet was expressing the completeness of Israel's sinfulness, seven being the number of totality or fullness. Verse 12, also an accusation, would then constitute the eighth wrong, giving a sense of going beyond all limits.

Many of the wrongdoings in Israel condemned by Amos in this section are dealt with more extensively in the rest of the book-the mistreatment of the poor, the greed and indulgence of the upper class, the lack of concern for justice and equity in society, and so on. This is the case with vv. 6b and 7a. Verses 7b and 8 seem to refer to special circumstances.

Verse 7b does not refer to prostitution, either regular or cultic. The former would not have profaned God's name and the latter was not practiced in Israel. The situation condemned by the prophet can best be understood in light of Exod 32:7-11. According to the Exodus text, a person might purchase a female and designate her for himself or his son as a sexual partner. If he designated her for his son then he had to treat her as a daughter; presumably if designated for himself, the son had to treat her as his father's wife. In both cases, sexual relations with her by both father and son would have broken a taboo.

Throughout much of the ancient Near East, marriage, betrothal, and offically sanctioned sexual arrangements were considered under the special protection of the divine. Adultery was considered the "great sin." Thus betrothals, marriages, and concubinage were understood as covenanted relationships divinely protected as if the Deity were the third party in such relationships. Sexual intercourse with a "designated" female, even a slave, by a male other than the covenanted partner was a desecration of the name of Yahweh, a trespass on a divinely protected relationship.

Verse 8a seems to condemn wealthy creditors who, rather than providing their own lounging materials while enjoying a meal of sacrificial flesh, were using garments belonging to debtors with no respect for their poor owners who could not afford the pleasure of such sacrifices. Verse 8b implies that fines perhaps improperly imposed by government officials in the form of wine were being consumed in the temple to the dislike of the prophet. Wine was customarily consumed with sacrificial meals. Thus the prophet probably objected to the use of a product not really one's own since the practice represented both a total lack of sensitivity and an excessive indulgence by the powerful and privileged.

In vv. 9–12, Amos reiterates some of the themes emphasizing God's special concern for Israel as a chosen people-the destruction of the inhabitants of Canaan (v. 9), the deliverance from Egypt, and guidance in the wilderness (v. 10). In addition, Amos points to the special guidance given through prophets and Nazirites (v. 11). The function of the prophet was proclamation; the task and function of the Nazirite remain uncertain. A Nazirite was required to abstain from any contact with grapes or products made from them, from cutting the hair, and from any contact with a corpse (Num 6:1–8). A vow was required to become a Nazirite (Num 6:2) and a desacralization ritual was undergone when the person reentered ordinary life (Num 6:13–20). While a Nazirite, the person belonged to the realm of the "holy" (Num 6:6, 8) and to this extent resembled a priest.

Amos accuses the people of having perverted and prevented the prophets and Nazirites from performing their roles (v. 12). Although he does not state it, he implies that the people were thus ungrateful for the past acts of salvation of God on their behalf.

The punishment to come upon Israel is described in vv. 13–16. The consequences of God's punishment (v. 13) will result in the people's inability to fight and defend themselves and their land. The "pressing down" of the Israelites in their place probably refers to the aggressive military action already underway against Israel and spoken of in 13–15. Surrounding nations were aggressively encroaching on Israelite territory, and Amos announces that the situation will worsen, with frightening effects on the Israelites (3:11 and 6:12).

In vv. 14–16, Amos describes the panic that will overwhelm the Israelite military. In the day of battle, the elite and most qualified of the foot soldiers and chariot corps will lose all those qualities that made for effectiveness in battle. Utilizing a sevenfold scheme, Amos enumerates the consequences that will overcome the swift, the strong, the warrior, the bowman, the fleet of foot, the horseman, and the stouthearted.

The Historical Background to the Oracles

The denunciations of all the foreign nations, except for Moab (2:1–3), appear to condemn these countries for ations against Israel and Judah. The prophet was probably alluding to events contemporary with and known by his audience. The most likely political-military scenario behind these denunciations would be the following.

In 841–840 BCE, Jehu submitted to or was declared ruler over Israel by the Assyrian king Shalmaneser III (858–824) and thus aligned Israel with a pro-Assyrian policy. This policy was followed by all the Israelite (and Judean) kings until the usurper Pekah seized the throne in Samaria in 734 BCE (2 Kgs 15:23–28). In the 760s and 750s Assyria was weakened by internal problems and by the encroachment of the Urartians who subjegated much territory to the northwest and northeast of Assyria and greatly reduced the commerce into Assyria. When Assyria was weakened, so was Israel. With Assyrian power weakened, states in Syria–Palestine moved toward organizing an anti-Assyrian coalition in the west. Judah and Israel retained their pro-Assyrian stance and were thus subjected to harassment and warfare by the neighbors and by Pekah whom Rezin of Damascus set up as a rival king in Israel (2 Kgs 15:37; 16:6 with NRSV marginal notes; 2 Chr 28:17–18). The actions described in Amos 1:3, 9, 11, and 13 reflect this aggression against Israel and Judah who were uncooperative with the regional anti-Assyrianism.

By the time Amos was preaching, Israel's economy and political standing were in a tailspin. Earlier in the reign of Jeroboam II, when Assyria was strong, Israel had enjoyed a period of prosperity and territorial expansion (2 Kgs 14:23–27). With the demise of good times and the hostility of local kingdoms, Israel was hard pressed; its upper classes, however, were attempting to continue their prosperous lifestyle but now by abusing the country's lower classes and by exploiting the national economy to its limit.

Conclusion

Amos opens his preaching with denunciations of local states. The foreign nations were condemned for breaking traditional and conventional standards of behavior by engaging in such activities as military atrocities, excessive slave trade, and tomb desecration. Although most of these actions were directed against Israel/Judah the prophet condemns them as wrongdoings in and of themselves. This assumes that out of international diplomatic and political-military relationships there had developed something approaching an accepted standard of norms or at least an understanding of what constituted infringements of normal, customary behavior. Some norms would have embodied conventions hammered out in response to the pragmatics of routine life.

Some have seen Amos's denunciations of foreign states as primarily an audience-attracting ploy. By denouncing other countries, Amos was sure to gain an audience both interested in his subject matter, since it involved matters of national welfare, and sympathetic to him, since he was advocating Israel's cause against the world. Once he had theatrically entrapped his audience, he could move to attack the real object of his scorn, namely, his own folk.

While Amos may have begun his prophetic preaching with the judgment and condemnation of foreigners as an audience-enlisting gimmick, this feature probably served a deeper and more significant rhetorical function.

Most likely, a number of issues were involved in Amos's rhetorical strategy in 1:2—2:16. First, the denunciations of the foreign nations were genuine statements of judgment with their own integrity. The crimes should be considered recent events known to the prophet and his audience. The atrocities condemned would have been sufficiently contrary to customary law that the prophet's references would have convinced his audience of the nation's guilt. Second, the declaration that Yahweh was to execute judgment against these guilty parties would have helped establish, if not the belief, at least the hope, that Yahweh would function as judge in matters of wrongdoing. In this case, since the nations were enemies of Israel, the audience would have been prone to accept the scenario of Yahweh as judge. Third, his strategy was then to move to the more controversial issue, namely, Yahweh's present condemnation and present and future judgment against Israel. If Amos had satisfactorily convinced his audience that known moral laws hold other nations accountable and infringements bring divine reprisal, then the same condition would pertain to Israel as well. If, in speaking on the other nations, Amos could convince his Israelite audience that Yahweh was in charge, had condemned their atrocities, and would bring punishment upon them, then he was in a better position to convince his hearers that Yahweh had also judged and would bring judgment on Israel.

Bibliography

Andersen, Francis I., and David Noel Freedman. *Amos*. AB 24A. Garden City, NY: Doubleday, 1989.

Barton, John. *Amos's Oracles against the Nations: A Study of Amos 1:3—2:5*. Society of Old Testament Monograph Series 6. Cambridge: Cambridge University Press, 1980.

Haran, Menahem. "Observations on the Historical Background of Amos 1:2-26." *Israel Exploration Journal* 18 (1968) 201–12.

Hayes, John H. *Amos—The Eighth-Century Prophet: His Times and His Preaching*. Nashville: Abingdon, 1988.

Knierim, Rolf. "'I Will Not Cause It to Return' in Amos 1 and 2." In *Canon and Authority: Essays in Old Testament Religion and Theology*, edited by George W. Coats and Burke O. Long, 163–75. Philadelphia: Fortress, 1977.

Lightfoot, John. *Whole Works of the Rev. John Lightfoot*. Vol. 2. London: Rivington, 1822.

Limburg, James. "Sevenfold Structures in the Book of Amos." *JBL* 106 (1987) 217–22.

Luckenbill, D. D. *Ancient Records of Assyria and Babylon*. 2 vols. Chicago: University of Chicago Press, 1926–27.

Noble, Paul. "Israel among the Nations." *Horizons in Biblical Theology* 15 (1993) 56–82.

Paul, Shalom. *Amos*. Hermeneia. Minneapolis: Fortress, 1991.

———. "Amos 1:3–2:3: A Concatenous Literary Pattern." *JBL* 90 (1971) 397–403.

Pritchard, James B., editor. *Ancient Near Eastern Texts Relating to the Old Testament*. 3rd ed. Princton: Princeton University Press, 1969.

Roth, W. M. W. *Numerical Sayings in the Old Testament*. VTSup 13. Leiden: Brill, 1965.

Steinman, Andrew E. "The Order of Amos's Oracles against the Nations: 1:3—2:16." *JBL* 111 (1992) 683–89.

Weiss, Meir. "The Pattern of Numerical Sequence in Amos 1–2: A Re-examination." *JBL* 86 (1967) 416–23.

Amos's Oracles against the Nations (1:2—2:16)

Wolff, Hans Walter. *Amos and Joel: A Commentary on the Books of the Prophets Amos and Joel*. Translated by Waldamar Janzen et al. Hermeneia. Philadelphia: Fortress, 1977.

8

Restitution, Forgiveness, and the Victim in Old Testament Law

A WIDELY HELD OPINION assumes that retaliation and retribution constituted the basic principles of ancient Israelite jurisprudence. This assumption in no small manner is based on the appearance of explicit references to the *lex talionis* within the Hebrew Scriptures (Exod 21:23-25; Lev 24:17-21; and Deut 19:21) and on the saying of Jesus found in Matt 5:38, which seems to imply *talion* as the accepted practice of his day.

I argue here that in cases between persons restitution not retaliation functioned as the basic principle underlying most Old Testament legal traditions. In like fashion, restitution of the injured party was a precondition of divine and human forgiveness and a basic component of the atonement ritual. Such considerations demonstrate that the victim not the perpetrator of injury was the center of attention in legal processes and that the reconstitution of normal relationships between parties was the primary goal of juridical actions.

Restitution not Retaliation

Many of the Old Testament laws focusing on interpersonal disputes appear in Exod 21:19—22:17, which forms part of a unit frequently designated the Covenant Code.[1] The first of these, 21:18-19, involves the case

---

1. Most scholars date the Covenant Code very early in Israelite history, perhaps during the pre-monarchical age. For arguments advocating an eighth-century dating,

Restitution, Forgiveness, and the Victim in Old Testament Law

of a man injured as the consequence of a fight. The injury described assumes that the victim will be bedridden for a time but then become able to walk around outdoors with the aid of a staff. The law requires that the assailant "must pay for his idleness and his cure" (so NJPS), or "shall pay for the loss of his time, and shall have him throughly healed" (so RSV), or "to pay for the loss of time, and to arrange for full recovery" (NRSV).[2] That is, the law requires the assailant to compensate the victim for his loss of time from work as well as his medical expenses. Such compensation functions as restitution, i.e., to restore the victim as nearly as possible to the state prior to the injury. Under such arrangements, the assailant went unpunished; that is, no retaliation was carried out.[3]

Exodus 21:22–25 speaks of a case involving the accidental infliction of misfortune upon a pregnant woman. Although the general sense of this material seems clear enough, the passage teems with philological and interpretive problems. Among these problems are: (1) the exact denotation of the plural in "if her offspring (plural) come forth"; (2) to whom the misfortune or harm may ensue, whether the embryo, the premature child(ren) or the mother;[4] (3) the meaning of the term *pelilim* in vs. 22 (RSV and NRSV: "the judges"; NJPS "reckoning" [of the age of the fetus])[5] and (4) the relationship of 21:22, which is stated in the impersonal third person ("when men . . . , the one who hurt . . . he shall"), to the *lex talionis* in 21:23–25, which is stated in second person address ("you shall give"). The general sense of 21:22–25 means that when a pregnant

---

see Smith, *Palestinian Parties and Politics*, 140–41; and Smith, "East Mediterranean Law Codes."

2. "If it (the wound or injury) gets healed and then gets sore again, gets healed and gets sore again, and even if this happens four or five times, he is still obliged to pay for curing it . . . just as he pays for the loss of time only when it is the result of the injury, so also when he is to pay for the healing he is to pay only for the healing of ailments resulting from the injury"; Lauterbach, ed. and trans., *Mekilta de-Rabbi Ishmael*, 3.55. All references to the *Mekilta* are to this edition.

3. Exodus 21:20–21 demonstrates that in ancient Israel injury to a slave was treated differently from injury to a free person since the slave was considered the "property" of the owner. These verses, however, illustrate that although slaves did not possess full rights, they did possess some human rights. See also Exod 21:26–27.

4. "Harm" (*'ason*) is understood as death in the *Mek.* 3.65–66. Greek translators seem to have understood the text with reference to the viability of the fetus. See Daube, *Studies*, 148 n. 6.

5. "Judges" is the common interpretation; see *Mek.* 3.66, where appeal is made to Deut 32:31 and 1 Sam 2:25. "Reckoning" was proposed by Speiser, "The Stem *PLL* in Hebrew."

woman is accidentally injured causing a premature birth or miscarriage then the husband of the woman[6] could receive compensation for the consequences inflicted upon his wife and/or the offspring. At any rate, there is no retaliation against either the man causing the injury or his wife.[7]

Two laws requiring restitution for the death of another's animal are found in Exod 21:33–36. In the first, a person who leaves a pit open allowing an ox or ass to fall into the pit is required to make restitution in the form of a payment sufficent to replace the dead animal. In the second, the issue concerns the killing of one person's ox by another's ox. Distinction is made in the restitution depending upon whether the animal causing the death has had a history of goring. In the first example, the live ox is to be sold and the money received as well as the dead animal divided equally between the owners. In the latter case, since the owner failed to oversee the ox adequately, the ox has to be replaced, "ox in place of ox" (*shor tachath hashshor*). Since the latter case, unlike the former, is not considered purely accidental or coincidental, the owner of the dead ox has to be restored to the state existing prior to the slaughter of his ox.

Beginning with Exod 22:1 (MT 21:37) is a section dealing with restitution of stolen animals (22:1, 4).[8] In the cases noted, the thief has to make restitution at the rate of twofold, fourfold, or fivefold. A stolen ox, when disposed of by slaughter or sale, has to be replaced at the rate of five to one, a sheep at the rate of four to one. If the stolen beast is recovered alive in the possession of the thief, then restitution is twofold, whether the animal be an ox, ass, or a sheep. If the thief does not possess the means to make restitution, then he may be sold (into indentured servitude) to provide the amount needed for restitution. The biblical text offers no explanation for the multifold restitution in the case of stolen animals. Later Jewish tradition assumed that the stolen animal is included in the number restored: "five oxen, that is, four in addition to the one stolen. And four sheep, that is, three in addition to the one stolen,"

---

6. The *Mekilta* preserves a discussion of whether payment should go to the natural father or the husband providing the two were not identical; see *Mek.* 3.64.

7. Unlike some near eastern codes. In the Hammurabi Code, for example §209—"If a seignior struck another seignior's daughter and has caused her to have a miscarriage, he shall pay ten shekels of silver for her fetus." §210—"If that woman has died, they shall put his daughter to death." For comparative texts to the Covenant Code, see Paul, *Studies*.

8. In the RSV these two verses are brought together on the assumption of a textual displacement.

Restitution, Forgiveness, and the Victim in Old Testament Law

and perhaps similarly with the twofold restitution.⁹ The requirement to restore multifold seems obviously to involve a penal element or punishment to discourage robbery and theft as well as destruction and sale of stolen property. It might be argued that in the case of the ox restitution has to provide for the loss of the animal's labor, but this could not be the case with a sheep and seems exorbitant in the case of an ox. Later Jewish tradition assumes that multifold restitution is not required when the thief confesses to the theft but only when guilt has to be proven.

> If a man said, 'I have stolen,' he must repay the value on his own admission, but he does not make double or fourfold or fivefold restitution. . . . This is the general rule: whosoever must pay more than the cost of damage done does not pay on his own admission. (*m. Ketuboth* 3:9; Danby ed., p. 249)

Israelite jurisprudence may have established the multifold restitution since the failure to admit guilt was to sin with a high hand.¹⁰ It should be noted that the multifold restitution goes to the victim and that the penalty involved in the payment beyond damages also accrues to the victim. In like manner, selling a person to recover the amount of the theft was not administered primarily to punish the thief but to restore the victim to the condition prior to the theft.

Restitution to the owner of a field or vineyard that was grazed over by another's livestock is required in Exod 22:5. The text stipulates that restitution shall be from the best or top yield of his field and vineyard but does not specify whether "his" refers to the owner of the grazing livestock (so RSV) or the owner of the field or vineyard (so NJPS).¹¹ A person is

---

9. *Mek.* 3.99.

10. The role of witnesses in establishing guilt plays a significant role in post-biblical Judaism; see *m. Baba Kamma* 7:1–6. The distinction between twofold and multifold restitutions is explained as follows in *Baba Kamma* 7:1—"More common in use is the rule of twofold restitution than the rule of fourfold and fivefold restitution, for the rule of twofold restitution applies both to what has life and to what has not life; while the rule of fourfold and fivefold applies only to an ox or a sheep," Danby trans. Rabbi Johanan ben Zakkai explained the difference between fourfold and fivefold restitution as follows: "God has consideration for the dignity of human beings. For an ox, since it walked with its legs, the thief pays fivefold. For the lamb, since he had to carry it on his shoulders, he pays only fourfold" (*Mek.* 3.99). Probably the fourfold and fivefold restitution was imposed because the stolen animals had been disposed of.

11. The resolution, according to Rabbi Akiba, was "Scripture comes to teach you that in appraising the damage we estimate it as damage done to the choicest field" (*Mek.* 3.110).

257

thus held liable for damage done by what is owned, i.e., by one's property. Exodus 22:6 holds a person responsible for damage as a consequence of what one does even when there is no intent to destroy.[12] In this case, fire that spreads to consume "stacked, standing, or growing grain" (NJPS) makes the starter of the fire liable for restitution.[13]

Exodus 22:7–9 concerns the responsibility incumbent upon one who receives money or goods left for safekeeping.[14] If the materials are stolen and the thief is caught,[15] the owner of the house has to undergo an appearance before God[16] in which an oath of innocence must be sworn (v. 8). The owner of the lost item has to accept the oath in lieu of the object and no restitution is required. Verse 9 appears to state a general principle dealing with any matter of *pesha'* (NJPS: "misappropriation"; RSV: "breach of trust") over which dispute might arise. The solution to such a problem is an ordeal of some sort (see Num 5:11–31), carried out

---

12. "Scripture comes to declare that in all cases of liability for damage mentioned in the Torah one acting under duress is regarded as one acting of his own free will, one acting unintentionally is regarded as one acting intentionally" (*Mek.* 3.110).

13. Rabbinic tradition used the examples of grazing over and burning to establish general principles concerning damage. In all cases, restitution was the primary goal: "You reason and establish a general rule on the basis of what is common to these two: The peculiar aspect of damage by grazing is not like the peculiar aspect of damage by burning, nor is the peculiar aspect of damage by burning like the peculiar aspect of damage by grazing. What is common to both of them is: that it is their characteristic to do damage, they are your property, and it is incumbent upon you to guard them [the cattle and the fire]. And when damage is done, the one causing the damage is liable to pay for the damage from the best of his land" (*Mek.* 3.112).

14. Talmudic tradition (*b. Baba Metzia* 93–95) argued that unless payment for safekeeping were involved then no liability was incurred if the object was lost or stolen.

15. Rabbinlc tradition distinguished between theft and robbery. The robber commits his act openly, seen by man and God, but the thief is careful not to be seen by man but does not mind being seen by God. The thief had to repay double but the robber pays back only the principle (see *Mek.* 3.115). In the Talmud, seven types of theft are noted:
   (a) Deceit ("stealing someone's mind") in a moral sense: no legal penalty provided;
   (b) Stealing things forbidden to be used: no restitution required, for one ought not to have these things in the first place;
   (c) Stealing certain things, like documents: simple restitution;
   (d) Stealing other things, like garments: double restitution;
   (e) Stealing a lamb: fourfold restitution at times;
   (f) Stealing an ox: fivefold restitution at times;
   (g) Stealing a human being (kidnaping): death penalty, See Plaut, ed., *The Torah*, 584.

16. "Elohim" in v. 8 is understood as "judges" in *Mek.* 3.116.

before God,[17] in which innocence and guilt would be determined (see Deut 17:8–13). The party determined to be in the wrong, i.e., declared guilty, has to make double restitution to the other.

Exodus 22:1–13 concerns the liability of and the terms of restitution by a shepherd or herdsman into whose hands an animal is left for safekeeping. When the animal left to the other's care dies, is injured, or stolen, the law holds the custodian liable if the loss is or could have been preventable. Again, the one into whose charge the animal has been placed is required to affirm innocence through an oath that has to be accepted by the owner in lieu of restitution in the case of the animal's death, injury, or "being driven away" without a witness. If the animal is stolen, however, he has to make restitution since the custodian failed to oversee the animal properly. No restitution is required for an animal torn by a wild beast since this is assumed to be unpreventable. Evidence of such attack by beasts has to be offered to authenticate the manner of death.[18]

Exodus 22:14–15 deals with the issue of restitution of things (animals) borrowed or hired. The borrower is liable to make restitution if the borrowed animal is injured or dies when the owner is not present. If the owner is present when the animal is hurt or dies, no restitution is necessary.[19] This ruling assumes that if the owner is present, then supervision of the animal is the responsibility of the owner and the borrower (or hirer) is not liable; without the owner's presence, liability lies with the non-owner.

A final law in the Covenant Code that concerns restitution is found in Exod 22:16–17. Here the case involves a man having sexual intercourse with an unbetrothed female. This particular case assumes two conditions: (1) the girl, whose marriage has not yet been arranged, is still fully under the care of the father, i.e., she is still considered to be his property; and

---

17. This text was used to argue that cases should be heard by three judges or by five (where three would give a majority opinion) since the text refers to the two parties and God; see *Mek.* 3.119–20.

18. See Amos 3:12, a text that the rabbis had already associated with Exod 22:13; see *Mek.* 3.125.

19. The lack of clarity in Exod 23:15b and its suggested meaning is explained as follows in rabbinic tradition: "The bailee for hire receives and gives benefit and the hirer also both receives and gives benefit. Now inasmuch as you have learned that the bailee for hire takes an oath concerning unavoidable accidents, but pays for the theft and loss, so also the hirer should take an oath concerning unavoidable accidents but pay for theft and loss. It is in this sense that it is said: 'If it be a hired thing, it came to him for his hire'" (*Mek.* 3.128–29).

(2) the girl is a willing participant in the sexual affair (as opposed to a case of rape or intercourse with a betrothed female; see Deut 22:23–29). The seducer is required to pay the marriage price for her and marry the girl if the latter arrangement is accepted by the father who can veto the marriage. Under either circumstance, the father receives payment of the marriage price for virgins (see Deut 22:29) since his property has been abused. The girl, of course, cannot be restored to her previous state of virginity. The closest arrangement to that is to provide the father, here considered the real victim, with the marriage present he would have received at the time of her marriage provided she had been a virgin.

Many of the cases considered in Exod 21:18—22:17 clearly fall into what today would be called civil cases whereas others would fall into the category of criminal cases. Among the latter would probably fall the cases involving injuring a neighbor in a fight (21:18–19), injuring a pregnant woman (21:22), and various forms of theft and misappropriation (22:1, 4, 7–9) although it is possible to see all of these being dealt with in civil situations. At any rate, features of civil cases (compensation and restitution) appear in what seem to be criminal law contexts. Thus it appears that our clear-cut distinctions between civil and criminal cases hardly existed in ancient Israel. In fact, it can be argued that in early Israel "there was no 'criminal law' in our sense, when the public itself exacts punishments for many offenses arising out of relationships between individuals."[20] Even homicide and adultery were private injuries. The basic principle operating in the laws we have examined was the principle of restitution of the victim. Only in the case of theft (22:1, 4) and misappropriation (22:9) was there multiple restitution and thus a penal element; but even in these cases compensation including the penalty went to the victim.

In addition to the content of the laws, philological considerations also support restitution as the basic principle in Israelite laws on interpersonal relations. Two Hebrew terms are used in the Covenant Code when speaking of making restitution, the *qal* form of the verb *nathan* and the *piel* of the verb *shlm*. The first, meaning "to give" or "to pay," occurs in Exod 21:19, 22, 30, 32. The latter occurs fourteen times (in Exod 21:34, 36, 37; 22:2, 3, 4, 5, 6, 8, 10, 11, 12, 13, 14; following the Hebrew enumeration of the verses). Unlike the very general and colorless verb *nathan*, *shlm* appears as the root in significant Old Testament words:

---

20. Plaut, ed., *The Torah*, 571.

shalom, "the state of well-being," *shelamim*, "the sacrifice of well-being."[21] The *piel* of *shlm* thus means "to make complete, whole, or sound," thus to restore one's well-being or to make restitution.[22]

The *Lex Talionis*

If restitution functions as the dominant principle in the Old Testament laws concerning damage to persons and property and the status of the victim is the dominant focus in juridical cases, then how is the appearance of the *lex talionis* in Scripture to be explained since talion by its nature is based on retaliation and makes the perpetrator not the victim of actions the center of attention? The appearance of the *lex talionis* in Exod 21:23–25; Lev 24:17–21; and Deut 19:21 cannot be denied. The issues, however, concern its application in cases other than intentional or accidental murder where, of course, restitution of the victim was an impossibility.[23]

The fullest statement of the *lex talionis* appears in Exod 21:23b–25: "life for life, eye for eye, tooth for tooth, hand for hand, foot for foot, burn for burn, wound for wound, bruise for bruise." Scholars have long noted that this passage appears as an interpolation in its context.[24] Several reasons support such a position. First of all, there is the matter of form. The *lex talionis* is an unconditional, apodictic law within a context of casuistic, conditional laws. This change in form could lead to the argument that vv. 23b–25 should follow vv. 12–17. Such a conclusion is contradicted by the second argument for the text's interpolation: the change in the person addressed. The other laws in Exodus 21 are formulated in impersonal address, "whoever," "when a man," whereas 21:23 is formulated in second person address, "you shall." This factor suggests that 21:23b–25 was not originally a component in a unit with vv. 12–17. Thirdly, the stipulations

---

21. See Milgrom, "Sacrifices and Offerings, OT," 769–70.

22. Daube (*Studies*, 133–44) has argued that the *piel* of *shlm* always denotes a literal restoration of the same object or one in kind but never refers to monetary equivalent. This gives the expression a more restricted use than merely with reference to restitution. For a critique of Daube, see Milgrom, *Cult and Conscience*, 137–40.

23. Genesis 9:6 lays down the regulation: "Whoever sheds the blood of man by man shall his blood be shed." The Israelites clearly distinguished between murder and manslaughter (Exod 21:12–14; Deut 19:4–10). Many of the provisions laid out in the Mishnaic tractate *Sanhedrin* were set out to protect the innocent.

24. See Alt, "The Origin of Israelite Law," 134–39; and Daube, *Studies*, 105–8.

in v. 22 presuppose compensation and restitution not retaliation as apparently do vv. 23–25. The content and procedure of v. 22 are directly contradicted by vv. 23–25. If the former (v. 22) had actually assumed the operational procedure of the latter (vv. 23–25), then v. 22 should have required that the wife of the perpetrator of the injury be treated as the woman caused to miscarry.[25]

The interpolation or appearance of the *lex talionis* in a context where it clearly does not belong, in so far as the application or any of its straightforward statements are concerned, raises the question of its function. Its function cannot be to lay out the stipulations and conditions pertaining in the laws preceding or following. Neither the law of aggravated miscarriage that precedes nor the law about injury to slaves that follows has anything to do with retaliation. They do not implement the requirements of the *lex talionis*. Thus the *lex talionis* plays neither a substantive nor a regulatory role in its present context. Its function, therefore, must be rhetorical.[26] Enforcement of its own stipulations is not its concern. Its presence merely lends support to the argumentation of its context, namely, the necessity to make restitution for injury to a mother or the fetus.

The talion principle also appears in Lev 24:17–21 in the follwing form:

> He who kills a man shall be put to death. He who kills a beast shall make it good, life for life. When a man causes a disfigurement in his neighbor, as he has done it shall be done to him, fracture for fracture, eye for eye, tooth for tooth; as he has disfigured a man, he shall be disfigured. He who kills a beast shall make it good; and he who kills a man shall be put to death.

A number of features about this text are noteworthy. (1) The larger context, in Lev 24:10–23, is concerned with the question of blasphemy or the improper use of the name of Yahweh. The central thrust of the overall text in its present form is the ruling that "you shall have one law for the sojourner and for the native." The episode involving the man who

---

25. For comparative near eastern texts, see Paul, *Studies*, 74–77; and Renger, "Lex Talionis."

26. Rhetorical usage refers to its employment in actual legal contexts where persons "bargained" for compensation and restitution, in seeking to compose their differences, with appeals to more drastic demands, i.e., an eye for an eye, and so forth, whereas in reality what was desired and settled upon was actually restitution. This rhetorical employment of the *lex talionis* in real cases is then reflected literarily.

blasphemed the name and cursed (Lev 24:10–12, 23) provides the context for the general ruling about execution for blasphemy (Lev 24:14) with its extension to cover the non-Israelite sojourner (Lev 24:16). (2) The episode of the blasphemer has the function of establishing a "narrated precedent," that is, a type case. A similar such episode and "narrated precedent" appears in Num 15:32–36 where a person is stoned for transgression of the Sabbath. In each of these stories, the following elements occur: (a) description of an offense (Lev 24:10–11a; Num 15:32); (b) culprit taken to Moses (Lev 24:11b; Num 15:33); (c) custodial holding until Yahweh's will could be determined (Lev 24:12; Num 15:34); (d) divine response stipulating punishment (Lev 24:13–14; Num 15:35); and (e) the stoning of the culprit according to the command of Yahweh (Lev 24:32; Num 15:36). (3) This analysis of the two "narrated precedents" suggests that Lev 24:15b–22 is a secondary insertion that has been joined to the narrative by the connective phrase in v. 15a. Just as vv. 15b–16 extend the punishment for blasphemy to include the sojourner and thus broaden the circle of responsibility so vv. 17–22 extend the protection of the law to the sojourner and thus broaden the circle of the law's applicability. The *lex talionis* and its application, therefore, are not the primary concern of the text but function rhetorically to support the central thrust of the text—the twofold extenstons of the law to include the sojourner in both protection and accouatability. (4) The rhetorical character of the *lex talionis* in this context is further suggested by the fact that the text makes no differentiation between murder and manslaughter,[27] a factor taken into consideration in both the Covenant and Deuteronomic Codes (see Exod 21:12–14; Deut 19:1–6).

The third appearance of the *lex talionis* is in Deut 19:21. The context for this passage is concerned with evidence in court and the offering of testimony by witnesses. After declaring that two witnesses or more are required to convict, the text deals with a malicious witness who, after offering false testimony, is said to be subject to the same verdict as would have been the case with the one against whom he offered false testimony:[28]

27. Whether the phrases *mot yumat* (Lev 24:17) and *yumat* (Lev 24:21) should be understood as mandating capital punishment or understood merely as permitting capital punishment is uncertain. The former is the common interpretation reflected in practically all modern translations. For the latter position, see Soggin, *Old Testament and Oriental Studies*, 174–75; and Buss, "The Distinction between Civil and Criminal Law in Ancient Israel," 55–56.

28. The interrogation of witnesses can be seen in the story of Susanna (50–59) and in *m. Sanhedrin* 4:5—5:4.

"You shall do to him as he had meant to do to his brother; so you shall purge the evil from the midst of you."[29] The statement of the *talionis* in v. 21 merely functions as a rhetorical device to reinforce the conditions already spelled out in v. 19.[30]

In all three cases where the statement of the *lex talionis* appears (Exod 21:23–25; Lev 24:17–21; Deut 29:21), it functions rhetorically rather than realistically. The law of *talion* is secondary in all three passages and performs a supportive rather than a prescriptive role. In the pursuit of personal justice and in actual court cases in ancient Israel, the *lex talionis* probably functioned as a weapon in bargaining or pleading one's case when it was not actual *talion* but compensation that was desired. Thus the expression of the *lex talionis* in the Bible does not function "to curb unlimited retribution, personal vendetta, and excessive retaliation"[31] (in spite of Gen 4:23), nor to establish "the principle of equal justice for all!"[32]

Two further considerations suggest that actual talion and retaliation were not basic principles in Israelite law and jurisprudence. First of all, Old Testament law does not stipulate mutilation as would have been the case if actual talion and retaliation were carried out; and biblical narrative does not contain a single story in which there is mentioned the implementation of the talionic punishments.[33] The one possible exception regarding bodily mutilation occurs in Deut 25:11–12 and concerns the case of a woman who rescues her husband from an opponent by seizing the latter by his genitals. The stipulated punishment appears to require the amputation of her hand.[34] Here the mutilation seems ro have been

---

29. The influence of an example is found in several places in Deuteronomy (13:11; 17:13; 19:20).

30. The fomulations in Deut 19:21 differ from those in Exod 21:23–25 and Lev 24:17–21. The latter use the preposition *tachat* ("life *tachat* life") whereas the former uses the preposition *b* ("life *b* life"). Whether this different usage implies some different meaning cannot be determined. Daube (*Studies*, 130) has argued that the former should be translated "in place of" ("life in place of life") but with compensation clearly in mind and that the Deuteronomic form does not use *tahat* because "to speak of compensation in this case was somewhat illogical, since as the accused has suffered no loss through the false witness—the latter's plot having failed—there is no room for compensation."

31. Paul, *Studies*, 76.

32. Albright, *History*, 74.

33. The case of flogging in Deut 25:1–3 does not fall into the area of a case of *talion* or retaliation.

34. An attempt is made to see the punishment of the woman as talionic by Eslinger, "The Case." He understood the unexpected Hebrew term *kap* (instead of *yad*) in v. 12

Restitution, Forgiveness, and the Victim in Old Testament Law

based on the nature of the case or rather its unusual nature rather than the talionic principle itself.[35]

Secondly, later Jewish and rabbinic interpretation understood the *lex talionis* as requiring not literal retaliation but compensation whereby the wrongdoer had to make good the damage that had been caused. That is, the object of the penalty imposed was the restitution of the injured not the punishment of the guilty; rabbinic exegesis understood the need to make restitution to the injured to include even the indignity inflicted upon the victim.

> If a man wounded his fellow, he thereby becomes liable on five counts: for injury, pain, for healing, for loss of time, and for indignity inflicted. 'For injury'—thus, if he blinded his fellow's eye, cut off his hand, or broke his foot, his fellow is looked upon as if he was a slave to be sold in the market: they assess how much he was worth and how much he is worth now. 'For pain'—thus, if he burnt his fellow with a spit or a nail, even though it was on his finger-nail where it leaves no wound, they estimate how much money such a man would be willing to take to suffer so. 'For healing'—thus, if he struck him he is liable to pay the cost of his healing; if by reason of the blow ulcers arise he is liable for the cost of their healing, but if they did not arise by reason of the blow, he is not liable. If the wound healed and then opened and healed again and again opened, he continues liable for the cost of his healing; but once it is properly healed he is no longer liable to pay the cost of his healing. 'For loss of time'—thus, he is looked upon as a watchman of a cucumber-field, since he has already been paid the value of his hand or foot. 'For indignity inflicted'—all is in accordance with the condition of life of him that inflicts and him that suffers the indignity ... A man is liable only when he acts with intention of causing injury. (*m. Baba Kamma* 8:1)[36]

Only Josephus, among ancient Jewish interpreters, suggests that both retaliation and retribution were means of settling accounts in cases of bodily damage. In summarizing the Mosaic law he writes:

---

as a euphemism for genitals (see Gen 32:26, 33; Song 5:5).

35. "A talmudic discussion suggests that the law did not apply when the woman's action was the only recourse to save her husband, and that in any case a fine was exacted in lieu of mutilation" (Plaut, ed., *The Torah: A Modern Commentary*, 1507). See *m. Baba Kamma* 8:1 and n. 36.

36. See the further discussion in *b. Baba Kamma* 83b; and *Mek.* 3.67–69.

> He that maimeth a man shall undergo the like, being deprived of that limb whereof he deprived the other, unless indeed the maimed man be willing to accept money; for the law empowers the victim himself to assess the damage that has befallen him and makes this concession, uuless he would show himself too severe. (*Ant.* 4.280)

Restitution and Atonement

Restitution to the victim formed the indispensable element in the ritual of atonement in ancient Israel. Although no texts provide a clear and full description of the atonement ritual and its components, such passages as Lev 5:1—6:7 (MT 5:1–26) and Num 5:5–10 do indicate its basic features. These features in the atonement ritual varied somewhat depending upon whether or not a victim or injured party was involved, that is, whether there was sin against a fellow human being as well as sin against the deity. In both cases, however, repentance or contrition was mandatory since "the priestly system prohibits sacrificial atonement to the unrepentant sinner, to the one who 'acts defiantly' . . . (Num 15:4)."[37]

Leviticus 5:1–6; 6:1–7; and Num 5:5–10 consider cases in which a person has not been placed on trial, found guilty, and been required to make restitution although one would assume that this would be the more normal course of events involving cases between persons. Rather, these texts deal with the pattern operative when a person has committed misconducts but has not been convicted of his crimes and then "feels guilty" or "becomes repentant" (Lev 6:4; RSV: "becomes guilty"; NJPS: "realizing his guilt") and wishes to make atonement. In normal, ordinary cases, a person would be forced to admit guilt as the consequence of arbitration or a trial. When the guilty party wishes to make amends and atonement in cases where another party or their property was involved, three steps were involved:

(1) "He shall confess his sin which he has committed" (Num 5:6)

(2) "He shall restore what he took by robbery, or what he got by oppression, or the deposit which was committed to him, or the lost thing which he found, or anything about which he has sworn falsely; he shall restore it in full, and shall add a fifth to it, and give it to him to whom it belongs, on the day of his guilt offering" (Lev 6:4–5).

37. Milgrom, "Atonement in the OT," 81.

Restitution, Forgiveness, and the Victim in Old Testament Law

(3) "And he shall bring to the priest his guilt offering to the Lord... and the priest shall make atonement for him before the LORD, and he shall be forgiven" (Lev 6:6–7).

Thus, the atonement ritual was composed of confession, restitution of the principal plus twenty percent,[38] and sacrifice. If these are viewed in terms of relationships one may say the following. (1) Confession is the means by which one narrates for oneself a new identity and then claims that identity. That is, confession is the means by which one comes to a new and truer relationship to the self and rights the self with itself. (2) Restitution is the means by which the victim is restored as nearly as possible to the condition existing prior to the misconduct or injury.[39] That is, restitution is the means whereby a proper and normal relationship (*shalom*) is restored between the two parties, the victim and the perpetrator of the misconduct. No doubt the payment of restitution was a public event in which the parties involved acknowledged the restoration of normalcy. Note that restitution was made "on the day of his guilt offering" (Lev 6:5) probably in a ceremony presided over by a priest. At the same time, there is no concern to punish the criminal except in the form of the payment of the extra fifth that went to the victim. (3) The sacrifice restores the relationship between the guilty party and God effecting atonement. The totality of the atonement ritual thus restored the disturbed threefold relationships produced by sinful activity.

The biblical and rabbinical tradition continuously recognized the integral relationship between repentance (confession), restitution, and sacrifice and saw these three elements as parts of a whole.

> Repentance effects atonement for lesser transgressions against both positive and negative commands in the Law; while for graver transgressions it suspends punishment until the Day of Atonement comes and effects atonement... For transgressions that are between man and God the Day of Atonement effects atonement, but for transgressions that are between a man and his fellow the Day of Atonement effects atonement only if he has appeased his fellow. (*m. Yoma* 8:8–9)

---

38. In rabbinic tradition, the fifth was considered as twenty percent of the principal plus indemnity. That is, a principal of one hundred shekels involved a total payment of one hundred twenty-five shekels (Plaut, ed., *The Torah*, 779). See *m. Ketuboth* 3:19, quoted above, for the fact that multifold restitution was not required where one made confession.

39. Perhaps the fifth functions as a payment for loss of usage or as an indemnity.

Bibliography

Albright, W. F. *History, Archaeology, and Christian Humanism.* Garden City, NY: Doubleday, 1964.

Alt, Albrecht. "The Origins of Israelite Law." In *Essays on Old Testament History and Religion.* 101–71. Translated by R. A. Wilson. Oxford: Blackwell, 1966.

Buss, Martin J. "The Distinction between Civil and Criminal Law in Ancient Israel." In *Proceedings of the Sixth World Congress of Jewish Studies,* 1.51–62. Jerusalem: Academic Press, 1977.

Danby, Herbert. *The Mishnah.* Oxford: Oxford University Press, 1933.

Daube, David. *Studies in Biblical Law.* Cambridge: Cambridge University Press, 1947.

Eslinger, Lyle. "The Case of an Immodest Lady Wrestler in Deuteronomy XXV 11–12." *VT* 31 (1981) 269–81.

Lauterbach, Jacob Z., editor and translator. *Mekilta de-Rabbi Ishmael.* Philadelphia: Jewish Publication Society of America, 1935.

Levine, Baruch. *Leviticus.* JPS Torah Commentary. Philadelphia: Jewish Publication Society, 1989.

Milgrom, Jacob. "Atonement in the OT." In *IDBSup,* 78–82.

———. *Cult and Conscience: The Asham and the Priestly Doctrine of Repentance.* Studies in Judaism in Late Antiquity 18. Leiden: Brill, 1976.

———. *Leviticus.* 3 vols. AB 3, 3A, 3B. New York: Doubleday, 1991, 2000, 2001.

———. *Leviticus: A Book of Ritual and Ethics.* Continental Commentaries. Minneapolis: Fortress, 2004.

———. "Sacrifices and Offerings, OT." In *IDBSup,* 763–71.

Paul, Shalom M. *Studies in the Book of the Covenant in the Light of Cuneiform and Biblical Law.* VTSup 18. 1970. Reprinted, Eugene, OR: Wipf & Stock, 2005.

Plaut, W. Gunther, editor. *The Torah: A Modern Commentary.* New York: Union of American Hebrew Congregations, 1981.

Renger, Johannes M. "*Lex Talionis.*" In *IDBSup,* 545–46.

Smith, Morton. "East Mediterranean Law Codes of the Early Iron Age." *Eretz Israel* 14 (1978) 38–43.

———. *Palestinian Parties and Politics That Shaped the Old Testament.* New York: Columbia University Press, 1971.

Soggin, J. Alberto. *Old Testament and Oriental Studies.* Biblica et Orientalia 29. Rome: Pontifical Biblical Institute Press, 1975.

Speiser, E. A. "The Stem *PLL* in Hebrew." *JBL* 82 (1963) 301–6.

9

Covenant

THE HEBREW TERM *BERITH*, often, and traditionally the only term translated as "covenant" in the Old Testament, has a wide semantic usage signifying in different contexts what could be and sometimes is rendered in English as "promise, pledge, obligation, agreement, contract, pact, or treaty." Although the OT speaks of many different covenants, the plural form of *berit* never occurs.

In spite of various proposals and their defenses, the etymology of the word remains uncertain. The most widely advocated suggestions are: (1) from the verb *brh* "to eat, feed"; (2) from the verb *brh* "to see, decide"; (3) from a preposition *birit,* unattested in Hebrew but found in Akkadian, meaning "between"; and (4) from a noun parallel to the Akkadian and Talmudic *biritu/byryt* "clasp, fetter."

The most likely Old Testament synonyms for *berit* are *'amanah* (from *'mn* to be firm, steadfast") in Neh 10:1; 11:23; *chozeh/chazat* (from *chzh* "to see"?) in Isa 28:15, 18; *shebu'ah/'alah* ("oath") in some texts (see Gen 26:3); and *'ed/'edut/'edot* (from *'dh* "to witness"?) in Gen 31:44–52; Josh 24:27; Isa 32:14 (reading *be'ad* as *ke'ed*), and in expressions like the "ark of the *'edut*." The latter would parallel the terms *adu/ade* in Akkadian and *'dn/'dy* in Aramaic. Such synonyms occur very infrequently in the Old Testament. Terms such as "peace" (*shalom*), "good, friendship" (*tob*), "law" (*torah*), and "oath" (*'alah*), which may occur in covenantal contexts, are not to be viewed as interchangeable synonyms for *berit* nor does their appearance in a text always presuppose that reference to a covenant stands as background to the text. Some terms, such as "peace," "friendship," and "brotherhood," were used however to refer to the conditions produced by covenant relationships.

In the Old Testament, the term "covenant" (*berit*) is employed with reference to three types of obligatory conditions. (1) In some cases, such as the covenant between God and Noah and the Israelite patriarchs, the obligation is self-imposed by the deity. (2) In other contexts, the obligation is imposed by the divine or the superior party on an inferior or another party (cf. Jeremiah 34 and Hos 2:18–23). (3) Elsewhere, as in the Sinai covenant, both parties are committed to reciprocal obligations (see Exod 34:10, 27).

The term "covenant" (*berit*) could thus be used to refer to a variety of solemn, binding obligations or agreements involving two or more parties in a relationship. (1) The obligation might be self-assumed by the primary party for the benefit of the secondary party. In this case, the covenant was more like a pledge or a promise. The expected attitude of the primary party to the obligation was one of fidelity and the attitude of the secondary party was one of acceptance and trust. (2) When the obligation was imposed on the secondary party, it represented a demand or condition placed upon the obligated party and required obedience. Generally such a covenant relationship was assumed to benefit the party imposing the obligation although obedience to the obligation might be seen as beneficial to the obligated party as well. (3) Conditions and commitments accepted by both or all parties produced a situation of mutual obligation intended to benefit all parties concerned. In all three cases, the gravity and solemnity of the parties' commitment could be enhanced by verbal declaration, swearing, or the taking of an oath.

Diverse terminology is used with regard to making, maintaining, and fulfilling a covenant: cut, give, establish, enter, observe, break, transgress, remember, forget, and so on. This suggests a lack of any limited, specific vocabulary employed to speak about the operations and attitudes toward covenant conditions.

Ancient Near Eastern Evidence

As in the Old Testament, the ancient Near Eastern evidence for covenants or treaties is diverse and reflects various conditions and relationships. Documentary evidence is known from the third through the first millennium (for a selection, cf. *ANET*, 199–206, 531–41, 659–61). Although

Covenant

the majority of known texts are preserved in Akkadian cuneiform, Hittite, Aramaic, and Greek examples also exist.

In Akkadian documents, especially during the first millennium BCE, treaties and their stipulations are referred to as *ade* (*'dn/'dy* in Aramaic), a term that, unlike *berit*, always occurs in the plural. The most common use of *ade* is to refer to conditions in which a subordinate party is bound through loyalty oath to a superior party at the initiative of the latter. The inferior party may be either a foreign vassal or a domestic group. Several Assyrian texts bind the entire nation, including members of the royal family, the aristocracy, and the general populace, to observe particular conditions, in regard to succession to the throne and loyalty to the king. However, *ade* is also used to refer to divine promises made by a god to a ruler, to agreements between gods, to treaties between rulers of equal status, and to agreements sought by an inferior party.

The general structural pattern underlying ancient Near Eastern treaties can be seen in Hittite texts from the fourteenth and thirteenth centuries, although it should be noted that these and subsequent treaties vary in very significant ways, no two treaties are identical, and elements in the pattern may be omitted or expanded. The six main elements of the treaty pattern are:

(1) a preamble identifying the parties

(2) a historical prologue noting past relationships between the parties (generally not present in first millennium texts)

(3) the stipulations imposed on the inferior party or shared by the parties involved

(4) provisions for safely depositing and consultation/reading of the treaty document

(5) a list of gods and other witnesses to the treaty, and

(6) curses and blessings.

Many of the texts allude to various rites that accompanied the concluding of the treaty, in particular, actions used to illustrate the calamities and curses that would befall the disloyal and disobedient party for failure to live up to the imposed stipulations. Oaths of loyalty, undergirded with the threat of divine sanction and supervision, were sworn by the inferior party on whom the stipulations were imposed. Failure to live up to the stipulated arrangements and conditions was considered rebellion/sin against both the superior party and the deities called upon to sanction the treaty.

The parties to the treaty are referred to in various ways in the texts. The superior party might be referred to in the third person and the inferior party in the second person, both parties in the third person, or the superior party in the second or third person and the inferior party in the first person. In some texts, the parties are described in the third person and the stipulations imposed to insure the loyalty of the inferior party utilize second person address.

Covenants in Genesis—2 Kings

Numerous covenants/treaties are referred to in the OT and the term *berit* occurs 286 times.

Covenants between God and Individuals

Although earlier commentators assumed that Adam lived under a covenant (of works), the first reference to covenant and the first use of the word *berit* appear in the Noah materials. Here the covenant seems to refer to the divine pledge made to Noah, to all creatures, and even to the earth as a whole (Gen 6:18; 9:9–16). In later interpretation, the Noachic covenant was understood as involving the conditions and stipulations imposed on Noah (Gen 9:1–7) and thus all humankind (cf. Isa 24:5); and these stipulations were broadened to include a number of conditions not directly stated in the text (cf. Acts 15:19–21, 28–29; *Genesis Rabbah* 34.8).

The covenant with Abraham, noted in Gen 15:18–19, appears to have been understood as a promise or pledge by the divine to give the land (of Canaan) to Abraham's offspring. Only the divine here is placed under any obligation and presumably the "smoking fire pot and flaming torch" (in v. 17) symbolize the deity and the divine commitment to the promise. This promise—to give the land to the patriarchs and their descendants—is spoken of throughout Genesis–Judges, sometimes using the word 'covenant' (Exod 2:24; 6:4, 5; Lev 26:42–45; cf. 2 Kgs 13:23) and at other times merely referring to the sworn oath/promise to give the land (Gen 26:3; 50:24; Exod 13:5, 11; 32:13; 33:1; Num 11:12; 14:23;

32:11; Deut 1:8, 35; 6:10; 11:9, 21; 19:8; 26:3,15; 28:11; 30:20; 31:7, 20–23; 34:4; Josh 1:6; 5:6; 21:43; Judg 2:1).

The covenant with Abraham described in Gen 17:1–14 is one of reciprocal obligations. Divine pledges include not only the promise of the land but also other commitments by the deity as well as the obligation of circumcision imposed upon Abraham and his descendants. Circumcision is presented as both an obligation and a sign of the covenant (17:11; cf. 9:13).

Numbers 18:8–9 speaks of Yahweh's covenant with Aaron, called a "covenant of salt" (18:19; cf. Lev 2:13; 2 Chr 13:5), which grants the Aaronites the priestly perquisites (see Neh 13:29 [cf. Num 18:21–24]; cf. Deut 33:9; Jer 33:21–22; Mal 2:1–9). Although the covenant statement only refers to God's gift of the holy offerings to the Aaronites (v. 19), the preceding passage describing these in vv. 8–18 refers to incidental priestly obligations, in the form of cultic directives (vv. 10, 17b) and might be understood as priestly obligations.

A covenant/promise of perpetual priesthood is given to Phinehas in Num 25:10–13 as a reward for his zealous and atoning work on behalf of Yahweh and the community (see 25:6–9; cf. Gen 26:5).

A further example of a divine covenant with an individual (and his descendants) is the covenant with David (2 Sam 23:5; Pss 89:3, 19–37; 132:11–18; cf. 2 Samuel 7). Probably the earliest expression of the divine covenant with David was conceived as a promissory pledge made by Yahweh to the Davidic house authenticating and justifying the family's right to rule (cf. 2 Sam 23:5–7). The covenant could also be and was later understood as placing obligations on the rulers of the Davidic line (cf. Pss 89:30–34; 132:12).

Covenants between Human Parties

Genesis 14:13 refers to a covenant of Abraham apparently between the patriarch and his allies (called "*be'alim* of the covenant") in the war against northern invaders. Abraham and Abimelech made a covenant at Beersheba (Gen 21:22–34) as did Isaac and Abimelech (Gen 26:23–33). Laban and Jacob made a covenant in Transjordan (Gen 31:43–54) and set up a cairn called Galed (= "cairn of witness" or "covenant" if *'ed* = Akkadian *ade*), followed by a shared meal, a sign of mutual cooperation. The invading Hebrews made a covenant with inhabitants of the land, the

Gibeonites (Josh 9:3–21), a practice discouraged in various passages in the Pentateuch (Exod 23:32; 34:11–16; Deut 7:2; see Judg 2:2). Joshua and the Israelites at Shechem covenanted to worship Yahweh (Josh 24:25). The people of Jabesh-Gilead sought to negotiate a covenant with Nahash the Ammonite (1 Sam 11:1). David and Jonathan covenant together on more than one occasion with the covenants declared to be "of Yahweh" or "before Yahweh" (1 Sam 18:3; 20:8; 23:18). David entered a covenant with Abner (2 Sam 3:12–13) and subsequently, "before Yahweh," with the elders of Israel (2 Sam 3:21; 5:3). Solomon and Hiram of Tyre concluded a covenant (1 Kgs 5:12), and both Kings Baasha of Israel and Asa of Judah did so with King Ben-Hadad I of Aram (1 Kgs 15:21) as did a later Israelite king with Ben-hadad II (1 Kgs 20:34). The priest Jehoiada made a covenant with the military captains (which involved an oath in the temple precincts, 2 Kgs 11:5), concerning a conspiracy against Queen Athaliah, and later presided over a covenant ceremony (involving the people, the new king, and Yahweh) to be Yahweh's people (2 Kgs 11:17—the reference at the end of the verse "and between the king and the people" is probably a scribal error). After the finding of the book of the law in the temple (2 Kgs 22:8), King Josiah and the people covenanted "before Yahweh" to obey the stipulations of the book, but nothing is said about with whom the covenant was made (2 Kgs 23:3). Jeremiah 34:8–22 tells of a covenant made between King Zedekiah and the owners of Hebrew slaves in Jerusalem (see v. 8). The covenant was made before Yahweh (v. 15) and could be spoken of as "Yahweh's covenant" (v. 18). Since breaking the covenant involved profaning the name of Yahweh (v. 16), an oath of loyalty to the covenant was probably sworn in the name of Yahweh. A particular feature of this account is the reference to passing through the severed parts of a calf (v. 18; cf. Gen 15:9–11, 17), probably as an act of self-imprecation.

Although the term "covenant" is not used with regard to Israel's and Judah's relationships to Assyria and Babylonia in 2 Kings, it can be assumed that such covenants existed since such international relations with Mesopotamian powers, especially with vassal states, were based on treaties. The closest terminology to concluding a covenant appears in 2 Kgs 17:3, which speaks of King Hoshea's becoming a servant to Shalmaneser V (726–722). That such covenants/treaties were concluded with Israelite and Judean kings is not only suggested by non-biblical evidence and international policy but also by Ezek 17:11–21 (cf. 16:59), which comments on the treaty between Nebuchadrezzar and Zedekiah. In speaking of this treaty, Ezekiel can describe the treaty and the associated loyalty oath as both Nebuchadrezzar's and Yahweh's treaty and oath (vv. 16 and 19). This indicates that such treaties were concluded and sworn in the name of Yahweh (cf. 2 Chr 36:13), thus making the Israelite deity a party to the arrangement. Thus disloyalty to the treaty was not only a sin against the sovereign overlord but also against Yahweh. Such treaties probably existed between Assyria and Israel from the time of Jehu's submission to Assyria in 841 (cf. *ANET*, 281).

Treaties/covenants between human parties, national kingdoms, and a ruler with his people, if sworn in the name of God, created what might be called a triangular relationship. The basic bond was between the covenanting parties but, through the oath, the deity became involved as a tertiary participant, as custodian and guarantor of a party's or the parties' fidelity. Breaking the treaty meant breaking an oath, a pledge to the deity.

The Covenant between God and Israel

Without doubt, the most prominent portrayal of covenant in the Old Testament is that between Yahweh and the Israelite people as a whole, which differs from the covenants with Noah, the patriarchs, Phinehas, and David. In the latter, the covenant was concluded with an individual although on behalf of subsequent descendants. It also differs from personal or national bilateral treaties in that the deity is a primary partner in the relationship.

Three sections of texts speak of the making of a covenant between Yahweh and Israel—Exodus 19-24, 34, and Deuteronomy 28-31—but none of these is presented as the renewal of an already existing covenant (however, cf. Exod 34:1; Deut 29:1). The first of these is made after the arrival of the Hebrews at Sinai, the second after the golden calf episode, and the third in the plains of Moab. All three blocks of material presume and reflect elements of a covenant based on reciprocal obligations and refer to a collection of divine commandments to be obeyed by the people (Exodus 20-23; 34:17-26; Deuteronomy 12-26), the writing down of these divine words (Exod 24:7, 12; 34:1, 27-28; Deut 31:9), the promise of blessings and the threat of curses (Exod 23:20-33; 34:10-16; Deuteronomy 28; cf. Leviticus 26), and the people's acceptance and pledge of obedience (Exod 19:8; 24:7; 34:31-32; Deut 26:17). Although the features reflected in these texts parallel elements in ancient Near Eastern treaty documents, it should he noted that such comparative features are drawn from both narratives and words of Yahweh or Moses, i.e., from both descriptions about the covenant-making itself as well as the presumed contents of a covenant document.

Covenant Thought in the Prophets

The eighth-century prophets—Hosea, Amos, Isaiah, and Micah—were certainly acquainted with and their preaching was informed by covenant/treaty perspectives. Their preaching, however, does not reflect the idea or the existence of a covenant between Israel and Yahweh sealed by loyalty oaths but rather of covenants between two parties in which Yahweh was the guardian of the covenant, having become a party through oaths sworn in the divine name. From the time of David and Solomon, the Israelite monarchs had entered into treaty relationships with other rulers, as was noted above, and these, especially vassal treaties with Assyria, would have been concluded with loyalty oaths in the name of Yahweh. Breaking these treaties constituted sin and brought down upon the offender the wrath of both Assyria and Yahweh and profaned the name of Yahweh, requiring the offending party to offer restitution or suffer punishment. It is possible that the practice of swearing officers and troops to a covenant of loyalty may also have been a part of Israelite life at the time (cf. 2 Kgs 11:4).

The prophets certainly assumed that Yahweh was Israel's God and Israel was Yahweh's people (cf. Exod 6:7; Lev 26:12), but this is simply an expression of the kingdom–deity relationship, not a relationship understood in the categories of covenant thought. While the two ideas are related, they are not identical and should not be confused.

Hosea uses the term covenant five times, in 2:18; 6:7; 8:1; 10:4; and 12:1. In 2:18, Yahweh presides over or imposes the making of a covenant between a female (probably Samaria since Israel as a people is always a male in the eighth-century prophets) and the beasts and birds and so forth. Here Yahweh imposes a covenant on two other parties. Agreements made either among the Israelites themselves or, less likely, with foreign states are referred to in 10:4. The other three references probably allude to Israel's covenant with Assyria. In 8:1, this treaty is referred to as Yahweh's treaty just as is the treaty between Nebuchadrezzar and Zedekiah in Ezek 17:19. "My law" or "my torah" would be a use of synonymous parallelism in which "my law" is equivalent to "my covenant." Whether the covenant referred to in 6:7 is Israel's covenant with Assyria or a loyalty covenant sworn by Pekah and broken when he rebelled against and attacked the Israelite monarch (cf. 2 Kgs 15:25) remains uncertain. Amos was certainly acquainted with the theological and legal considerations undergirding and embodied in international treaty thought and can refer to Tyre's failure to live up to treaty conditions (1:9). Behind much of Isaiah's and Micah's preaching lies the specter of the Assyrian treaty arrangements but their concern is somewhat different from that of Hosea since Isaiah and Micah preached in Judah where the covenant with Assyria remained generally intact. Only with the death of Sargon II in 705 and thus after the termination of a Judean–Assyrian treaty did Isaiah support rebellion against Assyria (Isaiah 24–27).

If the covenant perspective of the eighth-century prophets were based on conceptions associated with international political treaties, the matter is radically different for the seventh-century prophets, Jeremiah and Ezekiel. Both prophets speak of a covenant between Yahweh and the people (cf. Jer 11:1–10; 14:21; 22:9; Ezek 16:8, 60–63). Ezekiel still utilized the perspective of international treaty conceptions as well. His allegory of the eagles in chap. 17 provides the clearest insight into the triangular treaty arrangement in the Scriptures, especially in 17:11–21 in which the Nebuchadrezzar–Zedekiah treaty and oath are described as Yahweh's treaty and oath. It was the breaking of this treaty, not the Israel–Yahweh treaty, that the prophet proclaimed would bring judgment on Zedekiah (17:20–21).

The differences between the covenant preaching in the eighth-century prophets and the seventh-century prophets is to be explained as follows. In the three-quarters of a century separating the end of Isaiah's preaching (in 701–700) and the beginning (629–628) or early years of Jeremiah's preaching, Judean circles had given expression to the Israel–God relationship in terms of an Israel–God covenant. These circles are to be associated with what is called the deuteronomic-deuteronomistic movement, which eventually gave final shape to the book of Deuteronomy and a major history of Israel extending, probably, from Genesis through 2 Kings. The parallels between the covenant material in Deuteronomy (especially in chaps. 1–11 and 28–31) and the treaties of Esarhaddon, especially his so-called vassal treaties dating from 672 to 671 (cf. *ANET*, 534–41), suggest a connection between these two documents. Both Esarhaddon and his mother Zakutu swore their own people to fidelity and obedience. The form of this type of treaty, between sovereign and subjects, closely resembles that between Yahweh and Israel. In addition, Deut 28:68, with its reference to going to Egypt in ships, probably reflects Ashurbanipal's invasion of Egypt in 664–663 during which Judean troops, if not King Manasseh himself, accompanied him, some being carried in ships (see *ANET*, 294). The Old Testament's particular theology of a covenant between Yahweh and Israel was thus probably formulated in the mid-seventh century.

Marriage as Covenant

Two Old Testament texts, other indirect biblical evidence, and ancient Near Eastern materials suggest that marriage was understood in ancient Israel along the lines of a triangular covenantal arrangement in which the spouses were the primary partners and God was the custodian and guardian of the marriage relationship. Proverbs 2:17 describes the woman who forsakes the companion of her youth (her husband) as one who forgets the covenant (*berit*) of her God, implying both that marriage was a covenant and that the covenant was under the sanction of God. Malachi 3:14 speaks of God as witness to a marriage arrangement and the wife is referred to as the covenant woman. That marriage was so understood is also indicated by the fact that throughout the Near East, adultery was considered the "great" sin. Leviticus 19:20–22 also implies this triangular relation in marriage, here even in betrothal. An outside male who sexually interfered in a man–woman relationship was required to offer a reparation (guilt) offering (an *'asham*), which was demanded when one transgressed against God by profaning the divine name or desecrating something holy to the deity. This would suggest that an oath in the name of Yahweh was sworn (or assumed to be implied) in marriage-betrothal arrangements. Unfortunately we possess no full descriptions of Israelite marriages nor marriage documents in the Bible, so it is uncertain whether or not marriage loyalty-oaths were made in the name of the deity.

The New Covenant

The prophets speak of a future covenant that God will make with the people (Isa 61:8; Jer 31:31–33; 32:40; Ezek 34:25; 37:26). Only Jeremiah uses the adjective "new" in speaking of this future covenant (31:31).

Otherwise this future covenant is simply denoted as being "everlasting" (Isa 61:8; Jer 32:40) or "a covenant of peace" (or "friendship," Ezek 34:25; 37:26). The contexts of all these passages indicate that the prophets were addressing the issue of what conditions would need to prevail for the Israel of the future to be obedient to the divine will. The new or renewed covenant is to be part of a great transformation of both the people and the land. According to Jer 31:31–33, the new covenant will be inscribed upon the hearts of the house of Israel so that each person will instinctively and by nature know and heed the divine Torah.

Conclusions

A number of conclusions are in order regarding the nature and role of covenant in the Old Testament. (1) The broad semantic range of the term *berit* would indicate that "covenant" is not always the best translation of the term especially where "pledge/promise" or "obligation" better fits the context. The term *berit* functioned in a broader fashion than is implied in the term "covenant." (2) There is a diversity of covenants in the Old Testament, and a single structural pattern does not encompass this diversity. (3) The Old Testament contains no full covenant document per se. Hypothetical reconstructions of such are produced by combining narrative and "legal" material. (4) Comparisons between Old Testament texts and Near Eastern treaty texts, for example the Hittite vassal treaties (first done by Karge), are informative, but Old Testament materials should not be pressed into a hypothetical stereotyped Near Eastern treaty pattern. (5) The role of treaty agreements between kingdoms, with the theology and ethics implied by these, should not be overlooked. These treaties and their interpretation seem to have formed the basic background of the covenant references of the eighth-century prophets. (6) The idea of a covenant between Israel and Yahweh was probably a literary/theological phenomenon rather than a sociological or institutional reality. There is no evidence in Joshua—2 Kings of a covenant festival or a covenant renewal celebration in which a covenant between Yahweh and the people was regularly reenacted. (7) The present canonical form of the Hexateuch is patterned around a series of covenants (Noah, Abraham, Sinai, after the golden calf episode, in the plains of Moab, and at Shechem). The canonical form of the text should be interpreted in light of this fact.

Covenant in the New Testament

The New Testament writers inherited from the Greek of the Old Testament the use of the term *diatheke* as a translation for *berit*, although the Greek term tended to denote a last will or testament (cf. Gal 3:15, 17; Heb 9:15–17). This terminology is the source of the designations "Old" and "New" Testaments.

The early church saw its relationship to God in terms of a new covenant, which it closely associated with the death of Jesus and the observance of the Lord's Supper (or Eucharist). Covenant terminology and its association with the blood (death) (cf. Exod 24:8; Zech 9:11) of Jesus are anchored in both the Gospels (Matt 26:28; Mark 14:24; Luke 22:20 [absent from many ancient MSS]; see John 6:52–58) and Epistles (1 Cor 11:23–32). Early Christians used the idea of the "new" covenant (Heb 8:6–10; Luke 22:20) inaugurated by Christ, contrasting it with the "old" covenant. The "old" covenant is sometimes associated with the law or the Pentateuch (2 Cor 3:6, 14; Gal 4:24) or what might be called non-Christian Jewish religion. Elsewhere, the "new" covenant is related positively to the Abrahamic covenant (Acts 3:25; cf. Gal 3:17–18; but see Acts 7:8). Paul refers to the covenants of the Israelites (Rom 9:4) and associates the Christians with the divine promise to Abraham and God's fidelity to that promise (Rom 9:6–9; Gal 4:28–31). A central concern of the book of Hebrews is to demonstrate the superiority of the Christian covenant (7:22; 8:7–13). The new covenant could also be spoken of in terms of the "spirit" as a "spiritual bond" (2 Cor 3:1–6).

Bibliography

Baltzer, Klaus, *The Covenant Formulary: In Old Testament, Jewish, and Early Christian Writings*. Translated by David E. Green. Philadelphia: Fortress, 1971.

Barr, James. "Some Semantic Notes on the Covenant." In *Beiträge zur alttestamentlichen Theologie: Festschrift für Walter Zimmerli zum 70. Geburtstag*, edited by Herbert Donner et al., 23–38. Göttingen: Vandenhoeck & Ruprecht, 1977.

Beckwith, Roger T. "The Unity and Diversity of God's Covenants." *Tyndale Bulletin* 38 (1987) 93–118.

Frankena, R. "The Vassal-Treaties of Esarhaddon and the Dating of Deuteronomy." *OTS* 14 (1965) 123–54.

Gerstenberger, Erhard S. "Covenant and Commandment." *JBL* 84 (1965) 38–51.

Grayson, A. Kirk. "Akkadian Treaties of the Seventh Century B.C." *JCS* 39 (1987) 127–60.

Hillers, Delbert R. *Covenant: The History of a Biblical Idea*. Seminars in the History of Ideas. Baltimore: Johns Hopkins University Press, 1969.
Karge, Paul. *Geschichte des Bundesgedankens im Alten Testament*. Alttestamentliche Abhandlungen 2/1-4. Münster: Aschendorff, 1910.
McCarthy, Dennis J. *Treaty and Covenant: A Study in Form in the Ancient Oriental Documents and in the Old Testament*. 2nd ed. Analecta Biblica 21. Rome: Pontifical Biblical Institute Press, 1978.
Mendenhall, George E. *Law and Covenant in Israel and the Ancient Near East*. Pittsburgh: Biblical Colloquium, 1955.
Nicholson, Ernest W. *God and His People: Covenant and Theology in the Old Testament*. Oxford: Clarendon, 1986.
Oden, Robert A., Jr. "The Place of Covenant in the Religion of Israel." In *Ancient Israelite Religion: Essays in Honor of Frank Moore Cross*, edited by Patrick D. Miller Jr. et al., 429–47. Philadelphia: Fortress, 1987.
Parpola, Simo. "Neo-Assyrian Treaties from the Royal Archives of Nineveh." *JCS* 39 (1987) 161–89.
Parpola, Simo, and Kazuko Watanabe. *Neo-Assyrian Treaties and Loyalty Oaths*. State Archives of Assyria 2. Helsinki: Helsinki University Press, 1988.
Perlitt, Lothar. *Bundestheologie im Alten Testament*. WMANT 36. Neukirchen-Vluyn: Neukirchener, 1969.
Tadmor, Hayim. "Treaty and Oath in the Ancient Near East: A Historian's Approach." In *Humanizing America's Iconic Book*, edited by Gene M. Tucker and Douglas A. Knight, 127–52. Biblical Scholarship in North America 6. Chico, CA: Scholars, 1982.
Tsevat, Matitiahu. "The Neo-Assyrian and Neo-Babylonian Vassal Oaths and the Prophet Ezekiel." *JBL* 78 (1959) 199–204.
Weber, Max. *Ancient Judaism*. Translated and edited by Hans H. Gerth and Don Martindale. Glencoe, IL: Free Press, 1952.
Weinfeld, Moshe. "*berith*." In *Theological Dictionary of the Old Testament*, edited by G. Johannes Botterweck and Helmer Ringgren, 2:253–79. Translated by John T. Willis. Rev. ed. Grand Rapids: Eerdmans, 1975.
Zevit, Ziony. "A Phoenician Inscription and Biblical Covenant Theology." *Israel Exploration Journal* 27 (1977) 116–18.

10

Covenant and *Hesed*

The Status of the Discussion

THE 1920S GAVE BIRTH to several important developments in Old Testament studies.[1] The most significant was the rebirth of interest in Old Testament theology as a systematic discipline moving beyond descriptions of the history of Israelite religion, which had eclipsed Old Testament theology for the past four decades.[2]

A second major development was the impact of Max Weber's work on biblical studies. In 1917–19, Weber published a series of essays on

---

1. This was also the time when opposition to the Old Testament and Judaism was building to a crescendo. In 1921, Adolf Harnack wrote: "To reject the Old Testament in the second century was a mistake the church rightly repudiated; to retain it in the sixteenth century was a fate which the Reformation could not yet avoid; to continue to keep it as a canonical document after the nineteenth century is the consequence of religious and ecclesiastical paralysis" (*Marcion*, 248–49). The anti-Old Testament movement was a significant negative factor in the attempt to recover a relevant, systematic, and dogmatic Old Testament theology over against widespread anti-Judaism.

2. Significant discussions in the call for a revival of Old Testament theology were: Rudolf Kittel, "Die Zukunft der alttestamentlichen Wissenschaft"; Staerk, "Religionsgeschichte und Religionsphilosophie in ihrer Bedeutung für die biblische Theologie des Alten Testaments"; Steuernagel, "Alttestamentliche Theologie und alttestamentliche Religionsgeschichte"; Eissfeldt, "Israelitisch-jüdische Religionsgeschichte und alttestamentliche Theologie"; and Eichrodt, *Ist der altisraelitische Nationalreligion Offenbarungsreligion?*; Eichrodt, "Hat die alttestamentliche Theologie noch selbständige Bedeutung innerhalb der alttestamentliche Wissenschaft?" For a general discussion, see Hayes and Prussner, *Old Testament Theology*, 151–66.

ancient Judaism in the *Archiv für Sozialwissenschaft und Sozialforschung*.³ In these essays, Weber argued that ancient "Israel as a political community was conceived as an oathbound confederation,"⁴ an "amphictyony"⁵ in which the tribes were bound together in covenant with one another but in a covenant in which Yahweh was "the contractural partner to the ritualistic and social order of the confederacy."⁶ This covenant relationship was initially "bilaterally mediated through the prophet Moses" and while its primary orientation was military it included and incorporated laws regulatory "of the socio-legal order."⁷ Thus "all violations of the holy enactments were not merely violations of orders guaranteed by him as other gods guarantee their orders, but violations of the most solemn contractual obligations toward him personally."⁸ In premonarchic times, the Levites were teachers and guardians of the torah of the confederacy⁹ and pre-classical prophets were the guardians of amphictyonic law.¹⁰ The classical prophets were not creative idealists, innovative ethical monotheists, radical revolutionaries, nor advocates of self-help for the masses but rather were spokespersons of socioethical demands that presupposed and were based on the laws of the confederacy and the Levitical traditions.¹¹ As a result, "the Torah is always the completely self-evident presupposition of all prophecy. It is seldom explicitly referred to because it went without saying."¹²

3. After his death, these were published as volume three of his *Gesammelte Aufsätze zur Religionssoziologie* with the title *Das antike Judentum* (1921). An English translation appeared as *Ancient Judaism* (1952).

4. Weber, *Ancient Judaism*, 75.

5. Ibid., 90.

6. Ibid., 120.

7. Ibid., 131.

8. Ibid., 130.

9. Ibid., 169–70.

10. Ibid., 110–11.

11. Ibid., 278.

12. Ibid., 295. Julius Wellhausen had argued that the idea of a covenant between Israel and Yahweh based on stipulations imposed on the people and conditional upon their obedience to these stipulations was a late innovation of the seventh century and was dependent upon prophetic preaching. The following quotes illustrate his position. "The relation between the people and God was a natural one as that of son to father; it did not rest upon observance of the conditions of a pact." "Nor did the theocracy exist from the time of Moses in the form of the covenant, though that was afterwards a favourite mode of regarding it . . . Only when the existence of Israel had come to be threatened by the Syrians and Assyrians, did such prophets as Elijah and Amos raise

A third factor to be noted concerns the increasing focus on the role of the cult in ancient Israelite life. The most representative of this approach was Sigmund Mowinckel whose six volumes on the Psalms[13] and a work on the decalogue[14] highlighted the cult as the rallying point of Israelite life and faith and as the carrier and custodian of Israelite religious beliefs. In the latter book, he associated the narratives about the Sinai covenant making (Exodus 19–24) with cultic celebrations in monarchic Israel. He proposed that the covenant at Sinai and the giving of the law were annually re-enacted and re-experienced as part of the fall festival whose main focus was the dramatic re-enthronement-of-Yahweh ritual.[15]

A fourth development in biblical studies was a focus on etymological and lexicographical approaches to biblical theology.[16] Characteristic of this development were an emphasis on single words as the bearers of theological meaning and as embodiments of conceptual world-views, an obsession with the root meaning of terms, and a strong utilization of the so-called contrast between Hebrew and Greek conceptualization of the world and patterns of thought.[17]

---

the Deity high above the people, sever the natural bond between them, and put in its place a relation depending on conditions, conditions of a moral character. To them Jehovah was the God of righteousness in the first place, and the God of Israel in the second place, and even that only so far as Israel came up to the righteous demands which in His grace He had revealed to him ... In this way arose, from ideas which easily suggested it, but yet as an entirely new thing, the substance of the notion of covenant or treaty. The name *Berith*, however, does not occur in the old prophets" (*Prolegomena to the History of Israel*, 469, 417–18).

13. Mowinckel, *Psalmenstudien*, 6 vols.

14. Mowinckel, *Le Decalogue*.

15. The re-enthronement of Yahweh as the central drama in the fall New Year festival is expounded in his *Psalmenstudien II: Das Thronbesteigungsfest Jahwäs und der Ursprung der Eschatologie*, 1922.

16. Aspects of this development have been mapped and critiqued by Barr in *The Semantics* and other publications. Word study and etymological approaches to biblical study were of course nothing new. In the nineteenth century, for example, Girdlestone, in his *Synonyms of the Old Testament*, offered what constitutes a systematic theology in thirty chapters based on an ordering and analysis of about 300 biblical Hebrew words.

17. The first volume of the Gerhard Kittel, ed., *Theologische Wörterbuch zum Neuen Testament* appeared in 1933.

Most of these emphases were taken over by and integrated into Old Testament studies by Albrecht Alt,[18] Martin Noth,[19] Gerhard von Rad,[20] and other German scholars and were subsequently adopted and modified by English-language interpreters, especially the participants in the so-called "biblical theology movement."[21] Alt, Noth, and von Rad never succumbed to an excessive etymological-lexicographical approach to biblical studies. Their depictions of Israelite worship, however, probably bore more similarity to a German Protestant *Kirchentag* than to ancient Near Eastern cultic activity.

The impact of these new developments, in so far as the study of Israelite history and religion was concerned, was powerful and persuasive. Several elements became almost universally accepted axioms and operating assumptions in Old Testament study. (1) Premonarchic Israel was understood as a tribal confederacy/amphictyony covenanted together for religious and military purposes. The number of these tribes was assumed to be twelve although the number was a debated point. (2) The covenant was not only concluded between the tribes but also between the tribes and Yahweh as the god of the confederacy. (3) Covenant was not just a theologically or culturally functional idea but an actual sociological-institutional phenomenon. It was assumed that the tribes under their recognized representatives (the *nasi'im*) annually met at the central sanctuary (so designated by the presence of the ark) and formally carried out a covenant renewal service in which the great historical acts of divine salvation were rehearsed and the covenant laws were proclaimed and the covenant relationships reaffirmed. (4) The covenant law and institutions as well as the sacred traditions of Israel's *Heilsgeschichte* were presupposed during the monarchic period and formed the basis for prophetic preaching.

In the 1950s, international treaties between ancient Near Eastern states were brought into the discussion of the nature, age, and theology

18. Alt's important and influential early essays were *Der Gott der Vater*; *Staatenbildung der Israeliten in Palastina*; and *Ursprünge der israelitischen Rechts*, all available in translation in his *Essays on Old Testament History and Religion*.

19. Noth's work, *Das System*, was one of the most influential works in twentieth-century Old Testament study.

20. Von Rad's *Das formgeschichtliche Problem des Hexateuch* (available in English in *The Problem of the Hexateuch and Other Essays* and *From Genesis to Chronicles*) provides a succinct representation of his approach.

21. The "biblical theology movement" is described in Childs, *Biblical Theology in Crisis*; and Hayes and Prussner, *Old Testament Theology*, 209–18.

of covenant in ancient Israelite life.[22] Of special importance here were the so-called suzerainty or vassal treaties of the Hittites that first became available in the 1920s and 30s. In a highly influential essay, G. E. Mendenhall[23] argued that the Hittite vassal treaties, contemporary with premonarchic Israel (c.1400–1200 BCE), supplied the model for the Old Testament amphictyonic covenant and sought to demonstrate how the decalogue, Joshua 24, Exod 24:3–8, 9–11, and other texts parallel the structure or elements in the Hittite texts. The extra-biblical material was seen as substantiating conclusions already drawn about the role and antiquity of covenant and the covenant traditions in ancient Israel on the basis of biblical evidence. Subsequently published and newly discovered texts have since provided treaty documents from throughout much of the second and first millennia.

The impact of the emphasis on covenant, both institutionally and theologically, on Old Testament studies can be illustrated in the way prophecy and prophets came to be understood in some discussions. Whereas Wellhausen had viewed the prophets as contributing the basic content of Old Testament covenant thought and Weber had argued that covenantal thought and law were presupposed and utilized by the prophets, scholars such as Kraus,[24] Reventlow,[25] and Muilenburg[26] argued that the prophets were actually law preachers, occupied an "officer" in Israel associated with covenant renewal, participated in covenant renewal services, and that the prophetic literature shows clear signs of its employment in such services. Covenant perspectives had now expanded to include practically all aspects of Old Testament institutional life and literature except for the Wisdom materials.

At this point, I want to introduce a subsidiary issue into the discussion, namely, scholarly interpretation of the term *hesed* over the past few decades. Several Hebrew terms and expressions came to be associated closely with the ever engulfing world of covenant thought. Terms such as *ydʿ* ("to know"), *ʾhb* ("to love"), *sesullah* ("special possession"),

---

22. This had already been done in a limited way by Karge in 1910 in a frequently overlooked work (*Geschichte des Bundesgedankens*). At the time, ancient near eastern treaty evidence was very small.

23. Mendenhall, "Covenant Forms."

24. Kraus, *Die prophetische Verkundigung*.

25. Reventlow, *Das Amt des Propheten*, and additional works on Ezekiel and Jeremiah.

26. Muilenburg, "The 'Office' of the Prophet."

'b and *bn* ("father and son"), *'bd* ("slave"), *tb* ("goodness, friendship"), *shlm* ("peace, normalcy"), *rib* ("dispute"), and so on were all related to covenant thought in some way so that when these terms occurred, even in texts not mentioning covenant, one could draw on the larger picture to fill out the background to the expressions.[27] No term became so closely attached to covenant as *hesed*.

In 1927, Nelson Glueck's dissertation on *hesed* was published in Germany.[28] In this volume, he argued that *hesed* always refers "to conduct corresponding to a mutual relationship of rights and duties" and "in the older sources, the common usage of *hesed* never means an arbitrary demonstration of grace, kindness, favor or love" (pp. 54–55). *Hesed* reflects loyalty to a relationship and "represents the real essence of the covenant" (p. 45).[29] "God's *hesed* can only be understood as Yahweh's covenantal relationship toward his followers" (p. 102) and human "*hesed* is the reciprocal conduct of men toward one another and, at the same time, explicitly and implicitly, the proper relationship toward God . . . *hesed* is obligatory" (p. 69).[30] The importance of covenant found in Weber and other German scholars was combined with Glueck's understanding of *hesed* in Walther Eichrodt's influential *Theologie des Alten Testament*.[31] Eichrodt built his theology around the concept of covenant as an integrative principle. Although he concluded that the concept "enshrines Israel's most fundamental conviction, namely its sense of a unique relationship with God" (1.17), he often understood covenant in a very broad manner. With Glueck, he argued that "an immediate result of the conclusion of the *berit* was the duty of loyal mutual service; without the rendering of

---

27. Nicholson, *God and His People*, 59–65, provides a brief discussion with bibliographical data.

28. Glueck, *Das Wort hesed*; an English translation was published in 1967 under the title *Hesed in the Bible*, with a summary of research on the topic between 1927 and 1967 by Gerarld A. Larue (pp. 1–32).

29. Smith in his translation of and comments on Hos 2:19 and 6:6 had suggested that *hesed* should be translated as "leal love" (leal being a term used by Scots to mean "loyal") since "*hesed*, which means always not merely an affection, 'lovingkindness' as our version puts it, but a relation loyally and lovingly observed" (*The Book of the Twelve Prophets*, 1.255). Glueck, however, made no reference to Smith.

30. Although Glueck placed a strong emphasis on covenant, he nowhere refers to Weber's work. He was, however, heavily dependent on Elbogen, "'hsd' Verpflichtung, Verheissung, Bekraftigung," 43–46.

31. Eichrodt, *Theologie des Alten Testament* (3 vols.; 1933–39). The 6th ed. of vol. 1 (1959) and the 5th ed. of vols. 2 and 3 (1964) were translated into English as *Theology of the Old Testament* (2 vols.; 1961–1967).

hesed on both sides the maintenance of a covenant was in general unthinkable" (1.232–33).

In such etymologizing presentations of biblical theology as that by Snaith, the connection between *berit* and *hesed* came to be accepted as axiomatic: "It [*hesed*] expresses a firm adhesion to the conditions of the covenant."[32] This view was incorporated into the standard lexicon of Koehler-Baumgartner (1951), which suggested a definition reflecting mutual liability and solidarity. The same perspective is reflected in the RSV's attempt to translate *hesed* wherever possible as "steadfast love." *Hesed* had become a concept so intimately interwoven with covenant thought that the two were almost inseparable and their connection required no proof:
... *hesed* chiefly denotes the faithful, covenantal relationship to Yahweh which is neither compatible with the politics of coalition (5:11b), nor with submission to a greater nation (5:13), nor with the civil war between Ephraim and Judah (5:8,10)."[33] "[T]he vocabulary of Mic. 6: 8 (*hesed*) reflects ancient covenantal language."[34]

Both the role assigned a Yahweh–Israel covenant in ancient Israel and the association of *hesed* with covenant have been seriously (and I think rightly) challenged in recent literature. Here we can only note the general outline of such developments.[35] The erosion of the theory of a Yahweh–Israel covenant as a characteristic, institutional feature of early Israelite history and religion occurred in various waves.

(1) The Alt–Noth reconstruction of pre-monarchic Israelite history, as that of a twelve-tribe religious amphictyony centered around a common sanctuary, collapsed in the late 1960s and early 1970s.[36] After dominating Old Testament study for a generation, the theory failed to withstand a reexamination of its fundamentals in light of the biblical evidence.

(2) Comparisons between Old Testament covenant texts and ancient Near Eastern treaties led to the realization that, except in the case

32. Snaith, *The Distinctive Ideas*, 102.

33. Wolff, *Hosea*, 120.

34. Tucker, "The Law," 209.

35. See chapter 9 above. A good discussion of the issues surrounding covenant can be found in Nicholson, *God and His People* and Oden, "The Place of Covenant." A short discussion of the history of the interpretation of *hesed* is given by Andersen, "Yahweh, The Kind and Sensitive God."

36. See Mayes, "The Period of the Judges," and chapter 3 above, for a discussion of the issues.

of a secondary edition of the book of Deuteronomy and texts influenced by deuteronomic/deuteronomistic perspectives, no biblical texts really reflected the structural features of Near Eastern treaties sufficiently to be called a covenant/treaty document.[37] Parallels had frequently been produced by combining descriptive narratives and legal/covenant type stipulations within the Bible.

(3) Parallels between Deuteronomy and other covenant type biblical texts and Near Eastern treaties are closer to Neo-Assyrian treaty texts than to the Late Bronze Age Hittite texts.[38] Several seventh-century Assyrian treaties are now known in which the reigning monarch or queen mother binds the state's subjects to the observance of particular stipulations.[39] This pattern of treaty, probably also utilized by the Israelites, is typologically more comparable to a Yahweh–Israel covenant than interstate treaties.

(4) The absence of Yahweh–Israel covenant thought in the eighth-century prophets, as well as a late dating for the pentateuchal covenant material, has again been stressed by scholars.[40] Such a position, Nicholson argues, "does, indeed, take us back to Wellhausen: the distinctiveness of Israel's faith lies in the way it breaks the mould of a 'natural bond' between God and the people, and transfers the relationship on to the plane of moral response and commitment, and it was the prophets and their disciples in the Deuteronomic tradition who were the architects of this new vision" (p. 216).

(5) E. Kutsch has argued that the term *berit* never means "*Bund/* covenant" in the Old Testament and should always be translated as "obligation" or the like.[41] For him, *berit* denotes one of four types of obligation: (1) An obligation taken upon oneself (*eine Selbstverflichtung*), (2) an obligation imposed upon another (*eine Fremdverflichtung*), (3) a bilateral acceptance of obligation (*eine wechselseitise Verflichtung*), and (4) an obligation imposed by a third party (*eine Verflichtung durch einer Dritten*).

---

37. One of the first to demonstrate this was McCarthy, *Treaty and Covenant*. The 2nd ed. provides full bibliographical data.

38. See Frankena, "The Vassal-Treaties." All known Neo-Assyrian treaty texts have now been collected in Parpola and Watanabe, *Neo-Assyrian Treaties*.

39. Grayson, "Akkadian Treaties."

40. See Perlitt, *Bundstheologie im Alten Testament*; and Nicholson, *God and His People*.

41. In a series of studies, brought together in *Verheissung und Gesetz*. See Kutsch, "Bund." See also Barr, "Some Semantic Notes."

Kutsch, in my estimation, has overstated his case but performed a service in noting the broad semantic field covered by the term *berit*.

Unlike the influence of covenant theology, which went almost unchallenged in the 1940s and 50s,[42] the understanding of *hesed* as covenant vocabulary signifying performance of obligatory acts of loyalty was frequently opposed early on but without much effect.[43] Here it is only necessary to summarize some conclusions of the thorough reexamination of *hesed* and its usage carried out by Francis I. Andersen. He argues that *hesed* when used of God's action toward humans refers to what we might call mercy or lovingkindness (the latter translation going back to Coverdale) and when used of human to human actions it refers to acts of unobligated favor or exactly the opposite of the commonly assumed position. *Hesed* as human attitude or action toward God is absent from the Old Testament. His summary statements are worth quoting in full:

> (i) *hesed* denotes behaviour that copes with an emergency for which custom and contract provide no norms (*hesed* is not prescribed); (ii) *hesed* is an expression of love and generosity which a person need not have been expected to do (*hesed* is not obligatory); (iii) *hesed* behaviour is surprising, ingenious (the stories are told, and they are exciting, precisely because they are so unusual); (iv) the act of *hesed* is supremely meritorious, but the performer could not have been blamed for its omission; (v) *hesed* issues in covenant, rather than from covenant; (vi) there are even cases of *hesed* which arise from a conflict of love with loyalty, and involve the performer in acts of treachery or crime.[44]

To sum up. First, in the old stories, *hesed* mainly describes exceptional acts of one human to another, meeting an extreme need outside the normal run of perceived duty, and arising from personal affection or pure goodness.

---

42. One of the few who challenged the covenant reading of Israelite life and history during this period was Pfeiffer; see his "Facts and Faith in Biblical History."

43. In addition to Glueck's 1927 dissertation, a surprising number of dissertations and books have been written on *hesed*: Gulkowitsch, *Die Entwicklunq des Besriffes HASID im Alten Testament*; Bowen, "A Study of *hsd*"; Asensio, *Misericordia et Veritas*; Yarbrough, "The Significance of *hsd* in the Old Testament"; Stoebe, "Bedeutung und Geschichte des Begrifes *hasad*"; Sakenfeld, *The Meaning of Hesed in the Hebrew Bible*; Kellenberger, *Hasad wa'amat als Ausdruck einer Glaubenserfahrung*. Of these, Asensio, Stoebe, Kellenberger, and Bowen (to a degree) offered alternative interpretations to Glueck's position.

44. Anderson, "Yahweh, The Kind and Sensitive God," 44.

Secondly, the earliest revelations of God's character (or "name") highlight his *hesed* as primal, elemental, enduring, and associated with his love, grace, compassion, rather than with justice.

Thirdly, the prophets associate *hesed* with a cluster of virtues, including moral ones, giving it more associations with justice. The balance, however, still lies with compassion.

Fourthly, in the Psalms, *hesed* is the supreme attribute of God, associated with both justice and compassion.

Fifthly, in later writings, and especially as the word *hasid* comes to the fore as a designation of the godly man, *hesed* comes to denote piety in general, and this usage became even more prominent in the writings of the rabbis.[45]

Bibliography

Alt, Albrecht. *Essays on Old Testament History and Religion*. Translated by R. A. Wilson. Oxford: Blackwell, 1966.

———. *Der Gott der Väter*. BWANT 3/12. Stuttgart: Kohlhammer, 1929.

———. *Staatenbildung der Israeliten in Palastina*. Leipzig: Reformationsprogramm der Universität Leipzig, 1930.

———. *Ursprünge des israelitischen Rechts*. Berichte über die Verhandlungen der Sächsischen Akademie der Wissenschaften zu Leipzig. Philologisch-Historische Klasse 86. Leipzig: Hirzel, 1934.

Andersen, Francis I. "Yahweh, The Kind and Sensitive God." In *God Who Is Rich in Mercy: Essays Presented to Dr. D. B. Knox*, edited by Peter T. O'Brien and David G. Peterson, 41–88. Homebush West, Australia: Lancer, 1986.

Asensio, Felix. *Misericordia et Veritas, el Hesed y 'Emet divinos: Su influjo religioso-social en la historia de Israel*. Analecta Gregoriana 48. Rome: Gregorian University, 1949.

Barr, James. *The Semantics of Biblical Language*. London: Oxford University Press, 1961.

———. "Some Semantic Notes on the Covenant." In *Beiträge zur alttestamentlichen Theologie: Festschrift für Walther Zimmerli zum 70. Geburtstag*, edited by Herbert Donner et al., 23–38. Göttingen: Vandenhoeck & Ruprecht, 1977.

Bowen, Boone M. "A Study of *hsd*." PhD diss., Yale University, 1938.

Childs, Brevard S. *Biblical Theology in Crisis*. Philadelphia: Westminster, 1970.

Eichrodt, Walther. "Hat die alttestamentliche Theologie noch selbständige Bedeutung innerhalb der alttestamentliche Wissenschaft?" *ZAW* 47 (1929) 83–91.

———. *Ist die alt-israelitische Nationalreligion Offenbarungsreligion? Ein Vortrag*. Gutersloh: Bertelsmann, 1925.

———. *Theologie des Alten Testaments*. 3 vols. Leipzig: Hinrichs, 1933–39.

———. *Theology of the Old Testament*. Translated by J. A. Baker. 2 vols. OTL. Philadelphia: Westminster, 1961–1967.

Eissfeldt, Otto. "Israelitisch-jüdische Religionsgeschichte und alttestamentliche Theologie." *ZAW* 44 (1926) 1–12.

---

45. Ibid., 81–82.

Elbogen, I. "'*hsd*,' Verpflichtung, Verheissung, Bekraftigung." In *Oriental Studies Published in Commemoration of the Fortieth Anniversary (1883-1923) of Paul Haupt as Director of the Oriental Seminary of the Johns Hopkins University, Baltimore, Md.*, edited by Cyrus Adler and Aaron Ember, 43-46. Baltimore: Johns Hopkins University Press, 1926.

Frankena, R. "The Vassal-Treaties of Esarhaddon and the Dating of Deuteronomy." *OTS* 14 (1965) 123-54.

Girdlestone, Robert Baker. *Synonyms of the Old Testament: Their Bearing on Christian Faith and Practice*. London: Longmans, Green, 1871.

Glueck, Nelson. *Hesed in the Bible*. Translated by Alfred Gottschalk. Edited by Elias L. Epstein. Cincinnati: Hebrew Union College Press, 1967.

———. *Das Wort hesed im alttestamentlichen Sprachgebrauche als menschliche und göttliche gemeinschaftgemässe Verhaltungsweise*. BZAW 47. Giessen: Töpelmann, 1927.

Grayson, A. Kirk. "Akkadian Treaties of the Seventh Century B.C." *JCS* 39 (1987) 127-60.

Gulkowitsch, L. *Die Entwicklung des Begriffes HASID im Alten Testament*. Tartu Ülikolli Juuditeaduse Seminari Toimetused 1. Tartu: Mattiesen, 1934.

Harnack, Adolf von. *Marcion: Das Evangelium vom fremden Gott: Eine Monographie zur Geschichte der Grundlegung der katholischen Kirche*. Texte und Untersuchungen zur Geschichte der altchristlichen Literatur 45. Leipzig: Hinrichs, 1921.

Hayes, John H., and Frederick C. Prussner. *Old Testament Theology: Its History and Development*. Atlanta: John Knox, 1985.

Karge, Paul. *Geschichte des Bundesgedankens im Alten Testament*. Alttestamentliche Abhandlungen 2/1-4. Münster: Aschendorff, 1910.

Kellenberger, Edgar. *Hasad wa'amat als Ausdruck einer Glaubenserfahrung: Gottes Offen-Werden und Bleiben als Voraussetzung des Lebens*. Abhandlungen zur Theologie des Alten und Neuen Testaments 69. Zurich: Theologischer, 1982.

Kittel, Gerhard, editor. *Theologische Wörterbuch zum Neuen Testament*. Stuttgart: Kohlhammer, 1933–.

Kittel, Rudolf. "Die Zukunft der alttestamentlichen Wissenschaft." *ZAW* 39 (1921) 84-99.

Kraus, Hans-Joachim. *Die prophetische Verkündigung des Rechts in Israel*. Theologische Studien 51. Zollikon: Evangelische, 1957.

Kutsch, Ernst. "Bund." In *Theologische Realenzyclpädie* 7 (1981) 397-410.

———. *Verheissung und Gesetz: Untersuchunqen zum sogenannten "Bund" im Alten Testament*. BZAW 131. Berlin: de Gruyter, 1973.

Mayes, A. D. H. "The Period of the Judges and the Rise of the Monarchy." In *Israelite and Judaean History*, edited by John H. Hayes and J. Maxwell Miller, 285-331. OTL. Philadelphia: Westminster, 1977.

McCarthy, Dennis J. *Treaty and Covenant: A Study in Form in the Ancient Oriental Documents and the Old Testament*. AB 21. Rome: Pontifical Biblical Institute, 1963; 2nd ed. 1978.

Mendenhall, George E. "Covenant Forms in Israelite Tradition." *BA* 17 (1954) 50-76.

Mowinckel, Sigmund. *Le Décalogue*. Etudes d'Histoire et de Philosophie Religieuses 16. Paris: Alcan, 1927.

———. *Psalmenstudien*. 6 vols. Kristiania [Oslo]: Dybwad, 1921-24.

Muilenburg, James. "The 'Office' of the Prophet in Ancient Israel." In *The Bible in Modern Research*, edited by J. Philip Hyatt, 74–97. Nashville: Abingdon, 1965.
Nicholson, Ernest W. *God and His People: Covenant and Theology in the Old Testament*. Oxford: Clarendon, 1986.
Noth, Martin. *Das System der zwölf Stämme Israels*. BWANT 4/1. Stuttgart: Kohlhammer, 1930.
Oden, Robert A. Jr. "The Place of Covenant in the Religion of Israel." In *Ancient Israelite Religion: Essays in Honor of Frank Moore Cross*, edited by Patrick D. Miller, Jr. et al., 429–47. Philadelphia: Fortress, 1987.
Parpola, Simo, and Kazuko Watanabe. *Neo-Assyrian Treaties and Loyalty Oaths*. State Archives of Assyria 2. Helsinki: Helsinki University Press, 1988.
Perlitt, Lothar. *Bundstheologie im Alten Testament*. WMANT 36. Neukirchen-Vluyn: Neukirchener, 1969.
Pfeiffer, Robert H. "Facts and Faith in Biblical History." *JBL* 70 (1951) 1–14.
Rad, Gerhard von. *Das formgeschichtliche Problem des Hexateuch*. BWANT 4/26. Stuttgart: Kohlhammer, 1938.
———. *From Genesis to Chronicles: Explorations in Old Testament Theology*. Edited by K. C. Hanson. Translated by E. W. T. Dicken. Fortress Classics in Biblical Studies. Minneapolis: Fortress, 2005.
———. *The Problem of the Hexateuch and Other Essays*. Translated by E. W. T. Dicken. Edinburgh: Oliver & Boyd, 1966.
Reventlow, H. Graf. *Das Amt des Propheten bei Amos*. FRLANT 80. Göttingen: Vandenhoeck & Ruprecht, 1962.
Sakenfeld, Katharine Doob. *The Meaning of Hesed in the Hebrew Bible: A New Inquiry*. Harvard Semitic Monographs 17. Missoula, MT: Scholars, 1978.
Smith, George Adam. *The Book of the Twelve Prophets*. 2 vols. New York: Armstrong, 1896; rev. ed. 1929.
Snaith, Norman. *The Distinctive Ideas of the Old Testament*. London: Epworth, 1944.
Staerk, Willy. "Religionsgeschichte und Religionsphilosophie in ihrer Bedeutung für die biblische Theologie des Alten Testaments." *ZTK* 21 (1923) 389–400.
Steuernagel, Carl. "Alttestamentliche Theologie und alttestamentliche Religionsgeschichte." In *Vom Alten Testament: Festschrift für Karl Marti*, edited by Karl Budde, 266–73. BZAW 41. Giessen: Töpelmann, 1925.
Stoebe, Hans Joachim. "Bedeutung und Geschichte des Begrifes *hasad*." PhD diss., Münster University, 1951.
Tucker, Gene M. "The Law in the Eighth-Century Prophets." In *Canon, Theology, and Old Testament Interpretation: Essays in Honor of Brevard S. Childs*, edited by Gene M. Tucker et al., 201–16. Philadelphia: Fortress, 1988.
Weber, Max. *Ancient Judaism*. Edited and translated by H. H. Gerth and D. Martindale. Glencoe: Free Press, 1952.
———. *Gesammelte Aufsätze zur Religionssoziologie*. Vol. 3, *Das antike Judentum*. Tübingen: Mohr/Siebeck, 1921.
Wellhausen, Julius. *Prolegomena to the History of Israel*. Edinburgh: A. & C. Black, 1885.
Wolff, Hans Walter. *Hosea: A Commentary on the Book of the Prophet of Hosea*. Translated by Gary Stansell. Hermeneia. Philadelphia: Fortress, 1974.
Yarbrough, U. G. "The Significance of *hsd* in the Old Testament." PhD dissertation, Southern Baptist Theological Seminary, 1949.

Acknowledgments

THE AUTHOR, EDITOR, AND publisher wish to acknowledge with gratitude the permission to use in revised form essays that have been previously published.

Chapter 1 "The History of the Study of Israelite and Judaean History" was first published in John H. Hayes and J. Maxwell Miller, editors, *Israelite and Judaean History*, 1–69. Old Testament Library. Philadelphia: Westminster, 1977.

Chapter 2 "Wellhausen as a Historian of Israel" was first published in *Semeia* 25 (1982) 37–60. This volume was titled *Julius Wellhausen and His Prolegomena to the History of Israel* and edited by Douglas A. Knight.

Chapter 3 "The Twelve-Tribe Israelite Amphictyony: An Appraisal" was first published in *Trinity University Studies in Religion* 10 (1975) 22–36.

Chapter 4 "The Final Years of Samaria (730–720 BC)" was coauthored with Jeffrey K. Kuan and first published in *Biblica* 72 (1991) 153–81.

Chapter 5 "The History of the Form-Critical Study of Prophecy" was previously published in *SBL Seminar Papers* 1 (1973) 60–99.

Chapter 6 "The Usage of Oracles against Foreign Nations in Ancient Israel" was first published in *Journal of Biblical Literature* 87 (1968) 81–92.

Chapter 7 "Amos's Oracles against the Nations (1:2—2:16)" was first published in *Review and Expositor* 92 (1995) 153–67.

Acknowledgments

Chapter 8 "Restitution, Forgiveness, and the Victim in Old Testament Law" was previously published in *Trinity University Studies in Religion* 11 (1982) 1–23.

Chapter 9 "Covenant" was first published in Watson E. Mills, editor, *Mercer Dictionary of the Bible*, 177–81. Macon, GA: Mercer University Press, 1990.

Chapter 10 "Covenant and *Hesed*: The Status of the Discussion" was not previously published.

www.ingramcontent.com/pod-product-compliance
Lightning Source LLC
Chambersburg PA
CBHW021649230426
43668CB00008B/562